RISING PHOENIX, FALLING SHADOWS

THE YEAR IN AUSTRALIAN POLITICS

EDDY JOKOVICH · DAVID LEWIS

Rising Phoenix, Falling Shadows: The year in Australian politics
ISBN (paperback): 978-0-6456392-9-2

©2024 Eddy Jokovich & David Lewis

All rights reserved. No part of this book may be reproduced in any form or by any electronic or mechanical means, including information storage and retrieval systems, without written permission from the authors, except for the use of brief quotations in book reviews and promotional material.

January 2024. Published by New Politics, an imprint of ARMEDIA Pty. Ltd.

New Politics
PO Box 1265, Darlinghurst NSW 1300
www.newpolitics.com.au
Email: info@newpolitics.com.au

Production: ARMEDIA

Published and produced on the lands of the Wangal and Whadjuk people.

EDITORIAL NOTE ON THE USE OF AI TECHNOLOGY
We employ artificial intelligence tools in the editing process of our articles. These tools assisted with transcriptions of audio recordings, grammar correction, refinement and formatting.

 A catalogue record for this work is available from the National Library of Australia

CONTENTS

1. INTRODUCTION: THE YEAR IN POLITICS 10

JANUARY

2. THE VOICE TO PARLIAMENT REFERENDUM: A COMPLEX POLITICAL LANDSCAPE.......................15
3. THE CHALLENGES FOR THE FEDERAL LIBERAL PARTY 20
4. GEORGE PELL'S LEGACY: A DIVISIVE FIGURE IN AUSTRALIAN SOCIETY................................24
5. THE MISOGYNY OF NEWS CORPORATION: A LEGACY OF ATTACKS ON SUCCESSFUL WOMEN 28
6. NAVIGATING THE SHIFTING TIDES: OPINION POLLS AND THE VOICE OF PARLIAMENT...............33

FEBRUARY

7. THE ROBODEBT SCHEME: A TALE OF CORRUPTION, INEPTITUDE AND DECEPTION 38
8. REDEFINING CAPITALISM AND THE QUEST FOR ECONOMIC EVOLUTION 43
9. COMPLEX POLITICAL ISSUES SET THE START OF A NEW PARLIAMENTARY YEAR.....................48
10. THORPE'S DEFECTION AND THE INDIGENOUS RIGHTS DEBATE 53
11. THE WEEK IN PARLIAMENT: REFLECTIONS ON THE APOLOGY TO THE STOLEN GENERATIONS.....57
12. UNVEILING THE MAZE OF POLITICAL DONATIONS FROM GAMBLING COMPANIES 63
13. THE INSIDIOUS LINK BETWEEN AUSTRALIAN FEDERAL POLICE AND NEWS CORPORATION..........67
14. ANALYSING RECENT OPINION POLLS AND THE "HONEYMOON PERIOD" 71

MARCH

15. SUPERANNUATION POLITICS: UNVEILING RHETORIC, STRATEGIES, AND IMPLICATIONS 74
16. MEDIA REFORM IN AUSTRALIA: A CALL FOR COMPREHENSIVE CHANGE 78
17. THE ROBODEBT SCANDAL: UNRAVELING THE CONTROVERSIAL WELFARE DEBACLE...................81
18. UKRAINE CONFLICT: RUSSIA'S INVASION AFTER ONE YEAR WITH NO END IN SIGHT 85
19. THE WAR WITH CHINA MEDIA SENSATIONALISM AND RACIAL BIAS 88
20. THE AUKUS AGREEMENT: A COMPREHENSIVE ANALYSIS...92
21. WHY MAINSTREAM MEDIA IGNORED THE ROBODEBT ROYAL COMMISSION.............................96
22. THE VOICE TO PARLIAMENT: WILL IT SUCCEED? 102
23. SAFEGUARD MECHANISM AND POLITICS OF CLIMATE CHANGE 105
24. THE RISE AND INFLUENCE OF RIGHT-WING IDEOLOGY IN AUSTRALIA 109
25. THE END OF THE LIBERAL–NATIONAL COALITION REIGN IN NEW SOUTH WALES.....................113
26. A CRUCIAL TEST FOR WHISTLEBLOWER PROTECTION IN AUSTRALIA 118
27. PUTTING THE SPOTLIGHT BACK ONTO THE SOCIAL HOUSING CRISIS 121

APRIL

28. A LABOR VICTORY: ASTON BYELECTION AND A SHIFTING POLITICAL LANDSCAPE 124
29. YUNUPINGU'S LEGACY: FAREWELL TO A GREAT ADVOCATE FOR INDIGENOUS RIGHTS 127
30. LIBERAL PARTY IN CRISIS: INTERNAL STRUGGLES AND AN IDENTITY CRISIS........................131
31. UNRAVELING THE INLAND RAIL ENIGMA..134
32. GOVERNMENT ANNOUNCES MASSIVE FUNDING FOR AUKUS SUBMARINE DEAL....................138
33. NEWS CORPORATION'S LEGAL TROUBLES: A DIMINISHING INFLUENCE 142
34. COALITION CONTINUES TO STRUGGLE AS TACTICS COME UNDER FIRE 146

MAY

35. ALBANESE ATTENDS CORONATION AMIDST REPUBLIC DEBATE 149
36. LABOR'S BUDGET SETS THE STAGE FOR A LONG-TERM IN OFFICE...151
37. BUDGET REPLY: UNCERTAIN PATH FORWARD FOR THE LIBERAL PARTY 154
38. HOUSING CRISIS IN AUSTRALIA DEMANDS A NATIONAL APPROACH 157
39. RACIST MEDIA AND ATTACK-DOG NEWS CORPORATION..161
40. GLOBAL ADVOCACY GROWS FOR THE RELEASE OF JULIAN ASSANGE...................................165
41. MODI VISITS AUSTRALIA: TRADE TIES AND HUMAN RIGHTS CHALLENGES...........................169

JUNE

42. PWC SCANDAL SHEDS LIGHT ON CONSULTANTS AND CONFLICTS OF INTEREST....................172
43. MARK MCGOWAN RESIGNS AND LEAVES WESTERN AUSTRALIAN POLITICS.........................175
44. EXPLOSIVE FINDINGS IN ROBERTS-SMITH DEFAMATION CASE 179
45. FORMER MORRISON GOVERNMENT MISUSED $2 BILLION HEALTH FUND 182
46. GROWING CALLS FOR MURDOCH ROYAL COMMISSION AND MEDIA REFORM......................185
47. THE GROWING HECS DEBT: TIME FOR FUNDAMENTAL REFORM 189
48. THE CONTINUING HOUSING AFFORDABILITY CRISIS 192
49. STILL A MONSTER: DUTTON'S IMAGE MAKEOVER 196

JULY

50. SERIOUS CORRUPTION ICAC FINDINGS FOR BEREJIKLIAN AND MAGUIRE 199
51. INSURRECTION SPARKS CONCERNS ABOUT AUSTRALIA'S INVOLVEMENT IN UKRAINE 202
52. A GROWING DISSATISFACTION WITH THE FEDERAL GOVERNMENT 206
53. NATIONAL ANTI-CORRUPTION COMMISSION FINALLY COMES TO LIFE 209
54. ROBODEBT REPORT RELEASED: A DARK CHAPTER IN AUSTRALIA'S HISTORY 214
55. INTEREST RATES AT THE CENTRE OF AUSTRALIA'S POLITICAL DRAMAS 218

56.	FALLOUT FROM ROBODEBT INTENSIFIES AMID CALLS FOR MORRISON RESIGNATION	221
57.	THE COMPLEXITIES OF COMBATING MISINFORMATION IN POLITICS	225
58.	THE FADDEN AFTERMATH: A FAMILIAR RESULT LEAVES THE PARTIES UNCHANGED	228
59.	THE CONFLICTS OF INTEREST IN GOVERNMENT OUTSOURCING	230
60.	2026 COMMONWEALTH GAMES CANCELLATION SPARKS CONTROVERSY	233
61.	GOVERNMENT FUNDING FOR PRIVATE SCHOOLS DOUBLES, RAISING EQUITY CONCERNS	237
62.	THE CONSERVATIVE MEDIA'S ENDLESS ATTACKS ON LABOR AND THE VOICE	241
63.	DUTTON UNDER FIRE OVER OFFSHORE PROCESSING CORRUPTION ALLEGATIONS	245
64.	AUSTRALIA'S FIRST WELLBEING BUDGET: A PARADIGM SHIFT	249

AUGUST

65.	MORRISON'S ROBODEBT DENIAL FACES FIERCE CRITICISM	253
66.	CALLS INTENSIFY FOR A ROYAL COMMISSION INTO IMMIGRATION DETENTION	256
67.	GREAT BARRIER REEF IN DANGER: AUSTRALIA'S ENVIRONMENTAL EFFORTS ATTACKED	259
68.	DIVISIVE POLITICS: DUTTON'S FEAR AND LOATHING ON THE VOICE TO PARLIAMENT	262
69.	THE TROUBLING SAGA OF THE LEHRMANN TRIAL	267
70.	RENEWED PUSH FOR NUCLEAR ENERGY SPARKS A NEW EMPTY DEBATE	271
71.	THE REACTIONARY CPAC BIGOTS AND BANDITS HIJACK THE NATIONAL AGENDA	275
72.	THE DISPARITY OF CORPORATE PROFITS AND WORKER EXPLOITATION IN AUSTRALIA	279

SEPTEMBER

73.	THE HI-VIZ CORPORATE APPEASEMENT: POLITICS, AND CORPORATE INFLUENCE	282
74.	THE VOICE IS A BATTLE FOR AUSTRALIA'S SOUL BUT HOW WILL IT END?	287
75.	THE CHANGING INDUSTRIAL LANDSCAPE FOR GIG ECONOMY WORKERS	294
76.	FEAR OF CHANGE: A STALLING FORCE IN AUSTRALIAN POLITICS	299
77.	UNRAVELLING CONTROVERSY AND MISINFORMATION ON THE VOICE	303
78.	THE END OF INTEGRITY: POLITICAL JOURNALISM IN AUSTRALIA	309
79.	CLIMATE CHANGE AND EXTREME WEATHER WARNINGS: A CALL FOR URGENT ACTION	315
80.	THE MANIACAL DEBATE OVER NUCLEAR ENERGY IN AUSTRALIA	319
81.	RUPERT AND THE EMPIRE: A LEGACY OF NEGATIVE INFLUENCE AND BAD BEHAVIOUR	323
82.	DANIEL ANDREWS: A LEGACY OF LEADERSHIP AND MAINSTREAM MEDIA MADNESS	329

OCTOBER

83. THE FINAL WEEK OF THE VOICE CAMPAIGN: WHAT WILL THE RESULT SAY ABOUT US?.........334
84. THE DISABILITY ROYAL COMMISSION: A VITAL CALL FOR REFORM......................................339
85. THE VOICE: MISSED OPPORTUNITIES, RACISM, AND POLITICAL OPPORTUNISM....................342
86. THE NEW WAR ON GAZA: A HISTORICAL CONTEXT AND RECENT ESCALATION.....................347
87. REFLECTIONS ON THE DEFEAT OF THE VOICE TO PARLIAMENT REFERENDUM......................353
88. IS IT THE END OF THE ROAD FOR RECONCILIATION IN AUSTRALIA? 358
89. POST-REFERENDUM: BATTLING THE SHADOWS OF MISINFORMATION IN THE MEDIA 363
90. TRUTH IN POLITICAL ADVERTISING: GOOD FOR DEMOCRACY?..368
91. WHO SPEAKS UP FOR PALESTINIAN IN THE UNENDING CYCLE OF VIOLENCE? 374

NOVEMBER

92. THE WORLD SITS IDLY BY AS GAZA BURNS 379
93. MEDIA BIAS IN AUSTRALIA AND THE FUTILE BALANCING ACT..385
94. SPECULATION GROWS OVER PROSPECTS OF A MINORITY GOVERNMENT 391
95. REBUILDING BRIDGES: ALBANESE'S CHINA VISIT MARKS A TURNING POINT 397
96. HIGH COURT RULING SPARKS CONCERNS OVER COMMITMENT TO HUMAN RIGHTS..............401
97. THE ESCALATING CONFLICT IN GAZA AND THE INTERNATIONAL OUTCRY 406
98. HMAS TOOWOOMBA INCIDENT REIGNITES TENSIONS IN AUSTRALIA–CHINA RELATIONS.......412

DECEMBER

99. WILL COURAGE, CAUTION OR BRUTAL POPULIST POLITICS WIN THE NEXT ELECTION?..........418
100. THE DUPLICITOUS REPORTING OF GAZA AND SHIFTING PERSPECTIVES ON ISRAEL..............423
101. THE ONGOING DECAY AND IDEOLOGICAL DECADENCE OF THE MEDIA 429
102. LABOR STRUGGLES WITH END OF YEAR IMMIGRATION CHALLENGES 434
103. THE FRAGILE STATE OF CEASEFIRE IN GAZA AMIDST A HUMANITARIAN CRISIS....................439

ABOUT THE AUTHORS

EDDY JOKOVICH is editor of *New Politics*, and co-presenter of the New Politics Australia podcast. He has worked as a journalist, publisher, author, political analyst, campaigner, war correspondent, and lecturer in media studies at the University of Technology, Sydney and the University of Sydney; has a wide range of experience working in editorial and media production work and is Director of ARMEDIA, a publishing and communications company specialising in public interest media.

DAVID LEWIS is co-presenter of the New Politics Australia podcast, historian, musicologist, musician and political scientist based in Sydney. His lecturing and research interests include roots music, popular music, Australian, UK and US politics and crime fiction. He has published in *Music Forum Australia*, *Eureka Street*, *Quadrant*, *Crikey* and has edited several books.

NEW POLITICS AUSTRALIA is a weekly podcast, providing analysis and opinions on Australia politics. It can be found at Apple and Google podcasts, Amazon Audible and Spotify.

ALSO BY EDDY JOKOVICH + DAVID LEWIS

DIVIDED OPINIONS
THE NEW POLITICS ANALYSIS OF THE 2019 YEAR IN AUSTRALIAN POLITICS

As the mainstream media struggles to retain audiences and survive under new business models and shrinking revenue streams, independents are filling in the gaps left behind by the older mastheads. New Politics is one of the more important voices appearing in this new landscape, and *Divided Opinions* presents some of the best work from the monthly podcast, and a selection of articles published during 2019. Guaranteed to make you think; aggravate, or inform and enlighten—and maybe all at once—this is a must-read analysis of one of the most dynamic years ever in Australian politics.

Available in paperback and ebook.

Divided Opinions: The New Politics analysis of the 2019 year in Australian politics
ISBN: 978-0-6481644-5-6
ISBN (Amazon): 978-1-6611355-7-7
338 pages

POLITICS, PROTEST, PANDEMIC
THE YEAR THAT CHANGED AUSTRALIA

2020 was one of the most dramatic years in human history, shaped by the coronavirus pandemic that influenced society in so many different ways, combining health, politics, economics, business and education into the one sphere—and that proved to be difficult for many governments around the world to manage. *Politics, Protest, Pandemic: The year that changed Australia* is the story of the year in Australian federal politics, told through a collection of extended political essays from the New Politics Australia podcast series.
This is a must-read analysis of one of the most dynamic years ever in Australian political history.

Available in paperback and ebook.

Politics, Protest, Pandemic: The year that changed Australia
ISBN: 978-0-6481644-8-7
ISBN (Amazon): 979-8-7372030-8-5
414 pages

DIARY OF AN ELECTION VICTORY

LABOR'S RISE TO POWER

When the coronavirus arrived in early 2020, an anxious electorate threw its support behind Scott Morrison to guide Australia through the pandemic, leaving the Labor Party behind in a sea of irrelevance and Anthony Albanese with the role of political bit-player who could only watch from the sidelines, and hope that his political fortunes would change.

At the time, Morrison held record high electoral ratings and Albanese was told to not worry about the next election: it was already out of reach and best to focus on the 2025 election and beyond. Labor appeared to be doomed to yet another extended time in opposition and were left wondering when they could ever return to office again.

In 2022, Labor saw an opportunity: Morrison had made promises that he ultimately couldn't deliver and couldn't effectively deliver on the issues that should have been delivered. He was more intent on photo opportunities than the practice of good government and his leadership and government started to unravel, and it unravelled quickly. *Diary of An Election Victory* explores the key political moments of the 2022 election year, Morrison's demise, and Albanese's ascendancy and victory against the odds. It's a must-read analysis of one of the most dynamic and unusual election results ever in Australia's political history.

Available in paperback and ebook.

Diary of an Election Victory:
ISBN (paperback):   978-0-6456392-1-6
ISBN (hardback):   978-0-6456392-2-3
ISBN (Amazon):   979-8-3681569-7-2
304 pages

INTRODUCTION: THE YEAR IN POLITICS

2023 was supposed to be a better year. A new government, buoyed by a wave of independent candidates, promised new hope and change for the better. The decline of the COVID-19 virus signaled a return to some semblance of normality. There was a war in Ukraine, but much of the world remained relatively stable. Things were looking up. However, by the end of 2023, things had not panned out quite as Australia had hoped. The government, according to some accounts, was drifting—even "decaying", according to its less measured critics.

The Opposition floundered, and rumours swirled about the imminent replacement of its leader, Peter Dutton. Yet, at the end of 2023, he remains leader of the Liberal Party. Interest rates shot up, a move critics suspiciously attribute to the Reserve Bank. Even the replacement of the unpopular and out-of-touch Philip Lowe hasn't stopped the bank's aggressive interest rate policy.

We are in the midst of a housing crisis, fueled by failed neoliberal policies that treat every commodity as a profit-making asset, rather than something of broader value. Demand has outstripped supply, but merely building more accommodation is not the solution. Too many vacant properties, too much policy focused on maximising profits, and too many potential residences not being used as permanent accommodation have led to exorbitant rents and high mortgage interest rates, while a parliament filled with landlords has slowed or even halted meaningful reform.

The environment continues to deteriorate. 2023 is the hottest year on record—a conclusion reached in early December, surpassing 2022, which itself replaced 2021 as the hottest year. Extreme weather conditions have occurred worldwide, and while Australia had a relatively quiet year in terms of fires and floods, the concern remains high.

Big polluters, with financial and political interests, have ignored environmental issues, aided by a certain public apathy and even disdain for "greenies". Although most governments offer some form of solar rebate, these rebates have been cut. The nuclear industry presents a solution, but most support comes either from the Liberal and National parties perspective—who did nothing during their tenure—or from well-meaning individuals who fail to address the problems nuclear power presents, such as the lengthy commissioning process for nuclear generators and the issue of waste disposal. The risk of a meltdown may be small, but it remains a concern.

The ALP government of Anthony Albanese has been tasked with rectifying nine years of mismanagement and corruption. The ship of state turns slowly, and many who voted for the government demand quicker change. Various treaties and international agreements have been made or continued. The Australian journalist, Julian Assange, remains in prison, facing the real prospect of life imprisonment in the U.S., and possibly even the death penalty. The global economy has struggled, presenting challenges for the Treasurer, Jim Chalmers. Whether his extensive knowledge of economic theory can translate into practical solutions remains to be seen, but the signs are tentatively positive.

It is not unusual for governments to blame their predecessors for poor performance. In this case, it is somewhat justified. The incompetence and corruption of the Morrison Government, which included revelations that Scott Morrison had assigned himself at least five ministries without public announcement, was unprecedented. The Albanese government faces the significant task of cleaning up both Australia's governance and its reputation, both internationally but, most importantly, to its own citizens. Morrison's tenure was marked by broken contracts, misleading Parliament, absences at critical times, and ministers known more for their lack of integrity and capability than anything else. The more we learn about the Morrison government, the more distressing it becomes. Major constitutional reform may be needed to prevent a repeat of such a governance disaster. However, as we've learned through the experiences of the Voice to Parliament referendum, constitutional change is not easy and may be impossible in the current political landscape.

The Albanese government began with much goodwill and hope. One of its platforms was a referendum to give Indigenous people a Voice to Parliament. A referendum in Australia requires a majority of people in a majority of states and this provision, designed to prevent frivolous and unnecessary constitutional changes, also ensures that less populous states have an equal say in matters affecting them. The 'Yes' campaign for the Voice to Parliament was poorly executed, struggling to articulate precisely what the Voice would entail. Constant demands for 'detail' from the Leader of the Opposition, Peter Dutton, although politically motivated, also reflected community uncertainty.

The 'Yes' campaign appeared muddled and uncertain, and a major mistake was announcing the intention for the referendum and then waiting 18 months to hold it. The 'No' campaign, ostensibly run by the Opposition but comprising a diverse group including mining interests, conspiracy theorists, neoliberals, fascists, racists, and others, had a clear, albeit often misleading, message. Rumours circulated that the Voice to Parliament would provide Indigenous people the right to veto legislation (it wouldn't), provide free housing (false), and take over schools and push out non-Indigenous students (untrue). The most extreme conspiracy theories claimed it was a racially divisive plan, an attempt by the United Nations to remove Australian sovereignty, and a step towards 'The Great Replacement'—the baseless notion that people of colour, aided by various global entities, are trying to commit genocide against white people. Reasonable 'No' arguments were seldom heard, mainly because there were so few of them.

In the end, a weak and confused 'Yes' campaign, coupled with a relentless barrage of 'No' propaganda—regardless of how outlandish—led to the Voice's resounding defeat. Inner-city, university-educated individuals, up to 80 per cent of Indigenous people, and younger voters (aged 18–25) tended to support the Voice to Parliament, but this was insufficient. The defeat revealed an Australia that is resistant to change, and possibly harbours racist and regressive sentiments. The extent to which this reflects a lingering influence from the Howard government era, or signals a trend for Australia's future, is yet to be determined.

Like all governments, there were scandals, mostly minor compared to the previous government. The Prime Minister's son accepting a Qantas chairman's lounge membership was controversial. Albanese drew criticism for attending the wedding of Sydney radio DJ Kyle Sandilands and Tegan Kynaston, a decision seen as inappropriate given Sandilands' divisive reputation, though some speculated it was a reciprocal gesture for Sandilands' support during the 2022 election campaign.

More serious issues include the ongoing persecution of whistleblowers David McBride and Richard Boyle. Their cases are a blight on Australian governance; individuals who expose wrongdoing should be protected, not punished and both men face lengthy prison sentences for essentially doing the right thing. While McBride has now pleaded guilty to his charges and will be sentenced in 2024, this ongoing case remains a travesty. Attorney-General Mark Dreyfus had the power to dismiss the cases, yet for reasons unclear, he decided not to do so. As of the end of 2023, their prospects look grim, casting doubt on the Albanese government's commitment to progressive ideals and, certainly, on improving whistleblower laws in Australia.

INTRODUCTION: THE YEAR IN POLITICS

The Stage 3 tax cuts, favouring the highest income earners, remain a contentious issue. There was hope that the ALP government would repeal them—they are costly, and their beneficiaries are unlikely to support Labor—but it seems these will be implemented in the 2024 tax year. Their retention is baffling, as they are a legacy of the Morrison government from 2019.

The Albanese government's enthusiastic endorsement of the AUKUS agreement, an alliance between the United States, Britain, and Australia, is also questionable. As of the end of 2023, Australia has seen little benefit from this agreement, instead being drawn into expensive defence contracts with unclear or limited national defence benefits. Maintaining good relations with the United States and Britain is sensible, but not at the expense of Australian interests.

Two wars have dominated world events, with Australia involved in both. The Russian invasion of Ukraine continued into 2023, marked by the death of Prigozhin and an apparent stalemate. Australia has expressed support for Ukraine, viewing Russia, particularly under Vladimir Putin, as the aggressor.

The other major conflict involves events following a terrorist attack by Hamas on Israel on October 7. Both the bombing of Israeli citizens and the disproportionate response by the Netanyahu government are condemnable. Prime Minister Benjamin Netanyahu's actions seem driven more by political survival than any notions of a defence of Israel. The conflict has cost tens of thousands of innocent lives on both sides—over 18,000 Palestinian civilians—and some analysts fear it may escalate into a wider regional or global conflict. The Australian government's response has been controversial, with actions such as abstaining from a United Nations ceasefire vote, considering deploying a warship to the Persian Gulf, before eventually voting for a ceasefire. The initial decision to abstain from a ceasefire have been met with criticism from various quarters, including accusations of cowardice and the final about-face to support the ceasefire, too little, too late.

The Albanese government has had its achievements. The Prime Minister and Foreign Minister Penny Wong have worked hard to rebuild the international relationships damaged by previous governments. Efforts to strengthen ties with Pacific islands and rebuild relations with China, Australia's largest trading partner, have been notable. Despite China's human rights issues in areas such as Xinjiang, Tibet and Hong Kong, a strong relationship that can constructively critique yet maintain trade balance and friendship is crucial.

The National Disability Insurance Scheme has seen reforms, making it harder for dishonest providers to exploit the system. Labor's focus on aiding those who have suffered misfortune is commendable, and further reforms to broken systems are anticipated.

One of the government's biggest challenges is a mainstream media that is largely hostile to its interests and, primarily, the interests of working people. While the government occasionally receives positive coverage, most reporting begins with the Opposition's viewpoint, followed by explanations of why the government is wrong. The need for a royal commission into the media is apparent, particularly given the traditional bias in organisations such as News Corporation, Seven West Media, and Nine Media/Fairfax. The ABC, traditionally a neutral public broadcaster—at least on paper—has also shown a right-wing bias under the leadership of Ita Buttrose, and there are hopes that a new chair, to be appointed in March 2024, will return the ABC to this traditional value.

2023 was a year of contradictions, disappointments, hope, and strain. The cost of living rose, and optimism declined—it was a year of dynamic change, whose full impact may only be appreciated over the coming years.

***

JANUARY

THE VOICE TO PARLIAMENT REFERENDUM: A COMPLEX POLITICAL LANDSCAPE

13 January 2023

The Voice to Parliament referendum is becoming a more complex and contentious issue than it needs to be but it's important to begin by understanding the current political landscape surrounding this critical matter. The Voice to Parliament has emerged as a significant point of discussion and debate in Australian politics, harnessed by conservative forces that garnering attention and attempting to spark controversy at every turn.

While it is still the early stages of the year, the Voice to Parliament has already started to take centre stage in political discourse. The Prime Minister Anthony Albanese has initiated discussions on the timeline for a potential referendum, with August 2023 or "towards the end of the year" floated as a possible date. Indigenous Affairs Minister Linda Burney outlined the conceptual framework for the Voice to Parliament, shedding light on its intended structure and functionality. However, it is apparent that not all political players share the same enthusiasm for Reconciliation, as some appear more interested in maintaining the status quo.

One of the key dynamics at play is the necessity of bipartisan support for a successful referendum and history has shown that referenda with bipartisan backing tend to fare better—only eight of the 44 referenda questions that have been put the Australian electorate have been successful, and all had bipartisan support. The 1967 referendum, a watershed moment in Australian history, is one referendum that enjoyed this bipartisan support and saw an overwhelming 90 per cent of the population vote in favour of bringing Aboriginal affairs under federal jurisdiction removing references in the Australian Constitution that discriminated against Aboriginal and Torres Strait Islander people. Both sides of the political spectrum recognised the importance of treating Indigenous people more equitably and in the best interests of the nation.

However, the landscape has shifted since the 1990s, and the Liberal Party has increasingly adopted a strategy of opposition to Indigenous affairs and matters of race, an obstinate stance has been particularly noticeable in recent years. While this approach may have served certain conservative leaders well—John Howard and Tony Abbott—it raises questions about the party's long-term viability and relevance in a shifting political landscape.

The National Party, a Coalition partner of the Liberals, has been cautious about Indigenous representation. Notably, the member for Calare, Andrew Gee, has resigned from the National Party, citing his belief in the value of the Voice to Parliament. It appears that Gee's decision was rooted in both principle and political strategy, as he may have anticipated a changing electorate in his Indigenous-heavy constituency.

A significant question looms: Can the Voice to Parliament referendum succeed without bipartisan support? This scenario would mark a departure from historical precedent and, if so, potentially rendering the Opposition irrelevant. It underscores the Liberal Party's strategy, which seems to involve abstaining from the vote, so they can claim that they never intended to vote against Reconciliation, while working behind the scenes to hinder its progress.

Comparisons have been drawn to the Liberal Party's tactics during the 1999 Republic referendum, where the party refrained from taking a formal position but actively campaigned against it. However, this time, demographic shifts and evolving attitudes towards Reconciliation may create a different landscape. The Liberal Party's newfound position in the Opposition also influences the dynamics.

The Leader of the Opposition, Peter Dutton, has chosen to appeal to extreme conservative elements within the party, a move which seems to be aimed at solidifying his leadership within the party, even if it involves divisive rhetoric. Dutton's history, including his decision to walk out on the Apology to the Stolen Generation in 2008, also raises questions about the authenticity of his positions.

The supposed absence of a detailed plan for the Voice to Parliament's structure has also become a focal point of debate. While critics claim a lack of clarity, a substantial 290-page report, along with three preliminary reports, offers detailed insights into the proposal. Yet, this wealth of information often goes unnoticed, as the media focuses on the criticisms coming from the likes of Dutton, rather than substantive content.

The Voice to Parliament referendum is unfolding against a backdrop of political gamesmanship, historical precedents, and shifting demographics. The absence of bipartisan support, the Liberal Party's abstention strategy, and the focus on divisive tactics all add complexity to the debate. Moreover, the need for a clear plan and the exploration of alternative approaches underscores the significance of this issue.

THE CRITICS ARE GETTING LOUDER AND FIND A VOICE IN THE CONSERVATIVE MEDIA

The Voice to Parliament is a simple yet significant proposition, as emphasised by Albanese and Burney. At its core, it constitutes a constitutional amendment that seeks to ensure Indigenous people are consulted about laws directly affecting them. It doesn't empower the Voice to Parliament to amend laws or create new ones; that authority remains vested in the Australian Parliament. However, it does provide a structured avenue for Indigenous voices to be heard and considered in the legislative process.

Critics have raised concerns about the "lack of detail" surrounding the Voice to Parliament. Yet, it's worth noting that there is no shortage of comprehensive reports and documents that outline the proposal's specifics. Three major reports stand out: the Indigenous Voice Codesign Process, the final report of the Referendum Council, and the report for the Joint Select Committee on Constitutional recognition, co-authored by Labor's Patrick Dodson and Liberal Party's Julian Leeser.

What adds an intriguing dimension to the debate is the role of Ken Wyatt, the former Minister for Indigenous Affairs, who presented the proposals for the Voice of Parliament and the Uluru statement to Cabinet twice before the last election—Dutton was part of that Cabinet. It's perplexing that some Coalition MPs are now demanding more details despite having been privy to these discussions.

Wyatt's remarks shed light on the situation, as he highlighted the existence of substantial reports, explicitly laying out the principle-based approach, scope, practical implementation, and the relationship with government. He expressed frustration with the National Party's apparent ignorance of these details, emphasising that they had been given ample opportunity to engage with and implement an Indigenous Voice to Parliament.

This refusal by certain members of the Coalition to acknowledge the details and intentions of the Voice of Parliament may not sit well with the broader Australian population. While racism continues to be a complex issue in Australia, there appears to be a gradual shift away from the blatant racism that may have hindered such initiatives just a few years ago. The Voice to Parliament is gaining support from those who may have previously been skeptical or dismissive, as the old racist arguments against Indigenous self-determination lose their traction.

The argument that Indigenous communities "can't be trusted" to govern themselves, a sentiment often touted by *The Australian* newspaper and some elements of the Liberal Party, seems increasingly out of touch with the reality of a diverse and organised Indigenous population.

However, the ongoing misrepresentation of the Voice to Parliament by the Liberal Party and conservative media interests remains a concerning issue.

Despite the simplicity and flexibility of the proposed constitutional changes, some political actors have seized upon the opportunity to further their own agendas rather than working in the public interest.

Anne Twomey, a constitutional lawyer and legal academic at the University of Sydney, provides valuable insight into the nature of the referendum. She highlights that the referendum isn't about the intricate details of future parliamentary actions, instead, it focuses on inserting a principle into the Constitution: the establishment of a body that can make representations to Parliament on Indigenous matters. This principle allows Parliament to be better informed on Indigenous issues without freezing the details in the Constitution. The democratic process remains in place, allowing voters to express their preferences in subsequent elections.

The Voice to Parliament is a straightforward yet transformative proposal that aims to empower Indigenous voices in the legislative process. Critics who demand "more detail" should recognise the wealth of information available in existing reports. The refusal of some Coalition members to acknowledge these details and the misrepresentation of the Voice to Parliament's intent raise concerns about their commitment to Reconciliation and Indigenous self-determination. However, public sentiment appears to be shifting in favour of this crucial initiative, and while it might not end up being enough to win the referendum, it suggests that those who oppose it may find themselves on the wrong side of history.

THE ROAD AHEAD FOR THE VOICE TO PARLIAMENT

Considering the future of the Voice to Parliament referendum, it's essential to recognise the challenges and uncertainties that lie ahead. This critical issue demands careful and strategic management from all key stakeholders, including Indigenous groups, political leaders, and those who genuinely support the Voice to Parliament.

One key factor to consider is the shifting demographics and voting patterns of "Generation Z", as well as the diverse makeup of electorates across Australia. Speculation suggests that, based on current data, a referendum might not pass in states like Queensland or Tasmania. However, this would still leave four out of the six states needed for a successful referendum, along with a majority of votes across the nation. While this scenario is speculative, it underscores the potential for the Liberal–National Coalition to inadvertently wedge itself due to political ineptitude, intransigence, and opportunism. This situation could, paradoxically, benefit the "yes" campaign.

On the other hand, there's a possibility that the referendum could face a fate similar to the 1988 referenda, where four significant constitutional changes were easily defeated, largely due to the efforts of individuals from the Liberal

Party such Peter Reith, who used the "no" campaign at that stage, to boost his own political profile. The question that arises is, "What happens if this referendum is defeated?" Such an outcome would be a disheartening reflection of where Reconciliation currently stands in Australia—a cause that can easily be hijacked by conservative interests.

If the referendum were to fail, the Voice to Parliament could still be implemented, but it would lack constitutional recognition and remain at the discretion of the Prime Minister of the day. Future governments could choose to remove it, as John Howard did with ATSIC in 2004, with the support of the Labor Party under Mark Latham. This underscores the urgency of achieving constitutional recognition to safeguard Indigenous rights and self-determination.

Despite vocal opposition from a minority, led by figures like Jacinta Price and Warren Mundine, and debates about whether a Treaty should precede the Voice to Parliament, progress is being made. The state of Victoria, for example, is commencing Treaty negotiations with First Nation peoples. The potential for positive change remains, provided we can envision and work towards a more equitable future.

However, the road ahead won't be without its challenges. Every matter of skullduggery and political trickery in the conservative political playbook is likely to be employed, including media manipulation to sway public opinion. Media outlets may juxtapose negative portrayals of Indigenous settlements with discussions about the Voice to Parliament, subtly influencing how the public perceives the issue.

Despite these challenges, there is still hope for the success of the Voice to Parliament referendum. It may not be a unanimous victory, but a majority of states could support it. States like Western Australia and New South Wales may see close contests, while Queensland and Tasmania could provide surprises. Queensland, traditionally a Liberal–National stronghold in the federal sphere, could defy current polling trends, just as Tasmania's unique Indigenous issues may sway its vote.

The journey toward achieving the Voice to Parliament through a successful referendum is fraught with uncertainty. It will require strategic and thoughtful efforts from all stakeholders, including Indigenous leaders, political representatives, and the broader Australian community. While challenges and obstacles exist, the potential for progress and Reconciliation remains strong. The future of the Voice to Parliament referendum is uncertain, but it is a journey worth embarking upon to secure a more inclusive and equitable future for all Australians.

***

THE CHALLENGES FOR THE FEDERAL LIBERAL PARTY

13 January 2023

The federal Liberal Party has been a significant political force in the country's landscape, has played a crucial role in shaping Australian politics, and its policies and leadership have had a profound impact on the nation. However, recent events, including the release of a controversial election review and debates about the party's direction, have raised questions about its future.

Late last year, several issues emerged that are expected to have lasting consequences on Australian politics. Among these developments was the release of the Liberal Party's election review, which occurred just before Christmas, with the intention of avoiding widespread attention. The review has been met with mixed reactions, and it seems to be document marked by political paranoia and a strategy to combat the rise of "teal independents" in future election campaigns. The report also suggests that the Liberal Party should shift even further to the right on the political spectrum to distinguish itself from the Labor Party.

It is worth noting that election reviews are typically a critical postmortem process for political parties after they lose an election as they serve as a means of introspection, identifying shortcomings, and devising strategies for future success. In this context, the Liberal Party's election review seems to have stirred controversy and left some observers questioning its quality and credibility.

The review is notable for the emphasis it places on the need to move the party further to the right, a recommendation that has been met with both support and criticism. Proponents argue that the Liberal Party needs to differentiate itself more clearly from the Labor Party, while critics see it as a potentially divisive and polarising approach that may alienate moderate voters, at a time when the Australian electorate is seeking a more united vision of Australia, after a decade of manufactured division by the Liberal Party that saw it lose office at the 2022 federal election.

Furthermore, Liberal Party insiders have been vocal about the need to re-evaluate its leadership. While it's not uncommon for leaders to take a share of the blame after electoral losses, it is essential to understand the broader systemic issues that contributed to the outcome. In particular, the preselection of candidates has come under scrutiny, with some suggestions that the party struggled to field candidates of the same quality as the Labor Party. This has implications not only for electoral performance but also for the party's long-term viability and credibility.

On the other side of the political spectrum, the Labor government, under the leadership of Prime Minister Anthony Albanese, has been making significant strides. The quality of its Cabinet, including figures like Mark Dreyfus, Senators Penny Wong, and Katy Gallagher, has been marked and a significant departure from the collective efforts of the previous Coalition government. While it's early days—less than a year in office and it does take a while for new governments to lose their gloss and any incompetence to come to the fore—the Labor government's ability to maintain a relatively scandal-free record has also garnered attention, despite the efforts of media organisations, such as News Corporation, to fruitlessly unearth potential misconduct or controversies.

The federal Liberal Party finds itself at a crossroads, facing challenges and criticism from both within and outside the party. The release of the election review, with its call for a rightward shift, has generated significant debate about the party's future direction. While the Labor Party has been making notable progress, the Liberal Party must carefully navigate these challenges to remain a potent political force in Australian politics. The nature and dynamics of politics can change quickly but whether the party can successfully address these issues and regain its competitive edge in future elections will remain a subject of keen interest and debate.

THE HISTORICAL CONTEXT OF THE FEDERAL LIBERAL PARTY

To understand the contemporary issues facing the federal Liberal Party, it is essential to understand its historical context. The Liberal Party was founded in 1944, and inherited the remnants of the United Australia Party and sought to form a formidable conservative force in Australian politics.

The party's foundational principles have consistently included an emphasis on individual liberty, economic liberalism, and free-market policies. Its origins, in essence, lie in opposition to the Labor Party, which has traditionally represented the left-leaning and labour union-linked segment of the Australian political spectrum.

Throughout its history, the federal Liberal Party has seen several leaders who have left their mark on Australian politics. Sir Robert Menzies, Australia's longest-serving prime minister, is often regarded as one of the party's most influential leaders. Menzies championed policies that encouraged economic growth and a strong alliance with the United States during the Cold War.

In the years following Menzies' leadership, the Liberal Party continued to play a significant role in shaping Australian politics. However, it faced challenges, such as the minor split within the party in the 1970s, which gave rise to the formation of the Liberal Movement and the Australian Democrats, events which reflected internal divisions over issues such as social conservatism and economic liberalism.

In more recent times, the party has been led by figures like John Howard, who served as Prime Minister from 1996 to 2007, and Tony Abbott, who led the party from 2009 to 2015. John Howard was known for his conservative approach to both social and economic policies, while Abbott's leadership was marked by his emphasis on national security and a promise to repeal the carbon pricing scheme, colloquially known as the "carbon tax".

The Liberal Party's historical trajectory has often been intertwined with its main political rival, the Australian Labor Party. The competition between these two major parties has been central to Australian politics, shaping policies on issues like healthcare, education, taxation, and climate change.

The party's legacy is one of advocating for market-oriented policies, individual freedom, and strong national defence. However, it has also faced criticism over the years for perceived shortcomings in areas such as social justice and environmental protection. The party's challenge in addressing these criticisms while staying true to its core principles is an ongoing struggle that remains relevant in today's political landscape.

THE FUTURE OF THE FEDERAL LIBERAL PARTY

The future of the federal Liberal Party is a subject of immense importance, as it directly impacts the trajectory of Australian politics and the nation's policies. As the party navigates its challenges and contemplates its strategic direction, it must consider a range of factors that will influence its standing and effectiveness in the years to come.

One of the central issues confronting the Liberal Party is the ideological debate within its ranks. The call for a shift further to the right as suggested in the recent election review is indicative of the broader struggle to define the party's identity. Striking the right balance between conservatism and moderate policies will be essential for the party's future success.

Leadership is another crucial element that the Liberal Party must address. The party's former leader, Scott Morrison, plays a significant role in shaping its recent image and policies between 2018–22—Morrison's leadership style has faced criticism, but it is vital to recognise that leadership alone cannot address systemic issues within the party. A comprehensive evaluation of the selection of candidates, party culture, and ethical standards is essential to restore public confidence.

In a broader context, the Australian political landscape is evolving, as it always has, but in a far more dramatic fashion. Issues such climate change, social justice, and economic recovery are at the forefront of public discourse. The Liberal Party must adapt to these changing priorities while remaining true to its core values and striking the right balance between its traditional principles and addressing the concerns of a modern electorate will be crucial.

It is also important to acknowledge the inherent uncertainty of politics. While the Liberal Party faces challenges and criticisms today, the future is unpredictable. The party has demonstrated resilience and adaptability in the past, and it may well do so again. The ability to learn from setbacks and evolve is a hallmark of successful political parties.

The future of the Federal Liberal Party is fraught with challenges and uncertainties. It stands at a crucial juncture where its ability to adapt, evolve, and reconnect with its roots will determine whether it remains a viable political force in the ever-changing Australian political landscape. The lessons of the past must inform the party's path forward, as its ultimate success depends on more than just the pursuit of power; it hinges on its capacity to authentically represent the interests of the Australian people.

***

GEORGE PELL'S LEGACY: A DIVISIVE FIGURE IN AUSTRALIAN SOCIETY

20 January 2023

The death of George Pell has sparked a range of reactions in Australia, largely divided along political and ideological lines. Conservative politicians and mainstream media outlets, particularly News Corporation, have eulogised Pell as a "saint of our times" and portrayed him as a martyr persecuted for his beliefs during his 18-month imprisonment in a Victorian jail. On the other hand, those on the opposing end of the political spectrum, such as Premier of Victoria, Daniel Andrews, have taken a starkly different view, vehemently rejecting the idea of a state funeral or memorial service for Pell.

Andrews' refusal to grant a state funeral or memorial service for Pell, justified by his concern for the distress it might cause to the survivors of child sexual abuse, reflects a broader division in public opinion.

One can't ignore the prominent role of political polarisation in shaping the narrative surrounding George Pell's life and death. He was hailed as a hero by conservative interests in Australia, enjoying support from influential figures and institutions such as the Institute of Public Affairs, Rupert Murdoch, Tony Abbott, Peter Dutton, John Howard, Michael Sukkar, and Joe Hockey. However, the conservative celebration of his life by these figures often overlooked the many troubling aspects of Pell's legacy.

Pell, contrary to this conservative image as a hero, was a deeply flawed character. One of the most significant stains on his reputation was his failure to report child sexual abuse during his tenure in Ballarat, a city with a history of such abuses. He was part of the long-standing Catholic tradition of relocating offending priests from one parish to another, effectively shielding them from accountability. Furthermore, he displayed a disinterest in genuinely listening to the victims of child sexual abuse, adding to the growing outrage over his actions.

Pell's legal history further complicated the public's perception of him. While he faced allegations of historical child sexual abuse, many of these cases did not proceed to court. He was, however, found guilty of child sexual abuse in Victoria, only for the High Court to overturn the conviction 18 months later due to a technicality. This legal saga added to the controversy surrounding Pell and left many questioning the integrity of the justice system.

In addition to his role in the child abuse scandal, Pell's public stance on various issues also stirred controversy. He was a climate change skeptic, which put him at odds with the scientific consensus on the matter; he advocated for reducing the role of women within the Catholic Church, a position that drew criticism for its regressive stance on gender equality.

Pell, in many ways, came to symbolise the issues plaguing the Catholic Church in Australia and his actions and beliefs were seen as representative of the broader problems within the institution: the strategies he followed, which seemingly aimed to prolong legal proceedings until victims could no longer afford them, resulted in further victimisation and suffering. His own legal troubles and accusations of sexual abuse within his parish only added to the perception that he was a deeply flawed character.

It is essential to clarify that the criticism directed at Pell is not a condemnation of individual faith or the Catholicism, *per se*: it is the institution of the Catholic Church and organised religion that has been at fault here and many decent members of the church have expressed horror and conflict over his actions and legacy. However, the primary duty of care, especially in the context of the child abuse scandal, should be directed toward the victims. Their quest for peace and resolution, a process that some have yet to achieve, remains paramount in this complex narrative.

In essence, Pell's legacy is one marked by stark divisions in public opinion. His role as a conservative figurehead was celebrated by some but shrouded in controversy due to his actions, beliefs, and legal entanglements. While some mourn his passing, many cannot forget the pain and suffering endured by the victims of child sexual abuse, perpetuated by figures like Pell.

MEDIA, MORALITY, AND THE LONG SHADOW OF THE CHURCH

Conservative media outlets, primarily News Corporation and *The Australian* newspaper, have played a central role in shaping the narrative surrounding Pell's legal battles. They have been staunch advocates for his innocence, behaving at times as if they were part of a "Catholic mafia". Their narrative has emphasised the High Court's decision to overturn his conviction on a technicality, framing it as an exoneration. However, this perspective fails to acknowledge the nuanced legal nature of the decision. While the High Court did not declare Pell innocent, they found that the evidence provided at his initial trial was not of a high enough standard, leading to his acquittal.

In the midst of this media-driven narrative, conservative MPs have been vocal in their support for Pell, seemingly eager to align themselves with his legacy. Beyond his status as a right-wing ideologue, Pell held a significant political role as a link between the Catholic Church and the Liberal Party. This political alliance offered a mutually beneficial relationship, reinforcing the political motivations for praising him. However, these expressions of support often overlooked the darker aspects of Pell's life and actions.

Pell's legacy extends beyond his ideological alignment and political connections and his actions and decisions as a high-ranking member of the Catholic Church have left a troubling mark on the institution. He could have done more to support the victims of child sexual abuse, yet he chose to prioritise the interests of the church, making it as difficult as possible for victims to seek compensation and justice. This stance is a matter of great concern for those who have suffered at the hands of predatory priests.

The implicit acceptance of such actions and the broader issue of pedophilia within the Catholic Church has become a significant point of contention. Critics argue that by supporting Pell, conservative media and politicians are inadvertently condoning these heinous acts of child sexual abuse perpetrated by priests and brothers within religious institutions.

The seeming reluctance to acknowledge the problematic aspects of Pell's legacy becomes even more glaring when compared to the vociferous criticism that can arise within the political sphere for comparatively minor transgressions. The inconsistency in standards has raised questions about the threshold for what is deemed acceptable behaviour within certain political circles.

The Catholic Church's efforts to erase the memory of child sexual abuse victims further underscores the need to remember the deep-seated issues that Pell's legacy encapsulates. The removal of coloured ribbons that were tied onto the iron fences surrounding St. Mary's Cathedral—the location of Pell's funeral and the centre of his time as the Archbishop of Sydney—intended to honour the victims of child sexual abuse perpetrated by the Catholic Church and aggressively removed by church attendants and right-wing Catholic zealots—is a small but telling gesture of the church's desire to forget this dark chapter in its history.

The statistics surrounding child sexual abuse within the Catholic Church in Australia are staggering, with thousands of victims and alleged abusers involved. Pell's legacy cannot be disassociated from this pervasive issue that plagued the institution. His role in this context is what he should be remembered for, rather than being celebrated as a glorified ideologue who failed to prioritise the wellbeing of the most vulnerable in his care.

THE INTERSECTION OF FAITH, POLITICS, AND ETHICS

One of the remarkable aspects of this situation is the stark contrast between the actions of Pell and the image of Jesus Christ as presented in the gospels. The biblical portrayal of Jesus depicts a figure who associated with the marginalised, such as tax collectors, lepers, and prostitutes. He engaged in acts of humility, like washing the feet of those considered lesser, and even exhibited righteous anger, such as overturning tables in the marketplace. Pell represented the antithesis of these teachings and if a figure such as Jesus Christ were to appear in modern society, one can only wonder how they would be received.

The imagined scenario of a modern-day Jesus arriving in Sydney raises questions about how people interpret religious teachings. It underscores the idea that individuals often read into religious texts and figures what they want to see, shaped by their own perspectives and biases. It also serves as a reminder that the essence of a religious figure can be lost in the translation from scripture to contemporary beliefs and actions.

Pell's influence within the church chose to use that power to enrich the institution rather than to help the less fortunate, support the needy, or provide comfort to those in distress. It highlights a pervasive issue of churches amassing immense wealth at the expense of their primary mission of compassion and aid.

The political dimension of this legacy becomes more pronounced when considering the ties between conservative elements of the Catholic Church and certain political parties, notably the Liberal Party in Australia and these affiliations have raised concerns about the separation of church and state.

It is acceptable for politicians to be shaped by their ethical beliefs as long as these beliefs align with the broad majority of societal values. Ethical convictions, whether rooted in religion or other personal beliefs, can be influential in political decision-making, but they must remain within the boundaries of a secular and multicultural society.

The legacy of Pell is still unfolding. His death serves as a microcosm of the larger discussions surrounding the intersections of faith, ethics, politics, and the responsibilities of religious institutions in a secular society. It underscores the need for careful consideration of the separation between church and state, as well as the ethical boundaries that guide political decisions in a diverse and pluralistic society. The ongoing dialogue surrounding this complex figure's legacy reflects the broader challenges and debates facing modern societies in their quest for justice, compassion, and effective governance.

***

THE MISOGYNY OF NEWS CORPORATION: A LEGACY OF ATTACKS ON SUCCESSFUL WOMEN

27 January 2023

The world of media plays a pivotal role in shaping public opinion and discourse, significantly impacting the way society perceives its leaders, policies, and values. With great power comes an even greater responsibility, and it is disheartening to observe how certain media outlets, such as News Corporation, perpetuate a culture of misogyny and sexism in their reporting and commentary.

Jacinda Ardern's tenure as the Prime Minister of New Zealand was marked by remarkable accomplishments: she took office in 2017, forming a government and later securing a landslide victory in the 2020 election. What makes this achievement even more impressive is that she managed to secure a majority of seats for the Labour Party, a feat unprecedented in New Zealand's electoral history.

Ardern's leadership was not only characterised by political success but also by her effective handling of the Coronavirus pandemic and New Zealand's economy thrived under her governance. Nevertheless, like in Australia, New Zealand grappled with high living costs, soaring housing prices, and inflation issues. Despite these challenges, Ardern's tenure was an undeniably successful one, garnering international recognition.

However, when Ardern announced her resignation during the week, News Corporation unleashed a barrage of vitriolic comments, and the disparaging remarks included labels such as "vacuous queen of woke" and accusations of her being a "dreadful Prime Minister who failed". These derogatory comments, however, were not an isolated incident and are part of a disturbing pattern of sexism and misogyny that News Corporation has consistently perpetuated over the years.

It's essential to highlight that all these negative comments and articles were authored by male journalists employed by News Corporation and this pattern of sexism and gender bias is not limited to Jacinda Ardern. News

Corporation has a history of attacking successful women in politics, and their previous targets have included former New Zealand Prime Minister Helen Clark and former Australian Prime Minister Julia Gillard. These three women share several key characteristics—they were accomplished politicians, held left-wing political affiliations, and represented unions and workers' interests. Most significantly, they are women, and it is this very fact that appears to rattle News Corporation the most.

The recurring theme of misogyny within News Corporation's coverage and commentary is deeply troubling and it is these attacks undermine the achievements of accomplished women in leadership roles, perpetuating gender stereotypes and discrimination. The media's responsibility to foster informed public discourse is compromised when it engages in such biased and derogatory reporting.

The lasting image of Jacinda Ardern, donning a hijab and embracing the victims of the tragic Christchurch mosque shooting in 2019, where 51 people were murdered by an Australian extremist and terrorist, exemplified her compassionate and inclusive leadership. She showed the world how leaders should respond to crises with humanity and empathy and this act of compassion was met with admiration on the global stage. Still, in some corners of the media, including News Corporation, such actions were discredited, further illustrating the deeply entrenched gender bias within the organisation.

News Corporation's relentless attacks on successful female politicians, such as Jacinda Ardern, expose a deeply embedded culture of misogyny within the media conglomerate. It is crucial to recognise and address this issue, as the media's role in shaping public perceptions cannot be underestimated.

THE WIDESPREAD MISOGYNY IN NEWS CORPORATION AND BEYOND

It's evident that News Corporation's pattern of attacking progressive centre-left politicians knows no borders. Whether it's New Zealand, Finland, or Australia, the organisation seems unconcerned to the politician's country of origin: just another day at the office for News Corporation, especially within the Australian branch, which appears to serve as a retirement haven for aging male journalists of conservative persuasions. They never miss an opportunity to assail successful women, irrespective of their fields or positions.

The list of targeted women goes beyond politics and extends into other sectors. For instance, Christine Holgate, the former head of Australia Post, faced harsh criticism. Even Liberal women who didn't adhere to News Corporation's expectations were castigated: Bridget Archer, the member for Bass, was attacked when she crossed the floor last year. Julia Banks faced News Corporation's opprobrium when she resigned from the Liberal Party, as did Brittany Higgins when she made allegations of rape against the Liberal Party operative, Bruce Lehrmann. It seems that if you cross the Liberal Party or fail to align with their ideological agenda, News Corporation comes after you.

This pattern of sexism and misogyny is ultimately guided by Rupert Murdoch, the media mogul who often appears more interested in objectifying women than respecting their accomplishments. Yet, it's not merely a single individual but an entire cohort of News Corporation personnel, including Greg Sheridan, Dennis Shanahan, Andrew Bolt, and Paul Murray. Their rhetoric and behaviours are characterised by vileness, sexism, and abuse.

However, it's essential to acknowledge that while News Corporation's behaviour is particularly egregious, it does not exist in a vacuum and much of the media industry struggles with issues of sexism and abusive behaviour. But News Corporation seems to excel in perpetuating this disturbing culture. Occasionally, other media outlets like Fairfax/Nine Media publish articles that critique such behaviour, offering a valuable perspective on how these issues affect society. *The Guardian* also provides some coverage in this regard, albeit perhaps to a slightly greater extent.

Nevertheless, the common theme remains powerful women being targeted. Holding power accountable is a vital part of journalism's role, and no government or leader should be beyond scrutiny. It's expected that governments make mistakes, have ideas that initially seem good but turn out to be flawed in practice, and they should be criticised when necessary. This is true for Ardern's government, just as it is for Anthony Albanese's government or any other around the world. The problem arises when the assumption is that nothing a female leader does can be good simply because she is a woman.

Ardern's capabilities are evident, and her future in politics is far from over. While being a national leader is a challenging responsibility, she admitted that she had "nothing left in the tank" when she announced her resignation. Her decision to step down and not seek re-election is a clean break from the norm, where ex-prime ministers often linger, causing more harm than good to their parties or their countries. Ardern's choice to explore new avenues, perhaps in the not-for-profit sector or at the United Nations, is a stark contrast to those who simply refuse to let go.

THE IMPLICATIONS OF NEWS CORPORATION'S MISOGYNY AND FALSE REPORTING

The behaviour of News Corporation in the case of Jacinda Ardern serves as a stark example of how the media giant operates when a leader or a narrative doesn't align with their particular agenda. They resort to the creation of falsehoods and misrepresentations. This is a recurring pattern when it comes to centre-left political parties, and it fundamentally undermines the principles of objective journalism.

News Corporation's claim that Ardern left New Zealand's economy in shambles is at odds with the statistical reality. New Zealand's economy stands as one of the best-performing economies globally, with a growth rate of 6.4 per cent, slightly ahead of Australia and well beyond the OECD average of 3 per cent. The jobless rate of 3.4 per cent is the fourth lowest in the OECD, and inflation at 7.4 per cent is considerably lower than the OECD average of 11.6 per cent. These statistics challenge the false narrative that News Corporation has perpetuated about Ardern's economic performance.

It is crucial to remember that no political leader is perfect. Ardern's Labour Party is currently trailing in the polls, and her initial popularity has waned over the past year. Public opinion can vary significantly between an overseas audience and a domestic one, as seen in the case of other international leaders like Mikhail Gorbachev, the former President of the Soviet Union who was highly regarded in the international field, but widely despised domestically. However, Ardern did not reach the level of unpopularity experienced by some leaders towards the end of their tenures.

In the case of Ardern, News Corporation's portrayal of her as completely inept is far from being an analysis or accurate reporting and it reflects an ideological bias grounded in misogyny, propped up by false information and narratives. The question arises as to how much of this vitriol is a reaction to the perceived shortcomings of political leaders championed by News Corporation itself. This may manifest as an attempt to deflect from their own failures by pointing fingers at leaders like Ardern. However, it's essential to remember that the pursuit of truth should remain paramount and facts do not align with personal feelings or ideological biases. In this case, the facts challenge the false narratives constructed to disparage Ardern and her leadership.

As Ardern concludes her time as Prime Minister, she leaves New Zealand in a better place, a testament to her leadership and decision-making. Even excellent leaders do not always have the opportunity to leave on a high note. Unforeseen circumstances can lead to economic downturns or other unexpected challenges, resulting in leaders departing under a cloud of failure. Ardern, however, managed to step down at an advantageous moment, handing over a country in a favourable position to her successor. Whether this results in political success for her successor—Chris Hipkins—remains to be seen but, at least, Ardern has left at the time of her own choosing.

The New Zealand political landscape and mixed-member system is complex, making it challenging to predict election outcomes, but Ardern's remarkable ability to secure a majority in a system designed to foster collaboration was a testament to her political acumen. She is likely to be remembered not just in New Zealand but internationally for her leadership and achievements.

News Corporation's ideological bias, rooted in misogyny and perpetuated by false reporting, underscores the importance of critical media literacy and the need for objective journalism in an era of information proliferation. It is essential for the media to fulfill its role as a guardian of the truth and a responsible steward of public discourse, focusing on accurate and balanced reporting rather than perpetuating harmful narratives. Addressing the issue of misogyny in the media is not only crucial for the empowerment of women in politics but for the betterment of society as a whole.

***

NAVIGATING THE SHIFTING TIDES: OPINION POLLS AND THE VOICE OF PARLIAMENT

27 January 2023

While it's still early in 2023, Australia finds itself awash with a plethora of opinion polls into various aspects of its political landscape, offering insights into the country's federal voting intentions, perceptions of the Voice of Parliament, and sentiments about Australia Day. Among these polls, one conducted by Resolve has garnered significant attention.

The Resolve poll released its findings on the Voice of Parliament, which showed 60 per cent of respondents would vote in favour of the Voice of Parliament if a referendum were held over the weekend, while 40 per cent would vote against it. However, it's essential to note that the "yes" vote has experienced a slight decline from its standing at 64 per cent in September 2022, just over three months ago. Despite this dip, the level of support remains within the bounds required for the referendum to succeed.

The Resolve poll further delves into political voting intentions, revealing a different shift in the political landscape. Notably, support for the Coalition has receded—in this poll, the estimated two-party preferred vote for the Labor government stands at 60.5 per cent, while the Liberal–National Coalition lags behind at 39.5 per cent. The Morgan Poll echoes a similar sentiment, with the Labor Party enjoying a 59.5 per cent share of the two-party preferred vote, compared to the L–NP's 41.5 per cent.

Peter Dutton's diminishing support is also a conspicuous feature within these polls. Already occupying a precarious position, Dutton's popularity has dipped even further. As the leader of an unpopular Opposition, he spearheads an unofficial campaign against the Voice of Parliament and this campaign, while not explicitly voicing a "no" stance, seems primarily geared towards dissuading support for the Voice to Parliament.

In this dynamic political climate, there is an intriguing possibility on the horizon. The upcoming referendum on the Voice of Parliament might mark a departure from the norm as it could pass without official bipartisan support.

This prospect challenges traditional political expectations, and it is suggested that the Australian Greens could play a central role in this scenario. Senator Lidia Thorpe, a prominent figure for the Australian Greens, has expressed skepticism about the Voice of Parliament and its worthiness in the absence of a Treaty, and her argument centres around the notion that it should not be implemented until a Treaty is in place. While the viability of treaties remains a subject of debate, her perspective is not without merit, particularly regarding the timelines involved.

From a political and procedural standpoint, the argument for pursuing the Voice of Parliament without waiting for a Treaty seems more valid. Thorpe's reservations about the Voice of Parliament, such as the need for additional details, face scrutiny in light of extensive documentation, including articles and reports, that have been presented. The Australian Greens are, at this point, deliberating their stance on the issue.

While Dutton's efforts to create division within Indigenous voices have faced challenges, the role of the mainstream media in accentuating these divisions cannot be ignored. There's a growing narrative that Indigenous voices are divided, with some advocating for a Treaty before the Voice of Parliament—Senator Thorpe's position—others emphasising the need for the Voice of Parliament, while others are expressing doubts about the effectiveness of any of these measures. Figures like as Senator Thorpe, Senator Jacinta Price and Warren Mundine have been prominently cited in this context, each with their own agendas and different viewpoints and this discord within Indigenous voices could potentially jeopardise the success of the referendum.

DUTTON'S POLARISING POLITICS: UNPACKING THE CHALLENGES AND CONTROVERSIES

In examining the landscape of Australian politics in early 2023, it's essential to explore the potential repercussions of Dutton's strategy, which seems primarily designed to derail the "yes' vote for the Voice to Parliament referendum, and there is a palpable sense of despair about the effectiveness of his tactics.

One of the prevailing sentiments is that Dutton's unlikable and overtly negative disposition may ultimately render his strategy ineffective. His divisive and polarising style, while appealing to a specific segment of the population, may fail to resonate with the broader electorate and, as the leader of an unpopular Opposition and a party struggling in the polls, he might be predominantly reaching out to individuals already inclined to vote "no" to the Voice to Parliament. But in the field on Indigenous affairs in Australia, it's difficult to predict with certainty how these events unfold: it's very easy for conservative leaders and the mainstream media to destroy positive agendas for Indigenous people yet, despite this pessimism, there is a feeling that 2023 might be different to previous years and offer some hope for the future.

There is an undercurrent of concern on social media and within certain circles about whether Dutton's political strategies harbour racist tendencies and his historical record is replete with instances that would substantiate these concerns. Dutton's past actions, such as his controversial walk-out during the Apology to the Stolen Generations in 2008, his comical remarks about rising sea levels for Pacific island communities in 2015, and his rhetoric in 2018 about "African gangs" in Melbourne, have been widely criticised. Similarly, his false comments about rape victims in Manus Island and Nauru, his denial of visas for the Murugappan family, and his contrasting views on providing priority visas for white farmers from Zimbabwe have drawn scrutiny. Throughout these incidents, the common thread appears to be a focus on people's skin colour, which raises questions about Dutton's approach to these issues.

Whether or not Dutton can be labeled a racist is a matter of considerable debate. However, the perception of many within the voting public is that he harbours racist ideas, even if he doesn't align entirely with that characterisation. This perception can be deeply problematic for a political leader in a modern multicultural society, where inclusivity and sensitivity to diversity are valued. It underscores the complexities of leadership within a diverse and dynamic nation like Australia, where leaders must tread carefully to maintain public trust and unity.

Dutton's leadership has become emblematic of the challenges faced by the Liberal Party. As some see it, the party's choice of Dutton as a leader underscores a decline in ethical and moral standards within the Liberal Party, as the pursuit of victory at any cost takes precedence. This raises concerns about the party's future and whether it needs to undergo substantial reforms to restore its integrity and reconnect with the Australian public.

In light of these observations, there is a potential disconnect between the political strategies and media narratives and what is occurring within the broader Australian community. The divergent viewpoints, concerns about leadership style, and doubts about the intentions behind the Voice to Parliament referendum underline the complexity and volatility of contemporary Australian politics.

EVOLVING PERSPECTIVES ON AUSTRALIA DAY: REFLECTING ON SHIFTING DYNAMICS

It's evident that the issue of Australia Day remains a topic of significant debate and reflection within the country. Each year, the discussion around Australia Day is reignited, and this year is no exception. However, a noticeable shift in dynamics is occurring: unlike previous years, the conversation surrounding

Australia Day appears to be more subdued in 2023. This shift can be attributed, in part, to the absence of a jingoistic conservative Coalition government that often fueled culture wars.

Recent polling, including the Essential Poll, provides valuable insights into the evolving sentiments around Australia Day. According to the Essential Poll, 26 per cent of respondents support holding Australia Day on a different day, while 33 per cent suggest recognising Indigenous people on another day while keeping Australia Day on its current date of 26 January, with another 33 per cent advocating for no change at all. The fact that there is no consensus on the issue underscores the complexity and divisiveness of the topic.

It's evident that the controversy surrounding Australia Day has led to a transformation in how it is observed. Some local councils have opted not to hold citizenship ceremonies on 26 January, reflecting the growing acknowledgment of the day's historical significance and negative impact on Indigenous Australians. Corporate Australia has also weighed in, with companies like Kmart deciding not to sell Australia Day merchandise. Even in the realm of sports, Cricket Australia has made adjustments, no longer calling the match played on 26 January the "Australia Day match". The federal government has followed suit by amending public service rules, allowing people to work on 26 January if they wish to, as was the case prior to 1994.

Critically, Australia stands alone in the world in celebrating the colonisation of Indigenous land and the dispossession of Indigenous people on its national day. Opponents of Australia Day rightly refer to it as "Invasion Day", highlighting the painful history that it represents. The changing dynamics around Australia Day may suggest a growing awareness and a shifting societal view of this day's appropriateness.

Nevertheless, the issue of Australia Day remains deeply divisive. While 26 per cent of respondents support a change, it's important to remember that 74 per cent favour retaining the day as it is. For many immigrant families, Australia Day represents a momentous occasion, signifying the day they became citizens of the nation they have come to call home. This complexity underscores the multifaceted nature of the debate.

As the debate continues, there is a compelling argument for considering alternative dates to celebrate a national day. Proposals include commemorating the day of the Apology to the Stolen Generations, or the day of the Commonwealth referendum in 1967 to remove references to race within the Constitution, among other possibilities. This shift may offer a more inclusive and respectful way to celebrate the nation's identity, one that recognises the diverse historical and cultural perspectives that form the tapestry of modern Australia.

The decision of corporations like Kmart to abstain from selling Australia Day merchandise should not be viewed solely as a capitulation to political pressure or a liberal left-wing bias—it underscores a broader shift where companies exercise their right to align with values and principles that resonate with a diverse and informed customer base. Ultimately, these decisions are driven by a range of factors, including profitability, reputation, and the broader societal conversation. Such shifts highlight the nuances and complexities of modern corporate decision-making.

The future of Australia Day remains uncertain, and its celebration and observance may continue to evolve. The debate around this issue will persist as Australians continue to define their history, identity, and the need for a national day that is reflective, inclusive, and respectful of all its citizens. The outcome of this ongoing conversation will undoubtedly shape the trajectory of Australia Day in the years to come.

***

FEBRUARY

THE ROBODEBT SCHEME: A TALE OF CORRUPTION, INEPTITUDE AND DECEPTION

3 February 2023

The Robodebt Royal Commission has unearthed a treasure trove of shocking revelations, and witnesses, including ministers, political staffers, and public servants, have appeared before the commission to expose the sheer ineptitude, corruption, and deception that characterised the entire Robodebt scheme. What has come to light is not just a tale of financial mismanagement but a sordid chapter in the annals of governmental misconduct. The scheme, as it turns out, was not only a grave injustice to the Australian people but a fundamentally illegal endeavour hatched by the previous Liberal–National Coalition government.

The magnitude of the scandal is so astonishing that it has been speculated that if the truth about Robodebt ever saw the light of day at the time, it would be enough to bring down the Liberal–National Government and it for these reasons that the Morrison government decided not to release any details. Nevertheless, the evidence pouring forth from the Royal Commission paints a portrait of government officials who, at best, demonstrated a staggering degree of negligence and, at worst, engaged in blatant corruption. Public servants were equally culpable, marked by an alarming level of incompetence, while political staffers appeared shockingly ignorant and dense.

It's important to note that the Royal Commission does not have the power to prosecute individuals, as it is not a court of law. However, the urgency of the situation demands that punitive measures be taken to ensure that those responsible can never again serve in public office. The magnitude of the scandal necessitates justice, even if it's only to protect the integrity of public service and it's imperative that such actions are taken, and the Royal Commission's findings could be a critical turning point in achieving this.

While speculating on the specific individuals who might face charges could be prejudicial, it is a reasonable expectation that the Royal Commission may recommend charges against certain figures. The responsibility for pursuing these charges would then fall upon the Department of Public Prosecutions or the Australian Federal Police, depending on the nature of the charges recommended. Unfortunately, given the previous government's disregard for precedent, procedure, and legal traditions, there is a concerning possibility that the pursuit of justice may not be as straightforward as one would hope.

Throughout the previous government's tenure, it became clear that they had little regard for established precedents, procedures, or parliamentary traditions unless explicitly mandated. The public service's primary role is to provide free, fair, frank, and fearless advice to the government of the day and this advice is not supposed to be partisan in nature; it should remain consistent regardless of the government's political affiliation. For nearly a century, this principle has been upheld in Australia, ensuring that the public service played a vital role in holding the government accountable and assisting it in crafting effective policies.

Of course, not all policies are perfect, and not every questionable idea is halted in its tracks by the public service. However, the balance between the government's policy proposals and the public service's role in scrutinising them eroded during this period. The result was an unhealthy shift, where the government was no longer merely crafting policies but actively subverting the public service to implement illegal, immoral, and unethical agendas.

In the face of this ethical quagmire, public servants had a few courses of action—they could have chosen to resign and make a public statement condemning the government's actions. Or, they could have outright refused to carry out these morally objectionable tasks. It's disturbing to learn that some public servants, perhaps out of apathy or misguided loyalty, participated in these actions despite the long-term implications for the nation.

The revelation of culpability extends to the highest echelons of the public service, with senior public servants appearing equally responsible for this travesty as the two ministers directly involved—Scott Morrison and Alan Tudge. In fact, Tudge's testimony seems to have added another layer of chaos to the ongoing saga, casting an even darker shadow on the government's handling of the Robodebt scheme.

TRAGEDY, POLITICAL MANIPULATION AND MEDIA SILENCE

This unfolding story of the Robodebt Royal Commission is unlikely to culminate in a happy ending, with wrongdoers facing consequences, potentially including imprisonment. What has transpired is not merely a matter of fiscal mismanagement, but a sordid chapter in Australia's governance, and one that has illuminated the inner workings of the Morrison government.

One central point in the Robodebt scheme occurred in 2017 when the government had an opportunity to rectify the situation. Doubts had already surfaced regarding the legality of Robodebt within the public service, and the responsible course of action would have been to acknowledge their errors and misjudgments. However, the government chose to double down and employ spin and propaganda tactics to suppress the controversy. Tudge, the Minister for Social Services at the time, even went so far as to instruct his senior Media Advisor, Rachelle Miller, to "shut down the story", as can be seen with the testimony provided at the commission:

> **Rachelle Miller:** I developed a crisis media strategy at the request of the Minister, I would have done anyway. But that's what we did. He was very firm with me that I needed to shut this story down.
> **Counsel assisting, Justin Greggery:** Were you in contact with the Minister while he was on leave?
> **Miller:** Yes.
> **Greggery:** This is email contact?
> **Miller:** Yes. The minister became quickly aware that the Prime Minister was unhappy with, you know, the the sort of escalating media issue around this. But that media strategy was quite comprehensive that I developed in January, to shut down the story. And that involved placing stories with the more friendly media, the right-wing media about how the Coalition was actually catching people who were cheating the welfare system. And that media, including the likes of *A Current Affair*, or others, has a lot more reach. That is the commercial television programs, the 2GB radio, that type of thing has a lot more reach. The message that was getting to people on the ground was that the Coalition is cracking down on welfare cheats. Whereas in the left-wing Canberra circles, it appears to be quite a crisis. But we were getting feedback from the Prime Minister's Office that actually this was playing quite well, in your marginal seats, Western Sydney, that type of thing...
> **Greggery:** ...which was playing quite well?...
> **Miller:** The narrative of that Robodebt was actually playing quite well, in terms of people actually supported it. And were supportive of the notion of the government cracking down on anybody who was cheating the welfare system.

Miller's testimony at the commission exposed the extent of their efforts. They devised a crisis media strategy to quash the growing public concern, which included placing stories with media outlets they deemed more friendly to their cause, particularly the right-wing media. By portraying Robodebt as a crackdown on welfare cheats, they managed to manipulate public perception and minimise the growing crisis. This strategy proved effective in influencing the narrative, especially in key electoral constituencies.

Instead of addressing the underlying issue, the government allowed it to fester, using public relations tactics to silence criticism. In ordinary circumstances, such tactics might have succeeded, but the widespread impact of Robodebt left no room for the Coalition government to hide. Tragically, this scheme resulted in the loss of lives, with people taking their own lives as a direct consequence. Tudge's attempt to distance himself from these tragedies by highlighting the complexity of the cases is an insufficient excuse. The reality is that the government's inhumane and misguided policies played a significant role in these tragic outcomes.

The core issue at the heart of the Royal Commission is the legality of the Robodebt scheme. The lack of legal validation and verification for the scheme raises questions about plausible deniability among senior ministers. It is difficult to believe that no one within the government critically assessed the legality of Robodebt and it appears that the government was more interested in pushing the scheme forward for political reasons, such as perpetuating the narrative of welfare fraud and blaming the previous Labor government, even though their term of office ended in 2013. Despite the lack of evidence to support these claims, the right-wing media readily embraced this narrative. Unfortunately, the media's current coverage of the Royal Commission has been rather limited, especially when compared to their extensive and sensationalist reporting on the Trade Union Royal Commission in 2014.

This discrepancy in media coverage is perplexing, given the magnitude of the Robodebt scandal. The Royal Commission is arguably one of the most significant political scandals in Australia's history, with far-reaching consequences for its citizens. However, the limited attention it receives from mainstream media raises concerns about the transparency and accountability of the news reporting landscape. Independent media outlets, such as *The Guardian* and independent journalists such as Rick Morton, have been more thorough in their coverage. Still, the question remains: why is this crucial Royal Commission not receiving the attention it deserves, especially on the national broadcaster, the ABC?

While the Robodebt Royal Commission continues to shed light on the depths of government misconduct and the tragic consequences of their actions, it is imperative that the media plays its role in delivering unbiased and comprehensive reporting to keep the public informed and to ensure that justice is served.

A TIME FOR ACCOUNTABILITY: CONCLUDING THE ROBODEBT SAGA

It's undeniable that the 24-hour news cycle, while profitable for media conglomerates, has failed in its core mission to disseminate vital information but the constant repetition of inconsequential stories only serves to bury the truly important narratives. The Robodebt Royal Commission is a prime example of how a central investigation can be sidelined by the quest for sensationalism and the need to fill endless hours of programming. This choice not to cover the Commission comprehensively is a disservice to the public, who deserve to be fully informed about the government's actions.

One of the glaring issues surrounding the media's lack of coverage of the Royal Commission is the disconnect between the journalists who diligently cover the story and the news editors who decide not to include these reports in their broadcasts. This decision not only frustrates journalists who have put their heart and soul into uncovering the truth but also deprives the public of essential information that could shape their understanding of governance and justice.

The main purpose of this Royal Commission is to ensure that a scheme like Robodebt never occurs again. However, the current system of government, shrouded in cabinet confidentiality and delayed release of government archives—20 years—poses a significant challenge in preventing such occurrences. This revelation raises the question of what other illegal actions might have transpired during the Coalition government's nine-year tenure, and it's quite possible that their misdeeds extend beyond Robodebt, encompassing various rorts and acts of corruption that demand scrutiny and accountability.

The Robodebt scheme implicates multiple prime ministers, social services ministers, and senior public servants. The need for accountability and punishment, regardless of their current status in politics, is paramount and the severity of the consequences should be commensurate with the gravity of their involvement in this scandal.

Furthermore, senior public servants who failed in their duty, whether through dereliction of responsibility or complacency, should also face serious consequences. Accountability is the price to pay for their actions or inaction, as it was due to their negligence that lives were lost as a result of the Robodebt scheme.

The Robodebt Royal Commission offers an opportunity to send a clear message to those in positions of privilege and power and as a reminder that public service is a responsibility, not a privilege. The Australian people and the democratic process demand that elected officials prioritise the welfare of the nation over personal or political gain. Those who fail in this duty must face the consequences of their actions, ensuring that such grave injustices as Robodebt never recur.

***

REDEFINING CAPITALISM AND THE QUEST FOR ECONOMIC EVOLUTION

3 February 2023

In the complex field of modern economics, the Treasurer of Australia, Jim Chalmers, has sparked a debate with his article, "Capitalism after the Crises". Published in *The Monthly* magazine and subsequently republished in The Australian newspaper, this piece has ignited a firestorm of controversy. Critics, primarily from right-wing media outlets, have dismissed Chalmers' ideas as overly ambitious and potentially disastrous and accuse him of arrogance for suggesting that he alone has the power to redefine capitalism. However, before jumping to conclusions, it is essential to look deeper into the essence of Chalmers' proposals and consider the broader context of capitalism and its evolution.

Chalmers' central premise revolves around the introduction of "values-based" economics into the Australian community. While this may sound revolutionary to some, it is not an entirely novel concept, drawing inspiration from the theories and economic principles put forward by Mariana Mazzucato, an Italian economist known for her work on harnessing technological change, emphasising the public sector's role in fostering innovation, and expanding the scope of finance and economics to align closely with human behaviour and wellbeing. In essence, Chalmers advocates for a departure from the cold, quantitative world of numbers and statistics that often defines modern economics and, instead, focuses on shaping capitalism to serve a more profound purpose.

This approach opens the door to a range of possibilities for the Australian economy. However, as is often the case with groundbreaking economic ideas, Chalmers' vision faces vehement opposition from conservative quarters, including *The Australian*, *Daily Telegraph*, and the *Australian Financial Review*. These critics, it seems, lack the imagination to envision the future, failing to understand history, and overlooking the dynamism of economic systems. In a rapidly changing global economic landscape, Australia cannot afford to remain stagnant or wedded to outdated economic paradigms.

Historically, the role of a Treasurer in shaping economic policies and influencing the trajectory of capitalism is not new. Past Treasurers, from John Howard to Paul Keating, have left their mark on the economic landscape, molding it to fit their vision. It is only natural for a Treasurer to seek to imprint their own interpretation of capitalism on the economy, given the complexities of the economic terrain.

Chalmers' assertion that capitalism is not an end in itself but a tool for positive change, is a perspective that refers back to the foundational ideas of the economist Adam Smith. In the fervour surrounding capitalism, Smith's supporters often overlook the fundamental principle he espoused—that capitalism's worth lies in its capacity to generate profits and acquire capital, provided that these resources are employed to improve society as a whole. Capital accumulation, in and of itself, is insufficient; the real measure of capitalism's success is its ability to benefit the broader community.

Contrary to misconceptions, promoting the equitable distribution of wealth and resources does not equate to "communism" or "socialism", a simpleton argument that is usually pushed forward by conservative media. Rather, it is a quintessentially capitalist idea that emphasises the utilisation of profits from private enterprise, industry, and retail sectors to enhance the wellbeing of the majority. This approach incentivises hard work, leading to an overall improvement in society's quality of life.

Unfortunately, the past decade has witnessed the erosion of the safety net in society, and this highlights the pressing need to address issues such as unemployment and the inefficiency of underutilised labour. The current system is structured in a way that makes it relatively easy for individuals to amass immense wealth, provided they have the right opportunities. However, those who contribute more to society and occupy critical roles are often financially disadvantaged. This raises a fundamental question: shouldn't society support those who are essential to its functioning and wellbeing, such as healthcare professionals, teachers, builders, cleaners, mechanics, carpenters, retail staff and countless others who form the fabric of our communities?

These people are excluded from attaining a reasonable standard of living, but they are also penalised for failing to seize opportunities that are far from universally accessible. Chalmers' proposed reforms, although envisioned as a long-term endeavour spanning a generation, represent a potential shift towards a more equitable and sustainable economic model—one that has the potential to endure for several generations, much like the rise and dominance of neoliberalism in the past. Looking further into the concepts and principles of Chalmers' vision for capitalism, it becomes increasingly clear that the dialogue surrounding its potential merits is not just about challenging the status quo; it is about redefining the very essence of capitalism itself.

NAVIGATING THE CHANGING LANDSCAPE OF AUSTRALIAN ECONOMICS

The state of Australian business thinking presents a paradox in the evolving narrative of capitalism. While there are undoubtedly exceptional businesses within Australia, a prevailing inclination towards conservatism and a focus on cost-cutting and recovery accounting underscores a broader issue in the nation's economic mindset. This tendency is exemplified by the economy's heavy reliance on resources and the extraction-based model. In this context, Australia's economy stands as one of the least diverse in the world, ranking at 86th position in the World Complexity Index, placing Australia far behind Eastern and Western Europe, North and South America, and points to the pressing need for diversification.

Australia's growing population holds the promise of achieving economies of scale in various industries, including technology, yet, the reluctance of business leaders to embrace this new economic thinking stems from the perceived challenge it poses to their wealth base and the status quo they've upheld for decades. This conservatism, both in the business world and politically, threatens to leave Australia on the wrong side of history as the world undergoes rapid transformations.

Australia has witnessed instances of remarkable agility and innovation in its businesses, but all too often, these endeavours either do not stand the test of time or migrate overseas. Over time, they may become large, conservative, and slow-moving entities, stunting innovation and economic growth. This trend raises concerns about the "brain drain", where brilliant young Australians, including actors, scientists, writers, and more, seek opportunities overseas. The allure of international horizons, driven by a perception of greater possibilities, has drawn numerous Australian talents abroad, resulting in a loss of valuable cultural, intellectual, and technological voices domestically. It is important to reverse this trend and create an environment that fosters growth and encourages these talents to remain on home soil.

The decline in certain industries and fields, such as science, literature, and technology, is indicative of Australia's struggle to retain its intellectual and creative capital. This phenomenon is not solely about government funding; it requires a multifaceted approach that encourages individuals to stay and thrive in their chosen fields. This necessitates support from various stakeholders, including businesses, educational institutions, and the government.

Chalmers' essay is a blueprint for this transformation, encapsulating his vision for Australia as Treasurer, seeking to address pressing challenges by focusing on cleaner and more affordable energy, emphasising training and technology, stimulating business investment, and fostering progress in energy policy, skills development, education, and housing. These measures are intended to revitalise and restructure economic institutions and create a more dynamic, innovative, and diversified Australian economy.

Chalmers also aims to bridge the perceived gap between economic and social objectives, asserting that the two are not inherently contradictory. Instead, he advocates for a collaborative approach, where the public and private sectors work together to achieve national economic goals. This synergy is expected to modernise the Australian economy, fortify its institutions, and bolster democracy while rebuilding trust in the economic system.

The defining challenges of the coming decade, as Chalmers sees them, include the provision of cleaner and more affordable energy, effective education and training for a technology-driven workforce, and investment in sectors that enhance productivity and create opportunities for more people across the country. Chalmers asserts that the 2020s represent a pivotal moment in Australia's history, an opportunity to align its values, priorities, and objectives within its economy and society. The goal is to foster harmony and alignment between these facets, which have, for too long, operated in collision rather than synergy. A shift towards this approach carries the potential to bring far-reaching benefits to the Australian people, the nation's economy, and society as a whole.

EMBRACING CHANGE AND PREPARING FOR THE FUTURE

Chalmers' essay has the potential to become a defining moment in his political career, much like Kevin Rudd's iconic "Faith in politics" article about Dietrich Bonhoeffer in 2006 that preceded his prime ministership, ironically, appearing in the same publication as Chalmers'. Chalmers initiates a comprehensive conversation that traverses economic history, economic ideas, sociology, and world history. Politics, too, plays a significant role in this discourse, with Chalmers critiquing the previous Coalition government for wasting nearly a decade in office, essentially mocking good ideas while attempting to resurrect neoliberalism in Australia.

Indeed, the Australian economy stands at a juncture where rejuvenation, reform, and revitalisation are imperative. Over four decades have elapsed since the onset of neoliberalism worldwide, and the COVID-19 pandemic marks a clear endpoint to this economic era. The seismic shift triggered by COVID-19 necessitates a re-evaluation of economic thinking, providing an opportunity for Australia to redefine its path.

However, the Liberal Party's response has been marked by a persistent stream of negativity, ridiculing Chalmers for his efforts to reshape capitalism and introduce values-based economics. What is the point of the economy if it doesn't place human existence at the heart of its activity? Deputy Liberal Party leader Sussan Ley has led this charge and this perpetual negativism, though buoyed by media outlets that share similar perspectives, poses a significant risk to the party's future. When a political party chooses to sideline itself, without offering solutions, and abstains from contributing to the evolving narrative, it inevitably finds itself on the wrong side of history.

Historically, technological paradigms evolve and eventually face obsolescence or improvement. Traditional media, including print and free-to-air broadcast, are currently witnessing a shift towards new technologies such as streaming services. Forward-thinking businesses should acknowledge and adapt to these changes, much as smart business decisions should recognise the evolution of economic thinking.

Chalmers' success in achieving the goals he espouses is far from guaranteed, and the challenges facing the Australian economy will require time and thorough reform. The role of Treasurer demands not just effort but the ability to make those efforts bear fruit, yet, solid economic ideas, which are supported by good communication, should be implemented.

This is an opportune moment for these economic ideas to take root and sound economic management, political acumen, and a bit of good fortune are crucial for their success. However, Chalmers and the Labor government should not be overly concerned with the disarray within the Liberal Party, which seems poised for an extended spell in opposition, although this is always subject to change, given the ongoing volatility of Australian politics.

Instead, Chalmers and the Labor government should concentrate on preparing for substantial reforms that might take time to establish. Reforms will invariably cost political capital, but the prudent use of that capital on substantial, improving reforms is a worthy investment. The challenges of the present and the need for reform provide an ideal opportunity for the Labor Party to demonstrate its commitment to bettering the nation.

While these reforms may entail some short-term discomfort, they will ideally pave the way for longer-term improvements. The public's patience and support, provided the reforms prove effective, will be instrumental in ensuring their success.

Chalmers' essay has set in motion a conversation that extends well beyond economics. It encompasses political discourse, challenges conservative ideologies, and encourages Australia to adapt to the evolving global landscape. The window of opportunity is open, and it is now up to those in positions of influence to seize it. The future of Australia's economy and society hinges on the choices made in this defining decade, and the commitment to constructive reform is the beacon that can lead the nation toward a brighter future.

***

COMPLEX POLITICAL ISSUES SET THE START OF A NEW PARLIAMENTARY YEAR

11 February 2023

While each year in federal politics is different, and as Parliament reconvenes, it's apparent that the political landscape remains familiar—the government is eager to advance its policy agenda, the Opposition is striving to assert its relevance, and various other stakeholders are actively vying to shape the political outcomes. While there is a multitude of issues on the table, one topic that has garnered significant attention early in the year is the Voice to Parliament, which looms prominently on the political horizon.

The legacy of the past nine years of Coalition in office, marked by allegations of corruption and incompetence, still casts a shadow over federal politics, and the government's task includes not only steering the ship but also correcting past missteps. However, this journey is bound to be rife with blunders, missteps, and the growing pains that are inevitable as a new government navigates uncharted waters. In a political arena marked by complexity and nuance, missteps and controversies are likely to occur and some of these issues—such as the Stage 3 tax cuts—are residual traps set by the previous parliament, adding an extra layer of complexity to the political terrain.

The Voice to Parliament has emerged as a focal point of discussion in the early days of this year and it is expected to remain in the spotlight until a potential referendum occurs. This issue, however, has been marred by divisiveness, primarily due to the Coalition's attempts to frame it as a contentious matter. The Voice to Parliament is, in essence, a straightforward proposition that aligns with the wishes of the overwhelming majority of Indigenous people and should not be the focus of such division but, unfortunately in Australian politics, it is so easy to fabricate controversy and division over Indigenous affairs.

Nevertheless, there is a backdrop of contentious rhetoric from Peter Dutton, and media outlets such as Sky News, who are fervently opposing the initiative without presenting viable alternatives or clear articulation of their concerns. Their primary objection appears to be the clear association of the Voice to Parliament with the "Labor brand", prompting them to adopt an opposing stance. This stance has led to some internal divisions within the Coalition, with Liberal Party Senator Andrew Bragg arguing that the Voice to Parliament is an "Australian project" and a "Liberal solution" to Reconciliation, even though this has largely fallen on deaf ears within the party.

Opinion polls indicate substantial public support for the Voice to Parliament, despite the negative rhetoric from its detractors. It is worth noting that this situation might parallel the same-sex marriage plebiscite in 2017, which, despite similar opposition, ultimately succeeded. Critics like Dutton, Senator Jacinta Price, and Warren Mundine have been effective in communicating their "no" campaign, it's clear that they are trying to attract people beyond their existing support base with their relentlessly negative campaign.

The political stage is set for a year filled with challenges, potential reforms, and contentious debates. While the Voice to Parliament remains at the forefront, a multitude of other issues, from the Robodebt Royal Commission to economic concerns and immigration detention, promises a year of intricate political debate. The success of the government's agenda and the resolution of these debates remain uncertain, but what is clear is that 2023 is shaping up to be a year of significant political significance and change.

THE ROBODEBT SCANDAL, ECONOMIC CHALLENGES AND POLITICAL POSTURING

The Robodebt scheme is widely regarded as one of the most significant political scandals in Australia's history, characterised by its widespread implications and a staggering human toll.

The Robodebt Royal Commission, though currently on a short break, remains a topic of intense public interest. The hearings have revealed the profound impact of the Robodebt scheme, which tragically led to over 2,000 suicides, caused immense suffering to nearly 400,000 people, and resulted in a settlement cost of $1.8 billion for the government. The gravity of this scandal is not lost on anyone, and the fallout continues to reverberate.

What makes this issue even more complex is the role played by various stakeholders. The right-wing media's involvement, which has often been criticised for interfering in public perception and policy discourse, raises questions about its responsibility. Furthermore, external consultants, such as PriceWaterhouseCoopers, have been receiving substantial sums of taxpayer money for their services, sometimes without delivering on their contractual obligations.

This situation has prompted calls for additional investigations. Former Prime Minister Kevin Rudd has been advocating for a Royal Commission into the mainstream media in Australia, highlighting concerns about media influence and the framing of issues. Additionally, there have been suggestions to probe the role of external consultants like PriceWaterhouseCoopers, KPMG, EY, and McKinsey, in terms of value for taxpayer money and potential improprieties. The need for transparency in these dealings cannot be overstated, particularly in the context of such a significant scandal with far-reaching consequences.

In the realm of economic policy, interest rates have been a prominent feature in the political discourse. The recent rate increase marks the ninth since May 2022, a stark contrast to the Reserve Bank Governor Philip Lowe's earlier statement that interest rates would remain steady until 2024. This shift has not escaped public attention, as it directly affects households and businesses. While interest rate hikes are substantial news, other economic indicators paint a mixed picture. Share markets are on the rise, unemployment remains low, inflation, although elevated, has somewhat stabilised, and consumer confidence remains strong. Business confidence has experienced a slight decline, but it doesn't appear sufficient to undermine the government's standing on the economy.

In the end, these developments in the early days of 2023 illustrate the complexity and challenges inherent in Australian politics. The Robodebt scandal reminds us of the need for oversight, transparency, and accountability, particularly when taxpayer money is involved. Economic policy debates should be substantive, engaging with ideas, and offering alternatives. The onus is on the political leaders to rise to the occasion and provide the public with clear visions and effective governance.

OFFSHORE IMMIGRATION DETENTION AND THE NEED FOR HUMANITY

Despite the change in government, it appears that the fundamental policy regarding offshore detention remains largely unchanged. The government has extended contracts for immigration detention centres on Nauru and has yet to dismantle the system of offshore processing and temporary protection visas. This situation raises questions about the promises made by the Labor government during the 2022 election campaign, particularly the assertion that it is possible to be "strong on borders without being weak on humanity", a sentiment that was echoed by Home Affairs Minister Clare O'Neil during the week.

This glaring disconnect between rhetoric and action is evident: while the Labor government has articulated its intention to humanise the immigration detention system, the persistence of policies resembling those of the previous government paints a contradictory picture. It is crucial for political leaders to align their words with their actions and ensure that meaningful change occurs in the treatment of asylum seekers.

A poignant reminder of the suffering inflicted by these policies comes from the experiences of individuals like Behrouz Boochani, an Iranian journalist who spent six years in Australian immigration detention, first on Christmas Island and later on Manus Island under the "Pacific Solution" plan initiated by the Labor government in 2013. Boochani's eventual resettlement in New Zealand exemplifies how a nation can manage border control without compromising humanity.

Boochani's presence in the heart of Australian Parliament House, where he was promoting his book, *Freedom, Only Freedom*, is a powerful statement. When Peter Dutton was Minister for Home Affairs, he said that Boochani would "never set foot on Australian soil, yet here he was appearing at the institution which denied his human rights an asylum seeker, a move which showed that yet again, Dutton appears to always be on the wrong side of history, and on the wrong side of humanity.

It serves as a testament to the resilience of those who have endured the hardships of immigration detention. Boochani's call for a Royal Commission into the treatment of asylum seekers in Australia's detention centres is a cry for justice and a reckoning for the inhumane practices that have persisted for far too long.

This issue, like many others, is entrenched in the deep schism between the two major political parties in Australia. The Coalition has often seized upon human misery and the plight of asylum seekers for political gain, while Labor has struggled to find a coherent and humanitarian approach. In such a divisive political environment, it is the issue itself, involving the lives and dignity of vulnerable individuals, that suffers.

The challenges associated with immigration and border control are complex, and there are no simple solutions. However, it is essential to remember the moral obligation that nations have to refugees, as enshrined in international agreements. Humanity should be at the forefront of any policy dealing with asylum seekers. While there are no easy answers, it is evident that maintaining offshore detention centres, effectively acting as modern-day concentration camps, is a solution that helps no one, neither those seeking refuge nor the Australian people.

The hope is that the Labor government will re-evaluate the situation and take steps to rectify the ongoing crisis in offshore detention. The decision to extend contracts for detention centres is disheartening, and it is imperative that the government seeks a more humane and responsible approach. The plight of asylum seekers deserves a comprehensive and compassionate solution that respects the principles of human dignity and international agreements.

The beginning of the 2023 political year in Australia has revealed a host of critical issues, each with its unique complexities and challenges. From the Robodebt scandal to economic concerns, and the persistent problem of offshore immigration detention, these issues demand careful consideration, transparency, and ethical decision-making. The path ahead for Australian politics is a complex one, marked by the need for moral clarity and responsible governance.

***

THORPE'S DEFECTION AND THE INDIGENOUS RIGHTS DEBATE

11 February 2023

Senator Lidia Thorpe's recent defection from the Australian Greens has sent ripples through the federal politics, prompting a wave of reactions and speculation about its implications. Thorpe's decision to resign and sit as an independent Senator is significant, and it reflects a fundamental disagreement with her former party's stance on the Voice to Parliament.

The catalyst for Thorpe's departure was the Australian Greens' decision to support the "yes" campaign on the Voice to Parliament, a crucial issue within the broader Indigenous rights and Reconciliation debate. Thorpe, however, felt that prioritising Treaty was more essential and this schism within the party became the breaking point, leading to her resignation.

The notion of Treaty with Australia's Indigenous peoples is deeply intertwined with the historical context of European invasion and settlement in 1788 and the subsequent Federation in 1901. Unlike many other colonised nations, Australia has never established a formal treaty with its First Nations peoples. This omission has sparked persistent calls for Treaty, with many asserting that it is a necessary step toward addressing historical injustices, recognising Indigenous sovereignty, and reconciling the nation's past.

One of the most notable examples of such a treaty exists in New Zealand, where the Treaty of Waitangi was first agreed upon in 1840. Although the aftermath of the Treaty in New Zealand has been far from perfect, it remains a symbol of formal recognition and negotiation between the government and Indigenous Maori. In contrast, Australia, 193 years later, still resists the process of Treaty and Thorpe's resignation is, in part, a manifestation of this ongoing struggle.

Her decision to sit as an independent Senator on the crossbenches will undoubtedly reshape the Australian Senate and, with her newfound independence, Thorpe has the potential to become a significant player, as the government will need to negotiate with her to secure the passage of legislation.

Her ability to advocate for Indigenous rights, promote the Blak Sovereignty movement, and push for Treaty will largely depend on her effectiveness in navigating the intricacies of the Senate and building support for her agendas.

However, the outcome remains uncertain, and the ramifications of her defection are multifaceted. It is a challenge to sit as an independent Senator and to garner the necessary support to advance one's policy goals. While Thorpe possesses a national profile and a charismatic presence, she will face numerous hurdles, both within and beyond her control.

The Australian Greens, on the other hand, are left with the task of regrouping and moving forward after losing a prominent member of the party. The reactions to Thorpe's resignation have been polarised, with some criticising her decision and others supporting her right to leave a party that no longer aligns with her beliefs. In this complex situation, it is important to acknowledge the Indigenous perspective and recognise that Indigenous voices should be central to discussions about their rights and the path to reconciliation.

EXPLORING THE MERITS AND CHALLENGES OF INDIGENOUS RIGHTS IN AUSTRALIA

The debate surrounding the Indigenous Voice to Parliament, Treaty, and the broader Indigenous rights movement in Australia raises complex questions about political feasibility and the path toward achieving substantive change.

The Voice to Parliament, Treaty, the Blak Sovereign Movement, the Black GST (ending Genocide, acknowledging Sovereignty, and securing a peace Treaty), and the proposal for reserved positions in federal parliament all have their own unique merits and positions within Indigenous communities. These proposals reflect the diverse perspectives and needs of Indigenous peoples, showcasing the richness and complexity of their political beliefs.

Facilitating Indigenous Australia's chosen legal instruments is of paramount importance and the aspirations and demands of Indigenous communities should be respected and advanced as much as possible. However, the central question that arises is not merely about the merit of each idea but the practicality and political feasibility of achieving these objectives.

Within politics, there is always the art of what is achievable and compromise often takes precedence. The Indigenous Voice to Parliament, for example, can be viewed as a compromise aimed at addressing pressing issues, while recognising the political constraints and challenges. It might not fulfill all the expectations of Indigenous communities, but it represents a starting point that can be built upon and perfected over time.

On the other hand, the idea of Treaty is a significant step toward acknowledging Indigenous sovereignty and achieving justice. Victoria has already initiated the treaty negotiation process, but it's important to recognise that such negotiations take time. The history of the Mabo case in 1992, which eventually led to the Native Title system, illustrates how legal processes can be slow-moving. However, once the foundational structures are established, progress can be swift.

It's worth noting that "Treaty" means different things to different people and Indigenous communities have diverse political beliefs, as there are in any other segment of society. This diversity is evident in figures like Senator Jacinta Price and Warren Mundine, who hold varying perspectives on Indigenous issues. Additionally, groups like the Black GST, which includes prominent activists such as Marg Thorpe, Robbie Thorpe, Gary Foley, and Robert Corowa, offer their unique approach to addressing Indigenous rights.

The question of whether to wait for Treaty to be completed before implementing the Voice to Parliament or to proceed with both initiatives concurrently remains a matter of debate. These are complex issues that require careful consideration. It is challenging because Australia's political landscape offers limited and difficult opportunities for referendums, and getting the timing and substance right is crucial. Setting off with Treaty could potentially delay or hinder the progress of the Voice to Parliament, and given the uncertainty of future political windows, this might be the last opportunity for some time to enact meaningful change.

Critics of the Voice to Parliament have employed disingenuous arguments, such as the claim that its details are unclear, as a way to undermine its progress and Dutton's assertion that "nobody's answering my questions" falls into this category. However, such tactics are seen as dangerous and, ultimately, counterproductive. The Voice to Parliament, although not perfect, is considered by many as a significant step forward that can be further refined through legislative processes.

These initiatives, while not ideal in every respect, represent vital steps toward addressing historical injustices and advancing Indigenous rights and Reconciliation. The journey toward Indigenous self-determination and recognition is fraught with challenges, but it is imperative to seize the opportunities presented and move forward collectively. The intricate web of Indigenous rights, politics, and reconciliation necessitates thoughtful deliberation and action, and it is in this context that Thorpe's defection from the Australian Greens takes on added significance as part of the broader Indigenous rights discourse in Australia.

THE INDEPENDENT SENATOR: BALANCING POWER AND COMPROMISE

There are potential outcomes and implications that may arise from Thorpe's new status as an independent Senator. As a Senator for at least another five years, she has a significant window of opportunity to advance key Indigenous issues such as Blak Sovereignty, the Black GST, and Treaty. But will there be other receptive voices with the parliament that will take on and promote these initiatives?

The key challenge in Australia's political landscape is that decisions on these issues must be negotiated through the Parliament and ultimately approved by non-Indigenous communities or non-Indigenous representatives. This underscores the importance of the art of compromise, an essential aspect of political life, and a central role that Senators play, and it is this situation—an Indigenous community which comprises 3 per cent of the overall population, and depending on the rest of the electorate to approve decisions that affect their lives—that makes the issue so intractable.

While Thorpe was a member of the Australian Greens, the Labor government often needed the support of the Australian Greens and one other Senator, such as David Pocock, to pass critical legislation. Thorpe's defection changes the equation, requiring Labor to negotiate with the Australian Greens and *two* other Senators. This presents Lidia Thorpe with more tradable options and increased bargaining power and she can use her position to demand that the government initiate Treaty negotiations in exchange for her support on crucial legislation. If she can secure the backing of senators like David Pocock, her negotiating position becomes even more influential.

History has shown that when a government is desperate to pass its legislation, negotiations with key Senators can lead to significant concessions. The example of Senator Brian Harradine between 1996–99, who extracted benefits for Tasmania during negotiations over the GST legislation, demonstrates the potential power of a Senator in such circumstances.

However, it's important to recognise the limits of this power. Demanding too much from the government, however justifiable the demands may be, must be tempered by political realism. The government may opt to negotiate with other Senators, such as Jacqui Lambie, if Thorpe's demands seem too onerous, ultimately leading to a stalemate where no one achieves their goals.

Thorpe's career as an independent Senator holds both promise and uncertainty. Her ability to advocate for Indigenous rights and effect change will be determined by her strategic negotiation skills and the pragmatism with which she navigates the political landscape. While her departure from the Australian Greens has shifted the balance of power in the Senate, it is her ability to achieve what is politically achievable and the art of compromise that will shape her impact on Indigenous rights and Reconciliation in Australia. Whether her journey leads to a renewed term as a powerful Senator or fades into political irrelevance remains to be seen in the years ahead.

***

THE WEEK IN PARLIAMENT: REFLECTIONS ON THE APOLOGY TO THE STOLEN GENERATIONS

18 February 2023

There was another session of the federal Parliament this week, and many events and discussions unfolded, shining a spotlight on the diverse range of issues that take the attention of our elected representatives. The week was marked by Senate estimate committee hearings, which serve as a platform for scrutinising the government's actions and policies. Among the various matters discussed, one significant revelation took centre stage—the lapse of a major contract for offshore immigration detention centres in Nauru.

The most senior public servant in the Home Affairs department—Michael Pezzullo—found themselves at the heart of controversy as they failed to notify the government about this contract lapse and this failure raised questions about accountability and oversight within government departments, setting off debates about who should shoulder the blame for this oversight.

Meanwhile, the national energy market was a subject of fervent debate within the Parliament. Lawmakers grappled with critical questions about the country's energy future and responsibilities for ensuring a reliable and sustainable energy supply. These deliberations hold great significance, given the essential role of energy in the functioning of modern society.

In the midst of these discussions, a startling revelation emerged: the federal government had spent a staggering $7.6 million prosecuting whistleblowers, with a significant portion of these expenditures occurring during the tenure of the previous Coalition government. This revelation added fuel to the ongoing debate about government transparency, accountability, and the treatment of individuals who expose wrongdoing within organisations.

While these are all significant issues on their own, perhaps the most poignant moment of the week was the commemoration of the 15th anniversary of the National Apology to the Stolen Generations. It was a time to reflect on a dark chapter in Australia's history, a chapter that involved the forced removal of Aboriginal and Torres Strait Islander children from their families, communities, and country. The apology, delivered by then-Prime Minister Kevin Rudd, sought to acknowledge the profound grief, suffering, and loss inflicted on the Stolen Generations, their descendants, and their families.

> **Kevin Rudd:** "We reflect on their past mistreatment, we reflect in particular on the mistreatment of those who were stolen generations. This blemished chapter in our national history, the time has now come for the nation to turn a new page, a new page in Australia's history by righting the wrongs of the past. And so moving forward with confidence to the future. We apologise for the laws and policies of successive Parliament's and governments that have inflicted profound grief, suffering and loss on these our fellow Australians.
> We apologise, especially for the removal of Aboriginal and Torres Strait Islander children from their families, their communities and their country for the pain, suffering and hurt of these Stolen Generations, their descendants and for their families left behind, we say sorry. To the mothers and the fathers, the brothers and the sisters, for the breaking up of families and communities, we say sorry. And for the indignity and degradation thus inflicted on a proud people and a proud culture, we say sorry."

Rudd's apology was a landmark moment in the nation's history, characterised by its simplicity, sincerity, and symbolism. It contrasted starkly with the 11 years of intransigence displayed by the previous Prime Minister, John Howard, who had resisted such an apology on the grounds that the current generation should not be held responsible for the actions of the past. Contrary to Howard's predictions, the apology did not lead to a cascade of compensation claims, and it was embraced as a step towards healing by many Indigenous people and their communities.

The significance of the National Apology lay not in its financial cost but in its symbolic power. It acknowledged the continuity of the Australian Parliament since its inception in 1901 and recognised the Parliament's shared responsibility for past actions. The apology was a gesture that could not be revoked; it marked the first step on a long road toward reconciliation.

Nonetheless, the arguments against the apology back in 2008, claiming it was empty symbolism or too costly, find echoes in the current debates surrounding the Voice to Parliament. Peter Dutton, who had been a vocal opponent of the 2008 apology and walked out during Rudd's speech, has since apologised for his stance, acknowledging that he had "failed to grasp" the "symbolic significance" of the occasion. However, his current opposition to the Voice to Parliament raises questions about the sincerity of his change of heart.

As the week in Parliament unfolded, the nation was reminded of the complexities of government and the enduring importance of accountability, symbolism, and sincere acts of Reconciliation. It is a reminder that the past and present are inextricably linked, and the decisions made by our leaders today will shape the future of our nation. The question that remains is whether the lessons of the past will inform the actions of the present, ensuring that Australia moves forward with justice, compassion, and unity.

FISCAL PRIORITIES, STAGE 3 TAX CUTS AND COST OF LIVING PRESSURES

As the federal Parliament continued its deliberations, questions emerged about the Labor government's financial strategy and how it intends to fund its ambitious policy proposals. The list of initiatives includes proposed Medicare reforms, investments in social housing, and an ambitious infrastructure boost. However, the spotlight also falls on the proposed Stage 3 tax cuts set to begin in July 2024, which has generated significant debate and scrutiny.

The familiar refrain from the mainstream media revolves around funding these ambitious policy agendas, and the cyclical nature of these discussions often depends on the prevailing mood in the media landscape. However, it is essential to clarify that the source of funding for these initiatives remains a constant, irrespective of the political party in power. The money for government programs and projects primarily comes from the Reserve Bank of Australia, which can always provide the necessary financial resources when needed.

The central issue, then, is not where the money is coming from, but rather how the government chooses to allocate and spend these financial resources. Medicare reforms, investments in social housing, and infrastructure development are generally seen as valuable and necessary investments in the wellbeing and future of the nation. These areas of expenditure address essential public needs and contribute to societal welfare.

In contrast, the proposed Stage 3 tax cuts are raising a number of concerns. These tax cuts are not government spending; rather, they represent a reduction in government revenue, a form of foregone income. This move is particularly surprising, coming from a Labor government traditionally associated with policies aimed at reducing income inequality.

Questions arise about the wisdom of providing tax cuts to high-income earners, especially when the government claims to be committed to reducing economic disparities. Notably, polls in the past indicated that many individuals in the high-income bracket were open to forgoing tax cuts if the money were redirected toward critical areas such as healthcare, education, law enforcement, and infrastructure. The public sentiment suggests a preference for government resources to be allocated to essential services, which can have a substantial positive impact on society when effectively managed.

While the argument that these tax cuts are enshrined in law ("L.A.W. law," as former Prime Minister Paul Keating once famously put it) may be technically true, it is important to emphasise that laws can be repealed and modified. In this case, repealing tax cuts that primarily benefit high-income earners aligns with the government's commitment to reducing income inequality and promoting fiscal responsibility.

Cost of living pressures is a perennial issue in politics, one that politicians often exploit to gain political advantage. This issue takes on different meanings for different people and can encompass various economic concerns. It serves as a potent political message, especially for the Coalition, who have seized upon the narrative that "everything costs more under Labor".

However, it's crucial to recognise that prices in the economy are influenced by various factors, including the state of the economy, supply and demand dynamics, and external economic conditions. Prices do not inherently rise or fall under different governments but respond to a complex interplay of economic forces.

The federal Parliament's Senate Estimates hearings provide an opportunity for Senators to scrutinise the government's actions and policies, including those related to cost of living pressures. During recent hearings, Senators Bridget McKenzie and Matt Canavan, both from the National Party, directed their inquiries toward inane topics such staffing on Australia Day and the political activities of public servants.

While these questions might have their place somewhere in public discourse—where is not entirely clear—given the focus on cost of living pressures, it might have been expected that Senators from regional and rural constituencies would seek information on how the government plans to address the economic concerns of their constituents. These Senators represent communities where the cost of living is a significant issue, making it essential for them to prioritise this topic in their inquiries.

In the ongoing political discourse, the government's fiscal priorities and the effective allocation of resources will continue to be a subject of scrutiny and debate. The public and media will closely watch how the government balances its ambitious policy agenda, tax cuts, and addressing the real economic challenges faced by everyday Australians. The upcoming federal budget will provide a crucial opportunity for the government to outline its financial plans and demonstrate its commitment to addressing cost of living pressures while pursuing meaningful and effective policy initiatives.

WHISTLEBLOWERS, TAXATION REFORM, AND THE ASSANGE CONUNDRUM

One perennial challenge for any government is the risk of being excessively influenced by the media and the narratives they construct, as it is the media that often exerts pressure on politicians, shaping public perceptions and affecting the behaviour of elected officials. The egos and fears of politicians can lead them to be highly reactive to perceived negative media coverage, potentially diverting their attention from crucial policy priorities.

It is worth noting that inflation, a topic of current concern, is not primarily driven by high wages or increased discretionary spending, rather, inflation has been fueled by substantial corporate profits. This raises pertinent questions about the wisdom of providing tax cuts to high-income earners and the possibility of introducing measures such as super profits taxes and windfall taxes to mitigate excessive corporate gains. A broader discussion on tax reform in Australia is long overdue, given the complexity of the country's taxation system and measures such as simplifying tax laws and making it more equitable should be a fundamental goal in ensuring the economic wellbeing of all Australians.

Another financial matter that came to light during the week was the significant amount of taxpayer funds spent on prosecuting whistleblowers. The government incurred legal fees of $7.6 million, with a large portion spent on prosecuting Bernard Collaery and "Witness K", cases which ultimately ended with Attorney-General Mark Dreyfus dropping the charges. However, the cases against David McBride and Richard Boyle continue, having incurred substantial legal costs of $1.8 million and $233,000, respectively.

The ongoing prosecution of whistleblowers not only diverts taxpayer funds but also raises concerns about transparency and accountability within the government. While there may be valid reasons for the delay in resolving these cases, it is incumbent upon the government to expedite the process and bring these matters to a conclusion. The public has a legitimate interest in understanding the implications of such prosecutions on transparency and government accountability.

The case of Julian Assange—who is still languishing in Belmarsh Prison in London—presents a unique diplomatic challenge for the Australian government. Assange's ordeal, which spans many years, has involved various legal charges and international disputes. The Australian government's role in this matter primarily consists of diplomatic efforts to advocate for Assange's release. Prime Minister Anthony Albanese has voiced his view that the U.S. government should end its pursuit of Assange, but the matter remains highly complex and subject to ongoing diplomatic negotiations.

The case of Assange is both peculiar and perplexing. His legal troubles persist, even in the face of multiple legal victories that exonerated him from grave accusations. As he remains in confinement, the Australian government has a duty to persistently lobby for his release and ensure that justice is served.

The federal Parliament is a complex and dynamic arena where issues of all scales vie for attention. The role of MPs and Senators, the influence of the media, the management of the nation's finances, and the pursuit of justice for whistleblowers and individuals like Julian Assange are just a few of the multifaceted challenges and responsibilities faced by our representatives. In navigating these challenges, the government must strike a balance between public interest and the broader national agenda, maintaining a focus on addressing the most significant and pressing issues confronting the Australian people.

***

UNVEILING THE MAZE OF POLITICAL DONATIONS FROM GAMBLING COMPANIES

18 February 2023

Political donations have once again come into the spotlight, with recent revelations surrounding the Minister for Communications, Michelle Rowland—she had received a total of $19,000 in two separate donations from Sportsbet in the lead-up to the 2022 federal election. What adds a layer of complexity to this situation is that Rowland had previously served as the Opposition spokesperson on online gambling, and now, as Minister of Communications, she holds significant responsibility for the *Interactive Gambling Act* and the Australian Communications and Media Authority. The implications of these donations have sparked a debate on the ethics and legality of political donations from the gambling industry.

The crux of the issue lies in the fact that political donations often offer a direct avenue for financial influence on politicians. Politicians, in general, rarely—if ever—turn down the financial support coming their way, raising questions about the potential for undue influence in the legislative process.

What compounds the gravity of this issue is the nature of the donor: a gambling company. Sportsbet, in particular, is known for making substantial donations to both the Liberal and Labor parties and companies do not contribute financially without expectations of reciprocity, and it is naïve to believe that these contributions come without strings attached. The Minister cannot credibly assert that these substantial donations will not influence her perspective on gambling legislation.

While it is important to note that the Minister does not have sole control over legislation; decisions are typically made collectively by the Cabinet. This situation paints a disconcerting picture of potential conflicts of interest and political influence.

What further fuels public outrage is the fact that, from a legal standpoint, there is little to object to: no laws have been broken. The current reporting threshold for political donations in Australia stands at $14,500, and both of these donations from Sportsbet were, separately, well under that amount. The absence of legal repercussions exacerbates the public's sense of frustration and disillusionment with the political system.

In this context, it is evident that the issue extends beyond mere corruption; it is about the shortcomings in Australia's political donation framework. The disclosure laws urgently require reform, as do the political donation mechanisms themselves and these revelations prompt a deeper examination of Australia's campaign finance and political transparency landscape.

This is not the first time that political donations have elicited controversy. In the past, prominent figures liken former Prime Minister Tony Abbott, in a candid admission, spoke about accepting cash contributions intended to influence political decisions. Such stories shed light on the insidious nature of political donations and their use as tools to garner favour. The legal limit of $14,500 for disclosure further exacerbates the situation, creating opportunities for numerous smaller contributions, which, when aggregated, can significantly influence the political process.

Adding to the complexity, the gambling industry itself is contentious. While many individuals engage in gambling as a form of affordable entertainment, the industry is not without its darker side—problem gambling wreaks havoc on families, costing them millions of dollars every year. It is the problematic gamblers, the ones who cannot control their impulses, who bear the brunt of this insidious industry.

The advertising of gambling normalises the actions as a part of everyday life, often promoting odds during sporting events, either live events, or through broadcasting. The industry's influence on government actions raises questions about its role in shaping legislation and regulations. The need for stricter regulation, the elimination of gambling advertising, and increased transparency in political donations is now more apparent than ever.

In the wake of these revelations, many are calling for Minister Rowland's resignation, as her position is perceived as untenable. The confluence of significant donations from foreign-based gambling companies, lax regulations, and potential conflicts of interest demands immediate attention. The urgent need for comprehensive reforms in campaign finance and political donation laws is becoming increasingly clear. Publicly funded elections, despite their potential biases, offer a viable solution to eliminate the shadow of gambling money from Australian politics.

As this saga unfolds, the Prime Minister faces a critical decision: the credibility and integrity of the political system hang in the balance, demanding bold action to address the issue of political donations from gambling companies, while ensuring transparency, accountability, and the welfare of the nation's citizens remain at the forefront of legislative decisions.

THE PERSISTENT CHALLENGE OF POLITICAL DONATIONS AND THE QUEST FOR TRANSPARENCY

The issue of political donations in Australia is like a game of "cat and mouse", where the reporting threshold amount becomes the central point upon which each major political party sways. When the Labor Party takes the reins of power, they endeavour to reduce the reporting threshold amount. Conversely, the Liberal–National Coalition, when in office, tends to push for an increase in this threshold, to support donations from larger business interests. The motivation behind these strategies is clear: it serves the respective interests of the ruling party at any given time. These constant adjustments have perpetuated a system that is ripe for manipulation and have left the public yearning for transparency and fairness.

The calls for Rowland's resignation, not only from her ministerial portfolio but from the parliament itself, underscore the gravity of the situation and the question of whether she should relinquish her portfolio or return the donation received from Sportsbet has become a focal point of discussion. The inherent conflict of interest in holding a position of responsibility for online gambling while accepting donations from an online gambling company raises ethical concerns, however, the fundamental problem lies in the absence of any clear legal restrictions on ministers receiving donations related to their portfolios.

This recent episode with Rowland is just one example in a broader context of political finance concerns. The past has seen other instances, such as the case of former Labor Senator Sam Dastyari, where legal, but ethically questionable, donations were made to fund political activities. The transparency issue extends beyond the Labor Party, as the Liberal Party has faced scrutiny over the sources of its political donations. Third-party donations, such as those made by Gina Rinehart, serve to obscure the origins of funds further.

The general opacity surrounding political donations has left the Australian public questioning the motivations behind these contributions and their potential consequences. The ability of individuals and entities to donate without clear disclosure has fueled concerns about undue influence in the political process.

Efforts to address these concerns have been somewhat tepid—a Senate committee report on electoral matters in 2011 recommended a reduction in the threshold for anonymous donations down to $50, but these recommendations were never implemented. In most cases, smaller donors intend to support a party without expecting anything in return: it's primarily an effort to show their support for the political party of their choice. However, notable figures like mining magnates Rinehart and Andrew Forrest, who donate substantial sums, are likely seek a return on their investment, whether directly or indirectly.

To foster transparency and accountability in political donations, several key measures could be introduced. Setting a threshold on the maximum amount that any individual or entity can donate in a financial year or during the term of Parliament is a feasible step. Reducing the disclosure threshold to a mere $50 is a clear call to action, as is the adoption of real-time disclosure of all donations, as opposed to the current annual reporting system, and this would provide a more immediate and comprehensive view of financial contributions to political parties.

Despite these reforms, it is essential to recognise that political parties often find innovative ways to bypass rules, and unintended consequences can emerge. The quest for greater transparency might inadvertently drive political donations underground or onto the "dark web", yet, even in the face of these challenges, such reforms remain critical to preventing external entities from unduly influencing key government decisions.

The ultimate question is whether the major political parties, both Labor and the Liberal Party, possess the will to usher in these reforms. Achieving a system that is both fair and transparent is not only a noble aspiration but a fundamental component of a robust democratic process. The path forward may be fraught with complexities and uncertainties, but the pursuit of a cleaner and more accountable political donations landscape is an imperative that cannot be ignored. The time for change has never been more pressing.

***

THE INSIDIOUS LINK BETWEEN AUSTRALIAN FEDERAL POLICE AND NEWS CORPORATION

24 February 2023

The link between the Australian Federal Police and News Corporation has once again come under scrutiny, thanks to recent developments surrounding an alleged rape that took place in Parliament House in 2019. This troubling incident occurred just weeks before the federal election was announced, adding a layer of complexity to an already controversial case. What has particularly raised concerns is the role played by former Defence Minister Senator Linda Reynolds, who is now attempting to portray herself as a victim rather than someone who had a role in covering up the crime scene at the time.

However, the core issue that has emerged is the publication of the personal diaries of Brittany Higgins, which were provided to the police as part of the investigation into Bruce Lehrmann, the alleged perpetrator. These diaries, while provided to the federal police for investigative purposes, were not tendered as evidence in court, making them non-public documents, yet, these deeply personal and private diaries found their way into the pages of a News Corporation newspaper. This revelation has prompted an investigation by the ACT government into the conduct of the police during the Lehrmann trial and the release of this private material to a media outlet.

The publication of private diaries without permission or knowledge of the person involved raises significant ethical concerns and such an act can hardly be justified as being in the public interest. While it might have been defensible had these diaries been presented as evidence in court, this was clearly not the case. This breach of privacy is not only unethical but also raises questions about how News Corporation obtained access to these diaries and why they were deemed fit for publication without proper consent.

What adds further complexity is the absence of a similar level of attention given to the alleged perpetrator. While the case is ongoing, the focus on private documents and personal aspects of Higgins' life are intrusive and inappropriate. All sides involved in such sensitive cases should be shielded from the media spotlight until a civil court hearing takes place, except when it serves a genuine public interest.

The questionable actions of certain individuals within the News Corporation have come under the spotlight in recent times, remembering that this is an organisation with a history of controversial practices, such as the British phone-hacking scandal that involved tapping into a deceased girl's phone to retrieve voice messages. The Australian Federal Police has also been criticised for delving into people's private matters to uncover potential dirt and for running campaigns against individuals who threaten the status quo.

In the broader context, this case highlights the need for a thorough investigation into the Australian Federal Police as an institution. It is not just about one case; rather, it is about addressing systemic issues within the organisation. The suspicion that the Australian Federal Police may be protecting someone beyond the immediate case raises concerns about the transparency and integrity of the investigation and the stonewalling on various aspects of the case, including the release of CCTV footage and the handling of private "research" material within the jury room, only deepens these concerns.

The questionable actions of the police in this case, from wiping security tapes to steam cleaning the crime scene before involving law enforcement, suggest a broader issue at play. Whether it is an attempt to protect the political party or whether there were additional individuals involved, the situation is deeply distressing for all parties. The response of the Australian Federal Police raises questions about their priorities and their true role within the Australian politic.

The prevailing sentiment is that it may be time for a clean-out of senior members of the Australian Federal Police and a reformation of the entire system to ensure that the force is serving the interests of justice and the public, rather than being perceived as a partisan protector of political interests.

THE NEXUS OF LAW ENFORCEMENT AND MEDIA

The intertwining of the Australian Federal Police and News Corporation underscores a broader concern about the relationship between law enforcement and media organisations. This connection has evolved over time, starting with their origins as the Commonwealth Police, initially, perceived as a private police force or a militia designed to protect the sitting Prime Minister, dating back to 1917.

However, the force's evolution over the past five decades has brought it closer to the political and ideological thinking of conservative political parties, especially after 1996. This has been evident in various incidents, such as the raids on the ABC and journalists in 2019 and the use of the Australian Federal Police to raid the offices of Labor Party Senators and union offices in 2016. Additionally, the Australian Federal Police's involvement in investigating leaks related to the NBN project highlights its political entanglements.

While the force's actions might be argued as legitimate police work to uncover potential illegalities or wrongdoings, they have often been used to serve political agendas. The practice of leaking information to the media about upcoming raids, particularly when they don't lead to charges, raises questions about their role as a political tool rather than a neutral law enforcement agency.

The police force should focus on apolitical and unbiased law enforcement, ensuring equal protection and rights for all individuals. While it is natural for some police officers to have conservative views, this should not translate into biased or imbalanced treatment under the law.

The connection between the Australian Federal Police and News Corporation also raises great concerns, and while there is no direct accusation, the circumstances evoke memories of the British *News of the World* scandal that led to the Leveson inquiry in 2011.

The apparent influence of News Corporation, particularly Rupert Murdoch, on the Australian media landscape cannot be underestimated. In the eyes of many, this media conglomerate operates as a propaganda machine for conservative political parties, including the Liberal Party in Australia. The question arises: is this relationship compromising the integrity of the Australian Federal Police and the justice system as a whole? It may be time for a comprehensive investigation into these matters to ensure the media operates within the boundaries of ethical journalism.

Murdoch's influence, while extensive, should not be allowed to exempt him from scrutiny or accountability. To maintain a healthy democratic society, the media must be free and critical, but it should not infringe on the rights and privacy of individuals, especially in sensitive cases like the one involving Brittany Higgins.

The reluctance of politicians to address the issue of News Corporations's influence suggests a broader challenge and while it is crucial to have a free and critical press, it is equally important to address unethical behaviour and media outlets that cross the line. Striking a balance between a free press and accountability for unethical conduct is a complex task, but it is essential for the health of a democracy.

The Australian Federal Police needs to be reshaped to serve its fundamental purpose, free from political influence. At the same time, media organisations such as News Corporation must be held accountable for their actions, especially when they involve the publication of private, sensitive materials. Balancing a free press with ethical journalism and individual rights is a challenge that requires careful consideration, but it is a vital one for the maintenance of a healthy democratic society.

***

ANALYSING RECENT OPINION POLLS AND THE "HONEYMOON PERIOD"

24 February 2023

The recent opinion polls have sparked discussions about the standing of Prime Minister Anthony Albanese and the support for opposition leader Peter Dutton. While headlines have proclaimed "the end of the honeymoon for Albanese", it's important to analyse these developments within the broader context of Australian politics.

Firstly, despite the dip in support for Albanese, the Labor government maintains a significant lead in key polling indicators. In two-party preferred voting intentions, the Labor government is still ahead, with a 58 per cent to 42 per cent advantage over the opposition. Additionally, Albanese enjoys a considerable lead as the preferred Prime Minister and holds a net approval difference of 41 points against Peter Dutton. These statistics indicate that while there may be media attention on the decline in Albanese's personal ratings, the overall support for the Labor government remains robust.

The concept of a "honeymoon period" in politics is a cliché often used in the mainstream media, but it's essential to remember that such periods are largely driven by media narratives. The "honeymoon" phase represents the early period of a government's term when they are granted some leeway by the public and the period is ideal for a new government to start implementing its agenda and building goodwill with the electorate.

However, this is also the time when a government needs to demonstrate its ability to govern effectively and address key issues. While the media's focus on the "end of the honeymoon" may create the impression of a crisis, it is more crucial for the government to focus on governing competently and delivering on its promises.

Labor tends to panic when their polling numbers drop—as was shown when the numbers for former Prime Minister Kevin Rudd declined in 2010, although there were other reasons why the party removed him at their leader—and this can lead to leadership changes.

The true test for any government comes in its second year, as this is when the initial honeymoon phase starts to wane, and the government's performance is scrutinised more closely and the government's handling of the issues of the day and its ability to address problems, even those it didn't cause, will determine its electoral standing and longevity.

The Labor government, as outlined by Albanese's recent address at the National Press Club, seems to be focused on building greater security in the economy and people's lives through various policy initiatives. One of his key proposals mentioned is the reform of the superannuation system, particularly targeting the $53 billion in superannuation concessions for wealthy individuals. This issue reflects the government's commitment to creating a more equitable system and addressing budget concerns, especially in the context of reducing government debt.

Despite political opposition, the government's drive to reform superannuation should be viewed as a step towards creating a more equitable system and addressing fiscal challenges. It's crucial for the government to carefully navigate this issue and distinguish between genuine retirement planning and the use of superannuation as a tax haven.

The recent opinion polls and the media's focus on the "end of the honeymoon" period for the Albanese government should be viewed within the broader context of Australian politics. Of course, the government's standing within the electorate will drop over time, irrespective of how poorly the Liberal Party might be performing at this stage of the political cycle. The electorate is primarily concerned with economic wellbeing and, if there is a concern that the government is not addressing these issues sufficiently, then the support for the government will drop—that is one consistent factor in electoral matters for governments of all persuasions.

The government's focus, however, should remain on effective governance, addressing key issues, and building public trust, rather than reacting to short-term fluctuations in polling numbers. The second year of a government's term is a critical phase, and how well the government manages it will shape its political prospects and longevity. Addressing issues like superannuation reform while consulting a wide range of stakeholders, including those with different perspectives, will be crucial for effective governance and public confidence.

THE ALBANESE GOVERNMENT'S POLICY DECISIONS AND THE CRUCIAL ASTON BYELECTION

One notable issue raised is the potential amendment of the Stage 3 tax cuts by Prime Minister Albanese and Treasurer Jim Chalmers—these tax cuts have been a topic of contention, with concerns about their fairness and economic impact and while they have alluded to the need for these changes due to "difficult economic circumstances", the details remain uncertain, and there needs to be cautious about assuming that these tax cuts will be repealed or amended until concrete actions are taken.

Another significant concern relates to environmental matters, particularly the approval for 116 coal seam gas wells in Queensland. This decision, made by Environment Minister Tanya Plibersek, who has been relatively quiet in its announcement, raises questions about its environmental impact. Coal seam gas, often known as "fracking", is considered one of the most environmentally damaging forms of gas extraction and approving 116 such wells is seen as a significant environmental concern, especially when considering the cumulative impact on the ecosystem.

In addition, the connection between the approval and the company Santos, which has made substantial donations to political parties, raises concerns about the influence of corporate donations on political decisions—there are strong concerns within the electorate about political donations and its potential impact on the environment and governance, further emphasising the need for transparency and accountability in political funding.

The position of the Labor government is tenuous in these matters, attempting to balance environmental concerns with the interests of the mining sector and unions. This balancing act reflects the challenges facing political parties, especially in resource-rich countries like Australia. Achieving sustainable mining practices while addressing environmental concerns is difficult, and it does involve a delicate political balancing act, but the government does need to be called out for approving this amount of mining, at a time when it is trying to lessen the effects of climate change and reduce carbon footprints. It's a balance act that it might not be able to achieve.

These issues have the potential to impact the government's reputation and its relationship with the Australian electorate. However, the outcome of the upcoming byelection in the Melbourne seat of Aston will provide a clear indicator of the government's standing and whether the purported end of its honeymoon period is a reality or not.

***

MARCH

SUPERANNUATION POLITICS: UNVEILING RHETORIC, STRATEGIES, AND IMPLICATIONS

3 March 2023

The topic of superannuation, while often considered dull and uninteresting in most conversations, has taken centre stage in federal politics, with both the government and opposition fervently engaged in the debate, driven by differing motivations. The government's interest lies in closing a loophole to save the budget substantial amounts of money, while the opposition sees an opportunity to accuse the Prime Minister of breaking an election promise.

The proposed changes by the Labor government, which are set to come into effect after the next election, target a relatively small portion of the population, affecting roughly 80,000 people, accounting for only 0.5 per cent of all superannuation accounts. On the surface, it might appear as a minor adjustment that should not cause major concerns. However, the Liberal Party employs their time-tested strategy of magnifying minor issues into full-scale calamities to garner public support, drawing parallels with their 2019 campaign regarding share franking credits, wherein they convinced many that they would lose their credits, even if they had never owned shares.

The effectiveness of such scare campaigns tends to diminish when a party is in opposition, and the Labor government's proposed change is relatively straightforward to communicate—taxing superannuation accounts with over $3 million at a higher rate. To the average citizen, $3 million is a substantial sum, well beyond what most will accumulate in their entire working lifetime. From an equity perspective, this reform seems reasonable, retrieving funds from those who can comfortably afford it.

Nevertheless, critics have argued that the $3 million threshold may inadvertently affect individuals who are not wealthy, without clearly articulating why this would be the case. The shift in the job market towards the gig economy, contract work, and casualisation has resulted in decreased contributions to superannuation, particularly for those with fluctuating or multiple income sources. The mandatory superannuation system was initially implemented to reduce the strain on the pension system as the baby boomer generation retired. Encouraging individuals to establish private pensions—for those who could afford it—seemed to be a sensible policy to promote financial self-reliance.

However, the Liberal Party's historical opposition to compulsory superannuation raises questions about their current stance as supposed protectors of the system. They have consistently criticised industry super funds and their links with unions, despite their outperformance over retail super funds. Additionally, when they were in government, they allowed early access to superannuation funds during the early stages of the COVID pandemic, an action that challenged the stability of both the superannuation and housing markets.

NAVIGATING PURPOSE, POLITICS, AND TAX FAIRNESS

The superannuation debate in Australia has exposed not only the political strategies and ideologies of parties but also the fundamental question of the purpose and limits of the superannuation system. Superannuation, as originally designed, serves the purpose of providing a passive income during retirement and offers individuals the opportunity to secure their financial wellbeing in their later years, whether in conjunction with a pension or as a stand-alone retirement plan.

However, when superannuation accounts amass substantial sums, as in the case of the $3 million threshold, the original retirement plan becomes a vehicle for tax avoidance rather than retirement security. It is justifiable for the government to seek to close this loophole and the concept of fairness in the tax system dictates that those with the capacity to contribute more should do so. In this context, the proposal to increase the tax on superannuation accounts over $3 million from 15 per cent to 30 per cent is not only reasonable but also a measure that ensures a fair distribution of the tax burden.

The debate within the Liberal Party itself highlights the complexities of internal party politics. While some backbenchers such as moderates Russell Broadbent and Bridget Archer support discussing these reforms in the national interest, others, such as Shadow Treasurer Angus Taylor, seem intent on opposing them for political gain. The opposition's stance mirrors the approach employed by former Liberal Party leader Tony Abbott, whose *modus operandi* was characterised by "opposition for opposition's sake". While this approach may have served Abbott's political interests at the time in 2013, it is not necessarily a winning strategy for the Liberal Party in 2023 and is opportunistic and devoid of a coherent vision for the country.

Additionally, the threat of disendorsement against Archer, the member for the Tasmania seat of Bass, who has taken a constructive approach to the debate, highlights the challenges faced by those who strive to act in the national interest rather than simply promoting party interests. It raises concerns about the health of the democratic process and the role of elected representatives and if politicians prioritise party loyalty over the betterment of the nation, the system becomes susceptible to stagnation and a lack of meaningful progress.

Reflecting on the past nine years of Liberal government, one can hardly point to a substantial legacy or positive transformative policy. While it is not unusual for political legacies to have mixed outcomes, there is usually something tangible to point to. In the case of the recent Liberal governments, the legacy appears to be defined more by inertia than by impactful change, of restricting positive progress, rather than enhancing it. This raises questions about the party's purpose and its ability to govern effectively in the short to medium term.

The superannuation debate serves as a microcosm of the broader political landscape in Australia, showcasing the complexities, conflicts, and strategic considerations that define the political arena. As the debate continues, it remains to be seen how the various players will navigate the intricacies of political messaging and governance, and whether the proposed reforms will materialise as a meaningful change or remain a footnote in the nation's history.

BALANCING THE CHALLENGE OF A HOSTILE MEDIA AND PRIORITISING THE NATIONAL INTEREST

The superannuation reform debate also illustrates the complex landscape of Australian politics. The mainstream media, in many instances, amplifies the opposition's accusations, framing the reforms as a "tax hike" and fueling public skepticism. This poses a significant challenge for the government in achieving its objectives and communicating the merits of the reforms to the public.

One key question emerges from this situation: How can necessary reform be enacted in such a political environment? The dilemma faced by the Labor government, which previously ruled out changes to the superannuation system, showcases the difficulty of pursuing reform when it may be misrepresented and opposed during an election campaign. The question is whether to wait three more years to take the plan to an election, potentially facing similar obstacles, or to enact the changes that serve the national interest now.

The argument in favour of immediate reform is compelling. By taking decisive action, the Labor government can address a critical issue and remove political uncertainty from the equation. While the political heat generated by the opposition and media may be intense in the short term, allowing the reforms to settle and demonstrate their benefits can yield long-term political dividends.

This approach, however, is not without its challenges. Prime Minister Anthony Albanese must navigate the political consequences of such decisions and the electorate's response to these reforms is uncertain, and his political capital is diminishing, as it always does with political leaders. In addition, the Labor government should be prepared for a possible backlash from those affected by the changes which, in this case, seem to be the loudest voices in the debate, and are happy to magnified to a level far outside of their significance. To address this, the government might consider implementing grandfather clauses or transitional measures to mitigate the immediate impact on certain individuals.

The political landscape is changing, and the Labor government has an opportunity to shape its trajectory. The Liberal Party's standing among certain demographics, such as the Gen Z and Millenials, is eroding, while the party deals with questions about its long-term viability.

For the Labor government, there is a chance to garner support beyond the party's traditional base by demonstrating a commitment to sound fiscal management and fair taxation. By making efficient use of the revenues generated from these changes, such as investing in infrastructure, education, and healthcare, the government can align its policies with the public's stated priorities.

In the end, the Labor government faces a key choice: to focus on addressing important issues and serving the national interest or to remain preoccupied with managing the media and opposition's rhetoric. By seizing the opportunity to enact meaningful change, they can lay the foundation for a lasting and impactful legacy. It is a delicate balancing act, but it is in the hands of the government to decide whether they will prioritise the national interest over short-term political gain.

***

MEDIA REFORM IN AUSTRALIA: A CALL FOR COMPREHENSIVE CHANGE

3 March 2023

The role of the mainstream media in Australian has long been a topic of discussion, with concerns over issues ranging from press freedom and journalistic standards, to media ownership and diversity. A recent roundtable meeting convened by the Attorney–General, Mark Dreyfus, brought representatives from news agencies and media unions together to discuss matters of national secrecy laws and press freedoms for journalists and those involved in news gathering and political reporting. While it is undoubtedly crucial to address these concerns, it is essential to recognise that they are not the only issues at hand and there are more profound and often overlooked problems that require attention.

One such important issue is the lack of diversity in the Australian media, a media landscape considered to be one of the least diverse in the Western world. The dominance of a few major media conglomerates, including News Corporation, Seven West Media, and Nine Media, has led to limited perspectives and voices in the industry. The absence of independent media outlets like *Crikey* or *Saturday Paper* from the roundtable discussions further highlights the need for broader representation.

In addition to diversity, media ownership laws and a comprehensive code of conduct for the media demand urgent reform. Suggestions such imposing a cap on media ownership, limiting an entity's stake to 10 per cent of the industry, and establishing a revolving and independent press council with term limits could help mitigate potential biases that stem from long-standing relationships between journalists and politicians, and such measures would promote fairness and professionalism within the industry.

While discussions at the roundtable focused on government support for press freedoms and protections for journalists, it is equally important to address the issue of truth in journalism, where laws and regulations in Australia appear to be applied selectively, allowing the mainstream media to determine when they are to be adhered to. A more standardised approach to truth in journalism is needed to ensure that the public can trust the information they receive.

Moreover, the social media bargaining code, which was introduced with the intention of improving media diversity, has instead led to media concentration. This unintended consequence underscores the need to revisit this legislation and its impact on the media landscape. Another critical aspect that demands reform is the Australian Press Council—it is ineffective and requires significant restructuring, and to enhance its role in maintaining journalistic integrity, the council needs to undergo a substantial overhaul.

One of the most pressing issues is the fitness of media owners to hold licenses. Instances where media owners are deemed unsuitable to operate in the industry raise concerns about the standards and enforcement mechanisms in place. The reform agenda should include a thorough evaluation of media ownership licensing and, if necessary, the introduction of stricter enforceable codes of conduct.

The question remains: who should decide these standards, and how should they be enforced? The existing self-regulation approach is seen as inadequate. An independent press council for handling complaints, composed of representatives from both the media and the broader community, is one possible solution. This approach ensures a balanced view of issues and prevents undue influence from within the industry.

Moreover, a representative press council appeals or complaints board would contribute to the council's credibility by incorporating a diverse range of perspectives, including those of minorities and marginalised communities. Why are these voices not already included? This diversity is vital for addressing concerns that may not be readily apparent to the mainstream.

While discussions about improving press freedoms and journalist protections are commendable, they should not overshadow more extensive and deeply rooted issues within the Australian media landscape. Media reform in Australia must encompass a broad range of concerns, including diversity, ownership, truth in journalism, and the efficacy of regulatory bodies.

MURDOCH'S INFLUENCE AND THE IMPERATIVE FOR MEDIA REFORM

The case of Rupert Murdoch and his media empire, notably Fox News, offers a striking example of the need for media reform in Australia. The recent testimony by Murdoch in a defamation case in the United States highlights the role of powerful media figures in shaping public opinion and influencing political events. Murdoch's admission that Fox News endorsed the false narrative of a stolen U.S. election in 2020, despite knowing that this was not the case, raises important questions about media responsibility and accountability. This revelation about the head of one of the world's most influential news corporations underlines the urgency of media reform in Australia.

The influence of Murdoch and News Corporation in Australian media is considerable, and it is a mistake to ignore the impact of his holdings in the country. In an age where information knows no borders, Australians have access to global news outlets that often provide a more diverse and unbiased perspective. The dominance of media conglomerates like Murdoch's is a unique challenge that Australia faces, and it can limit the range of voices and opinions available to the public. In contrast, countries with stronger truth in journalism laws and a commitment to diverse media ownership—such as Canada and New Zealand—have managed to maintain the relative integrity of their news landscape.

The road to media reform is undoubtedly a complex and multifaceted one, but it is essential for preserving the integrity of journalism and maintaining public trust. The recent roundtable discussions, while commendable, must be followed by concrete actions and reforms that address the deeper issues affecting the Australian media landscape.

The call for a Royal Commission is one approach, but it may not be the most expedient one—legislative reforms that tackle issues like media ownership, diversity, and truth in journalism laws could bring about quicker and more effective change. It is in the best interest of the government to act swiftly on media reform to ensure that the public's trust in journalism is restored and maintained.

The issues surrounding media reform need to encompass everything from media ownership to journalistic integrity and accountability. The revelations about Murdoch's role in shaping public opinion in the United States underscore the power that media figures hold and the importance of addressing such issues comprehensively. As the landscape of journalism continues to evolve, it is crucial for Australia to adapt and enact reforms that foster a diverse and trustworthy media environment for the benefit of all Australians. Only through comprehensive reform can Australia's media industry develop into a more transparent, accountable, and equitable institution, serving the interests of both journalists and the public.

***

THE ROBODEBT SCANDAL: UNRAVELING THE CONTROVERSIAL WELFARE DEBACLE

3 March 2023

The controversial Robodebt scheme has been a subject of great scrutiny and criticism and the ongoing Robodebt Royal Commission has shed some light on many concerning aspects related to the scheme. Taking this into account, it is perplexing that this scandal, one of significant national consequence, has not received the level of attention and public outcry that it deserves. The intricate web of issues surrounding Robodebt is too substantial to ignore, and its implications extend beyond welfare recipients and into the very core of governance and responsibility.

One of the central figures in the Robodebt scandal is Stuart Robert, the former Government Services Minister. The evidence presented during the Royal Commission indicates that Robert was made aware by the Secretary of Human Services that the Robodebt scheme was, in fact, unlawful and, instead of taking appropriate action to rectify this, he responded dismissively, suggesting that it was merely a legal opinion and even expressed his intention to double down on the scheme. This response raises fundamental questions about the role and accountability of government officials and it highlights a willingness to disregard legal and ethical concerns in pursuit of political agendas.

The actions of Reneé Leon, the former Secretary of Human Services, further illuminate the deeply problematic nature of the government's response to the scheme's unlawfulness, where she testified that officials who supported the Minister's agenda were rewarded, while those who provided negative advice were punished. Leon herself faced dismissal after suggesting the scheme was unlawful. This not only demonstrates a clear disregard for the law but also creates an environment where public servants fear repercussions for acting in accordance with their professional and ethical responsibilities.

The behaviour of Robert as Minister, and that of the former Prime Minister, Scott Morrison, during their appearances at the Royal Commission is disconcerting. When questioned about the accuracy of the statistics used to justify the Robodebt scheme, Robert offered dismissive and evasive responses and his approach mirrored a broader issue within the Coalition government at the time, where political expediency appeared to take precedence over transparency and truth.

At the heart of the Robodebt scandal is the willingness of the Liberal–National Coalition Government to push through an agenda that, despite being morally, ethically, and legally questionable, was pursued with unwavering determination. This reveals a systemic problem within the government where, at times, it seems necessary for the public to be protected from its own elected officials. Governance demands a duty of care for citizens, and the persistent disregard for this duty throughout the Robodebt saga is deeply troubling.

Within this scandal, there is a painful human cost: welfare recipients, already struggling will many pressures and life issues, faced punitive measures from the Robodebt scheme, leading some to take their own lives. The exact number of casualties remains disputed, but even one life lost to such a extreme program is a tragedy. The Robodebt scandal reveals not only a lack of care but also an alarming level of arrogance and entitlement among those in power, and the belief that they could act with impunity, irrespective of the harm caused, is a stain on the principles of good governance and public service.

The Robodebt scandal is a grave reflection of the challenges that exist within government systems and highlights the need for a robust system of checks and balances to ensure that the wellbeing and rights of citizens are protected. The Robodebt Royal Commission continues to unveil shocking revelations, and it is crucial that these issues are addressed and rectified to prevent future instances of such disregard for ethics, legality, and public welfare. The scandal serves as a stark reminder that citizens must remain vigilant in holding their governments accountable and to paraphrase the philosopher John Stuart Mill, "all evil needs is for good people to do nothing".

A TALE OF INJUSTICE, IDEOLOGY, AND INDIFFERENCE

The continued attention and scrutiny of the Robodebt Royal Commission isn't just a fixation, it's a necessary examination of a depraved government scheme that affected so many people and the disbelief that many feel about the scheme's implementation and the suffering it caused is a testament to the need for accountability and justice. This Royal Commission has uncovered a consistent theme of indifference to the suffering of welfare recipients, a disregard for the illegalities of the scheme, and a striking level of incompetence across various levels of ministries and government.

Aside from the bizarre and punitive action contained within this scheme, the most perplexing aspect of Robodebt is its negligible financial impact in the context of the overall government budget. The scheme managed to recoup approximately $750 million over three years, a relatively minuscule sum in comparison to the vast government expenditure that hovers around $600 to $700 trillion annually. In essence, the amount recovered didn't even justify the resources expended in the implementation and subsequent legal challenges which, of course, begs the question: what was the driving force behind the relentless pursuit of this questionable policy?

The evidence points to an ideological pursuit rather than a fiscal one. The Robodebt scheme was, in essence, an instrument to punish the poor and vulnerable and points to the ideology of the modern Liberal Party, which tends to champion the interests of the wealthy while being less concerned with the welfare of the most marginalised in society.

Moreover, it is evident that legal advice on the scheme's validity was consistently ignored by government. Every piece of advice received by the government indicated that the scheme was unlawful and would not withstand a legal challenge and in light of this, there would be an expectation that a responsible government to reconsider and reassess the policy's impact. Yet, the Coalition government not only persisted but also refused to question the legitimacy of their accusations against welfare recipients.

The discrepancy between the number of people accused of rorting the system and the actual number found guilty of doing so is staggering and the data shows that the accusations of "rorts" were grossly overblown, leading to immense hardship for innocent individuals. While the money that was illegally taken by the government has been repaid in many cases, it never should have been extracted in the first place, and shows a complete disregard for the wellbeing and dignity of those who rely on welfare support.

The potential political motivations behind Robodebt's implementation also raise strong concerns. It is conceivable that the scheme was designed to hand the Labor government a political and financial burden, undermining their budgetary capabilities and the political calculations behind such a move may be a cynical ploy to gain an upper hand in future elections. While this issue remains speculative, it underscores the complex and often Machiavellian dynamics that operate within the political landscape, especially for the Liberal Party.

The Robodebt scandal is a striking illustration of government negligence, indifference, and an apparent willingness to sacrifice the welfare of citizens for political or ideological gains. The ongoing Robodebt Royal Commission is a vital process to uncover the truth and determine accountability and it is essential that the Commission thoroughly investigates the actions and decisions that led to this deeply flawed scheme and, if warranted, takes measures to hold those responsible to account. The lack of mainstream media interest in this critical issue is concerning, as it remains a matter of significant public interest and importance. The principles of justice and fairness demand that the lessons learned from Robodebt serve as a catalyst for positive change in government policies and practices.

***

UKRAINE CONFLICT: RUSSIA'S INVASION AFTER ONE YEAR WITH NO END IN SIGHT

3 March 2023

The war in Ukraine, caused by the invasion by Russia, has defied initial expectations of a short and quick conflict and extended past its first year and is showing no signs of imminent resolution. As the Prussian general and war theorist Carl von Clausewitz famously stated, "war is an extension of politics by other means," and this conflict exemplifies the complexities that often underlie armed conflicts. The prevailing belief that wars will continue until both sides are exhausted and recognise the futility of their endeavours holds true for Ukraine. However, one year on, it is evident that Russia is the primary loser in this protracted confrontation.

The situation in Ukraine bears striking resemblances to Russia's involvement in other conflicts, such as Afghanistan and Chechnya where, in both cases, Russia's military interventions, initially intended to be short-lived, transformed into extended, brutal conflicts. These historical parallels raise questions about the competence and effectiveness of the Russian military, revealing that having a massive army does not necessarily guarantee success in modern warfare.

At its core, the war in Ukraine can be understood as part of Vladimir Putin's efforts to reshape European geopolitics but despite the Russian president's ambitions, the endeavour has not yielded the desired results. Rather, the war has imposed a heavy human toll, with estimates of casualties ranging from 100,000 to 300,000 people, including military personnel and civilians on both sides. In addition, the conflict has displaced around six million people, a staggering number that underscores the humanitarian crisis that has unfolded.

Tragically, as is the case in most conflicts, it is the ordinary civilians and soldiers who bear the brunt of the suffering, while the political leaders often remain removed from the immediate consequences of their decisions. The war in Ukraine has prompted intriguing alliances and polarised opinions, with some surprising voices in support of Vladimir Putin, including patriotic Americans and Australians who argue that Ukraine is rife with Nazi sympathizers. While there are military units in Ukraine with far-right affiliations, the extent of this ideology's prevalence across the entire country remains uncertain.

One notable outcome of this conflict is the transformation of Ukraine's President Volodymyr Zelenskyy, who, before the war, was an unpopular leader. In the face of the crisis, Zelenskyy has emerged as a wartime leader, echoing the transformation of Winston Churchill during World War II, when he transitioned from being widely underestimated to being celebrated as one of Britain's greatest prime ministers.

However, the fog of war and the sophisticated propaganda machinery employed by both sides make it challenging to discern the truth. Ukrainian victories are countered with Russian claims of success, and the situation on the ground seems in constant flux, with claims being made that Ukraine either on the brink of falling, or Russia being on the verge of retreat. The uncertainty extends to those on the ground, further emphasising the difficulties in obtaining an accurate picture of the conflict.

Russia's initial hopes for a swift and perhaps limited victory, potentially confined to regaining disputed regions with Russian majorities, have given way to a protracted, entrenched conflict. The Ukrainian people's resolute determination to resist Russian encroachment stems from a deeply rooted history of tension between Ukraine and Russia, which only momentarily subsided during the era of the Soviet Union, and re-emerged after the collapse of this empire in 1991. These historical undercurrents continue to shape the dynamics of the conflict, underscoring the complexity of the situation.

THE ELUSIVE PATHWAY TO PEACE

The war in Ukraine presents a dilemma with no obvious exit strategy for either party and a decisive victory seems unlikely for either Russia and Ukraine. The Ukrainian army's size and capabilities may not be sufficient for a decisive victory, and Russia's military appears to be in disarray, making a clear-cut triumph equally challenging to attain. The prospect of a unifying international figure, a mediator with the stature of someone such as former U.S. President Jimmy Carter, seems elusive. While another U.S. President Barack Obama possesses the intelligence and capability to resolve this issue, his strained relationship with Vladimir Putin undermines his effectiveness as a peace negotiator in this situation.

Australia has been a significant contributor to the conflict, providing substantial support, including military hardware, amounting to $655 million.

This assistance is expected to continue, underlining Australia's commitment to the situation. However, the bulk of support for Ukraine comes from the U.S. government, with $44 billion in contributions; and the United Kingdom follows with $5 billion. In this context, the conflict takes on the appearance of a proxy war between the U.S. and Russia, reflecting broader geopolitical dynamics.

China's offer to mediate and its 12-point political settlement proposal represents an alternative diplomatic avenue and President Zelenskyy has indicated his willingness to discuss some of these points. However, it's worth noting that the U.S. government may prefer the war's continuation rather than Chinese intervention, given the broader geopolitical implications of China's involvement in the conflict.

The war in Ukraine is a multifaceted issue with geopolitical dimensions that extend far beyond the region itself. Unfortunately, it appears that this conflict will persist for the foreseeable future and the lack of a clear resolution path, coupled with the uncertainty and misinformation surrounding the conflict, suggests that an end is not in sight. This enduring tragedy affects not only Ukrainians and Russians directly involved but has repercussions across the world, making it a protracted crisis with global implications.

Geopolitical dynamics, the absence of a clear mediator, and the competing interests of various world powers have contributed to the war's intractability but the hope is that a peaceful resolution will eventually prevail, bringing relief to the people of Ukraine and an end to this tragic chapter in European history.

***

THE WAR WITH CHINA MEDIA SENSATIONALISM AND RACIAL BIAS

10 March 2023

Amidst growing discussions about the "possibility of war" with China—pushed forward by the leader of the opposition, Peter Dutton—Australian media outlets have recently ignited controversy by promoting the idea of preparing for conflict. The *Sydney Morning Herald* and *The Age*, both owned by Nine Media, have been at the forefront of this discourse, further added to by News Corporation's contributions. This narrative is part of Nine Media's 'Red Alert' series, a five-person panel's collective effort to explore the question of whether Australia is prepared for war with China.

The 'Red Alert' panel comprises former senior Defence Department official Peter Jennings, university lecturer in Strategic Studies and criminology Lavina Lee, former Federal Chief Scientist Alan Finkel, the chair of the National Institute of Strategic Resilience Leslie Seebeck, and retired Army Major General Mick Ryan. While the panel lacks any official authority, it brings together a group of former officials with predominantly white Anglo backgrounds, with no specialist expertise on China. This fact has raised concerns, as it excludes perspectives from any individuals with Chinese heritage and questions their expertise on Chinese politics.

In addition, several panel members, such as Peter Jennings and journalist Peter Hartcher, have taken a hawkish stance on the idea of a war with China, and this bias has led to accusations of sensationalism and irresponsible journalism.

The broader question that arises is why such a discussion on the prospect of war with China has emerged in the first place. Australia and China have maintained a traditionally positive relationship since 1972 when Gough Whitlam officially recognised China as a state and established an embassy in Beijing. Subsequent leaders, including Malcolm Fraser and John Howard, never rescinded this recognition and although there have been challenges and controversies within the Chinese community during Howard's tenure, especially he made calls to limit Asian immigration in 1988 while he was leader of the opposition, the overall diplomatic and economic relationship has been prosperous.

China stands as Australia's largest trade partner, and the country is home to a significant population with Chinese heritage, some of whom have been present in Australia for over a century. This historical context underlines the complexity and depth of the relationship between the two nations.

It's evident that this push for a war narrative is influenced by a historical pattern seen in the conservative media, where war and conflict have been seen as profitable for media outlets. As newspapers lose influence among the younger demographics, the strategy of stirring up conflict to gain readership remains a contentious issue and while the media industry adjusts to new audiences and their news consumption habits, there is skepticism about whether the calls for war with China genuinely represent public sentiment or if they serve other self-centred interests.

SENSATIONALISM AND GEOPOLITICAL REALITIES

It is important to recognise that throughout history, there have been consistent tensions between major world powers, often reflecting the dynamics of the global stage. The Cold War era witnessed a protracted conflict between the United States and the Soviet Union, a period marked by intense rivalry, ideological confrontation, and geopolitical posturing. The ever-present threat of war provided a backdrop for the military-industrial complex, not only in the United States but across the globe and this pattern of geopolitics, which requires a perceived adversary to fuel military interests, has persisted for generations.

It is worth noting that despite the intensity of the Cold War, neither the United States nor the Soviet Union engaged in direct military conflict. The Cuban Missile Crisis in 1962 was perhaps the closest the world came to an all-out war between superpowers but this history provides a crucial context for any discussions about war with China, emphasising that superpowers seldom engage in direct confrontations.

Similarly, tensions between China and Australia have arisen, especially during the tenure of the Coalition government, which began after 2013. Australia's relationship with China has faced challenges, but efforts have been made to repair it gradually but these issues do not necessarily equate to an impending war.

The recent rhetoric of war with China is characterised by sensationalism and lacks a clear, credible explanation of how such a war might unfold, what the precipitating factors might be, or the specific circumstances involved. This approach is taken by the mainstream media—certainly in this instance—is the classic example of "clickbait" material, rooted in the interests of organisations such as the conservative Australian Strategic Policy Institute, which promotes defence industry interests and is aligned with the political interests of the Liberal Party.

Connections between political figures and the defence industry in Australia have also raised concerns. Former Liberal Party Minister Christopher Pyne's involvement with military manufacturers, and former Liberal Party treasurer Peter Costello's chairmanship of Nine Media, demonstrate a web of interests—in the military and the media industries—that benefit from pushing the argument that Australia is "unprepared" for war with China and these affiliations have led some to question the motivations behind such rhetoric. What exactly does being "unprepared" for a war with China mean in any case? China's armed forces personnel is 55 times larger than Australia's; has 153 times the amount of battle tanks; 16 times larger air force and a military budget six times larger. What is even the point of making a public comparison between the two countries, when there is such a massive imbalance, and how would Australia prepare itself in a military conflict with China? The pressing concern remains the potential consequences of such sensationalism, which can incite fear and uncertainty among the public.

The global landscape is shifting, with the United States experiencing relative decline and China's ascent as a major power. Consequently, tensions are expected, but neither side has a significant interest in committing to an all-out war, as was the case during the Cold War era between the U.S. and Soviet Union. The risks are immense, and the costs of such a conflict could be catastrophic. Australia's role in this context, as some critics argue, may not be as significant as portrayed in the sensationalised narrative.

The debate surrounding war with China is complex and multilayered, encompassing historical context, geopolitical dynamics, and vested interests. But the sensationalist tone of the media discourse is essentially an exercise in trouble-making and pursuing vested interests. The need for a nuanced, fact-based discussion that accounts for the complexities of international relations is more critical than ever, particularly when considering issues of such gravity.

KEATING DENOUNCES THE MEDIA SENSATIONALISM ON CHINA

Former Prime Minister Paul Keating has openly criticised the media outlets for their role in promoting what he deems as the most egregious and provocative news presentations in his over five decades in public life. Keating's critique resonates with many who believe that the sensationalist tone of the discussion has reached alarming and unnecessarily provocative levels.

However, despite the outrage and debate this sensationalism has generated, it may not carry significant weight or influence, particularly on the global stage. The economic relationship between Australia and China is substantial, with two-way trade valued at $235 billion annually, consisting of $153 billion in Australian exports and $82 billion in imports from China and both nations have a vested interest in maintaining this economic relationship and would be cautious about jeopardising it, despite whatever self-interest exists at Nine Media.

Nonetheless, the sensationalism in the media continues to perpetuate problematic narratives. The "Red Alert" title echoes historical tropes like "reds under the bed" and the "Yellow peril" mania in the earlier parts of the twentieth century and feeds into a racist undercurrent that has persisted in Australia's history. This media approach not only contributes to racist undertones but also puts pressure on the Chinese communities within Australia, who often bear the brunt of such media-driven paranoia.

Racism remains a prevalent driving force in Australian politics and discourse, which is particularly concerning given the diversity of the domestic population. The under-35 demographic is generally more inclusive and less influenced by such narratives, marking a shift in the nation's cultural and social dynamics and, as this demographic continues to grow and gain political influence, the outdated and short-term ideas propagated by certain media outlets will face increasing resistance.

The sensational rhetoric regarding "war with China" in Australian media raises complex issues that go beyond mere journalistic responsibility. It touches on the deeper problem of perpetuating problematic narratives and the impact on diverse communities within Australia. The nation's future will be shaped by the evolving dynamics of its population, and how it addresses these issues will have a significant bearing on its long-term trajectory. It is a call for introspection and responsible journalism in an era when the consequences of misinformation and sensationalism can have far-reaching implications.

***

THE AUKUS AGREEMENT: A COMPREHENSIVE ANALYSIS

17 March 2023

The AUKUS agreement, a trilateral security partnership involving Australia, Britain, and the United States, has generated substantial public attention and debate since its announcement. While some details have emerged, much of the agreement remains shrouded in secrecy. However, it is clear that the AUKUS agreement is a significant and ambitious undertaking, with the announced price tag of $368 billion over 30 years, primarily for the acquisition of nuclear submarines.

One of the central components of the agreement is the acquisition of nuclear submarines by the Australian government and the plan involves the purchase of at least three nuclear submarines, possibly supplemented by three secondhand submarines in the early 2030s. Over the following decades, there is a commitment to construct one new submarine every two years, potentially resulting in a fleet of around ten submarines by the late 2050s. This sizeable investment in submarine technology raises concerns about the agreement's long-term relevance and its alignment with future geopolitical circumstances.

A critical question that arises is whether large-scale submarine technology will still be strategically important in 30 years and given the rapidly evolving nature of military technology and the shifting global landscape, the AUKUS nations must carefully consider whether this substantial investment aligns with future defence needs. Moreover, the agreement's staggering cost has sparked debate, particularly regarding the allocation of resources. The availability of $368 billion for submarines contrasts with the recurrent struggle governments face when financing critical domestic sectors such as healthcare, education, and infrastructure.

In a broader context, it is essential to recognise that defence encompasses more than just military capabilities, it extends to biological, environmental, and cultural defence. Cultural defence, in particular, involves safeguarding a nation's cultural identity against external influences or efforts to assimilate it into larger cultural entities. While military defence is necessary for protecting sovereignty, a balanced approach should be adopted to address all facets of national security and wellbeing.

The AUKUS agreement reflects a sense of overemphasis on military defence, particularly concerning potential future threats, and the subtext here always circulates over China. However, the perception of China as an imminent aggressor in the region is highly subjective. Different sources and opinions exist regarding the nature of China's intentions, but many highlight the significance of China as a trading partner and potential ally, and prudent foreign policy should aim to engage with, rather than antagonise, these types of partners.

The role of Australia in this context is essential: as a middle power, Australia has an opportunity to play a constructive role in mediating between major powers and by emphasising diplomacy, cultural, and social influence, Australia can contribute positively to the South Pacific region. The AUKUS agreement, in contrast, might raise doubts about Australia's neutrality and regional peacemaking efforts.

The AUKUS agreement has sparked a range of questions and concerns, especially the substantial cost, the uncertainty of its long-term relevance, and the potential to strain Australia's diplomatic position in the region. In addition, the agreement's implications for domestic budgeting and resource allocation are under scrutiny, especially in contrast to other pressing national needs.

POLITICAL, GEOPOLITICAL, AND MEDIA DIMENSIONS

At its core, the AUKUS agreement is a political endeavour, with the various actors seeking to secure their interests and bolster their political standing. The decision to invest heavily in military technology, especially nuclear submarines, is driven by a need to anticipate potential future threats, however, it appears that the worst-case scenario has become a primary consideration, apparently, a full-on conflagration with China. While prudent planning is essential, the question looms: should nations allocate such vast resources based on unlikely, extreme scenarios? In comparison, when it comes to climate change—which is a far greater threat to humanity—governments seem to have taken a "best-case" scenario approach, despite the pressing global threat it represents.

The technological aspect of the agreement raises questions about the future of submarine technology—the agreement's investment in nuclear submarines may be obsolete in 20, 30, or 40 years, as emerging technologies such as cluster and drone systems could prove more effective and cost-efficient. Geopolitical dynamics, too, may evolve significantly in the coming decades, as history has shown that global power structures are subject to change. The collapse of the Soviet Union in 1991, once seen as a major existential and physical threat, serves as a poignant reminder of how rapidly geopolitical landscapes can shift.

Another layer to the AUKUS agreement is its role in supporting the military industry and maintaining employment in the three participating countries: Australia, the UK, and the U.S. The justification that the agreement sends a message of containment to China remains nebulous and secretive and its potential to be redefined by future governments highlights its lack of accountability and transparency. As shifts in political leadership occur over the next 50 years, the agreement could be reshaped in ways that are difficult to predict and it is this ambiguity that introduces an element of uncertainty into the long-term strategic implications of AUKUS.

Despite the weighty considerations involved, the manner in which the agreement has been managed and communicated raises concerns. While some aspects may be enshrined in contracts that cannot be easily renegotiated, the public relations surrounding AUKUS have been questionable. The agreement was introduced through a "feel-good" narrative, presenting it as excellent news for Australia and the political optics of this announcement are evident, as wartime leadership personas have historically been coveted by leaders. However, the lack of transparency and constructive dialogue with the public leaves room for skepticism.

The AUKUS agreement is a complex mixture, compiled from political considerations and geopolitical uncertainties, and while the need for robust defence planning is undeniable, the agreement's details and its alignment with future realities remain subjects of scrutiny. The manner in which it is managed and communicated has led to skepticism and questions about its long-term implications.

IMPLICATIONS AND AUSTRALIA'S ROLE

Former Prime Minister Paul Keating, known for his forthright views, criticised the AUKUS deal and had strong words for the media's handling of the issue, questioning the media's bias in its choice of specialists and their presentation of an allegedly one-sided view on China. He also emphasised that great power diplomacy should focus on overarching issues rather than delving into each other's domestic challenges. Keating suggested that AUKUS is the Labor Party's worst foreign affairs decision since the conscription referendums of 1916 and 1917, and asserts that if he were still Prime Minister, he would have never allowed the AUKUS deal to happen.

As a middle power, Australia's decisions in the realm of international affairs are often influenced by larger, more powerful nations, particularly the United States. The historical example of Gough Whitlam's attempts to shift Australia toward a more autonomous direction in the 1970s and the repercussions he faced underscores the limitations of unilateral decisions in foreign policy. AUKUS, whether viewed positively or negatively, is a reflection of the geopolitical constraints Australia operates within.

The AUKUS deal is an expensive deal. The concerns over underfunded schools, hospitals, and other essential sectors, contrasted with the exuberance surrounding the agreement, highlight a misalignment between the far-more-important national priorities and defence expenditures, which essentially exist in the realm of the hypothetical and conceptual frameworks of events that may never happen. It's difficult to reconcile this anomaly.

In the end, the AUKUS agreement is a complex and multifaceted arrangement with global implications. It reflects the evolving dynamics of international relations, the constraints placed on middle powers like Australia, and the challenges of striking a balance between defence and domestic priorities. The discussions and debates surrounding AUKUS underscore the importance of public discourse, accountability, and transparency in shaping a nation's foreign policy.

As AUKUS continues to unfold and influence Australia's role on the world stage, it remains essential to scrutinise its long-term consequences, consider alternative approaches, and ensure that the nation's decisions align with its broader national interests and values. In the coming years, the debate surrounding AUKUS will continue to be a primary aspect of Australian foreign policy discussions and global diplomacy.

***

WHY MAINSTREAM MEDIA IGNORED THE ROBODEBT ROYAL COMMISSION

17 March 2023

The Robodebt Royal Commission has largely escaped the widespread attention of the mainstream media, leaving many questioning the factors responsible for this conspicuous absence. The Commission has now concluded its hearings, with its findings scheduled for release at the end of June, leaving the public eagerly anticipating the results. To understand why media coverage of this critical issue has been somewhat muted, we must look at the intricacies of media dynamics, politics, and audience demographics.

One of the factors contributing to this minimal media coverage of the Robodebt Royal Commission is the intersection of political affiliations among media proprietors and news editors. The Australian media landscape is vast yet limited in its diversity, comprising various outlets with ideological perspectives which lean towards conservative political parties, most notably, the Liberal Party. Media organisations often reflect the perspectives of their owners and editorial teams, which influence their editorial choices and priorities. In the case of Robodebt, its ramifications extended beyond mere policy discussion; it became a matter of government accountability and potentially wrongdoing. This inherent political dimension may have led some media outlets to approach the topic with caution, aligning with their political interests and allegiances.

Furthermore, commercial pressures related to advertising revenue play a pivotal role in shaping media coverage. The media industry relies heavily on advertising income to sustain operations and fund journalism and advertisers typically target specific audience demographics to maximise the effectiveness of their campaigns. As a result, media outlets are driven to cater to the interests and preferences of the audience segments that generate the most advertising revenue. In this context, Robodebt, which primarily affected individuals on social security payments and pensioners, didn't align with the core demographic that advertisers sought to reach, mainly an older, more conservative, and wealthier cohort. Consequently, some media outlets might have chosen to downplay or ignore the issue, as it did not correspond to the financial interests of their primary advertisers, or the political interests of their owners.

Another dimension to this issue is the class difference within the media industry itself. Journalists often come from middle and upper-class backgrounds, which creates a disconnect between the newsroom and the experiences of those affected by Robodebt. This disparity in lived experiences may have made it challenging for some journalists to fully grasp the significance of the issue. However, it is essential to recognise that this class difference, while a factor, is not the primary reason for the muted media coverage.

A more substantial concern arises from the broader challenges facing free-to-air media. With the decline of traditional advertising revenues and the rising popularity of digital platforms and social media, free-to-air media outlets face a unique set of challenges. To remain financially viable, they often target a smaller, older, and more economically stable audience. This demographic may not be as directly impacted by an issue like Robodebt, potentially leading to a perception that there is limited interest in the topic among their viewers.

This divergence in editorial priorities becomes evident when contrasting outlets like *The Guardian* and the *Saturday* Paper, known for their willingness to cover stories of government malfeasance and social injustice, with larger media conglomerates such as Fairfax and News Corporation, which have largely refrained from in-depth coverage of the Robodebt Royal Commission. The role of smaller media outlets in providing more comprehensive coverage underscores the need for diversity of perspectives within the media landscape.

The Robodebt issue, however, affected a more extensive spectrum of the population than what might initially meet the eye. Many people who had previously received government benefits found themselves unexpectedly burdened with massive debts due to the flawed implementation of the program. This widespread impact should have made Robodebt a compelling story for newspapers—one highlighting injustice, government malfeasance, and corruption and it should have attracted the attention of journalists seeking to expose such issues.

However, the media landscape also faces a shifting dynamic as legacy media contends with the rise of social media and new media. This divide can influence the focus of news coverage, with established outlets potentially less inclined to cover issues like Robodebt that may not align with their business models or traditional journalistic values. In contrast, newer, digitally native platforms often prioritise different stories and offer alternative perspectives.

The limited media coverage of the Robodebt Royal Commission is a complex issue influenced by a confluence of factors. It involves political affiliations, commercial pressures, class differences, and the evolving media landscape. Despite the significant ramifications of the Robodebt program on the lives of many Australians, the mainstream media's engagement with this issue has been far from exhaustive.

COMMISSIONER HOLMES' INSIGHTS ON THE ROLE OF SOCIAL MEDIA IN NEWS DISSEMINATION

Commissioner Catherine Holmes' insights into the media coverage of the Robodebt Royal Commission shed light on the changing dynamics of news dissemination and the evolving role of social media in shaping public perception, and her comments highlight a crucial aspect of the contemporary media landscape, where the traditional media often struggles to fully engage with complex, multifaceted issues such as Robodebt.

Holmes acknowledges that traditional media tends to focus more on high-profile moments, such as when former government ministers testify during the Commission's public hearings. This selective attention might be driven by sound commercial reasons, as media outlets cater to specific demographics that align with their advertisers' interests. When issues like Robodebt are multifaceted and require a deep dive into extensive evidence, traditional media may find it challenging to provide in-depth coverage, and they may consequently prioritise other topics.

However, Holmes also underscores the importance of social media in this context. Social media platforms have become spaces where individuals, often with a deep commitment to a particular issue, provide a real-time summary of evidence along with occasional commentary. These "Twitter commentators", bridge the gap between social media and mainstream commentary and their efforts to convey the proceedings of the Royal Commission, as well as their varying perspectives on the evidence, have contributed significantly to public understanding. Holmes acknowledges the invaluable public service rendered by these dedicated individuals.

Importantly, Holmes' commentary highlights the changing media landscape where social media plays a complementary role alongside traditional media. While she doesn't propose that social media should replace traditional news sources, she advocates for their symbiotic coexistence. The Commissioner's recognition of social media's value serves as a call for mainstream media to adapt and integrate new media dynamics, but it's clear that many within the legacy media landscape have been dismissive of social media's potential.

The Commissioner's words have ignited a broader debate about the future of news reporting and dissemination—she didn't need to make the comments, and it wasn't part of her purview to critique the media. However, it does raises questions about who decides what news is seen or heard in an age where mainstream media is often criticised for being predominantly white, Anglo-Saxon, and male-dominated, and her implication is that the mainstream media is at risk of becoming increasingly irrelevant to a diverse and evolving audience.

The decline of the media industry in Australia is not a new phenomenon, and it's attributed to various factors, including shifting audience preferences and the challenges of digital disruption and is exacerbated by editorial decisions that emphasise sensationalism, clickbait and opinion, over objective reporting, potentially alienating traditional readerships.

The media landscape is undergoing a transformation, with social media playing a pivotal role in shaping public discourse and understanding complex issues. While social media is not without its problems, it cannot be ignored. It is essential for traditional media outlets to evolve and adapt to the changing dynamics of news consumption if they wish to remain relevant in a rapidly evolving information age. The ongoing debate about the future of news and media's role in society underscores the need for innovation and adaptation within the industry to ensure its continued vitality.

CHALLENGES AND OPPORTUNITIES IN MODERN JOURNALISM

The evolving landscape of mainstream media and its role in shaping public discourse is a multifaceted and complex issue. It is essential to clarify that not all of the mainstream media can be dismissed as "terrible"—there are undoubtedly pockets of excellence and dedication within the traditional media landscape, which continue to produce valuable and credible journalism. However, the overarching concern lies in the media's increasing detachment from the broader public discourse on important political matters.

The rise of alternative sources of news and reporting within the community, such as social media, podcasts, and independent media websites, indicates a shifting paradigm in information consumption. These alternative platforms have gained prominence as sources of information on pressing political matters, bypassing the selective editorial choices often seen in traditional media. They offer a space for diverse voices and perspectives, contributing to a more inclusive and dynamic public discourse.

The criticism directed at mainstream media is not just about its perceived irrelevance but, more importantly, its reluctance to cover crucial issues. The reluctance of mainstream media outlets to extensively cover topics like Robodebt has not prevented this information from reaching the public, as it found its way through social media and alternative media outlets. This trend underscores the resilience and adaptability of the information ecosystem, even in the face of mainstream media's shortcomings.

One significant factor contributing to the mainstream media's skewed coverage is the class differences within newsrooms, where editors and journalists often hail from more privileged backgrounds. This class bias is evident in the editorial decisions made within media organisations. Issues that primarily concern higher-income individuals tend to receive more attention, while those affecting marginalised or lower-income communities receive less coverage. This perpetuates a cycle where the media reflects the interests and perspectives of the wealthy and propertied classes, reinforcing an inequitable public discourse.

For example, reporting on topics like interest rate hikes, budgetary matters, and tax cuts often dominates media coverage, in part because these issues align with the financial interests of both media organisations and their predominantly higher-income audience. This bias also extends to the hyperactivity witnessed in coverage of franking credits during the 2019 federal election, which largely favoured more affluent segments of the population—the coverage of the franking credits issue in 2019 was three times higher than the coverage of the Robodebt Royal Commission in 2023 and, given the make-up of the mainstream media, it's easy to see why.

Capitalism is a tool that can facilitate economic growth and innovation, but it can also have adverse consequences when it prioritises profit over public interest. In the case of mainstream media, the drive for advertising revenue can influence editorial decisions, sidelining important issues like government actions impacting pensioners and individuals on social security payments.

The changing media landscape underscores the necessity for adaptation. Newspapers and other traditional media outlets are a vital part of the information ecosystem, providing a crucial community service. However, they must evolve and incorporate new technologies to remain relevant in an age where information is readily accessible through digital platforms. If traditional media fails to embrace technological advancements, it risks obsolescence.

While acknowledging that there have been excellent journalists in the mainstream media, it is crucial to recognise that these journalists often operated within the constraints of editorial decisions and commercial interests. The gap left by major newspapers, which failed to provide comprehensive coverage of important issues, contributed to the proliferation of alternative media sources.

The evolution of the media landscape in Australia is reflective of a broader global trend. While there are still pockets of quality journalism within the mainstream media, the industry as a whole has faced challenges in adapting to changing reader preferences and technological advancements. The rise of alternative media sources has filled a void created by the mainstream media's selectivity, indicating that the public is seeking more diverse and comprehensive coverage. The future of journalism in Australia and around the world lies in the ability of traditional media outlets to embrace change, adapt to contemporary circumstances, and prioritise public interest over profit.

***

THE VOICE TO PARLIAMENT: WILL IT SUCCEED?

24 March 2023

As Australia approaches an important stage in its ongoing national conversation about Indigenous representation and Reconciliation, public opinion and political machinations are coming to the forefront of the debate. The Voice to Parliament, aimed at recognising the First Peoples of Australia by establishing an Aboriginal and Torres Strait Islander Voice in the constitution, is on the horizon and has garnered substantial support, but faces some challenges on its path towards referendum, to be held at some point this year.

At present, public opinion is a significant factor in the equation—recent opinion polls indicate the Voice to Parliament enjoys 59 per cent support among the Australian public and this level of support, while significant, has dipped from previous highs, suggesting that the issue may be entering a more precarious phase. This support also varies by state, with backing in four of the six states, which is essential for the proposal to pass when it eventually reaches the referendum stage. However, it's crucial to note that this margin is tight, and the outcome remains uncertain.

To gain a better understanding of the challenges facing the Voice to Parliament, it's worth looking back at a historical referendum. In 1977, a proposal for simultaneous Senate and House of Representatives elections seemed reasonable and straightforward, receiving a "yes" vote of 62 per cent across all of Australia. However, it was not without opposition, as the Premiers of Queensland and Western Australia, Joh Bjelke-Peterson and Charles Court, campaigned against it and those two states, along with Tasmania, received less than 50 per cent support. Although a large majority supported the proposal, three of the six states voted against—a majority of the votes *and* a majority of the states are required for success—and the referendum question was defeated, demonstrating that even seemingly simple proposals can face substantial opposition in particular regions.

Comparing the historical precedent to the current situation, it's apparent that the Voice to Parliament referendum may face similar challenges. However, there are crucial differences in the nature of the proposal. Prime Minister Anthony Albanese, who has been a vocal advocate for the Voice to Parliament, recently announced the specific referendum question that will be put to the Australian people. The question is straightforward and directly aligned with the principles outlined in the Uluru Statement from the Heart, which seeks to foster unity and co-operation among all Australians on the path to a better future.

Albanese emphasised the significance of the moment, recognising the patience and optimism of those involved in the process and stated that the proposed alteration to the constitution will "recognise the first peoples of Australia by establishing an Aboriginal and Torres Strait Islander Voice", and Australians will be asked whether they approve this alteration. The wording of the question is clear, but the challenges that lie ahead are less so.

A major uncertainty in the lead-up to the referendum is the stance of the federal Coalition, which has stated that it will support the Bill to enable the referendum in exchange for funding to produce a pamphlet about the Voice to Parliament, more than likely as part of a campaign to defeat the proposal.

As the debate surrounding the Voice to Parliament continues to evolve, the next steps are crucial. Public opinion remains a driving force, but the referendum's fate will ultimately be determined by the actions and commitments of political leaders. The prospect of constitutional recognition of the First Peoples of Australia hangs in the balance, making it a matter of significant national importance that will require careful observation and analysis as the nation moves closer to this historic vote.

THE UNCERTAINTIES AND CHALLENGES AHEAD

As the nation prepares for the Voice to Parliament referendum, the path forward remains clouded by uncertainties and challenges. The Australian public's support for the proposal is not as overwhelming as some might have hoped, and the looming spectre of political opposition adds another layer of complexity to the debate.

The wording of the referendum question itself has drawn attention. It is deliberately nebulous and constitutional experts, such as Professor of Constitutional Law Anne Twomey, have suggested that this is essential to provide flexibility for future governments and changing circumstances. A more specific question could potentially give opposing voices an opportunity to dissect and exploit the finer details, as was the case in the 1999 Republic referendum and, while a broader proposal aims to avoid this pitfall, it may also create ambiguity and room for misinformation to flourish.

While it's unclear what approach the Coalition will take in the lead-up to the referendum, it's expected that they are likely to campaign against it, although perhaps more tacitly. The political landscape, particularly within the Coalition, is far from unified on this issue. The recent history of former Prime Minister Malcolm Turnbull, who, despite his efforts, faced resistance within his own party, demonstrates the challenges of securing support for progressive measures such as a Voice to Parliament, whereas the currently Liberal Party leader, Peter Dutton, has a strong record of indifference on Indigenous rights, further complicating the situation.

History has shown that the Australian public tends to be cautious about constitutional changes. It's a high bar to clear, and aside from the failed conscription referenda of 1916 and 1917, there is no other precedent for a referendum that has been presented to the electorate, lost, and then returned for future consideration. This is the one chance for the Voice to Parliament to be enshrined in the Constitution, and any doubts or misconceptions could potentially derail this historic opportunity.

One alternative proposal that has been suggested is to begin with a Treaty between Indigenous and non-Indigenous Australians as a first step and while this approach has its merits, proponents of the Voice to Parliament argue that it offers a practical path toward achieving a Treaty that the broader Australian population can then accept. The complexities and nuances of this debate highlight the need for careful consideration and balanced discussion as the nation moves toward a potentially transformative decision.

In the end, the Voice to Parliament referendum represents a historic juncture in Australia's long journey toward Reconciliation and recognition of its First Peoples. The path forward will require navigating a complex terrain of political dynamics, public opinion, and the challenges of achieving meaningful constitutional change, all while maintaining a spirit of co-operation and unity to build a better future for all Australians.

***

SAFEGUARD MECHANISM AND POLITICS OF CLIMATE CHANGE

24 March 2023

Australia has long been a battleground for one of the most pressing global issues of our time: climate change. While the rest of the world has been diligently working to reduce carbon emissions and transition towards a more sustainable future, Australia's political landscape has been marred by a turbulent history of climate policy shifts and questionable effectiveness.

The Safeguard Mechanism, a lingering remnant from the Abbott government's tenure which ended in 2015, epitomises the nation's struggle to find a coherent and effective strategy for mitigating carbon emissions. Designed as a system where companies were to be financially incentivised to pollute less, it fell far short of its intended impact. Instead of a reduction in emissions, Australia witnessed an unintended consequence—companies being paid for their pollution, and, alarmingly, even increasing their carbon footprint. It was a climate policy misfire that left many questioning the Coalition's commitment to tackling the existential threat of climate change.

The Labor government, recognising the urgent need for reform, has embarked on a path to salvage the Safeguard Mechanism. A logical course of action would have been to scrap the flawed program and institute an entirely new one, but political considerations have made it a more intricate process. In the realm of climate change, every move is scrutinised and dissected by the public and political opponents, and the fear of backlash appears to be steering the government toward retrofitting the Coalition's program rather than crafting an entirely new solution.

The reasons for this somewhat cautious approach can be traced to Australia's recent history of divisive climate politics. Despite claims that the "climate wars" are over, the Labor government remains haunted by the spectre of the carbon price reduction scheme of 2011, famously demonised and incorrectly labelled as a "carbon tax". The political fallout from that episode continues to cast a long shadow, compelling the current government to tread lightly on matters associated with carbon pricing.

Amidst these intricate debates and political challenges, a critical point of contention revolves around the Safeguard Mechanism's complexity, particularly concerning the nature and quality of carbon offsets. The Australian Greens are demanding an end to new coal and gas projects, a stance that aligns with climate science and international climate agreements but may not align with economic and political realities.

Negotiations between the Australian Greens and the government are ongoing, with the outcome uncertain. The urgency of the matter is underscored by the climate itself, as Sydney experiences unseasonably high temperatures even in what should be the autumn season and it is these unusual weather patterns that serve as a stark reminder of the climate crisis's very real and immediate consequences.

Adding to the complexity, the Labor Party finds itself in a precarious position, caught between the interests of its traditional base in the unions, many of which represent workers in fossil fuel industries, and the undeniable need for a just and timely transition to more sustainable energy sources. This duality encapsulates a broader challenge faced by nations worldwide—reconciling economic and political interests with environmental responsibilities.

The issue of jobs and industry transition is central to the debate. Many unionists in mining and forestry sectors, understandably concerned about their livelihoods, look to the Labor Party to safeguard their employment and job security. However, it is becoming increasingly evident that these traditional industries are approaching the end of their useful life in their current form. While mining will continue to be a necessity for essential materials such as lithium, zinc, and silicon, the nature of these jobs will evolve, which requires a strategic and comprehensive plan to ensure a just transition for the workers involved.

Typically, debates surrounding the future of these industries centre around coal mining. However, as global pressure to reduce carbon emissions intensifies, the broader question arises: how does Australia manage the transition to a more sustainable and environmentally responsible economy without sacrificing its workforce and economic stability? This issue lies at the core of the current climate policy conundrum facing the nation.

In this complex and politically charged climate, Australia finds itself at difficult crossroads. The Safeguard Mechanism, a symbol of past climate policy failures, is being cautiously revisited by the Labor government as the nation deals with the complex interplay of environmental imperatives, economic interests, and political considerations.

LABOR'S CLIMATE CONUNDRUM

As the debate over Australia's climate policy continues, it is increasingly evident that the Labor Party, in either the position of government and opposition, struggles with a challenging and often uneasy relationship with coal. This issue is far from a simple city-versus-country divide, where inner-city progressives advocate for phasing out coal, while those in the outer regions, particularly those areas controlled by the New South Wales Labor right, champion its retention. The reality is more nuanced.

Within the Labor Party, there exists a spectrum of viewpoints on coal mining, reflecting the diverse landscape of regional interests and economic considerations and many rural Labor members are vocal proponents of transitioning away from coal mining. They argue for a shift to more efficient and environmentally friendly methods of power production that align with the global imperative to reduce carbon emissions. In a world rapidly embracing renewable energy, these voices represent a push for innovation and sustainability.

Conversely, there are vested interests deeply entrenched in traditional coal mining practices. These stakeholders have invested billions in the industry, and they are understandably hesitant to relinquish their financial commitment. While the world moves toward greener alternatives, these interests resist change, in part due to their substantial investments and, to a certain extent, fear of economic disruption.

This division within the Labor Party reflects a broader challenge confronting not only the party but also the nation as a whole. The Labor Party, founded in 1891 to champion the interests of working class people, now faces a vastly transformed political and economic landscape. The working class comprising the manual labour and blue-collar workers of today is not only smaller but also enmeshed in an evolving, technology-driven economy, making that shift away from traditional industries like coal mining an intricate task for the party.

The party, once rooted in the ideals of protecting a working class heavily engaged in manual labour, now operates in an era of automation, artificial intelligence, and a service-oriented economy. The shift from the coal mines to a 21st-century job market represents a profound change, one that necessitates a thoughtful and measured transition.

However, the Labor Party, while maintaining a particular stance on climate change and acknowledging the need for a greener future, finds itself constrained by political and economic realities. This dilemma becomes particularly pronounced as the party transitions from the role of an opposition force, where it can make sweeping promises, to the responsibilities of government, where it must deliver on those promises while balancing competing interests.

The present predicament faced by the Labor Party is characterised by an absence of a clear and comprehensive plan for dealing with the complex ramifications of transitioning away from coal and other carbon-intensive industries. In essence, the vision of change has yet to be articulated, leading to criticisms that there is a lack of detail regarding how jobs will be protected and transitioned in the wake of such a transformation.

This absence of clear planning stems, in part, from a reluctance to confront the inevitable changes that climate action will necessitate. Labor, like the broader population, faces the reality that it can no longer rely on the same industries and employment opportunities that have shaped its history.

However, the challenge also presents an opportunity for the Labor Party to fulfill its core mission—protecting those who need it most. Ensuring that the transition is not only smooth but also offers a dignified and secure future for workers in declining industries is essential. The party's historical role as a guardian of the less secure and vulnerable segments of society can be retained by facilitating retraining programs, offering unemployment assistance, and enabling early retirement for those affected by industry shifts.

In the face of these complexities, the Labor Party must embark on a process of collaboration and dialogue with the various factions and unions within its ranks. By working together to find innovative solutions, the party can navigate the shifting economic landscape in a way that aligns with its values and, ultimately, secures the interests of the Australian workforce. The Labor Party, renowned for its ability to protect the most vulnerable, has the potential to be a guiding force in the transition toward a more sustainable and equitable future, offering a testament to adaptability and leadership in a rapidly changing world.

***

THE RISE AND INFLUENCE OF RIGHT-WING IDEOLOGY IN AUSTRALIA

24 March 2023

In recent years, Australia has witnessed the resurgence of right-wing ideologies that have sparked intense debates and concerns across the nation. While the political landscape has historically been dominated by centrist and centre-right parties, the emergence of far-right elements, often associated with extremist movements, is causing unease among many Australians and their political leaders.

The Nationalist Socialist Network, a name that conjures memories of Nazi Germany in the 1930s, has reared its head in contemporary Australia, drawing attention and raising alarm. This group, known for its far-right and white supremacist beliefs, has been responsible for causing trouble and inciting controversy and their recent activities have raised questions about the extent to which such extremist ideologies have gained a foothold in Australian society.

One particularly concerning aspect of the rise of right-wing extremism in Australia is the convergence of such movements with other controversial causes. Notably, the Nationalist Socialist Network aligned itself with an anti-transgender rally organised by Moira Deeming and Kellie Jay Keen-Minshull, who also goes by the name "Posie Parker". This alliance between the far-right and anti-trans activists has further polarised public opinion and added to the growing concern about extremist ideologies taking root in the country.

Deeming, an elected member of the Victorian Parliament, has been a polarising figure since her election in the 2022 Victoria election. Many within the Liberal Party had reservations about her candidacy, warning that she would prove to be more trouble than she was worth and, as predicted by her critics, Deeming's actions and affiliations have been met with widespread disapproval, pushing the Victoria branch of the Liberal Party to the brink of expelling her. The controversy surrounding Deeming's political career illustrates the challenges facing mainstream parties when it comes to extremist elements within their ranks.

Keen-Minshull has also played a prominent role in the recent wave of right-wing activism in Australia. Her decision to travel to Australia from Britain and join forces with the Nationalist Socialist Network has drawn criticism and raised questions about the motivations behind her involvement. Some observers have drawn parallels between Parker's actions and those of other controversial figures, such as the British far-right polemicist and commentator, Katie Hopkins, who have sought refuge in Australia to promote their divisive rhetoric.

The backlash against Keen-Minshull activities extended to Hobart, where she attempted to organise another rally but was swiftly met with resistance and ultimately driven out of Tasmania. Australian Greens Senator Nick McKim strongly condemned Keen-Minshull actions, labeling her as a "pathetic and disgusting excuse for a human being". Senator McKim's remarks highlight the divisive and confrontational nature of the issues at the center of these right-wing movements.

The anti-trans movement in Australia, often characterised by its confrontational and divisive tactics, is made up of a group of professional troublemakers, including figures like Deeming, Keen-Minshull and the failed political candidate, Katherine Deves and these figures have found a platform for their views in certain sections of the media, particularly outlets sich as Sky News and News Corporation. The mainstream media's role in amplifying the voices of these far-right figures raises concerns about the extent to which media platforms are contributing to the radicalisation of public discourse in Australia.

In addition to media coverage, certain right-wing movements have received unexpected attention from the public. Christian Lives Matter, a group that has gained notoriety for its extreme views and actions, has been implicated in incidents of violence against the LGBTQ+ community. These incidents highlight the dangers of extremist ideologies spreading beyond fringe groups and gaining a foothold in the broader community.

The rise of right-wing ideologies in Australia is not unique to the nation but rather part of a global trend. The far-right's attraction to Australia could be partially attributed to the perception that it offers a receptive audience, particularly within certain media circles. However, it's essential to acknowledge that Australia's broader population often remains relatively peaceful when it comes to protests, with the centre-left typically opting for peaceful demonstrations. The nation's political climate, though not immune to controversy and conflict, is distinct from some of the more violent and tumultuous scenes witnessed in other parts of the world.

THE RESURGENCE OF DIVISIVE ISSUES AND THE STRUGGLE OF THE LIBERAL PARTY

The complexities of right-wing ideologies in Australia is taking a trajectory that mirrors some of the divisive issues seen in American politics, a shift that reflects the reality that the political right, in its conventional form, might be finding it increasingly challenging to provide a coherent and compelling vision for the nation. In response, it appears that right-wing politics is beginning to differentiate itself through social and moral issues, rekindling debates that were thought to have been settled long ago.

One such issue that has resurfaced is the question of race. Several years ago, Melbourne experienced a wave of controversial rhetoric regarding so-called "African gangs", a narrative that was strongly pushed by the current leader of the Liberal Party, Peter Dutton, a narrative which stirred fear and division within the community, ultimately emphasising the importance of addressing racial tensions with sensitivity and evidence-based policy solutions, rather than telegraphing these sentiments through the media for political gain.

Additionally, abortion rights, once seen as a settled matter in Australia, are making a return as a national issue. The resurgence of debates surrounding "men in women's sports", the use of unisex toilets and change rooms, and transgender issues further exemplify how marginal topics are being amplified and placed back onto the national agenda.

Even in 2023, the presence of neo-Nazis on the streets of Melbourne is a grim reminder of the challenges Australia faces in maintaining a harmonious and inclusive society. These marginal issues, while of limited significance to mainstream society, have been magnified beyond proportion, serving as a reminder of the need for responsible discourse and policy-making in the country.

The Liberal Party has found itself in a precarious position amid these controversies, as it attempts to define how it fits politically in contemporary Australia. Some of its members have associated with neo-Nazi groups, causing significant concern among the broader public and while it is important to note that not all members of the Liberal Party hold such views, the fact that some within the party have aligned themselves with extremist ideologies is a troubling development.

John Pesutto, the leader of the Victoria Liberal Party, has shown leadership on these issues by moving to Deeming from the party, however, this action has faced resistance within the party itself. The Liberal Party's internal struggle over issues related to extremism and far-right ideologies reflects the broader challenges of navigating right-wing politics in an increasingly polarised landscape.

Australia's struggle with extremist ideologies and divisive issues raises questions about why such debates continue to persist. World War Two, which occurred 80 years ago, is a stark reminder of the consequences of extremist ideologies and the sacrifices made to combat them and the continued presence of extremist elements, including neo-Nazis, on the streets of Melbourne highlights the need for vigilant efforts to counter radicalisation and hate.

Moreover, the emphasis on "freedom" within right-wing discourse begs the question: Shouldn't individuals be free to identify as they wish? The ongoing debate about gender identity and sexual orientation is a reminder that individuals should have the freedom to express their identity in ways that feel authentic to them. Gender identity and expression, like many other facets of individuality, should not be a matter of public concern, but rather a personal and private choice.

As a society, we must ensure that individuals have the freedom to live as their authentic selves without fear of discrimination or vilification. Letting people be who they are is an essential principle of a tolerant and inclusive society.

The resurgence of right-wing ideologies and divisive issues in Australia has raised significant concerns and challenges for the nation. The Liberal Party's internal struggles, the amplification of marginal issues, and the ongoing presence of extremist elements serve as critical markers in the broader debate over the future of right-wing politics in the country. As Australia struggles to deal with some of these issues, it must strive to maintain a balanced and inclusive society that respects individual freedoms and promotes unity.

***

THE END OF THE LIBERAL–NATIONAL COALITION REIGN IN NEW SOUTH WALES

31 March 2023

The recent change of government in New South Wales marks the end of a 12-year reign by the Liberal–National Coalition, and while it remains unclear whether the incoming Labor government will secure a majority or manage in a minority position, the implications of this shift are significant and extend beyond the borders of New South Wales.

Of particular note is the dwindling presence of the Liberal Party in Australian politics. With Tasmania as the sole remaining Liberal Party stronghold, former Prime Minister John Howard's optimistic assertion that the party will inevitably return as a political force appears, at this stage, to be empty rhetoric. Of course, the mainstream political parties in Australia always seem to survive, despite predictions of their demise, but the challenges faced by the Liberal Party are not confined to New South Wales but are indicative of broader, long-term issues afflicting the party across the nation.

Tasmania's Liberal Party stands as a unique exception within the Australian political landscape. Unlike its counterparts in New South Wales and Victoria, the Tasmanian Liberal Party is characterised by its relatively competent leadership and resistance to ideological extremes and cult-like influences. This distinction harks back to a more moderate style of politics reminiscent of pre-Howard Liberal leadership, exemplified by figures such as Andrew Peacock, Malcolm Fraser, and John Hewson.

The Liberal Party's troubles extend far beyond New South Wales, with disastrous results in Queensland, near obliteration in Western Australia, and significant internal disarray in Victoria. The inability of the party's leader, Dominic Perrottet, to secure a victory in the New South Wales election underscores the challenges it faces in regaining public trust.

The result of the New South Wales election mirrors the trends observed in the federal election the previous year, with a significant presence of independent and minor party candidates. The Labor Party has emerged as the winner in terms of seats, although it is expected to fall slightly short of securing a majority. To form a government, it will likely need to forge alliances with the New South Wales Greens or independent representatives.

Remarkably, despite not securing a majority, the New South Wales Labor Party captured 54.3 per cent of the two-party preferred vote, a reflection of its widespread appeal and strong support base and this outcome raises questions about the peculiarities of the state's electoral system, where the party with the most votes—54.3 per cent of the vote in Australia usually results in a landslide victory—does not necessarily secure a majority government.

The return of Labor to power after a 12-year hiatus in New South Wales holds significant implications for the state's political landscape. While governing in a minority position presents its own set of challenges, it may lead to more deliberative and inclusive legislation. The balance of power held by independents or the New South Wales Greens may force Labor to address issues such as gambling and coal mining, areas where the party has been cautious in the past. Such changes could have far-reaching implications for both New South Wales and the Labor Party.

The recent election campaign was not without its flaws, and the Labor Party faced an uphill battle in a media landscape often perceived as anti-Labor. However, there are signs of potential within the party's ranks. Figures such as Premier-elect Chris Minns and the new Treasurer Daniel Mookhey have shown promise, and there is hope that the Labor Party can evolve into a more effective and transformative government. The outcome of their governance remains uncertain, but the potential for a brighter future is not entirely out of reach.

MEDIA'S 'HORSE RACE' POLITICS: FLAWS IN THE ELECTION COVERAGE

The recent New South Wales election may have concluded with a victory for the Labor Party, but it also exposed a concerning pattern of media coverage that treats politics like a sporting event. Such an approach tends to create an illusion of competitiveness, even when one side is overwhelmingly ahead. This trend was similarly evident in the Victoria election in 2018, where mainstream media outlets predicted a close race and even suggested that Premier Daniel Andrews was in danger of losing his own seat. In the end, Victoria's Labor Party not only secured a resounding victory but also ensured a comfortable win for Andrews in his seat of Mulgrave.

The New South Wales election revealed a similar story. Labor leader Chris Minns experienced a substantial 20 per cent swing in his favour, and the Labor Party dominated both in terms of votes and seats, and the two-party preferred vote also favoured Labor. While they did not win an outright majority, the fact remains that they were the only party capable of forming a government. When election results are called decisively on election night, as they were by election analyst Antony Green, it is difficult to justify labeling it a "close contest". This highlights the pervasive problem of "horse race" journalism, as described by U.S. media academic, Jay Rosen, where politics is portrayed as a competitive game, even in situations where the outcome is clear.

This manner of reporting has been criticised as a disservice to the public, as it obscures the actual dynamics at play and misrepresents the state of the race. In New South Wales, none of the opinion polls indicated a closely contested election, and the assertion of a "close race" is belied by the reality that only one party could realistically form a government.

In addition to concerns about media coverage, the aftermath of the election has exposed some shortcomings within Australia's public broadcaster, the ABC. Its flagship current affairs program, *7.30*, failed to provide coverage of the election results the following Monday. For an event as significant as a state election—the second biggest electoral event in the country, after federal elections—this omission raised questions about impartiality and journalistic responsibility.

The decline of the Liberal Party is a recurring theme in the aftermath of this election. As a political historian notes, the party's struggles can be traced back to 1943, following a decisive electoral defeat by the United Australia Party, the precursor to the Liberal Party. At that time, the party underwent a transformation under the leadership of figures such as Robert Menzies. The United Australia Party faced corruption issues, lacked a clear policy platform, and had lost touch with the electorate. The Labor Party, under leaders like John Curtin and Ben Chifley, emerged as a formidable force.

Fast forward to the present, and the Liberal Party's trajectory is far from inspiring. It has experienced a succession of leaders—Tony Abbott, Malcolm Turnbull, Scott Morrison, Peter Dutton—and each of the leader inherited a party in decline for various reasons, and the absence of a unifying and dominant figure like Menzies poses a significant challenge. The call for suggestions on who could lead the party out of its current predicament reflects the uncertainty surrounding the Liberal Party's future. One thing is clear: it is a defining moment for the party, and its next steps will shape the political landscape in Australia for years to come.

CHALLENGES AHEAD: LABOR'S RESURGENCE AND LIBERAL PARTY'S NEED FOR REFORM

The election in New South Wales, with its apparent habit of narrowly returning the Labor Party to office, is reminiscent of historical precedents. Neville Wran's ascendancy as Premier in 1976 and Bob Carr's in 1995 were both marked by initially slim victories, only for these Labor leaders to solidify their rule over extended periods, ten years in both instances. The history of New South Wales politics suggests that such consolidation is likely to happen again.

Many have drawn parallels between the current political landscape and the situation in 2007, which marked the last time Labor enjoyed such comprehensive dominance across all levels of government in Australia. Back then, Labor held 60 per cent of all seats and secured 53 per cent of the two-party preferred votes across all federal, state and territory jurisdictions. When examining the recent election outcomes in 2023 and aggregating the results across all levels of government, the figures are not dramatically different: Labor currently holds 56 per cent of all seats and has received 54 per cent of the two-party preferred votes. The key divergence lies in where these votes are coming from.

Younger voters strongly favour the Labor Party, and more moderate Liberals are increasingly inclined to support independent or centrist candidates and this shift suggests that these voters may not return to the Liberal Party anytime soon. The scenario in 2008, when Western Australia's election was won by the Liberal Party just nine months after Labor's comprehensive victories, may not be repeated this time and the party is facing a more profound challenge today than it did in 2007.

The path to recovery for the Liberal Party seems to require substantial policy reform. The promise of neoliberal economics, with the belief that it would benefit everyone in the long run, has, for many, proven to be a failure. Citizens in Sydney struggle with road tolls, high property prices, a rental crisis, strained public transport, a beleaguered hospital system, and an education system in need of reform. Public sentiment has shifted to the point where people are demanding change and more of same will not result in electoral success.

To revitalise the party, some within its ranks may recognise the need for a different approach, one that encourages individuality, entrepreneurship, and poverty alleviation without relying solely on the market. A return to the Liberal Party's roots, where it embraced a Keynesian approach to economic policy, might be in order, an approach which prioritises infrastructure, healthy populations, and accessible services and recognises that government should provide inclusive services that meet the needs of all citizens. While these might not reflect the core values of the modern Liberal Party, if this is what is being demanded by the electorate, it would be foolish to ignore these concerns.

The Liberal Party must undergo significant internal reform, starting with preselections to ensure that it attracts capable and principled candidates. It cannot afford to use the party as a political grazing field for the unemployable elite. By doing so, the Liberal Party could restore its strength and contribute to a healthier political landscape in Australia, fostering greater success for the party and the country as a whole.

***

A CRUCIAL TEST FOR WHISTLEBLOWER PROTECTION IN AUSTRALIA

31 March 2023

In a landmark case that has stirred significant debate and controversy, the trial of whistleblower Richard Boyle is set to proceed after a recent ruling by the presiding judge. The judge's decision signifies a critical moment in the unfolding narrative of whistleblower protection in Australia and raises critical questions about the handling of cases involving individuals who expose alleged wrongdoings within government agencies.

Boyle's journey into the realm of whistleblower protection began when he exposed the Australian Taxation Office's relentless pursuit of debt from vulnerable individuals and struggling small businesses teetering on the brink of collapse. His revelations shed light on a deeply troubling practice that had persisted since 201 and the ramifications of his actions have been nothing short of life-altering, as he now faces the ominous prospect of a lengthy prison sentence.

Boyle's decision to reveal these issues has come with profound personal sacrifices: he has encountered not only legal adversity but also financial strain and a cloud of uncertainty that looms over his future. This immense personal cost underscores the immense courage required of whistleblowers and raises fundamental questions about the protection and support systems in place for those who choose to expose government misconduct.

The controversy surrounding Boyle's case is further exacerbated by the fact that, in 2018, the ATO extended an offer to him—a settlement was proposed, contingent on his silence, without an admission of liability on the part of the ATO. Boyle, however, opted to reject this settlement, firmly believing that the Australian public had a right to know about the alleged wrongdoing he had uncovered. His principled stance emphasises the importance of transparency and accountability within government agencies and highlights the moral dilemma often faced by whistleblowers.

Despite the passage of time and a change in government in 2022, the promised reforms to whistleblower legislation remain conspicuously absent. The Labor government, which assumed office almost a year ago, made clear commitments to address the shortcomings in whistleblower protection laws, yet progress has been frustratingly slow. This situation raises concerns about the government's commitment to safeguarding the rights and security of those who dare to expose unethical or illegal activities.

The looming question now centres on the role of Attorney–General Mark Dreyfus in this protracted case. As the highest legal officer in the country, Dreyfus holds significant sway in determining the course of action in matters of legal and ethical importance. The key query is whether, given the ATO's willingness to forgo pursuing the case back in 2018, the Attorney–General should intervene to prevent further legal action against Boyle. It is a decision that could either affirm the government's dedication to whistleblower protection or cast a shadow of doubt on its sincerity in this regard.

In the broader context, Boyle's case serves as a litmus test for the Australian government's commitment to upholding whistleblower rights and addressing the flaws in existing legislation. The outcome of this trial will undoubtedly resonate throughout the country, influencing the willingness of potential whistleblowers to come forward and, ultimately, the course of future efforts to foster transparency and accountability within governmental bodies. It remains to be seen whether the government will take decisive action in resolving this matter and, by extension, signal its dedication to whistleblower protection.

CRITICAL TEST FOR WHISTLEBLOWER PROTECTION: BOYLE'S CASE CHALLENGES AUSTRALIA'S LEGAL FRAMEWORK

As the case against Boyle continues to unfold, it is clear that Australia's whistleblower protection framework is facing a critical test. Boyle's legal team sought immunity under the *Public Interest Disclosure Act*, a piece of legislation originally introduced by Mark Dreyfus during his tenure as Attorney–General in 2013. The fact that Boyle, who exposed alleged misconduct by the Australian Taxation Office, is not granted immunity raises significant questions about the effectiveness of this Act in safeguarding the rights of individuals who act in the public interest.

A striking development in Boyle's case has been the reduction in the number of charges brought against him. Originally, the Public Prosecutor had levied a staggering 66 charges against him, which have now been pared down to 24. Notably, Dreyfus decided to drop the charges against Bernard Collaery and "Witness K" last year, demonstrating his discretionary power as the senior legal officer in the country. This discretionary authority also extends to the current case against Boyle.

In the past, it was suggested that the Attorney–General might hesitate to drop the case due to concerns about unintended consequences, potential legal complications in other cases, or setting a precedent. However, the core issue in Boyle's case revolves around the ethical, moral, and legal transgressions allegedly committed by the Australian Taxation Office. The agency's readiness to forgo pursuing the case back in 2018 raises questions about the necessity of continuing the legal battle against Boyle.

It is imperative to recognise that the alleged misconduct was not solely the responsibility of the current government but also extended to the previous administration. Therefore, there should be no loss of face in discontinuing the prosecution. The prevailing strategy appears to raise doubts about the government's willingness to address the concerns of whistleblowers and their role in exposing malfeasance. It is essential to consider the potential impact on public perception and the desire for real change when voters cast their ballots.

The case of Richard Boyle transcends individual circumstances and goes to the heart of whistleblower protection, government transparency, and accountability. The choices made by the government in addressing this case will inevitably shape the nation's stance on the rights and protections afforded to individuals who courageously speak out against wrongdoing within government agencies. It remains to be seen whether the government's actions will reflect a genuine commitment to addressing the concerns of whistleblowers and fostering a culture of openness and accountability or if, as some may fear, it represents more of the same. For a public that yearns for change, the stakes are high, and the spotlight is firmly on this crucial legal battle.

***

PUTTING THE SPOTLIGHT BACK ONTO THE SOCIAL HOUSING CRISIS

31 March 2023

The recent compromise between the Australian government and the Australian Greens on the Safeguard Mechanism legislation has drawn attention to a broader spectrum of policy issues, including the state of social housing in Australia. While the government's amended climate bill aims to deter new coal and gas projects, the government contends that it won't hinder future investments. This compromise appears to offer something for both parties, but the messaging around it varies for different audiences.

The key feature of the amended Safeguard Mechanism is its goal of reducing baseline emissions by 4.9 per cent and sets the stage for Australia's response to climate change. However, another important issue looms in the background: the status of the Labor government's social housing policy.

The policy, which aims to create a future housing fund worth $10 billion, with annual proceeds of around $500 million allocated to building 30,000 social housing properties across Australia, has encountered a roadblock. On the surface, this might seem like a substantial initiative, but when put into perspective, it falls short of addressing the nation's social housing needs.

The plan translates to an average of just two properties in each suburb and locality across Australia and contrasts with the estimated requirement of 650,000 social housing projects, as highlighted by the Australian Greens, who argue that the current approach is inadequate and advocate for direct funding, rather than relying on the proceeds from an investment fund.

What is perplexing is the Australian Green's decision to stall this legislation, especially given that the Labor Party had campaigned vigorously on the issue of social housing during the last federal election. Promising both an economic boost and a solution to a critical housing supply problem, the policy seems to have hit a snag.

The timing of addressing the social housing crisis couldn't be more opportune. With the Liberal Party facing challenges and the Labor Party enjoying favourable polling, this is a moment to seize the initiative. The Australian Greens, with their presence in the Senate, offer a potential ally on this issue.

Social housing should ideally be a cornerstone of any Labor policy, given the personal experiences of key figures within the party, such as Prime Minister Anthony Albanese, who grew up in council housing and understands the transformative impact such housing can have on individuals and communities. Basing the funding for social housing on investments introduces unnecessary uncertainty and potential pitfalls, and it's akin to making a promise without committing fully to it, as investments are inherently subject to market fluctuations and risk.

The potential benefits of a substantial social housing initiative are numerous. Building or renovating the needed 650,000 residences would not only provide homes for those in need but also stimulate the economy, as was seen with the school hall construction projects that played a vital role in avoiding the worst of the global financial crisis in 2008–10, where investments in infrastructure have a ripple effect, benefiting various sectors and local businesses.

The positive impact extends beyond the economic sphere. The ongoing homelessness crisis and the plight of older women—who have been the largest group of people within the community seeking shelter—underline the critical importance of addressing social housing needs. Providing subsidised rentals to these vulnerable populations can also significantly improve their mental and physical wellbeing.

The question that remains unanswered is why the government is not pursuing this issue with the same tenacity that they've applied to other policies. The benefits of substantial social housing investment are evident, and the time for action is now. Addressing this critical need should be a shared goal across the political spectrum, emphasising the potential for positive outcomes both socially and economically. In a time when a multifaceted crisis demands bold solutions, the role of social housing in shaping Australia's future cannot be understated.

AUSTRALIAN GREENS SEEK SOLUTIONS DESPITE RESISTANCE

The criticism from the Australian Greens about the proposed housing fund relate to the financial viability of such a fund which is dependent on market conditions, which are subject to fluctuations. These criticisms are valid—if the fund existed in the previous financial year, it would have generated no income at all, due to the negative growth of the share market.

Senator David Pocock's suggestion of a $20 billion fund with no annual spending cap underscores the need for more substantial and flexible financing to tackle the social housing crisis effectively.

Beyond the debate on social housing, a broader conversation about housing policy is necessary. A national approach is essential, given the disparities between state and local policies that often contradict federal efforts. The historical context, dating back to colonisation in 1788, has shaped Australia's housing landscape, highlighting the urgency for comprehensive reform.

Innovative concepts, such as tiny houses, smaller properties, and the development of villages and urban communities, are potential solutions to address the housing crisis. These ideas could be explored and negotiated by the Australian Greens, who are increasingly becoming adept political negotiators. Their willingness to collaborate and seek compromise is a positive sign for their long-term relevance in Australian politics.

As the Australian Greens navigate the challenging terrain of compromise and negotiation, they may occasionally face criticism from their own ranks. Some party members may question the wisdom of agreeing to certain measures, however, the growing recognition that constructive collaboration can yield results and influence change is a significant step forward.

The contrast with the Liberal Party's approach, marked by a steadfast refusal to co-operate and based entirely on negativity and opposition, underscores the importance of the Australian Greens' evolving strategy. They aim to remain relevant, striving to effect change and advance their core beliefs by agreeing to proposals that align with their values. This adaptability and pragmatism demonstrate a commitment to making a positive impact in Australian politics, rather than becoming a marginalised voice.

The debate over social housing funding in Australia is part of a broader conversation about housing policy that demands a national approach. The willingness of the Australian Greens to negotiate and compromise is a notable shift, reflecting their aim to remain influential and effective in shaping the nation's future. While challenges persist, their ability to work constructively may hold the key to making progress on critical issues like affordable housing.

***

APRIL

A LABOR VICTORY: ASTON BYELECTION AND A SHIFTING POLITICAL LANDSCAPE

6 April 2023

The Aston byelection result has resulted in a significant loss for the Liberal Party, and is the first seat won off the opposition by an incumbent government for over 100 years. Depending on one's perspective, the result can either be seen as a significant win for the Labor Party or a substantial loss for the Liberals. However, amidst the post-election analysis, the attention has largely been misplaced, fixated on what went awry for the Liberals rather than acknowledging the strategic moves made by the Labor Party.

In contrast to the Liberal Party's missteps, the Labor Party is credited with making the right decisions—from choosing the ideal candidate to crafting an effective campaign strategy. The election saw a sizable swing of 6.4 per cent in two-party preferred voting against the Liberal Party—in addition to the 7.3 per cent swing achieved in the 2022 general election—leading to the loss of a seat that had long been considered a stronghold for them. The key question arises: what did Labor do differently to secure this victory?

The primary problem for the Liberal Party revolves around the choice of candidate and the overall campaign strategy, fielding the wrong type of candidate and pursuing an ineffective campaign. The selected candidate's close ties to News Corporation were deemed detrimental, and this strategic misstep is seen as a significant factor contributing to the loss of a previously safe seat.

Roshena Campbell, the Liberal candidate, faces scrutiny not only for her News Corporation association but also for being perceived as a "parachuted" candidate without strong local roots. The potential for Campbell to be an excellent local representative remains uncertain, given the circumstances of her candidacy and the loss of Aston is considered a missed opportunity for the Liberal Party, with doubts about their ability to reclaim it in the future.

On the flip side, Labor's success is attributed to several factors. First and foremost, they presented a strong local candidate—Mary Doyle—a critical element that cannot be overstated. The preference for strong local candidates over national or celebrity figures cannot be overemphasised, with the belief that individuals deeply connected to the community, such as well-regarded mayors or prominent business figures, bring a sense of honesty, integrity, and a better understanding of local issues.

This sentiment extends to the broader political landscape, where the criticism of far-right candidates in traditionally moderate seats is seen as a contributing factor to the decline of the Liberal Party in various regions. The Liberal Party's embrace of far-right elements has led to a decline in membership, particularly in states like Western Australia and Queensland.

Moreover, the changing political landscape also shows a shift away from neoliberal ideologies and the waning influence of far-right ideas, and these fringe beliefs, particularly those held in Queensland, are losing traction, signifying a broader rejection of extreme ideologies.

In terms of media influence, traditional endorsements and mass media sway no longer hold the weight they once did. The era of figures like Rupert Murdoch shaping political outcomes through newspaper endorsements, while strong, is less influence than in previous years and the Aston electorate's rejection of the Liberal candidate essentially endorsed by the *Herald Sun*, underscores a changing dynamic where voters resist being dictated to by media entities.

The Aston byelection was more than just a local contest; it is seen as a microcosm reflecting the evolving political landscape. While the Liberal Party struggles with strategic missteps, the Labor Party's success is attributed to a strong local candidate and a campaign that resonated with the changing political sentiments. The broader implications suggest a departure from conservative and far-right ideologies and a diminishing influence of traditional media endorsements in shaping electoral outcomes.

SHAPING A NEW POLITICAL ERA

The current success of the Labor government stands in stark contrast to the struggles of the Liberal Party under the leadership of Peter Dutton. The Labor government, presenting as a competent and less divisive outfit, has gained favour with the electorate and while this is always subject to change in the context of fickle electorates and can evaporate quickly, governments need to harness electorate goodwill and take advantage for as long as possible. The Labor government's current focus on addressing community needs rather than perpetuating political drama—as was a current theme under the previous Coalition government—is a significant factor in this current success.

The changing dynamics within the Liberal Party and the evolving socio-economic landscape also form a critical backdrop to the Aston byelection, suggesting a party that is struggling with its identity and struggling to accommodate a diverse range of liberal perspectives that were once central to its appeal. The absence of a clear spot for the urban liberal, the small business person, or those favouring small government reflects a broader disconnect that the Liberal Party faces with its traditional support base.

The Labor government has done much right since returning to office, but it has to remembered that it has been in office for less than a year, and there is something substantially wrong with a government if major problems do develop during this time. There are other areas where improvement is necessary: The inadequacy of Newstart and the single parent payment highlight policy areas that the Albanese government has yet to address adequately. The also extends to matters of national security, with reservations expressed about the AUKUS deal diverting substantial funds to nuclear submarines at the expense of more pressing community needs.

The unspoken issue of COVID management also needs attention, highlighting the government's relative silence on the matter despite the persistent challenge of thousands of daily cases.

However, while there are areas that require attention and improvement, the electorate as reflected in current opinion polls and the Aston byelection result, supports the perception that Labor's approach, despite its imperfections, is resonating well with the Australian public at this current point of time.

***

YUNUPINGU'S LEGACY: FAREWELL TO A GREAT ADVOCATE FOR INDIGENOUS RIGHTS

6 April 2023

The passing of Yunupingu marks the end of an era for Australia, as the nation bids farewell to an advocate for Indigenous land rights and a formidable leader in the pursuit of justice and equality. His life's work, spanning decades, has left an indelible mark on the trajectory of Indigenous rights in Australia.

Yunupingu's journey onto the national stage began prominently with the Gove Land Rights case in 1971. Though the initial legal battle did not yield the desired outcome, it set in motion a series of events that would significantly alter the landscape of Indigenous rights in the country. The ensuing Woodward Royal Commission laid the groundwork for the *Aboriginal Land Rights Act*, a central piece of legislation that, in turn, paved the way for the landmark Mabo decision in 1992. This legal evolution underscored Yunupingu's persistent commitment to reshaping the narrative surrounding Indigenous land ownership.

The impact of Yunupingu's efforts extends beyond legal victories. His legacy is intertwined with the broader tapestry of Australian society. As the Australian of the Year in 1978, he stood as a symbol of recognition for the importance of Indigenous voices in shaping the nation's future and his unwavering dedication to the cause of self-determination for Indigenous people remained steadfast throughout his life. Serving on the Referendum Council, contributing to the development of the Uluru Statement from the Heart, and co-designing the Voice to Parliament, Yunupingu played a vital role in framing the discourse around Reconciliation.

The tributes that flowed in the wake of his passing highlight the profound impact Yunupingu had on the Australian political landscape. The Indigenous writer and academic, Marcia Langton, acknowledged his role as a cultural bridge and a leader during tumultuous times, emphasising his vision for constitutional recognition.

Marcia Langton: "So this wonderful man came into the world when his people were in the middle of the most tumultuous part of the history. He became a leader, both in his own culture and a bridge across between the cultures and between governmental systems. And he was able to steer people in the right direction and with great wisdom and grace.
So his idea of constitutional recognition, he explained to Noel Pearson and me some years ago, and he wanted a balance. We're all heartbroken that he didn't live to see the outcome, so I do hope that the referendum is successful, because it will be in very large part as a result of his work and in honour of him. And it gives all of us more inspiration to be as strong as he was in striving for a real sense of equality under the Constitution."

Yunupingu's advocacy for constitutional recognition was not a theoretical stance; he actively organised his community to present petitions to Prime Ministers Gillard and Rudd, demonstrating a hands-on approach to the pursuit of justice.

Prime Minister Anthony Albanese's recollection of a conversation with Yunupingu further underscores the personal connection that leaders felt with this giant of a figure.

Anthony Albanese: "I regarded as a great honour when his family reached out for me to have a conversation with him on the day that we announced the wording with the Referendum Working Group that will go forward in legislation now. And after a committee will, that's the words that will be considered before the parliament for a referendum. At the end of this year, I had the opportunity and great honour of speaking to him that afternoon, he was surrounded by his loved ones, and by his community, and he said to me on that afternoon, and I'll never forget it, he said to me, 'you spoke truth'. And that was one of the most heartwarming things that anyone could possibly have ever said to me in my life. He was an extraordinary leader. We mourn with his people today.
And we pay tribute to a lifetime of advocating for the rights of Aboriginal people in this country. He was a key focal point of the development of the Uluru Statement from the Heart, a wonderful, gracious request to advance reconciliation in this country. And when that happened in 2017, he spoke about lighting a fire. I think that today's a day that I certainly recommit myself to do everything we can to make sure that that referendum is carried at the end of this year."

The sentiments expressed by various leaders, including Liberal Party MP, Julian Leeser, highlight the universal respect and admiration Yunupingu commanded. His leadership extended beyond rhetoric; it was grounded in tangible accomplishments. As the longtime chairman of the Northern Land

Council, Yunupingu combined advocacy with action, fighting for rights and freedoms while actively working to deliver practical outcomes such as land, education, jobs, and opportunity.

In the face of this loss, Australia stands at a crossroads in its ongoing journey towards reconciliation, treaty, and a more equitable future. The path forward may be fraught with political complexities and differing opinions within both the Indigenous and wider communities. However, the groundwork laid by Yunupingu serves as a roadmap for a modern Australia, where Indigenous voices are not only heard but actively contribute to the nation's identity. The challenge now lies in honouring his memory by continuing the pursuit of the ideals he championed throughout his extraordinary life.

THE NATIONAL DEBATE ON THE VOICE TO PARLIAMENT

The aftermath of Yunupingu's passing has thrust the issue of Indigenous rights and the proposed Voice to Parliament into the forefront of political discourse. The eulogies and expressions of condolences from political figures such as leader of the opposition Peter Dutton and Leeser have, however, revealed a disconcerting dissonance between words of respect and their subsequent political actions.

It is disheartening, if not offensive, to witness leaders pay tribute to Yunupingu's lifetime dedication to Indigenous causes and then witness the outright refusal to support the Voice to Parliament—a modest proposal seeking to establish a mechanism for Indigenous voices to be heard in the nation's parliament. The incongruity between praising Yunupingu's courageous efforts and rejecting a fundamental aspect of his vision exposes a stark contrast between rhetoric and action.

The commentary on the actions of figures such as Dutton and Leeser reflects a frustration with what is perceived as political opportunism and a lack of genuine commitment to Indigenous causes. The accusation that these politicians exploit the moment for political gain, while simultaneously refusing to endorse proposals Yunupingu dedicated his life to, casts a shadow on their sincerity and commitment to positive change.

The failure of the Liberal Party to support the Voice to Parliament is not merely a critique of political decisions but a broader reflection on the state of Australian politics and a reluctance to engage constructively with proposals, regardless of their merit, simply for the sake of opposition.

The decision to not support the Voice to Parliament is a missed opportunity for change for the Liberal Party, especially in the wake of the Aston byelection defeat, and is seen as a failure to signal a shift towards a more responsive and constructive political approach. Instead, the perceived doubling down on opposition is interpreted as a retaliatory measure against public sentiment.

In the face of this political landscape, the words of the Premier of Victoria, Daniel Andrews, ring with a sense of urgency and frustration. His condemnation of the Liberal Party's stance on the Voice to Parliament as "appalling" and a failure to acknowledge the injustices of the past as a unifying act reinforces the broader societal discontent with the current trajectory.

> **Daniel Andrews:** "This is our moment, we need to give Aboriginal and Torres Strait Islander people a voice and deliver in full on the Uluru Statement from the Heart. And it is absolutely breathtaking. It is appalling for the Liberal Party to say that this is an act of division. This is an opportunity and an obligation for national unity. That's what this is putting right the injustices of the past or at least taking a big step towards doing that. Do you think that you get unity by telling First Nations leadership who gathered and lay down that Uluru Statement from the Heart, telling them that they will wrong? That's a unifying act, is it? It is absolutely appalling. And the Liberal and National Party, despite any weasel words, stand condemned—to campaign against this is just wrong.
> That's my view, people have to make their own judgments. A part of leadership is calling out racism, bigotry, and just a mean spiritedness and nastiness. They are a nasty outfit. If we can't find it in our hearts, as a modern progressive Australia to acknowledge the terrible horrors of our past, then we will never have a shared future together. The final lines of the Uluru Statement simply asked for that all Australians walk with First Nations Australians. Is that too much to ask?"

The plea for a shared future, walking hand in hand with First Nations Australians, echoes the sentiment that the Voice to Parliament represents an opportunity for national unity and Reconciliation. The rejection of this opportunity, as articulated by Andrews, is not just a political misstep but a moral failing that jeopardises the prospect of a collective journey towards a more inclusive and equitable Australia.

***

LIBERAL PARTY IN CRISIS: INTERNAL STRUGGLES AND AN IDENTITY CRISIS

6 April 2023

In a recent revelation, former Liberal Party strategist Tony Barry—now a director of the political communications and research company, RedBridge Group—has exposed the internal struggles and identity crisis plaguing the party. Barry's candid admission that extensive focus group testing has dubbed the Liberal Party as the "nasty party" and likened Liberal Party leader Peter Dutton to an "ugly baby" speaks volumes about the party's image problem.

The roots of this perceived toxicity are traced back to the success of the federal Liberal–National Party in Queensland, where the Liberal–National Party holds a commanding 21 out of 30 seats. This is Dutton's stronghold. The concern, however, is that the Queensland model doesn't necessarily reflect the sentiments of the entire nation. Queensland is unique, and its politics cannot be applied universally to Australia.

Queensland Liberal–National Party MPs, who exert significant influence within the party, are not representative of the diversity that should characterise the Liberal Party nationally. Instead, they are accused of fostering a divisive and exclusionary atmosphere, displaying a propensity to favour their own kind while showing disdain for others. The fear is that the political strategy emanating from figures like Dutton could lead the Liberal Party down a destructive path, alienating voters and undermining the party's long-term viability.

Liberal Party member Bridget Archer, representing Bass in Tasmania, has become a vocal dissenting voice within the party. Archer expresses her frustration at the party's failure to act on critical issues, emphasising the importance of taking a stand and avoiding vacating the political field. Her call for a referendum on key matters has been met with resistance within the party, showcasing the internal dissent that threatens to fracture the Liberal Party further.

Despite her efforts to be a political "voice of reason", Archer faces the thread of disendorsement by the party before the next election and this move puts her at a crossroads, contemplating leaving the party to continue serving as an independent in Parliament, following in the footsteps of others such as Andrew Wilkie, who holds the Tasmania seat of Clark.

The pressing question now is whether the Liberal Party is at a crossroads of its own, where the voices of reason are drowned out by the influence of a select group of MPs, particularly from Queensland. As the party struggles with issues such as same-sex marriage, transgender rights and the Voice to Parliament, it stands at a crucial juncture. The concern is that, if the party continues down its current path of narrow right-wing conservatism and abandons true liberalism, it risks being left behind on these critical issues, alienating a broader section of the Australian electorate and compromising its future relevance in the country's political landscape. The Liberal Party is facing a stark choice: adapt to the changing political landscape or risk irrelevance.

DISSENT HIGHLIGHTS PARTY'S CROSSROADS

The continuing dramas within the Liberal Party is not confined to ideological battles; it extends to a geographical divide as well. While the Western Australia, Tasmania and South Australia branches of Liberal Party have expressed support for the Voice to Parliament, the Queensland faction, spearheaded by figures such as Dutton, stands as an exception. This divergence in stance underscores the internal divisions within the party regarding key issues, with some attributing the discord to political expediency, timing, or genuine belief in the cause.

The dissenting voices, like that of Archer in the seat of Bass, argue that figures like Dutton are putting themselves at odds with the broader party and the broader community. Moreover, the emergence of independent candidates such as the "teals"—individuals who would have identified with the traditional Liberal Party but feel compelled to run independently due to a perceived shift away from their values—raises questions about the party's direction and whether there exists a political void that aligns more closely with their views.

As the tide of history moves along, the federal Liberal Party appears to be struggling to keep pace. The looming byelection in Fadden—and in the seat of Cook if the rumours of an impending resignation from parliament by Scott Morrison are to be believed—add another layer of uncertainty. Cook, a traditionally safe Liberal seat, might face challenges, given recent swings towards the Labor Party in the area. Fadden, experiencing changing demographics, could also be a battleground. The potential loss of these seats, while unlikely, would not only shake the Liberal Party but also significantly bolster the Labor government.

There is a possibility of major reforms on the horizon, reflecting the turbulent state of Australian politics. The Liberal Party, seemingly resistant to learning from its recent experiences, may be on the verge of a transformative, albeit tumultuous, period. As the nation enters a time of political flux, there could potentially be an ugly and awe-inspiring spectacle of change, adding to the period of uncertainty for the conservative side of politics.

***

UNRAVELING THE INLAND RAIL ENIGMA

13 April 2023

The Inland Rail Project, initially presented as a transformative infrastructure initiative, has recently come under scrutiny due to a staggering doubling of its projected cost within a span of two years. From an initial estimate of $16 billion with a completion date set for 2027, the projected cost has now soared to $31 billion, with an extended completion timeline of 2031. This revelation raises pressing questions about the project's financial management, transparency, and the underlying factors contributing to this substantial cost escalation.

Barnaby Joyce's association with the Inland Rail Project adds an intriguing layer to the narrative. As the former Deputy Prime Minister and Minister for Infrastructure and Regional Development, Joyce was a driving force behind the project. However, allegations have surfaced regarding his potential conflict of interest, with claims suggesting that he sought to alter the project's route to benefit his personal landholdings near Narrabri in northern New South Wales. The sizeable 1,000-hectare land tract in question raises suspicions of insider knowledge, as it seems improbable that anyone would invest in such an expanse without anticipating a future government project.

The revelation of a cost blowout prompts speculation about the project's initial budgeting and financial management. Two possibilities emerge: either the project was deliberately under-costed to secure approval, with future governments left to deal with funding challenges, or there has been severe mismanagement in handling funding arrangements and contracts. Both scenarios point to potential ethical lapses and even allegations of corruption, particularly given Joyce's historical connection to the project.

Comparisons to other infrastructure projects in New South Wales, such as the rail from Parramatta to the city, further underscore the prevalence of cost overruns in large-scale endeavours. The New South Wales Government's acknowledgment of a 30 per cent cost increase, from $17 billion to approximately $25 billion, demonstrates the pervasive challenges faced by major infrastructure initiatives. The decision to temporarily halt the project for reassessment reflects a responsible approach to addressing financial uncertainties, albeit with inevitable consequences for those directly impacted by the project's delays.

Historically, the concept of an inland rail network has been on the table since the 1890s, gaining renewed attention after the formation of the Northern Territory. However, the relevance of rail transport in an era dominated by trucking and reduced reliance on rail freight is a pertinent question.

Joyce's personal political stake in the Inland Rail Project is evident as he viewed its potential success as a crucial achievement in his political career. However, doubts persist about the viability and lasting legacy of a project marked by cost escalation, environmental concerns, inadequate engagement with Indigenous communities, and accusations of prioritising business and mining interests over community wellbeing.

A critical analysis of the Inland Rail Project is contained in the *Delivery of Inland Rail: An independent review*, prepared by Dr Kerry Schott and commissioned by the Prime Minister. The report, prepared by a seasoned executive with extensive experience in both business and government sectors, sheds light on various issues, including environmental impacts, Indigenous consultations, and accountability. The $2.5 billion already spent on the project underscores the urgency of addressing these challenges and ensuring accountability for the project's trajectory.

In media interviews, Joyce deflects blame for the cost blowout, challenging the credibility of the figures and casting doubt on the integrity of the reviews conducted. His reluctance to engage with the critical report prepared by Schott raises questions about transparency and accountability in the project's leadership. The ensuing dialogue between Joyce and the ABC's Steve Austin, reveals a defensive posture, with Joyce emphasising the project's environmental benefits while downplaying criticisms of mismanagement and lack of proper oversight.

> **Steve Austin (ABC presenter):** "So you're blaming the four different reviews that took place, particularly the Millmerran stretch, delaying the project, affecting the costs of blowouts."
> **Barnaby Joyce:** "And any delay means you're gonna have to pay more for more for steel, more for contracting everything that the cost of everything goes up. The more you delay, the more it costs..."
> **Austin:** "...but Barnaby Joyce, this went from $16 billion—I thought it was 14, but let's say $16 billion, according to the new minister, to $31.4 billion, that's astronomical."

Joyce: "Let's have a look at the numbers. Why don't they say a trillion dollars—if you can't actually provide the details of exactly how this is made up? Then it's just a number."

Austin: "Well, Dr. Schott has in her over 100 page report, as I understand it—have you read that report by Dr. Schott?"

Joyce: "No, I haven't."

Austin: "Why not, given it to your project you're so proud of?"

Joyce: "I'm happy, I'm happy, well I'm very proud of it. Because if we don't get it, we're going to … it takes about 750,000 tonnes of carbon emissions out if he wanted to have the green movement of goods and this is the way to do it. We've also got a business plan to get bulk commodities into Gladstone as well. I think that's incredibly important."

Austin: "Did you ignore the advice to get the right people involved from the start? Because Dr. Kerry Schott has been critical in her report, on this point."

Joyce: "Kerry Schott in her role with basically green energy. And I've thought lock horns in the past. I'm not surprised that Kerry Schott who was the grand architect of the renewable power which is costing us…"

Austin: "… can I get you to answer that her criticism was that you didn't get the right people involved from the start, and that's what's caused the delays in the cost blow out…"

Joyce: "…No, that's, that's a that's a pathetic, that Kerry would say that—a board has overview, but the actual cost that you don't select the accountants and you don't select the quantity surveyors—that is done in a corporate structure of the Inland Rail. And what's more, if if there was a cost blowout, they were looking at $31 billion, we would have definitely known about it. So they've come up with this magic figure, basically as a mechanism to try and delay it further, kicking into the long grass so you can continue with the trucks powering through the middle of Brisbane."

FINANCIAL TURMOIL, GOVERNANCE FAILURES AND POLITICAL ENTANGLEMENTS

The revelation of the staggering $31 billion cost for the Inland Rail Project has ignited a cascade of criticism and raised fundamental questions about the project's viability and the management practices of the previous Coalition government. The Australian Rail Track Corporation has attributed the cost blowout to inadequacies in the original project design and initial scoping details, as well as the appointment of unsuitable individuals to senior positions within the project. These issues underscore the importance of competent oversight by governments, irrespective of their political orientation, when undertaking large-scale infrastructure projects.

The Inland Rail Project should be placed within a broader context of alleged corruption and incompetence left behind by the previous Coalition government. The recurrence of controversies, from secret ministries to million-dollar payments for unreceived reports, paints a picture of a government marked by questionable practices. The Inland Rail Project is portrayed as the latest in a series of Coalition government projects marred by mismanagement, financial irregularities, and a legacy of problematic decision-making.

This narrative dovetails with a perceived tradition where outgoing governments, particularly Liberal administrations, leave behind challenges or "booby traps" for their successors. Whether intentional or a consequence of incompetence, the impact is the same—incoming governments are burdened with the task of remediation, diverting attention and resources from their policy agenda. The Inland Rail Project exemplifies a mix of strategic calculation and sheer ineptitude, creating a vexatious situation for the current Labor government.

The consequences extend beyond financial implications. The Inland Rail Project, projected to be a monumental achievement, is seen now as a potential financial disaster and a future white elephant, with many questions about the project's economic viability left unanswered, suggesting that it might not recoup its costs anytime soon, rendering it unsellable and burdening the government with a costly infrastructure relic.

As the current government navigates these challenges, new administrations often utilise investigations to highlight the failings of their predecessors and bolster their own credibility. However, the sheer scale of the cost blowout, a $15 billion increase within two years for a project initially budgeted at $16 billion, transcends mere political posturing.

It's unclear whether this ongoing review is setting the stage for the project to fall under the purview of the National Anti-Corruption Commission, and whether political figures like Joyce could face scrutiny in the anticipated hearings. But it's yet another reminder of how haphazard the previous Coalition government was when it came to managing large-scale infrastructure projects.

***

GOVERNMENT ANNOUNCES MASSIVE FUNDING FOR AUKUS SUBMARINE DEAL

29 April 2023

The Australian government has announced an additional $4.1 billion for long range missiles, $9 billion towards the AUKUS submarine deal, and an extra $6 billion as part of the review of the Australian Defence Force. This funding comes just after ANZAC Day and is part of a larger $42 billion spending plan over the next decade.

The Defence Strategic Review was commissioned by the Albanese government a few months after it arrived in office last year. The timing of the release of this review, just before ANZAC Day, has led to criticism that the government is using the occasion to boost military funding.

While national security and defence spending are important, some Australians are questioning the prioritisation of defence over other issues such as health, education, and transport. Defence spending is often considered a "beast that keeps needing to be fed," with little cutback compared to other sectors.

There are concerns that this funding will not adequately address veteran welfare and the transitioning of soldiers into civilian life. Critics argue that the funding focuses more on big-ticket items that politicians can use as political props.

There is also criticism of Labor governments using military alliances and arrangements for political gain. The current government has been criticised for its involvement in the Quad meetings and extending the AUKUS deal. There is also disappointment from some Labor voters who are questioning if they made the right decision in supporting the current government. Critics are also calling into question the foreign minister's performance in promoting defence spending.

The government has not addressed these criticisms directly, and there is uncertainty about the long-term strategy for defence spending. Some are calling for a review of priorities to ensure that funding is distributed more evenly across different sectors, including cultural defence, border defence, medicine defence, and biological defence.

SINGLE PARENT PAYMENTS TO CHANGE?

Changes to single parent payments and pension support are expected in the latest Budget news, with the government suggesting modifications to the current system. While the exact details of these changes remain unknown, experts and politicians alike are calling for action on other areas, such as the rate of Jobseeker payments.

Former Secretary to Treasury Ken Henry and former Reserve Bank Governor Bernie Fraser have both voiced their support for a substantial raise in Jobseeker payments, as have several Labor backbenchers. On election night in 2022, Prime Minister Anthony Albanese emphasised the need to support the disadvantaged and vulnerable, stating that "no one should be left behind". However, despite their previous suggestions for change while in opposition, the Labor party has been criticised for being dismissive of the issue now that they are in government.

The pressure for change is building, and if not addressed, it could lead to a leakage of votes and support for the Australian Greens and other independent parties in future elections. While some argue that there are other areas where support could be provided, such as through universal service provision or rental assistance, the refusal to raise Jobseeker payments substantially could be a major political problem for the Labor government.

In the context of other substantial spending, such as the $240 million support package for building an AFL stadium in Hobart, the optics of this situation are not good. It remains to be seen what changes will be made to the single parent payments and pension support system, but it is clear that action is needed on the rate of Jobseeker payments to ensure that those in need are not left behind.

In the wake of the controversial decision to rebuild a sports stadium in New South Wales, questions are being raised about the necessity of a new stadium in Hobart, one of Australia's smaller capital cities. While many argue that a modern stadium could attract a variety of events and provide a space for community gatherings, others are concerned about the cost and whether the benefits would outweigh the expenses.

Critics of the proposed stadium are pointing to the previous NSW Government's experience, where a decision to rebuild a stadium instead of minor modifications cost them dearly. The backlash from the public eventually led to the government's downfall, and some believe that a similar fate could befall the federal government if they proceed with the Hobart stadium.

Despite these concerns, some still believe that a new stadium in Hobart could be a valuable addition to the city. By attracting concerts and other events, the stadium could provide a much-needed economic boost, while also serving as a community gathering place.

However, the question remains whether the people of Hobart are willing to foot the bill for such a project. With the cost of living on the rise and many struggling to make ends meet, the idea of spending millions on a new stadium may not sit well with some residents.

As the debate rages on, it remains to be seen whether a new stadium will be built in Hobart or if the idea will be shelved in favour of other priorities.

CALLS FOR AUSTRALIAN GOVERNMENT TO TAX RESOURCES MORE ADEQUATELY

There have been increasing calls for the Australian government to start taxing resources more adequately and receiving a better return on these resources that are owned by all Australians. This comes amidst concerns about the country's $1 trillion national government debt and endless cost of living debates.

Mining and resource companies have been the primary beneficiaries of Australia's abundant natural resources, and it's time for them to pay their fair share of taxes. According to a recent report, Australia collected only $2.6 billion in tax revenue through the Petroleum Resource Rent Tax, while Qatar, which has similar energy exports to Australia, collected a massive $76 billion this year alone.

Some critics believe that the Labor government should follow the example of other countries with substantial mineral and mining resources and tax these companies to a level comparable with other nations. This would generate much-needed revenue that could be used to fund critical programs such as social housing and Jobseeker payments.

While some people have suggested waiting for the budget announcement, it's essential to remind the government that this is a long-term budget problem that needs to be addressed urgently. The government must take action and stop being limited by budget restraints.

Despite the potential backlash from the mining and resource industries, it's time for the government to put the interests of all Australians first and tax these companies fairly. The possibilities of what we could do with the additional revenue are endless, and it's time to take action now.

LABOR GOVERNMENT TO REVEAL BUDGETARY ISSUES ON BUDGET NIGHT, HIGHLIGHTING ITS TRUE NATURE

As Australia eagerly awaits the upcoming budget, the Labor government has hinted at addressing some critical budgetary issues. The budget, set to be revealed on 9 May, is considered one of the most important ones in recent times, with experts speculating that it will unveil the true nature of the Labor government.

Treasurer Jim Chalmers had earlier put out a budget in October 2022, but it was deemed as more of a warm-up act. This budget is expected to be a more definitive show of whether the Labor government is a 'business-as-usual type' of government or a real reformist government.

Prime Minister Albanese had earlier mentioned modeling himself on the Hawke government, which was known for being a visionary and expansive government. However, critics suggest that the Albanese government has not displayed the same level of boldness and adventure as the Hawke government.

There have been suggestions that the upcoming budget will be the Labor government's first significant opportunity to demonstrate the type of government it intends to be. With only a few seats required in the next election to move the government to a minority, experts recommend that the Labor government should not waste time and start reforming from the outset.

Looking at previous successful reformist state governments like those run by Annastacia Palaszczuk (Queensland), Daniel Andrews (Victoria), and Mark McGowan (Western Australia), the federal Labor government should be prepared to take bold steps in the first term.

The government has a sympathetic Senate, but things can change at any moment, and the government needs to take advantage of the favourable circumstances while they exist—now is the time to do the reforms and make an impact.

The budget night promises to be an interesting one, with expectations about whether it see the Labor government's true nature and whether it will be a real reformist government that makes the necessary changes for Australia's future.

***

NEWS CORPORATION'S LEGAL TROUBLES: A DIMINISHING INFLUENCE

29 April 2023

In recent legal developments, News Corporation finds itself entangled in defamation cases on two fronts—one in the United States and another in Australia. The divergent outcomes of these cases offer a striking commentary on the evolving perception of News Corporation's influence, casting shadows on its reputation as a right-wing propaganda unit.

In the United States, News Corporation, primarily represented by Fox News, has settled a defamation case with Dominion Voting Systems. The settlement, totaling a staggering $797 million US—$1.2 billion Australian dollars—amounts to a quarter of News Corporation's current cash reserves. The case revolved around the dissemination of false information regarding the 2020 presidential election, with Fox News accused of spreading unfounded claims that the election was rigged and stolen from Donald Trump and the Republican Party.

Meanwhile, in Australia, a contrasting narrative unfolds. Lachlan Murdoch has chosen to drop his defamation case against *Crikey* news, a decision that was framed as an attempt to deny *Crikey* additional publicity, despite the fact that the news outlet had already experienced a surge in subscriptions, raising nearly $600,000 through a GoFundMe campaign. This unexpected turn of events marks a departure from News Corporation's historical inclination to staunchly defend itself in legal battles, signaling a shift in their approach.

The repercussions of these legal battles extend beyond monetary losses and legal concessions. Observers point to the larger implication that News Corporation's influence might be waning, as evidenced by its seeming reluctance to engage in protracted legal battles. This retreat from a combative stance is in stark contrast to the company's previous strategy of doubling down on litigation and defence, raising questions about the sustainability of its long-standing dominance in the media landscape.

Adding to News Corporation's legal woes is another pending defamation case in the United States—Smartmatic versus Fox News. The staggering claim of $2.7 billion US suggests that, if successful, this case could inflict substantial damage on the media giant. Speculation is rife that the Dominion case's settlement might be a prelude to the potential fallout from the Smartmatic case, with the latter expected to leverage revelations from the former to strengthen its claims.

As News Corporation navigates these legal challenges, signs of internal turmoil are evident. The abrupt dismissal of Tucker Carlson, one of the network's highest-rated hosts, raises questions about the company's internal dynamics. Carlson's departure, attributed not only to his controversial conspiracy theories but also to alleged mistreatment of staff, underscores the gravity of the situation. Moreover, rumours circulate that other prominent hosts might follow suit, triggering concerns among figures like Andrew Bolt, Peta Credlin, and Paul Murray on Sky News about the potential impact on their own positions.

In Australia, Lachlan Murdoch's acknowledgment of being unpopular raises intriguing questions about the strategic considerations behind legal actions. His assertion that the defamation case against *Crikey* was pursued to avoid granting the news outlet additional sponsorship suggests a calculated move to sue someone perceived as unpopular. This revelation adds an intriguing layer to the unfolding legal saga and invites speculation about the broader implications for News Corporation's standing in both the United States and Australia.

THE MEDIA INDUSTRY STRUGGLES AMID SHIFTING CONSUMER INTERESTS AND DIGITAL DISRUPTION

The recent legal setbacks for News Corporation are not occurring in isolation but rather against a backdrop of a gradual decline in legacy media influence, not only for News Corporation but for the industry at large. The ability to shape political narratives and public opinion, once a stronghold for media giants like News Corporation, has undergone a discernible erosion. While it would be an oversimplification to claim a total loss of influence, the company's recent defeat in the defamation case, resulting in a substantial $797 million US settlement, signals a significant blow.

Beyond financial implications, News Corporation grapples with a decline in audience numbers and shifting consumer habits. Legacy media, accustomed to audiences relying on traditional news outlets for information, is witnessing a generational shift. Younger demographics, more tech-savvy and discerning, seek diverse perspectives from niche outlets rather than relying solely on mainstream sources. The internet has facilitated a global comparison of news, prompting audiences to explore international perspectives directly from the source, bypassing the filters imposed by media moguls.

The gradual decline of News Corporation's influence is not merely a recent phenomenon but part of a larger narrative concerning the changing landscape of media consumption. It took News Corporation considerable time to establish itself as a media powerhouse, but, as history has shown, even empires have a "use by date" and an endpoint. The comparison to the Packer empire's exit from the media business within a decade after Kerry Packer's death serves as a cautionary tale, emphasising the potential swiftness with which media landscapes can transform.

However, the demise of one media empire does not necessarily translate into an automatic improvement in media quality. The existence of a demand for sensationalism and right-wing media, coupled with financial incentives, means that new players will likely emerge to fill any vacuum left by News Corporation. The cautionary tale extends beyond the company itself to the broader media landscape, suggesting that the issues with mainstream media may persist even if ownership structures change.

A fundamental misunderstanding of the internet's impact has played a role in legacy media's decline. While the industry anticipated the internet's disruptive potential, it underestimated the sophistication of younger generations and their ability to access news globally. Legacy media's struggle to adapt to this new reality is evident in their failure to comprehend the competitive nature of the internet, where readers can easily compare global news sources, free from the influence of a few media moguls.

The shift in how news travels, from the outdated 24-hour news cycle to real-time interactions, is a hurdle that legacy media struggles to overcome. The inability to adapt quickly, coupled with the loss of agility and innovation over time, poses a substantial challenge to traditional media models. Just as age affects an athlete's speed, the lifetime of a business model inevitably diminishes its ability to keep pace with evolving consumer preferences and technological advancements. Whether News Corporation can weather this storm and adapt to the changing media landscape remains uncertain, but its recent legal setbacks and the broader industry trends suggest that the road ahead may be fraught with challenges.

NEWS CORPORATION'S NEGATIVE IMPACT ON AUSTRALIAN JOURNALISM

As News Corporation struggles with its current legal battles and potential future challenges, the impact of its influence on journalism in Australia over the past two decades comes under scrutiny. The period coincided with an extended tenure of Coalition government since 1996, raising questions about the intertwining of media influence and political landscapes.

A notable consequence has been the migration of numerous News Corporation journalists to the ABC and the now Nine Media (formerly Fairfax Media). This shift, encompassing not only on-air talent but also senior managers, has fundamentally altered the focus of the ABC. The injection of a commercial mindset and targeting the highly cherished A–B demographic—even though the ABC doesn't have a commercial market imperative—has led to a perceived loss of the ABC's distinctiveness, transforming it into what some critics describe as a dumbed-down news operation, mirroring mainstream media trends.

The legacy of News Corporation, according to critics, lies in fundamentally changing the landscape of news and current affairs for the worse in Australia. The emphasis on appealing to specific commercial demographics has, in their view, diluted the quality of journalism. While niche markets still exhibit an appetite for good journalism, the likelihood of finding such quality within legacy media is perceived to have diminished.

Despite concerns about the direction of journalism, some defenders argue that the ABC still hosts quality programming. Shows like *Landline* are praised for their fairness and balance, even if their appeal might be limited to specific audiences. Programs such as *AM* and *PM* maintain their quality, offering a more nuanced and in-depth approach to news coverage.

However, skepticism surrounds other ABC programs like *Q+A*, which many on social media describe as "unwatchable" unless a compelling panel is featured. The critique extends to the composition of panels, often featuring unqualified individuals and presenting inane questions from the audience. While there is hope for the ABC, there is a call for vigilance in maintaining the quality of shows like *Q+A* and *Insiders*.

Suggestions for improvement include ensuring diverse and qualified panels on *Q+A* and featuring independent journalists on *Insiders* instead of those affiliated with commercial entities. The call for a broader range of perspectives, including regional correspondents from different states, aims to enhance the diversity and depth of discussions. The recurring use of the same News Corporation figures is criticised as contributing to a lack of variety and substance on certain programs.

As the media landscape continues to evolve, the intersection of journalism, politics, and corporate influence remains a focal point of public discourse. The outcomes of News Corporation's legal battles may shape not only the company's future but also influence the trajectory of journalism in Australia. The broader question looms about whether the industry can navigate these challenges and rediscover its commitment to high-quality, independent reporting.

★★★

COALITION CONTINUES TO STRUGGLE AS TACTICS COME UNDER FIRE

29 April 2023

Recent opinion polls—Newspoll and Essential—have confirmed the poor standing of the Coalition and the Leader of the Opposition, Peter Dutton. The news is getting worse for the Coalition, as they continue to oppose every government program and announcement with a negative response, without providing a viable alternative.

The Shadow Treasurer, Angus Taylor, commenced with an announcement that the inflation rate coming down to 7 per cent was "terrible news", and that the Labor government "doesn't understand the pain" that the electorate is going through. Similarly, the Shadow Finance Minister, Senator Jane Hume, criticised the government's two-for-one prescription program, which essentially halves the cost of medicines, citing concerns that it won't do much to alleviate the cost of living pressures. However, the Coalition had seriously considered introducing the same plan when they were last in government.

Even with the government's Voice to Parliament proposal, the Coalition has responded negatively, asking for more details, then asking for more or something different to what they asked for. This constant opposition for the sake of opposition has led to criticism, with the public calling for a constructive opposition that offers support when needed and builds a policy and an alternate vision for how government should be done.

The failed Abbott ministries serve as a reminder of the result of continual opposition—continuing even when they were in government—with the Morrison and Turnbull ministries also facing criticism for similar tactics. Effective oppositions in the past, such as the Whitlam and Howard oppositions, opposed what needed to be opposed while supporting what needed to be supported with cogent and actual argument. They built a policy and an alternate vision for how government should be done, ultimately leading to success.

The current Liberal Party has shown little interest in this approach, with a sole focus on getting back into power as quickly as possible. However, with the anti-corruption commission coming and the potential for former Coalition leaders to feature in any hearings, it may be time for the party to consider mass resignations and the restarting of the party with better candidates.

As the Labor government faces pressure in developing the budget, an effective opposition that offers constructive criticism and provides alternatives is needed to hold the government accountable while building a vision for the country. The Coalition must reassess its opposition tactics and provide a viable alternative if they hope to regain public support.

DO SMALLER PARTIES AND INDEPENDENT CANDIDATES OFFER A SOLUTION?

The rise of smaller parties and independent candidates is changing the face of Australian politics, and could be a sign of the failure of the two-party system, according to some political experts. With the major parties experiencing a decline in their primary vote, and demographic changes leading to shifting voting patterns, it's becoming easier for smaller parties and independents to win lower house seats. This was evident in the 2022 federal election, where the Australian Greens won a lower house seat off the Liberal Party for the first time, and several teal independents also picked up seats previously held by the Liberal Party.

As a result, there's a growing likelihood of more minority governments in the future, with multiparty coalitions become the norm rather than the exception. While this may be a relatively new concept for Australia, it's a model that's worked well in other countries such as Germany and New Zealand.

Despite these challenges, there is much enthusiasm within the electorate for the smaller parties and independent candidates, who are bringing fresh perspectives and meaningful reform ideas to the political landscape. They're also offering an incentive for people to participate in politics, with the belief that getting into Parliament isn't as insurmountable as it might have been in the past. With the major parties facing an uphill battle to remain relevant and electable, the success of smaller parties and independents could be the key to their long-term survival.

It is clear that the Australian political landscape is facing significant challenges. The emergence of minor parties and independent candidates, coupled with declining support for the major parties, is redefining politics. It is important to note that this trend is not limited to the Liberal Party, as the Labor Party also faces similar issues. To address these challenges, there is a need for reform to the voting system to ensure that it is fair and inclusive for all parties and candidates and such reforms could help to promote greater diversity in Australian politics and provide more opportunities for minor parties and independents to have a voice.

However, it is important to ensure that any changes to the political system occur naturally and are in the best interests of Australia as a whole. The major parties have played an important role in Australian politics for many years, and while their relevance may be declining, they are likely to remain a major force in the foreseeable future.

The challenges facing the Australian political landscape are significant, but with thoughtful and considered reforms, we can ensure that our democracy remains strong and vibrant for years to come.

***

MAY

ALBANESE ATTENDS CORONATION AMIDST REPUBLIC DEBATE

6 May 2023

In an event that has sparked discussions about Australia's constitutional future, Prime Minister Anthony Albanese has travelled to London to attend the Coronation of King Charles. However, some voices in Australia have questioned the appropriateness of the Prime Minister's attendance, suggesting it would have been more fitting for the Governor-General, the King's representative in Australia, to solely represent the country at the event.

During his visit to London, Albanese also sat down for an interview with conservative broadcaster, Piers Morgan, where he was questioned about his republican tendencies and the potential transition of Australia to a republic. Albanese, a self-proclaimed lifelong republican, expressed his belief that it is possible to hold republican views while still respecting existing institutions, emphasised his respect for King Charles and considered it an honour to represent Australia at the Coronation.

Albanese acknowledged the diversity of opinions regarding Australia's constitutional arrangements but firmly stated his view that Australia should have its own head of state. He has advocated for an appointed head of state and proposed a process that involves democratic institutions, such as the House of Representatives and the Senate, having a say in the selection. He also suggested the ongoing dispute over the suitable model for a republic has been a major obstacle in advancing the republican cause in Australia.

A recent opinion poll released by the Australian Republican Movement sheds light on public sentiment regarding the monarchy and the values it represents. The poll indicated that 66 per cent of respondents believe that King Charles does not align with their values, while 64 per cent perceive the monarchy as contrary to Australian values of equality and "a fair go". However, despite these opinions, there appears to be significant hesitation among the Australian public when it comes to voting in favour of a republic. The lack of consensus on the model for a republic—as was suggested by

Albanese—further contributes to the challenges faced by proponents of change. Consequently, it is clear that the journey towards Australia becoming a republic is far from straightforward, and significant milestones must be achieved before that vision can be realised.

The broader discussion surrounding the monarchy-versus-republic in Australia raises fundamental questions about tradition, secularism, and national identity. Critics argue that the monarchy is a medieval tradition that does not align with the values of a secular society and question the compatibility of divine right with a secular democratic system. The desire to break free from this perceived anachronism and forge a distinct Australian identity free from the monarchy is gaining traction among proponents of a republic.

However, the timing and mood of the electorate are crucial factors in advancing the republican cause. The failure of the 1999 Republic referendum serves as a reminder that the conditions must align for success. Some argue that Australia's current political landscape, marked by dissatisfaction with past governments, reflects a broken system that needs addressing. While there is recognition of the need for leadership and conviction politicians to spearhead the movement, the prioritisation of other significant referendums, such as the Voice to Parliament, may impact the timeline for the republican agenda.

Referenda are complex and carry significant weight, often representing a once-in-a-generation opportunity for change. Despite favourable opinion polls and the desire of the Australian people, success is never guaranteed. This reality underscores the importance of careful strategising and timing—Albanese may be playing the long game, strategically planning the Republic referendum for a later term, possibly after addressing other pressing issues.

As Australia witnesses the Coronation and contemplates its constitutional future, the Australian Republican Movement continues to call for change. The Movement's aspiration for an Australian head of state and the desire to reshape the nation's identity may take time and concerted effort. The ongoing debate surrounding the monarchy-versus-republic in Australia reflects a broader global trend as other Commonwealth nations transition towards republics: 36 of the 56 Commonwealth nations have already become republics and there are several other nations—Jamaica and possibly Scotland after continuing disruptions caused by Brexit and the revolving door of British prime ministers—are planning to make the transition soon.

While Australia remains divided on this issue, the conversation is far from over, and the path to a republic is likely to be navigated with careful consideration and strategic planning.

***

LABOR'S BUDGET SETS THE STAGE FOR A LONG-TERM IN OFFICE

13 May 2023

In a Budget release that emphasises a cautious approach, Treasurer Jim Chalmers unveiled the Labor government's financial plan for the coming year. The Budget, while receiving mixed reviews, reflects the party's commitment to fulfilling its promises made during the 2022 federal election campaign. However, some critics argue that the Budget falls short in certain areas and misses opportunities for substantial reform.

One of the notable highlights of the Budget is the extension of the single parent payment, which will now continue until the youngest child turns 14. This move has been welcomed as a positive step towards supporting families. Additionally, Jobseeker payments have been increased by $20 per week, though some believe this increase is still insufficient to meet the needs of those relying on the welfare system.

However, the Budget also faces scrutiny for what it lacks. Expectations for increased revenue from the mining sector, particularly through improvements to the petroleum resources rent tax, have not been fully met. Critics point out that the projected $2.4 billion in additional revenue over the next four years falls short of expectations, given the substantial increase in iron ore revenues in the current financial year.

Despite its political nature, the most significant aspect of the Budget is its prediction of a $4 billion surplus. While this surplus is seen as an accomplishment, concerns arise regarding the support offered to individuals at the lower end of the socioeconomic scale.

From an economic perspective, the Budget demonstrates responsible financial management. However, there is room for improvement, as some argue that the cautious approach could hinder progress. The government's gradual shift in policy aligns with the belief that it is easier to rectify mistakes if the "ship of state" turns slowly, rather than implementing radical changes in hasty fashion. Nevertheless, critics argue that this approach underestimates the public's desire for decisive action, especially considering the previous Coalition government's unpopularity.

Reflecting on the mainstream media coverage of the Budget, there is a sense of disappointment regarding the lack of economic analysis; instead, the focus has shifted towards political analysis. This media narrative also provides partisan and simplistic interpretations of budget deficits and surpluses—Labor governments often face the perception that any positive outcomes are attributed to 'luck' or factors beyond their control, while budget deficits are typically viewed as negative. On the other hand, Liberal governments tend to receive more favourable assessments, whether they deliver deficits or surpluses, and these narratives shape public perception and influence political discourse.

Traditionally, the Liberal Party has been perceived as the "better economic manager", often pointing out the lack of surpluses under Labor governments. However, this Budget surplus challenges that narrative, showcasing the Labor Party's ability to achieve fiscal balance. The surplus, though modest, eliminates the notion that only the Liberal Party can deliver economic stability. During their nine years in office between 2013–2022, the Liberal–National Government failed to achieve a surplus, and this factor is further bolstering the Labor Party's claims of economic competence.

This Labor government's budget demonstrates a sense of purpose and commitment to the promises made during the 2022 election campaign. The focus is on laying strong foundations for a better future and addressing immediate cost-of-living pressures. Initiatives aimed at transitioning Australia into a renewable energy superpower reflect a forward-looking approach to sustainable growth and job creation.

While some supporters may express disappointment with the Budget's cautious approach, it aligns with the government's commitment to responsible governance. The Labor government understands the need for big reforms but also recognises the importance of delivering on promises made. The challenge lies in striking a balance between caution and proactive decision-making, ensuring that Australia moves forward while addressing the lingering effects of the previous government's policies.

From a political standpoint, the Budget also presents challenges for the Liberal and National parties. The surplus achieved by the Labor government diminishes their argument of being superior economic managers. Their focus now shifts to addressing inflation and cost-of-living pressures, but these issues alone may not sustain their political message for the next few years. With negotiations required in the Senate to pass Budget measures, the Labor government's plans may receive support from the Australian Greens, who have expressed some concerns but are likely to find common ground.

LABOR'S BUDGET SETS THE STAGE FOR A LONG-TERM IN OFFICE

While the Labor government's budget may not satisfy everyone's expectations, it is seen as a reasonable building block for the future. The long-term vision and commitment to key issues such as renewable energy indicate a desire for progressive change. The challenges faced by any government, unexpected events, and evolving circumstances should also be taken into account when evaluating the achievements and shortcomings of political leadership.

Looking ahead, the Labor government's Budget sets the stage for a potential longer-term period in office, with the budgetary foundations now in place. The true test lies in executing their plans effectively and meeting the expectations of the Australian people. Only time will tell how this Budget—and subsequent Budgets—shape the nation's trajectory, but for now, it serves as a significant step towards a brighter and better Australia.

***

BUDGET REPLY: UNCERTAIN PATH FORWARD FOR THE LIBERAL PARTY

13 May 2023

In the midst of discussions surrounding the recent budget and the opposition's reply, the immediate political prospects of the Liberal–National Coalition remain uncertain. While the Budget Reply speech failed to provide substantial insights into the party's direction, it is important to note that, at this stage of the political cycle, such details are not usually expected. However, the lack of clarity regarding the Coalition's agenda, particularly if they are to regain power, is concerning.

The announcement of Stuart Robert's retirement from politics adds another layer of complexity to this situation. Although the date of his departure is yet to be determined, it is likely to happen sooner rather than later. Robert represents the Queensland seat of Fadden, which is a stronghold for Peter Dutton and the Liberal–National Party, holding 21 of the 30 seats in Queensland. With Fadden secured by a margin of 10.6 per cent by the L–NP, it would be difficult for them to lose the seat. Nonetheless, Robert's retirement raises questions about the future of the party and the path they hope to carve out for themselves.

The rumours still persist regarding former leader Scott Morrison's potential departure from politics—Morrison has taken up an advisory role with the Center for New American Security, a smaller military thinktank based in the United States. These upcoming changes in federal politics indicate a period of transition and uncertainty on the horizon.

Robert's retirement from politics can be seen as a positive move. As one of the ministers responsible for the Robodebt scandal, along Scott Morrison, his departure presents an opportunity for the Liberal–National Party to define its future trajectory. It also signals a chance to address the controversial actions taken by Robert and Morrison in relation to Robodebt and for the types of candidates it chooses in future preselections.

Looking at the internal dynamics within the Liberal Party, there seems to be a glimmer of hope. Katherine Deves overlooked for the vacant Senate seat in NSW—reportedly, she was told not to stand—may be a sign of wiser and cooler heads prevailing. Perhaps there are some in the Liberal Party who recognise that the electoral appeal of far-right ideologies is diminishing. Losing many elections across federal, state and territory jurisdictions should be a wake-up call, urging the party to consider alternative approaches. The upcoming byelections in Fadden and Cook will be telling, as they could shape the party's future direction.

Robert's questionable conduct, including accumulating unjustified expenses and the Robodebt debacle, does not leave a positive legacy. His fallout with Morrison over the Robodebt issue also further isolates him in opposition, leaving him with few allies. Considering the allegations surrounding Robert and any future National Anti-Corruption Commission investigations, it is likely that he will be one of the prominent figures involved—it should be noted that these are only allegations at this stage, but they suggest that Robert's exit from politics is a welcome development.

DUTTON IS JUST REVISITING THE HOWARD YEARS

In his Budget Reply speech on Thursday night, Leader of the Opposition, Peter Dutton, attempted to rally his base supporters—possibly an appeal to One Nation supporters—however, his speech failed to impress and raised concerns about the direction of the party. Dutton's attacks on the idea of a "big Australia" and immigration, along with his criticism of the increase in public servants in Canberra, reflected a continuation of the policies of past Liberal leaders such as Scott Morrison, Tony Abbott, and John Howard. Unfortunately for Dutton and the party, this approach is outdated and out of touch with contemporary politics.

One of Dutton's main messages focused on the failures of the Labor Party, particularly on higher power prices, higher unemployment, and higher taxes. While there may be some validity to the argument about power prices, the claims of higher unemployment and higher taxes lack substantial evidence. It appears that Dutton is resorting to the same old tactics that have become synonymous with the Liberal Party, failing to offer fresh ideas or progressive solutions.

Demographically, the Liberal Party is facing a disastrous situation. The under-35 demographic shows little support for the party, unlike in the past when it enjoyed higher levels of support from young voters. The declining trend in younger voters aligning with the Liberal Party is alarming and indicates a lack of foundation upon which the party can build as individuals grow older and more conservative. While it is true that numbers, not just age, matter in politics, the fact remains that the Liberal Party is struggling to attract and retain a diverse voter base. Unless a substantial change occurs within the party, they face an uphill battle in future elections.

There are speculations within the Liberal Party about alternative leadership options, particularly the deputy leader Sussan Ley. Although there isn't an active push to make her the leader at present, the party seems to be preparing for potential changes in leadership if the situation deteriorates further. Ley's engagement in a listening tour and increased participation in parliamentary Question Time reflects her aspirations for leadership. However, it is worth noting that the Liberal Party, like any political entity, must be ready for any leadership transition, even as a contingency plan.

Another figure mentioned is Shadow Treasurer, Angus Taylor, but his recent inconsistencies and lack of credibility have tarnished his reputation. He fails to make a serious contribution to the party's future.

The Liberal Party is undoubtedly in a difficult position. Dutton, is struggling to resonate with the public, and the party's frontbench appears demoralised. While political parties need to be prepared with alternative leadership, it is surprising that Ley is considered a leader-in-waiting, even though she is the deputy leader—Ley's past controversies, such as "accidentally" buying a unit on the Gold Coast during a parliamentary business trip, have left a negative impression. Her lack of popularity among the wider community hinders her chances of becoming an electorally acceptable face for the Liberal Party.

Additionally, Taylor's involvement in questionable activities, such as his involvement in Eastern Australia Agriculture—an entity established under a cloak of secrecy in the Cayman Islands—and alleging forged travel documents in an attempt to support a political campaign for his wife, Louise Clegg, to run for position of Lord Mayor of Sydney, has further damaged his standing. The party needs a leader who can tap into the zeitgeist and reinvigorate the Liberal brand, but such a figure is currently lacking.

The Liberal Party is facing an uncertain future. It must confront the reality of its dwindling support among younger voters and the need for new ideas that align with the current era. While Ley might be the likely candidate for leadership—if it does come to that—the truth is that whoever leads the party at this moment is bound to be irrelevant. The Liberal Party must undergo significant changes to regain relevance and appeal to a broader spectrum of voters.

***

HOUSING CRISIS IN AUSTRALIA DEMANDS A NATIONAL APPROACH

20 May 2023

Housing has emerged as a pressing issue in federal politics, capturing the attention of policymakers and the public alike. Australia is currently grappling with a multifaceted housing crisis that encompasses soaring housing costs, unaffordable mortgages, skyrocketing rents amidst a historically tight rental market, a growing homelessness problem, and a shortage of social housing. Particularly alarming is the affordability challenge faced by younger individuals, for whom property prices in major cities remain out of reach, especially for single people. The severity of the situation is apparent across the country, demanding immediate attention and effective solutions.

While there have been calls for the federal government to take a more proactive role, the complex nature of housing policy presents a significant challenge. Housing responsibility primarily lies with state and territory governments, and despite the majority of governments being Labor-led, each jurisdiction has its own housing policies shaped by varying political pressures and vested interests. Further complicating matters are the divergent local council regulations and requirements that influence housing development and planning decisions.

Recognising the need for a unified approach, it is time for the federal government to consider convening a national housing summit, providing a platform to engage stakeholders from all levels of government, housing industry experts, community representatives, and advocacy groups to collectively define the problems and explore comprehensive solutions. By understanding the unique perspectives and challenges faced by different stakeholders, policymakers can devise an overarching direction to address the housing crisis.

One fundamental issue is the stigma surrounding public housing, which perpetuates misconceptions and hampers the potential for inclusive and sustainable solutions. It is essential to combat this stigma and recognise that housing assistance, like other forms of welfare, is meant to provide necessary support to those in need. Public housing should be viewed as an integral part of the solution, ensuring secure and affordable housing for all.

Critics argue that rental laws need to be reassessed to strike a fair balance between the rights and responsibilities of landlords and tenants. Landlords contend that renters hold all the power, while tenants often feel powerless against landlords. In truth, both perspectives contain elements of truth. An examination of rental laws and regulations with an aim to establish fairer practices is necessary to alleviate the existing tensions.

To encourage housing affordability and discourage hoarding of vacant properties, reforms are required, such as reducing tax incentives associated with keeping houses unoccupied. It is estimated that a significant number of homes, particularly in Sydney and Melbourne, remain unoccupied, with reasons ranging from properties being listed on Airbnb to prolonged absence by owners—and in some cases, owners of new apartments would prefer them to remain vacant for several years, until the value of the property appreciates, and then selling the property for a profit. Addressing this issue by incentivising occupancy would not only lower rents but also contribute to alleviating homelessness.

It is also crucial to acknowledge the vulnerable groups disproportionately affected by the housing crisis. Women over the age of 55 constitute the largest growing demographic among the homeless population, highlighting the need for targeted interventions to prevent homelessness among this group. Additionally, individuals with mental health issues face challenges in maintaining stable households. Policies must prioritise the provision of appropriate support and resources to ensure their wellbeing and housing stability.

Essentially, at the heart of the housing crisis in Australia is a shortage of available homes, whether due to insufficient construction, unoccupied properties, or other factors. Increasing the housing supply emerges as a critical step, but determining the type, location, and quantity of housing presents its own set of challenges. Previous policies, such as first homeowner grants, have inadvertently inflated property prices rather than achieving their intended purpose. Piecemeal and politically-motivated solutions have failed to provide a comprehensive and cohesive vision for housing policy, necessitating a shift towards a long-term perspective.

To forge effective solutions, it is imperative to accurately identify and define the problem at hand. A comprehensive understanding of the housing crisis will enable policymakers to adopt targeted and sustainable measures. By transcending political interests and approaching the issue with compassion and foresight, Australia can establish a housing policy framework that addresses the immediate challenges while laying the foundation for a more equitable and affordable housing landscape in the future.

A DELICATE BALANCING ACT IN THE HOUSING SECTOR

The interconnected nature of the challenges facing the housing market, has resulted in a wide range unintended consequences resulting from previous policy adjustments by governments—such as a rise in property prices, when the purpose of such policies, has been to lower prices. The need for ethical considerations in addressing these issues also needs to be considered, particularly in relation to negative gearing benefits and living density changes.

Calls to end or restrict negative gearing benefits for housing have gained traction, with proponents arguing that such measures would align with more ethical and moral principles—why should owners of many multiple residences be expected to receive taxpayer-supported benefits, when there are many people homeless?

However, concerns have been raised about the potential impact on housing supply. Past experiences, such as the changes to capital gains tax in 1989 by the Hawke government, which led to a rental crisis before the policy was reversed, serve as a reminder of the delicate balance within the housing market.

Research suggests that the current housing market challenges have been influenced by a shift in living density preferences. The pandemic prompted individuals to opt for homes with fewer occupants, rather than shared accommodations and although seemingly a minor change, this shift has generated significant ripple effects throughout the housing sector.

While legislation cannot enforce specific living density requirements for each house, there is a possibility of passing regulations to ensure that vacant houses are occupied. However, this example of living density highlights the intricate nature of the housing sector, where even minor policy adjustments can have far-reaching consequences.

Housing is a right, not a privilege, and that everyone should have access to suitable accommodation. Addressing homelessness and insufficient housing is emerging as a primary concern in public policy, highlighting the vulnerability of those in need. A comprehensive housing policy should prioritise the wellbeing of the most vulnerable members of society.

The Labor government's social housing fund policy has been met with mixed reactions, as some question its adequacy to address the housing crisis. Urgent action is needed to address the immediate shortage of approximately 600,000 social housing units, projected to reach nearly a million by 2040.

In addition to expanding the availability of social housing, re-evaluating outdated housing development practices is deemed essential. The dominance of profit-driven developers and the nostalgic notion of quarter-acre blocks with three-bedroom houses should be challenged. Embracing diversity in housing options, such as tiny houses and communal living arrangements, can contribute to sustainable and community-oriented development.

To address the increasing difficulty of property ownership for younger generations, there needs to be a strengthening of leasing and renting laws and longer lease options, such as five or ten years, with reasonable provisions for early termination, could provide stability for both tenants and landlords.

Ultimately, housing is a multifaceted issue requiring compassionate and sensible solutions. By addressing interconnected challenges, such as living density, affordability, community-building, and ecological sustainability, substantial progress can be made in the housing sector.

The housing crisis in Australia demands urgent attention and concerted efforts from all levels of government and society, especially the federal government. A national housing summit could serve as a pivotal moment for stakeholders to come together, align their visions, and chart a path forward that prioritises affordability, access, and support for the most vulnerable. By recognising the complexities and nuances of the housing crisis, Australia has an opportunity to shape a future where secure and affordable housing is a reality for all its citizens.

***

RACIST MEDIA AND ATTACK-DOG NEWS CORPORATION

30 May 2023

Racism in the media is a deeply entrenched issue that requires urgent attention. The recent case of ABC journalist Stan Grant, who has taken indefinite leave after facing a torrent of racist abuse, highlights the pervasive nature of discrimination faced by people of colour, women, and individuals from migrant backgrounds in the media and political spheres. Grant's decision to step away from his role comes as a culmination of ongoing racist attacks he has experienced throughout his career.

It is important to recognise the role played by News Corporation, led by Rupert Murdoch, in perpetuating racism within the media landscape. News Corporation has a history of amplifying racism, as seen in their coverage of incidents such as Adam Goodes—hounded out of the AFL in 2015—the Black Lives Matter movement, the 'African gangs' agenda pushed by the Liberal Party during 2019, and the current debate surrounding the Voice to Parliament. Their influence in shaping public opinion and promoting divisive narratives cannot be ignored.

However, it is not only News Corporation perpetuating racism in the media. Many other media outlets—including the ABC, Nine Media, Seven Network, Ten Media, and *The Guardian*—often fail to adequately address and combat racism. While some pay lip service to the issue, others—such as News Corporation—display outright hostility. This lack of action and accountability allows racism to persist within the industry, hindering progress towards a more inclusive society.

The power of social media exacerbates the problem, acting as a platform for hate speech and racist abuse. While discussions about combating racism often emerge in response to such incidents, little is done to address the root causes. It is crucial for the media industry to confront its own role in perpetuating racism and take concrete steps to rectify the situation.

Grant's departure also raises concerns about the support offered by ABC management. He criticised the lack of support he received amid the abusive attacks and expressed disappointment in the ABC's failure to address the role of News Corporation in fueling this racism. Grant's sentiments were echoed by ABC News head Justin Stevens and managing director David Anderson, who accused News Corporation of relentlessly attacking the public broadcaster.

The relationship between the ABC and News Corporation has long been contentious, with News Corporation often criticising the ABC. The recent revelations at Senate estimate hearings, where ABC executives were questioned by Senator Sarah Hanson-Young, shed light on the extent of News Corporation's influence and the lack of action taken by ABC management.

Senator Sarah Hanson-Young: "News Corporation have been attacking the ABC for years. And it's basic sport for them—beat up on the public broadcaster. They have a they have a track record of going after individuals: they've done it to women; they've done it to women of colour; they've done it to First Nations people. They go after them. They whip up the frenzy of haters and then they sit back and watch good people be torn down. And you can't sit here today and tell me that you haven't seen that pattern happen until now. Surely, this is not new.

Justin Stevens: A few things, Senator—the first is the Murdoch family and the ABC have had an interesting relationship since the 1930s—there's nothing new there. Secondly, the coverage of the ABC, and the criticism of the ABC news coverage was not limited to News Corp; Nine and other publishers were very critical as well—"

Senator Hanson-Young: "Do we see the nine newspapers, trawling through ABC journalists, social media feeds?"

Stevens: "I'm not sure..."

Senator Hanson-Young: "Why does the ABC continue to provide a platform for representatives from News Corp when they so clearly, as a corporate entity, have such disdain for the public broadcaster?

David Anderson: "There's some good journalists News Corp—we've got good journalists in our ranks that have come from News Corp. But there are some journos that we do want to put on to, whether it's *Insiders* or whether we have *Q+A*, whether it's *The Drum*, for we are seeking their view and perspective."

One crucial step towards combating racism in the media is reassessing the association between the ABC and News Corporation. Constantly inviting News Corporation journalists onto ABC programs should be reconsidered, as it provides a platform to a corporate entity that consistently displays public disdain and humiliation for the public broadcaster. Instead, the ABC should prioritise supporting marginalised voices and fostering a more inclusive and equitable media landscape.

Addressing racism requires a comprehensive approach that goes beyond overt acts of discrimination. It requires examining the language, narratives, and perspectives used in media coverage. The media industry must strive to be more inclusive, ensuring that diverse voices are not only heard but also respected and valued.

It is time for the media industry to reflect on its role in perpetuating racism and take meaningful action to bring about positive change. By supporting independent journalism and demanding accountability, we can work towards a society that values diversity, fosters respectful dialogue, and challenges discriminatory practices in all forms.

THE BATTLE FOR BALANCED REPORTING

It has to be remembered that News Corporation in Britain came under fire for unethical practices—the tapping of a deceased girl's phone, with the aim of uncovering private messages, with many of the individuals responsible for this breach of ethics still retaining their positions within the company. This incident highlights that it was not an isolated event or a mere lapse in judgment by a few individuals, but rather a systemic problem within the organisation. In the context of this obvious lack of ethics, ABC programs such as *Insiders* should consider banning journalists from News Corporation appearing as panellists.

During the recent broadcast of King Charles' coronation, the ABC organised a panel discussion on colonialism and its impact on Indigenous Australians. Invited guests, including Stan Grant, Craig Foster, Teela Reed, and Julian Leeser, engaged in a conversation about this critical topic. Surprisingly, the abuse and backlash were primarily directed at Stan Grant, despite him being an invited guest rather than the organiser of the panel. Conservative groups, including News Corporation, the Australian Monarchist League, and supporters of the royal family, spearheaded the offensive against Grant.

Critics argued that the timing of the discussion, which coincided with the coronation, was inappropriate. However, the conversation about the effects of colonisation and the future of the monarchy in Australia is crucial and should not be limited by ceremonial events. The strong negative reaction from conservatives reflects a resistance to open dialogue and a refusal to acknowledge the complexities of Australia's history.

The response from News Corporation has been a doubling down on their attacks against the ABC, attempting to distance themselves from any association with the racist abuse directed at Stan Grant and other individuals. This denial of responsibility is disingenuous, as News Corporation has played a significant role in shaping public discourse and perpetuating divisive narratives.

While acknowledging that the ABC is not perfect, it is evident that racism in the media remains a persistent problem. Stan Grant highlighted the lack of support from ABC management during this challenging time. This lack of understanding and empathy can be attributed to the absence of Indigenous representation in senior management and the board of the ABC, and this limited diversity within these decision-making positions perpetuates a dismissive attitude towards racist attacks and prevents meaningful change.

Addressing these issues requires a comprehensive overhaul of the ABC's board and management. As a nation, Australia must mature and foster a broader range of debates that reflect the diversity of its population. However, vested interests often impede progress, with News Corporation acting as the mouthpiece for those resisting change.

Senator Hanson-Young has introduced legislation for a federal inquiry into News Corporation—the outcome of this inquiry at this stage remains uncertain, but it represents an opportunity to examine the influence and practices of Rupert Murdoch and News Corporation in Australia. At 92 years old, it is essential for Murdoch to understand the criticisms leveled against him and the negative impact he has had on Australian media and politics, before he passes away.

In an ideal world, Murdoch would have faced legal consequences after the Leveson inquiry in 2011. The decline of print media, exacerbated by online platforms, has already weakened the power of traditional press barons like Murdoch and the dwindling subscription numbers and waning influence of News Corporation indicate a shifting media landscape.

As Australia strives for a more inclusive and equitable society, media organisations must recognise the need for greater diversity in their ranks. It is time for the mainstream media to evolve and accurately reflect the multicultural fabric of the nation. While change may be slow, it is crucial to challenge the prevailing orthodoxy and work towards a media landscape that embraces all perspectives. Only then can Australia truly mature as an independent nation and move away from the divisive media narratives that have plagued its history.

***

GLOBAL ADVOCACY GROWS FOR THE RELEASE OF JULIAN ASSANGE

27 May 2023

Julian Assange remains a focal point of global attention as efforts intensify to secure his release from Belmarsh prison in London, where he has been held since 2019. The latest developments involve his wife, Stella Assange, a human rights defender, lawyer, and activist, who took centre stage at the National Press Club and participated in a rally in Sydney's Hyde Park during the week. These events are part of an ongoing campaign to shine a light on Assange's plight and rally support for his freedom.

While background diplomacy has been in play from both Coalition and Labor governments, the consensus is that soft diplomacy alone may no longer be effective in securing Assange's release. A notable 48 Australian members of parliament and Senators have collectively called on the United States government to halt its pursuit of Assange; additionally, media associations worldwide in democratic nations have echoed this plea, underscoring the widespread belief that his continued incarceration serves no meaningful purpose.

The debate surrounding Assange's actions and status as a journalist has been a contentious one. Some critics argue that he is not a journalist at all, pointing to his alleged interference in the 2016 U.S. presidential election by publishing information that supposedly favoured Russia and harmed the electoral chances of the Democrat candidate, Hillary Clinton. However, those advocating for Assange's release emphasise that the fundamental issue at hand is the release of classified material related to the Baghdad airstrike in 2007, which resulted in the deaths of 18 innocent Iraqi citizens and two journalists. The leaked video footage, made public by WikiLeaks in 2010, placed Assange into the crosshairs of the United States government.

Notably, the whistleblower who originally leaked the footage, Chelsea Manning, faced charges under the U.S. *Espionage Act* and served time in jail, but Manning was released in 2017 under a commutation from then-

President Barack Obama. The apparent disparity in the treatment of Manning, who actually leaked the material, and Assange, who published the material, has fueled criticism and raised questions about the consistency of the legal process.

Amid these complexities, concerns persist regarding Assange's human rights. His confinement in the Ecuadorian embassy in London for six years, followed by eviction under vague justifications of his "messiness" and "rudeness" within the embassy, has been a subject of scrutiny. Critics question whether these reasons justify the eviction of a political prisoner, emphasising the need for transparent and fair treatment.

As the call for Assange's release grows louder, advocates argue that the secrets he exposed are no longer relevant, and his prolonged imprisonment serves no justifiable purpose. The debate transcends political affiliations, focusing on the universal principles of human rights and the right to a fair and timely trial. As the world watches and deliberates, the central question remains: is it time for Julian Assange to come home?

THE DIPLOMATIC CHALLENGES IN THE QUEST FOR ASSANGE'S RELEASE

Despite the limitations the Australian Government faces in directly influencing Assange's case, efforts persist to secure his release. The High Commissioner of Australia to the United Kingdom, Stephen Smith, has been actively engaging with British authorities, and the government continues to make representations to the United States regarding Assange's situation. The Prime Minister, Anthony Albanese, recently responded to queries from independent MP Andrew Wilkie during question time, shedding light on the government's stance.

Wilkie pressed the Prime Minister on why he had not met with Stella Assange, who was present in Parliament House, and also inquired about the government's efforts to reunite Assange with his family, questioning why more substantial action had not been taken. In response, Albanese emphasised that his meetings were determined by the priorities that would yield tangible outcomes rather than mere demonstrations. He asserted that his focus was on effective actions and diplomatic efforts to break through the prolonged issue of Assange's incarceration.

While Albanese's response may come across as dismissive to some, the Prime Minister highlighted the bipartisan consensus that has emerged, especially following the leader of the opposition's comments the previous week. The shared sentiment is that the ongoing incarceration of Julian Assange serves no purpose. Albanese maintained that he had conveyed Australia's view to both the U.S. and British administrations diplomatically, underscoring the government's commitment to finding a resolution.

Despite the challenges, historical precedent suggests that Australia has been successful in securing the release of its citizens from oppressive regimes. Past cases involving countries such as Libya, Cambodia, Bulgaria, Colombia, Egypt, Saudi Arabia, though not universally successful, demonstrate Australia's diplomatic capacity to navigate complex situations. The question now is whether Australia can leverage its alliance with the United States to make a more compelling case for Assange's release.

Stella Assange, addressing the National Press Club during the week, emphasised the pivotal role Australia plays as the United States' most important ally.

> **Stellar Assange:** "Australia is the United States most important ally.
> That's clear, maybe this wasn't the case 10 years ago. So it's important to recognise that that Australia plays an important role, and can secure Julian's release. Julian's life is in the hands of the Australian Government. And it's not my place to tell the Australian government how to do it, but it must be done.
> Julian has to be released. And I place hope in Anthony Albanese to make it happen. This is the closest we've ever been to securing Julian's release, and I want to encourage and do everything in my power to help that."

STELLA ASSANGE URGES AUSTRALIA TO OFFER WHISTLEBLOWER PROTECTION

As Stella Assange raises the possibility of Julian's imminent release, the uncertainty surrounding the timeframe lingers, with the potential for a resolution to materialise swiftly or extend over an indeterminate period. Drawing parallels to the unexpected releases of Mamdouh Habib and David Hicks from Guantanamo Bay in 2005 and 2007, it obvious that diplomatic dynamics can swiftly shift, leading to unforeseen developments in high-profile cases. However, there needs to be the political will in the first instance.

Stella Assange's optimism is underscored by the belief that Australia, as a staunch ally of the United States, holds the key to demonstrating a commitment to protecting whistleblowers. To substantiate this commitment, she contends that the Australian government must not only work towards Julian Assange's release but also cease the trials of other whistleblowers, such as David McBride and Richard Boyle. Despite the differences in the issues these individuals expose, Stella Assange emphasised the overarching goal: to end the persecution of truth-tellers and safeguard the human rights of Australian citizens.

The call to action is clear: if Australia aspires to be more than a subservient ally to the U.S. and the UK, it must champion the rights of its citizens. The plea is not just about freeing Assange but ensuring that individuals revealing uncomfortable truths about government actions are protected. Drawing a parallel to the way Australian diplomatic efforts rally behind citizens facing legal challenges in foreign countries, Stella Assange underscores the disparity in treatment when it comes to Julian Assange. The urgency lies in upholding Assange's rights, bringing him back to Australia, and ensuring a fair trial, just as any other Australian citizen would rightfully expect.

The plea is a simple one: let Australia transcend its current role and be a defender of citizen rights on the global stage, the essence of the matter lies in ensuring due process and fairness. Stella Assange remains hopeful for a positive resolution, underscoring the ongoing struggle for justice and the anticipation that a conclusive end to this protracted saga is on the horizon.

***

MODI VISITS AUSTRALIA: TRADE TIES AND HUMAN RIGHTS CHALLENGES

27 May 2023

The Indian Prime Minister, Narendra Modi, has embarked on a crucial visit to Australia, with the primary aim of fortifying trade ties between the two nations and collaborating on the development of a green hydrogen program. Although the specifics of this initiative remain unclear, it aligns with the global movement toward producing green hydrogen, distinguished by its reliance on renewable energy sources.

Originally scheduled as part of a broader gathering, Modi's visit to Australia was rescheduled after US President Joe Biden cancelled his attendance. The bilateral relationship between Australia and India holds significant importance for various reasons. Notably, there are approximately 800,000 individuals of Indian heritage residing in Australia, with 720,000 of them born in India. The burgeoning Indian economy, positioned to rival China's, underscores the strategic importance of fostering ties between the two nations.

Amidst the economic collaborations and cultural exchanges, concerns about human rights issues in India come to the forefront. India, like China, faces scrutiny for alleged human rights violations. Modi, a charismatic and popular leader with a 70 per cent approval rating in India, has been both praised and criticised for his governance. His populist and nationalistic approach resonates with many, particularly the Hindu majority, while simultaneously drawing criticism for his treatment of religious minorities.

The Indian leader's visit prompted reflections on the enduring nature of the Australia–India relationship and beyond the fluctuations in leadership and government, the bond between the two countries must transcend political changes. However, there arises a crucial question: should Australia, as a responsible ally and advocate for human rights, address these concerns with its Indian counterparts?

As Modi, a figure both admired and criticised, steps onto Australian soil, the need for a nuanced approach is apparent. While India's influence on the global stage is undeniable, maintaining a strong relationship should not come at the expense of addressing human rights and governance issues. The historical ties between the two nations, dating back to trade relationships during India's independence struggles, lay a foundation for mutual understanding. Still, as Australia navigates its alliances with major players like the United States and China, striking the right balance becomes imperative.

The narrative surrounding Modi's governance is not without its complexities: his tenure as Chief Minister of Gujarat in 2002 during anti-Muslim riots remains a point of contention, even though he was officially exonerated in 2010. Additionally, accusations of the curtailment of press freedoms and discriminatory laws against religious minorities present challenges that merit careful consideration.

As Australia welcomes Modi, it is faced with the delicate task of acknowledging the shared history and cultural connections while not shying away from addressing uncomfortable topics. Diplomacy demands a nuanced approach, recognising that engaging in dialogue about values and human rights is not a rebuke but an expression of concern. The visit serves as a platform for Australia to assert its values while reinforcing the importance of maintaining a multifaceted, yet principled, relationship with India.

BALANCING HUMAN RIGHTS ADVOCACY WITH INTERNATIONAL REALITIES

As Australia welcomes world leaders like Modi, the need for introspection is critical. While it is crucial to maintain diplomatic ties and celebrate international collaboration, there is a growing call for Australia to lead by example, both in its domestic policies and its approach to engaging with other nations on human rights issues.

The recent footage of Prime Minister Anthony Albanese's reception for Modi, likening the Indian Prime Minister to Bruce Springsteen at a rally, raises questions about the appropriateness of such comparisons. While acknowledging the significance of Modi's visit as a leader of a close and important ally, the manner in which these events are conducted warrants careful consideration. Leading by example means not only engaging in talks but also demonstrating a commitment to the principles of human rights.

Australia, though a member of the G20, is undeniably a low-level power compared to giants like the United States, China, and India. In light of its relatively limited influence, it becomes imperative for Australia to wield its diplomatic power judiciously. Lecturing other nations on human rights without addressing its own issues—the historical and current treatment of

Indigenous people, for example—could potentially undermine Australia's credibility on the international stage, as seen in recent exchanges with China over the Uighur issues.

The ongoing Reconciliation with Indigenous communities in Australia is a case in point. While no country is perfect, Australia's efforts to address historical injustices, such as the establishment of the Voice to Parliament, demonstrate a step towards positive change. The acknowledgment of Indigenous people in the constitution is a critical move, not only for the benefit of the international community but, more importantly, for the wellbeing and rights of Indigenous Australians.

In navigating the complex landscape of international diplomacy, Australia has the opportunity to set an example. Rather than merely pointing out the flaws in other nations, Australia can highlight its own initiatives to improve human rights conditions and encourage collaborative efforts. This involves not only talking about change but actively implementing policies that foster a more just society.

As the world struggles with various human rights challenges, Australia has the chance to contribute to meaningful conversations and actions. By making noticeable changes to its own human rights record and openly discussing these efforts, Australia can inspire others to join in creating a world where respect for human rights is a shared value. The journey toward a more just and equitable global community starts at home, and Australia's commitment to positive change will undoubtedly shape its standing in the broader context of international diplomacy.

***

JUNE

PWC SCANDAL SHEDS LIGHT ON CONSULTANTS AND CONFLICTS OF INTEREST

4 June 2023

In a week dominated by revelations surrounding PwC—one of the world's largest accounting firms—attention has been drawn to the alarming leaking of secret information from the Australian Taxation Office to other consulting firms and PwC's clients. The leaked information, which potentially holds valuable insights into the Australian government's plans regarding multinational corporations and taxation, has sparked a heated debate on the issue of government outsourcing. It is now becoming evident that the disclosures made so far merely scratch the surface, with indications of more revelations to come, not just concerning PwC but other consulting firms as well.

The magnitude of this issue becomes apparent when examining the exorbitant amounts of money spent on consultants and outsourcing: during the final year of the Morrison government, an astonishing $20.8 billion was allocated to these services. To put this into perspective, this figure is equivalent to employing 54,000 full-time staff or 37 per cent of the entire federal government public service. While the Albanese government has expressed its intention to address this issue and curtail excessive outsourcing, immediate reductions are not feasible due to ongoing contracts that cannot be terminated abruptly, some of which have a duration spanning several years.

It is essential to acknowledge that certain areas of government activity require the specialised expertise of the private sector and reintegrating these functions back into the public service quickly poses significant challenges. It is now clear, however, that no amount of confidentiality agreements with external providers can guarantee the protection of sensitive material belonging to the federal government, emphasising the urgent need for a comprehensive review of the outsourcing practices.

A critical aspect that emerged during Senate hearings this week is that relationship between the 'Big Four' accounting firms—PwC, KPMG, EY and Deloitte—and political donations to parties on both sides of the political spectrum—over $4 million over the past decade. The conflict of interest arising from such financial contributions casts doubt on the fairness and impartiality of policy-making processes and there is a need for more robust regulations prohibiting these donations, considering their potential influence over governmental decisions and elections.

The Australian Greens Senator Barbara Pocock questioned Peter de Cure from the Tax Practitioners Board during the Senate hearings, and his responses shed light on the inadequacy of the current system's response to the actions of PwC. The failure to consider whether PwC breached professional codes, particularly in acting honestly and with integrity, has raised serious concerns about the resolve and effectiveness of oversight committees. The absence of any referrals for financial penalties, despite the gravity of the situation, adds to the growing skepticism surrounding the regulatory mechanisms in place.

The ongoing Senate hearings continue to uncover shocking details, and it is anticipated that more revelations will follow. Beyond the questionable behaviour of individual consultants at PwC—such as the former head of international tax, Peter Collins—the larger issue at hand is the overreliance on external expertise, which has steadily increased since the 1980s. Influenced by neoliberal ideologies and a desire to distance themselves from anything remotely associated with communism after the fall of the Berlin Wall in 1989, governments embraced the outsourcing trend, often to an extreme extent. However, the time has come for a substantial reduction in this reliance on the private sector, as the detrimental effects of excessive outsourcing become increasingly evident.

The issue of outsourcing also extends beyond consultants to the management of procurement from the private sector on behalf of the government. In the case of PwC, the lack of effective checks and balances allowed for the leakage of sensitive government information, exposing potential vulnerabilities in the system.

The current situation has brought into question the role of other bodies, such as the Australian Federal Police, in overseeing and addressing potential breaches. The revelation that the AFP received information about a confidentiality breach involving PwC back in 2018, without taking substantial action, highlights the need for a thorough investigation into the relationship between PwC, government agencies, and regulatory bodies. The integrity and trustworthiness of the government are vital for the effective functioning of democracy, and any compromise in these areas could have serious consequences.

Beyond the PwC scandal, there is a growing realisation that a broader re-evaluation of outsourcing practices is necessary. Privatisation, ethics, and the alignment of private sector interests with public goals are all critical aspects that demand attention. While the private sector can play a role in certain areas, infrastructure development and vital services are best managed by the government to ensure the public interest is served and prevent profit gouging at public expense.

Although calls for a Royal Commission have been made, some argue that a complete overhaul of the system, while maintaining essential services, may be a more effective approach. Rebuilding government operations from scratch with transparency, accountability, and the public interest at the forefront, could address the underlying issues that have led to the current state of affairs.

With the potential for further revelations and ongoing Senate hearings, the debate surrounding the role of consultants and the future of government outsourcing is likely to intensify in the coming weeks.

The Albanese government faces the challenge of striking a balance between utilising external expertise when needed and safeguarding national interests. It is a delicate task that requires careful consideration and a commitment to transparency, integrity, and the public interest.

***

MARK MCGOWAN RESIGNS AND LEAVES WESTERN AUSTRALIAN POLITICS

3 June 2023

Mark McGowan, one of the most accomplished and enduring figures in Australian politics, has announced his resignation as the Premier of Western Australia. His departure comes after an illustrious career spanning six years as premier and a remarkable tenure in the Parliament since 1996. McGowan's decision to step down was revealed in a candid resignation speech where he cited exhaustion and a lack of energy to effectively continue leading the state.

In his address, McGowan expressed his love for the role, recounting the satisfaction derived from implementing the party's agenda and navigating the complexities of political leadership. However, he acknowledged the relentless nature of the job, describing it as all-consuming and emphasising the toll it took, particularly during the challenging years of managing the COVID-19 pandemic. Despite his belief in the Labor party's capability to secure victory in the upcoming 2025 election, McGowan conveyed his inability to muster the required energy and drive for what would have been his eighth election campaign, the first campaign commencing in 1996.

The decision to resign on one's own terms is rare in political leadership, a trend more commonly associated with electoral losses, challenges to leadership, or scandals. McGowan joins a list of notable state premiers who have voluntarily stepped down, including Geoff Gallop in Western Australia, Stephen Bracks in Victoria, Peter Beattie in Queensland, and Bob Carr and Neville Wran in New South Wales. At the federal level, such resignations have been infrequent, with Robert Menzies being the last to do so in 1966.

Political leadership, as underscored by McGowan's departure, is a demanding role that often accelerates the aging process due to the myriad decisions, pressures from various quarters, and the constant scrutiny from the media and electorate. Enoch Powell's assertion that "all political careers might end in failure" resonates here, albeit with a nuanced understanding that many leaders prefer to exit on their own terms rather than face internal challenges or adverse circumstances.

Reflecting on McGowan's legacy, it becomes evident that he has departed at the zenith of his political career. He leaves behind a state where he significantly impacted the political landscape, notably contributing to the serious decline of the Liberal Party in Western Australia, especially in the 2021 state election, where it was reduced to two seats in Parliament. Despite facing criticisms regarding his ties to the mining industry and accusations of favours to media figures such as Kerry Stokes, McGowan maintained a high approval rating and solidified his party's position in the state.

The void left by McGowan's resignation presents an opportunity for reflection on the dynamics of political leadership in Western Australia, setting the stage for a new chapter in the state's political landscape.

SHAPING WESTERN AUSTRALIA'S FUTURE

McGowan's departure marks the end of an era for Western Australia—his success as a leader, evidenced by his massive community support, sets him apart in Australian politics. Yet, the mainstream media's traditional reluctance to commend leaders from the Labor side of politics has framed the narrative surrounding his legacy.

As time unfolds, the true impact of McGowan's leadership will become clearer, allowing for a more objective assessment of his accomplishments and shortcomings. Drawing a parallel with the legacy of former Prime Minister John Howard, who faced both praise and criticism in retrospect, underscores the necessity for a nuanced evaluation of political legacies over time.

McGowan's resilience during tumultuous times, such as the legal challenges posed by Clive Palmer during the pandemic, showcased his ability to weather storms and make decisions in the best interest of Western Australia. His adept management of the COVID-19 crisis, adopting stringent measures reminiscent of New South Wales, contributed to the state's favourable outcome compared to the eastern states.

The economic landscape also stands as a testament to McGowan's leadership, with the state's treasury left in good stead and property and job situations appearing far more favourable than in the eastern states. These initial observations suggest that McGowan may be remembered as one of Western Australia's great premiers, pending further scrutiny and revelations that may emerge over time.

The departure of a highly successful leader like McGowan inevitably raises questions about the future political landscape. With an unprecedented approval rating of 91 per cent at one point, his resignation creates a void that could impact support for the Labor Party, potentially posing challenges for the new Premier, Roger Cook. However, it remains uncertain whether this decline in support will be substantial enough to effect a change of government at the 2025 state election.

History provides examples of the aftermath of successful long-term leaders resigning. In Victoria, Steve Bracks' resignation preceded John Brumby's loss in the next election. Similarly, in Queensland, Peter Beattie's resignation led to challenges for his successor, Anna Bligh. McGowan's departure aligns with a pattern observed in state politics over the past 15 years, where resignations have been more prevalent compared to federal politics.

State leadership may be more demanding than its federal counterpart, considering the direct link between state governments and essential services such as schools, hospitals, and roads. The challenges faced by state leaders, compounded by the intense scrutiny and responsibility, could be a contributing factor to the trend of resignations observed in recent years.

STABLE AND COMPETENCE IN GOVERNMENT BUT WILL IT CONTINUE?

The day-to-day grind of managing state affairs, dealing with infrastructural projects like road construction, hospital extensions, and social housing, is a reality that political leaders face. The mundane tasks of governance, such as resolving waste collection issues or local council disputes, may not capture public attention, but they remain a significant part of a leader's responsibilities.

Questions have emerged about how a change in state leadership in Western Australia might influence federal politics in the region. The perception was that McGowan's popularity played a significant role in Labor's success in the 2022 federal election, given the similarities between the state and federal seats in Western Australian—this effect cannot be underestimated. However, it is essential to recognise the inherent differences between state and federal politics, each governed by distinct issues, characters, and circumstances.

Even if the Labor government were to lose seats in Western Australia during the next federal election, the impact might be limited. The challenge for the new premier, Roger Cook, lies in following the footsteps of a leader with extraordinary popularity and McGowan's unique appeal may prove challenging to replicate—Cook may face unrealistic expectations to match his predecessor's levels of public favour, and this is always a difficulty for a new leader following in the footsteps of a leader who had unprecedented success, during unprecedented circumstances. Despite calls for patience and understanding that such popularity is often unsustainable, the political landscape rarely allows leaders the luxury of time for settling in.

While commentators may urge patience and an opportunity for Cook to develop his own leadership style, the immediacy of political judgments often prevails. The desire for continued success in Western Australia and beyond will be crucial for Cook's tenure.

In the broader context of national sentiment, support for Cook's leadership may extend far beyond Western Australia, with the exception of certain media outlets—Seven West Media and News Corporation. The public's hopes for a successful tenure and effective governance under Cook's leadership are shared not only by Western Australians but also by those across the country who recognise the importance of stable and competent state leadership. Whether this ends up being the case, is a different matter.

***

EXPLOSIVE FINDINGS IN ROBERTS-SMITH DEFAMATION CASE

10 June 2023

In a high-profile defamation case that captivated the nation, the release of findings in the Ben Roberts-Smith trial has sent shockwaves through Australia. The evidence presented during the trial, which involved major media outlets, war crimes, domestic violence accusations, and the intervention of influential figures, has exposed a dark underbelly of the Australian military's actions in Afghanistan and tarnished the reputation of a once-revered war hero.

The trial centred around the publications by Nine Media in *The Age*, *Sydney Morning Herald*, and the *Canberra Times*, which alleged that Roberts-Smith had committed heinous acts during his service in Afghanistan. The court's findings, based on the balance of probabilities, validated the veracity of these claims, including the disturbing revelation of four murders of civilians, the coercion of fellow soldiers to execute a prisoner, and the appalling act of kicking an unarmed handcuffed Afghan villager off a cliff.

Moreover, the court also found that Roberts-Smith had lied about his threatening behaviours towards a woman with whom he was having an affair, implicating him in domestic violence accusations.

AN EXPENSIVE DEFAMATION CASE

This trial encompassed a wide range of contentious issues, including war crimes, the conduct of the Special Air Service overseas, and the involvement of a Victoria Cross recipient who holds a significant presence at the Australian War Memorial in Canberra. The case also took on the dimensions of a battle between media owners, with Kerry Stokes, owner of Seven West Media, financing the substantial $25 million legal costs in support of Roberts-Smith.

The trial's outcome dealt a severe blow to Roberts-Smith's reputation, leaving it irreparably damaged. Moreover, it has opened the floodgates for the potential revelation of further war crimes committed in Afghanistan, amplifying concerns over the actions of the Australian military during its deployment.

Some have argued that if Roberts-Smith had remained silent about the damning evidence published by Nine Media, the public might have eventually forgotten about these allegations, and his reputation would have remained intact. However, the crucial point is not about reputation management but rather the pursuit of justice. Regardless of the misguided nature of the defamation case, it successfully brought the truth to light, unmasking a deeply flawed and morally questionable individual.

PUBLIC INTEREST JOURNALISM

Credit must be given to the journalists involved in uncovering and reporting on this story. Nick McKenzie and Chris Masters, through their relentless investigative journalism, showcased exemplary work under immense pressure. While mainstream media often draws criticism for its shortcomings, the quality of their reporting in this case deserves recognition. It demonstrated the importance of holding powerful individuals accountable and exposing the truth, even in the face of resistance.

Critics of Roberts-Smith have contended that the evidence against him should not be dismissed simply because outsiders were not present on the battlefield. The evidence provided in court did not stem from inexperienced journalists making assumptions but rather from combatants who were present during the incidents and were able to compare behaviours in harrowing circumstances. Their testimonies overwhelmingly pointed to wrongdoing, lending credibility to the court's findings.

Notably, the trial also witnessed the involvement of other media outlets, such as News Corporation, which offered support to Roberts-Smith while denigrating the soldiers who testified against him. They propagated the notion that only those who had experienced combat could judge Roberts-Smith's actions.

However, it is important to acknowledge that criticisms can be made by individuals who have not been in combat. The military operates under a rules-based order, and certain actions, such as killing civilians and non-combatants, constitute war crimes. While such crimes often go unpunished, this case serves as a reminder that accountability should prevail when evidence is presented.

The trial also exposed the flaws in the defamation laws of Australia, which have traditionally protected powerful individuals. In this instance, the legal process allowed crucial information about potential war crimes to enter the public domain. Though unintentional, Roberts-Smith inadvertently played a role in bringing these allegations to light.

A REASSESSMENT OF AUSTRALIA'S HERO WORSHIPPING

The trial shed light on the dynamics within the regiment and how Roberts-Smith's perception of support from his colleagues proved unfounded. Given his familial ties to another high-ranking Australian soldier—his father—Roberts-Smith was seen by some as highly privileged, potentially granted access and privileges not extended to others. While this perception may be subjective, it highlights broader issues within Australia, including the acceptability of certain behaviours and the need for a reassessment of how military veterans are cared for and revered. It challenges the notion of hero worship and reminds us that even those hailed as battle heroes can possess significant flaws.

Ultimately, the trial's outcome reinforces the importance of listening to those with firsthand knowledge and experience. When individuals who were present on the ground and witnessed Roberts-Smith's actions attest to their inappropriateness, their voices must be heard. This trial has not only brought justice to those who acted with integrity but also exposed a disturbing chapter in Australia's military history that demands reflection and change.

***

FORMER MORRISON GOVERNMENT MISUSED $2 BILLION HEALTH FUND

10 June 2023

In a shocking turn of events, the Morrison government has come under intense scrutiny for its mishandling of $2 billion in health funding programs during its final four years in office. The revelation, centred around the Community Health and Hospitals program, adds to a growing list of questionable practices exhibited by the former government. The pervasive pattern of poor guidelines, politically motivated grants, and a complete disregard for genuine need has left Australians questioning the ethical standards of some of their elected officials.

The Morrison government's legacy has increasingly become synonymous with scandal, presenting a never-ending source of ammunition for the Labor government. Every few months, new revelations of unethical and potentially illegal behaviour emerge, suggesting a systemic issue within the Morrison administration. Such developments undoubtedly provide substantial material for the National Anti-Corruption Commission, which is poised to tackle these matters head-on.

The disconcerting aspect of this situation lies not only in the scale of misspent funds but also in the government's evident lack of concern for the wellbeing and health of the Australian population. It was apparent that as long as the money flowed to their intended recipients—political donors and business supporters of the Coalition—the government showed little regard for the broader consequences. The implications of these revelations for the public service are equally worrisome, as senior officials who should have ensured better practices now face scrutiny.

A CONTINUING TALE OF CORRUPTION

For years, critics have branded the Liberal–National Coalition government between 2013 and 2022 as corrupt, incompetent, and unethical. The recent revelations about the misspent health funding only serve to reinforce these claims. The Australian National Audit Office, responsible for uncovering this damning information, previously investigated the 'sports rorts' affair in 2019 and the Leppington Triangle scandal, where exorbitant amounts were paid to a Liberal Party donor for land undervalued by millions.

It is hard to ignore the political dimensions surrounding these revelations. The timing of the release aligns neatly with the upcoming launch of the National Anti-Corruption Commission on 1 July 2023, and the impending byelection in the seat of Fadden on 15 July, caused by the resignation of former Liberal–National Party Minister Stuart Robert, who is likely to appear before the anti-corruption commission in relation to some of these matters. The Labor government will undoubtedly seize the opportunity to extract maximum damage from these revelations, potentially swaying public sentiment against the Coalition.

One particularly alarming aspect of the released information pertains to a $4 million grant awarded to the Esther Foundation. This Christian rehabilitation centre has faced numerous complaints, including allegations of sexual abuse, denial of food, restrictions on communication with friends and family, and LGBTQI suppression techniques. Indigenous residents were also subjected to demeaning beliefs that their skin colour and cultural heritage were possessed by the devil. Despite these serious concerns, the Morrison government saw fit to grant the organisation a substantial sum of taxpayer money, exposing their incompetence and misplaced priorities.

Former Prime Minister Scott Morrison's assertion in 2019 that he "doesn't invest in things that don't work" stands in stark contradiction to the reality of his government's actions. The allocation of $4 million to a controversial religious group exemplifies the inadequacy, incompetence, and corruption that plagued the Morrison government.

SCANDALS STILL REVERBERATE A YEAR LATER

The sheer volume of scandals associated with the previous administration is overwhelming. It is no wonder that people have grown weary of these never-ending controversies. The repercussions of the Coalition's misconduct in government continue to reverberate through Australian society, a year after their departure from office. With the establishment of the National Anti-Corruption Commission, it is anticipated that the exposure of such malpractice will persist for some time into the future.

It is vital to remember how egregiously the Morrison government treated the Australian public during its tenure. Elected officials took the citizens for granted, exploiting their trust for personal gain and, as the saying goes, 'they took us for mugs'. The intertwining of religion with government affairs, especially when it produces dodgy and harmful practices, warrants rigorous examination, deconstruction, and eradication from public life. Those involved must be held accountable, and the affected individuals should be rehabilitated, ensuring a more functional and responsible government for the future.

While personal faith and beliefs should be respected, when they begin to encroach upon the broader society, it becomes imperative to subject them to criticism, investigation, and scrutiny when necessary.

As Australians brace themselves for further revelations and investigations, they demand a government that prioritises their wellbeing, upholds ethical standards, and restores faith in the political system. The Morrison government's legacy of mismanagement, corruption, and incompetence should serve as a stark reminder of the importance of transparency, accountability, and integrity in public office.

***

GROWING CALLS FOR MURDOCH ROYAL COMMISSION AND MEDIA REFORM

10 June 2023

The push for an inquiry into the Murdoch media empire in Australia has gained momentum, and the looming prospect of such an inquiry is long overdue and potentially beneficial for the public. Critics of the current media landscape, including prominent figures such as Senator David Pocock and the Australian Greens Senator Sarah Hanson-Young, argue that the Murdoch media, particularly News Corporation, wields a cancerous influence over both the Australian media landscape and the political arena. The call for an inquiry is seen as a crucial step in addressing this perceived stranglehold on information dissemination and political discourse.

Senator Hanson-Young has taken a proactive stance by introducing a Bill in the Senate aimed at establishing an inquiry into the role of News Corporation in Australia's media landscape, and also shed light on the pressing need for such an inquiry. The Senator highlighted the multitude of issues plaguing media diversity in the country, emphasising the disproportionate concentration of media ownership. Beyond this, she pointed to outdated regulations that are ill-equipped to address the rapidly evolving media landscape. The way in which audiences consume news has also undergone a significant transformation, with a surge in news consumption coupled with a growing skepticism toward the information being disseminated.

The Senator underscored the "trust deficit" that currently characterises media consumption, where audiences, despite consuming more news than ever before, approach it with skepticism, and the prioritisation of clickbait and sensationalism over public interest further compounds the challenges facing the media landscape. Central to the Senator's argument is the overarching concern about media concentration, particularly the formidable influence wielded by the Murdoch press and empire in Australia. She stressed the necessity for modern and purposeful regulations to address the complex interplay of factors affecting the media environment.

The momentum for such an inquiry is not entirely new. In 2021, former Prime Minister Kevin Rudd initiated a petition calling for a Royal Commission into the Murdoch media, garnering an unprecedented 500,000 signatures. While Rudd has since been appointed as Australian Ambassador to the United States, another former Prime Minister, Malcolm Turnbull, has taken up the cause, becoming a vocal critic of the Murdoch empire. However, there is contradiction here, that these leaders, while in office, took no substantive action on media reform.

The complex relationship between political leaders and media moguls, exemplified by ongoing trips to meet Murdoch in his central office in New York for potential Prime Ministers seeking his approval, raises questions about the feasibility of achieving meaningful media reform within the confines of government power. This conundrum raises the question of whether media reform is an elusive goal for governments, especially when the potential backlash threatens their political survival.

HANSON-YOUNG'S CALL FOR REFORM AND COLLECTIVE ACTION

The concerns raised by Senator Hanson-Young also shed light on the irony surrounding the reluctance of key figures, notably Rudd and Turnbull, to confront the negative impact of the Murdoch media empire on democracy during their tenures as prime ministers. Both have acknowledged their fear of challenging the undue influence of the Murdoch press while in office, a sentiment echoed during a Senate inquiry chaired by the Senator. The crux of the matter lies in the evident need for media reform, given the inadequacy of existing rules and regulations that struggle to contend with the formidable power wielded by Murdoch and his media empire, one that is likely to continue under his successor, Lachlan Murdoch.

The call for a Royal Commission is a potential pathway forward, and such an inquiry could shine a light on the transgressions of the Murdoch press, including revelations in the United States regarding the role of Fox News in the Capitol riots and the propagation of conspiracy theories by Donald Trump. Furthermore, the Murdoch media's impact on global responses to the climate crisis also needs to be considered, highlighting the urgency of addressing the negative role played by media conglomerates in shaping public discourse on critical issues.

However, there is the challenge in effecting change solely through government-led initiatives, as well as the palpable fear among members of parliament to openly confront the undue influence of the Murdoch press. While frustration with this influence is expressed behind closed doors, reluctance persists in making public declarations. This highlights the necessity of building community expectations to ensure that government officials are not the sole drivers of reform, underlining the need for a collective effort to address the issue comprehensively.

Within the broader media landscape, it has to be acknowledged that not all journalism is equal and there is some exceptional material being published, with the recent example of Nine Media's reporting on Ben Roberts-Smith and the activities of the SAS in Afghanistan: this was a triumph for public interest journalism, demonstrating the importance of holding powerful figures to account. However, there is a lack of effective regulatory mechanisms, where institutions such as the Press Council and the ACMA are ineffective and lack regulatory power to enforce change. Additionally, there are concerns about defamation laws—while they can serve to protect individuals, they are sometimes misused to stifle information that is in the public interest.

THE BATTLE AGAINST NEWS CORPORATION'S GRIP ON DEMOCRACY

The pervasive influence of News Corporation on Australia's media landscape, extends beyond mere criticism of progressive politicians, people of colour, or those not aligning with their political agenda. In a recent Senate Committee Hearing, Senator Hanson-Young noted a particular level of disdain reserved for the ABC, an institution that has faced consistent attacks from the Murdoch empire dating back to 1932. The ongoing assault raises questions about the ABC's approach to inviting News Corporation journalists to participate in political discussion programs, given the apparent conflict of interest and the underlying agenda to undermine the public broadcaster.

There is a critical role for a strong and independent public broadcaster in maintaining a robust media landscape. The ABC has been deliberately targeted by News Corporation in a campaign to erode public trust, diminish political effectiveness, and ensure News Corporation always is the final arbiter of any public or political discourse. The ABC needs to assert its independence, cease allowing itself to be undermined, and confront Murdoch's media empire, and adopt a more assertive stance to safeguard its integrity and role in public discourse.

What is the vision of an ideal media landscape in Australia and what would it look like? There is the need for a combination of factors, including strong regulations, a balance between freedom of the press and media behaviour control, and addressing the core issues of media concentration, lack of regulation, and the undermining of public interest: there are toxic consequences in allowing Murdoch's media empire to wield unchecked influence without regulatory accountability, and this influence needs to be controlled.

Looking at global models, there are systems already in place in the Nordic countries, where strong public broadcasters coexist with a diverse commercial and independent media sector, all under the purview of a common regulator. Such frameworks, ensure co-funding from both the private and public sectors, fostering a collective interest in delivering quality news, an approach which seeks to avoid a "race to the bottom" and counteracts the profit-driven motives that prioritise sensationalism over journalistic integrity.

The existing toxic cocktail of media concentration and lax regulation serves Murdoch's business model but critically undermines the public's right to reliable news. Without significant reforms, such as a Royal Commission to expose and drive change, the media landscape will continue on its current trajectory, perpetuating the erosion of journalistic standards and the public interest. The call to action is clear: a comprehensive and collective effort is needed to reshape Australia's media landscape, ensuring it serves the public good and upholds the principles of democracy.

***

THE GROWING HECS DEBT: TIME FOR FUNDAMENTAL REFORM

10 June 2023

The Higher Education Contribution Scheme, implemented by the Labor government in 1990, has come under scrutiny due to the increased level of debts accumulated by graduates, and higher rates of inflation this year. With the indexation of HECS debts set at 7.1 per cent, it is alarming to note that while substantial debt payments are being made, the overall debt amount for graduates in same cases is actually increasing. This predicament creates an endless treadmill for graduates, as their debts seem destined to persist indefinitely without any real reduction. It is time to question and challenge the value and longevity of the HECS system, as well as initiate a comprehensive reform of higher education in Australia.

Education, regardless of its level, benefits the entire community, not just those who receive it. The HECS system has been in place for over three decades, and astonishingly, it has remained largely unquestioned and unchallenged by successive governments during that time. However, the landscape of university and higher education demands fundamental reform to address the existing issues.

Higher education in Australia, once reserved for those who could afford it, was revolutionised by former Prime Minister Gough Whitlam's policies aimed at opening up education opportunities. Before 1973, under the Coalition government, a scholarship scheme was in place, which often led to individuals being bound to specific careers, limiting their personal growth and professional opportunities in the future.

Whitlam's reforms changed this by providing individuals with the ability to shape their careers according to their own desires and skills, and opening up the sector to a broader range of people in the community, especially from working class and migrant communities. It allowed people who were better suited for professions such as law and medicine to pursue those paths, regardless of their socioeconomic backgrounds.

Interestingly, the Fraser government, despite its initial opposition, retained many of Whitlam's reforms. However, it was during the tenure of Labor Minister John Dawkins—a graduate from Perth's elite private school, Scotch College—that the HECS system was introduced, essentially, a betrayal of core Labor values. While it is true that the cost of degrees was significantly lower back then, it still resulted in deterring certain individuals from pursuing higher education.

Conservative governments have sometimes demonstrated an aversion to a well-informed and intelligent populace. A good degree, regardless of discipline, teaches critical thinking, evidence evaluation, and constructing persuasive arguments. It equips individuals with the skills to differentiate between strong and weak arguments. Naturally, this kind of informed thinking is not always welcomed by those in power. Whitlam, despite his elitist background, championed the notion that everyone should have access to the finer aspects of life, such as opera, art galleries, and literature. Everyone should be encouraged to have access to greater educational opportunities, if this is what they wish to pursue.

It is important to note that the original goals of the HECS system, aimed at expanding the university sector, have already been achieved. In 1990, only 8 per cent of the population held a university degree, but that figure has now risen to 30 per cent. This is good for the Australian society and, in essence, the objectives set forth by HECS have long been accomplished.

However, the system has transformed into a grossly unfair one, burdening graduates with excessive financial contributions toward the education system. The current HECS debt owed to the government stands at a staggering $48 billion, with estimates projecting it to reach $180 billion by 2026. This astronomical amount of debt is solely shouldered by one sector of the community: the graduates. No other segment of society carries such a heavy debt burden owed to the government.

Proponents of HECS often argue that graduates earn more than non-graduates and should, therefore, contribute more to the taxation system. However, this argument falls short when considering the fact that graduates already pay more taxes if they earn higher incomes. Furthermore, the income gap between graduates and non-graduates has been steadily decreasing. In 2006, the salary gap was $15,000, but it has now reduced to $10,000. Taking into account deferred entry into the workforce, HECS debt repayment, and higher tax rates, equity between a graduate and a non-graduate is achieved after approximately 20 years. Therefore, the purported financial advantage of a university education is not as significant as it is often portrayed.

It is perplexing that Labor members of parliament, many of whom benefited from free education prior to 1990, fail to advocate for its reinstatement. The justification for this stance becomes even more elusive when considering the allocation of substantial funds, such as the $360 billion directed toward AUKUS and other questionable endeavours. Why would we not want our populace to be well-informed, educated, and competitive in the global economy?

The time for change is now. The original goals of the HECS system have been accomplished, and universities have expanded significantly. However, what we truly need is a stronger focus on vocational education—TAFE—rather than proliferating universities. A highly educated society and workforce benefit both the community and the economy, as the challenges of our complex and sophisticated world continue to grow. While university education is not suited for everyone, the advantages of a university-educated society are undeniable.

Reforming the HECS system should be a priority. Considerations include implementing a freeze or cap on indexation, averaging it over a longer period to alleviate the burden on graduates. Alternatively, abolishing all current HECS debts or, better yet, eliminating the system altogether and making university education free are potential solutions. Many countries worldwide, especially in Europe, have embraced free university education for some time. Australia itself had such a system between 1973 and 1989 and New Zealand has taken progressive steps by providing the first year of university for free and gradually extending it to cover all undergraduate courses. Clearly, solutions exist, and it is imperative to address this issue before it causes significant hardship for many individuals in the years to come.

Australia needs to prioritise the reform of its higher education sector and re-evaluate the purpose and functioning of the HECS system. The economic, social, and cultural benefits of an educated society cannot be understated and by investing in education and removing the barriers imposed by excessive debts, we can shape a future where everyone has the opportunity to pursue knowledge, contribute meaningfully to society, and thrive in an ever-evolving and increasingly sophisticated world.

***

THE CONTINUING HOUSING AFFORDABILITY CRISIS

17 June 2023

Housing affordability remains a pressing issue throughout Australia, prompting the Labor government to introduce amendments to its Housing Australia Future Fund legislation in a bid to garner support from the Senate, approve the legislation, and commence the social housing building program that Prime Minister Anthony Albanese promised in the lead-up to the 2022 federal election.

The proposed changes aim to secure the backing of the Australian Greens and several other Senators, signaling a concerted effort to address the country's housing challenges. However, the suggested amendments still fall short of the drastic measures required to combat the crisis.

One of the key amendments put forward is the removal of the fund's proposed cap, accompanied by a pledge to allocate a minimum of $500 million annually towards social housing initiatives. While this commitment is an improvement, experts argue that it is woefully insufficient. Depending on the type of housing, this would create between 2,000 to 5,000 dwellings per year, whereas based on the current demand across Australia, an estimated 640,000 dwellings are needed immediately. It is clear that a more comprehensive approach is urgently required.

The Australian Greens—a key political player in the Senate if the Labor government wishes to have its legislation enacted—have decided to postpone their vote on this legislation until October and are expected to push for more substantial changes, emphasising that addressing housing affordability extends beyond social housing alone and that the magnitude of the crisis necessitates action across multiple facets of the housing sector.

Insufficient infrastructure provided by governments to support new housing developments further compounds the challenges faced by communities. An example is found in south-western Sydney suburb of Canterbury, where 3,000 apartments were constructed without adequate accompanying social services and community amenities.

Developers in this case were mandated to include social amenities but provided a supermarket and several cafes, instead of crucial facilities such as additional hospitals, police stations, medical services, and schools. This oversight has resulted in considerable difficulties for both existing and new residents of Canterbury, who have struggled with the ramifications of rapid expansion. Similar issues have arisen in other parts of the country, demanding a comprehensive re-evaluation of housing policies.

To tackle these complex issues, governments must convene a summit that goes beyond the developers' perspective, a summit which should include town planners, environmental thinkers, anthropologists, and sociologists to collectively determine the best strategies for managing cities and achieving affordable accommodation.

This approach should aim to alleviate problems such as overcrowding, inadequate public transportation, and limited access to essential social services such as hospitals and police stations. Currently, too many individuals are grappling with the scarcity of suitable housing, particularly in major cities where their skills and contributions are highly sought after.

Balancing the interests of small investors and preserving the value of existing properties while simultaneously enabling affordable homeownership poses a considerable challenge for the government. It is crucial to strike a delicate balance to ensure the financial stability of homeowners without further exacerbating the housing crisis.

As the housing affordability crisis continues to escalate, the Labor government's proposed amendments to the Housing Australia Future Fund represent a step in the right direction. However, greater efforts and a multifaceted approach are essential to alleviate the burden on individuals seeking affordable housing. The path forward requires proactive collaboration and innovative strategies to ensure that housing affordability becomes a reality for all Australians.

URGENT ACTION IS NEEDED

Advocate groups such as Shelter NSW have been at the forefront of this battle for housing affordability for some time, tirelessly lobbying for improved housing conditions for lower-income communities. According to Cathy Callaghan, senior policy adviser with Shelter NSW, the dire situation facing many Australians today is a culmination of government actions and inactions over the past few decades.

"Government policy over the last 20 years has been dominated by a philosophy that the private housing market will take care of housing, and governments have stepped away from its traditional role to provide housing through public social housing," says Callaghan. "We've seen policies that have really, in some cases, made the problem worse."

Recent years have also witnessed an alarming rise in homelessness, even among traditionally middle-class individuals. Stories of women in their 50s and 60s, who once led regular lives, finding themselves suddenly homeless have become distressingly common. Additionally, the sight of hundreds of people queuing for rental properties highlights the intensity of the housing shortage.

To tackle these pressing issues, Callaghan believes it is crucial to determine which level of government should take responsibility for finding solutions. "There needs to be a national strategy and plan, where we have national political and civic leadership that repositions housing as an essential service and not as a financial product. But probably the biggest thing that that governments could do right now, particularly in New South Wales, is step back into the game of being responsible for building and growing the stock of social housing."

Callaghan also feels that addressing the housing crisis requires a multifaceted approach that considers various factors contributing to the problem. "There's some underlying structural issues in the Australian taxation system, for example, that disproportionately ramps up investment in housing as a speculative product.

"The changes that were made under the Howard government around the capital gains discount, that's widely credited as being something that made housing much more speculative, brought investors in and saw people wanting to buy homes, competing with other investors. And even just the way the retirement income system is structured, everything assumes you own your own home. There's been very little recognition that we have a large and growing population that rents and will rent probably for their lives."

Other piecemeal solutions, such as first homeowner grants and government subsidies for buyers, have proven ineffective and often worsen the problem, whereas co-ordinated, big-picture initiatives are necessary to effect real change. The federal Labor government has shown promising signs of prioritising housing and homelessness, emphasising the need for a co-ordinated and strategic approach across the country.

While implementing solutions will undoubtedly take time, Callaghan points to certain factors that can signal progress and show whether any significant improvements are being met. "The Census, for example, counts every five years the rate of homelessness in the country—in the last Census in New South Wales, are over 122,000 people identified, self-identified as homeless. If we had a better system of housing in this state, we will see that figure go down.

"We also have some clear ways of tracking the degree of housing stress—if households are paying more than 30 per cent of their gross household income, whether it's mortgage or rent, then they define as being in a state of housing stress. And we know that households that are in housing stress, are forced to compromise on other critical spending, like their health, like food. If we will see rates of housing stress come down, we would see people not forced to make those unreasonable choices between paying rent and eating food or playing a power bill.

"And one key indicator would be the safety net of social housing restored and become—and it is in other countries—a substantial player in the rental market. This would mark a vital step toward resolving the crisis."

As governments deliberate on housing decisions, they must consider the broader implications and long-term consequences. With projected population growth, careful planning and integration of social and affordable housing into new developments will be critical to avoid compounding the existing housing issues.

It is crucial to act swiftly and decisively to combat the housing crisis in Australia. Only through a co-ordinated, comprehensive approach, backed by strong leadership and genuine political will, can the country hope to provide secure and affordable housing for all its citizens.

***

STILL A MONSTER: DUTTON'S IMAGE MAKEOVER

24 June 2023

In a bid to revamp his public image, the federal Liberal leader, Peter Dutton, has embarked on an extensive makeover campaign. Following in the footsteps of his predecessors—John Howard and Anthony Albanese all had political success after their respective image makeovers—Dutton aims to present a more appealing persona to the electorate.

Dutton's recent efforts have seen him don a new pair of glasses and release a seven-minute documentary-style video highlighting his positive attributes, with particular emphasis placed on testimonials from his wife, Kirilly Dutton. In the video, Kirilly praises Dutton's commitment to family, his love for his children, and his support for her successful small business. The couple portrays a "normal" home life, engaging in simple, wholesome activities like attending their children's sporting events and enjoying the outdoors.

However, critics argue that these orchestrated attempts to present Dutton as a kind and empathetic individual clash with his actions throughout his political career. They point to instances such as his controversial walk-out during the Apology to the Stolen Generations in 2008, divisive comments regarding "African gangs" during the 2018 Victoria election, a history of hardline policies targeting refugees and asylum seekers, and his dismissive attitude towards the Voice to Parliament. These actions, combined with allegations of corruption, cast doubt on the authenticity of Dutton's newfound empathy.

The video release has sparked a broader discussion about the effectiveness of such image makeovers in politics. It is not uncommon for politicians to attempt to reshape public perception through similar means, as evidenced by previous campaigns led by figures like Howard and Albanese. However, the cynicism surrounding Dutton's efforts stems from the stark contrast between the portrayed empathy and the lack thereof demonstrated in his political actions.

If a politician feels the need to produce a seven-minute video featuring people praising their character, it probably indicates an underlying insecurity or lack of authenticity. Dutton's video, a desperate attempt to improve his polling numbers, attempts to project him as a likable figure to counter the negative public sentiment. Nevertheless, critics contend that true empathy and kindness cannot be manufactured and must be demonstrated consistently through actions.

Dutton's ongoing struggle to resonate with the electorate is evident in his consistently low personal support ratings, hovering around 17 per cent, and the Liberal and National parties two-party preferred voting percentages ranging from 42 to 45 per cent. With the next federal election due in 2025—two years away—the pressure to turn the tide is mounting. Speculation has emerged about potential leadership challenges within the Liberal Party, with some suggesting figures such as deputy leader Sussan Ley, may be positioning themselves as alternatives.

While Dutton's image makeover may signal a sense of panic and desperation, it remains uncertain whether it will be sufficient to reverse his low levels support. Public perception of politicians is primarily shaped by their public actions, and no amount of spin or promotional videos can easily alter entrenched perceptions.

DUTTON AND THE RELIGIOUS PROBLEM IN VICTORIA

Victoria's political landscape also presents a significant obstacle for Dutton and the Liberal Party, as the state's performance often impacts federal voting intentions. Recent polling reveals a persistently low level of support for the Liberal Party in Victoria—in state and federal polling—with around 39 per cent support, compared to the Labor Party's 61 per cent. These numbers highlight the pressing challenges faced by Dutton and his party. Adding to the woes is the struggle of the opposition leader in Victoria, John Pesutto, who is grappling with his own set of issues.

There is a growing influence of religious groups within the Victorian branch of the Liberal Party, where Mormons, Pentecostals, and other conservative Christian factions have taken control of key party branches. This situation has raised concerns about the representation of the views of these groups in Parliament, especially when they do not necessarily align with the broader electorate's sentiments.

A significant development in this context is the upcoming state byelection in the seat of Warrandyte, where the Liberal Party has preselected Nicole Werner, a Pentecostal preacher and activist, as their candidate. While there is nothing inherently wrong with religious individuals participating in politics—not all people of faith are conservative and there are some very progressive religious voices out there—the concern arises when their views disproportionately influence policy decisions, outweighing their representation within the electorate.

Werner's previous electoral performance in the seat of Box Hill during the 2022 Victorian election is noteworthy: despite a 9 per cent swing against her on the primary vote in a seat the Liberal Party should have won, she has been given another preselection opportunity. This raises questions about the Liberal Party's commitment to merit-based selection, which they often tout as a core principle.

Critics argue that Werner's second preselection highlights the significant influence religious groups hold within the Victorian branch, potentially stifling the representation of diverse viewpoints. It also suggests that the party may not be genuinely listening to the electorate but rather prioritising the preferences of select interest groups.

The concerns surrounding the rise of religious groups within the Liberal Party extend beyond Werner's candidacy. The overall composition of the Victorian branch has led to a disconnect between party members and the wider community and this divergence poses a significant challenge for the Liberal Party, as they risk alienating voters and failing to resonate with the electorate.

LIBERAL PARTY NEEDS A RETURN TO LIBERAL PROGRESSIVISM

In response to these issues, there is a need for the Liberal Party to evolve and become more progressive in the traditional sense of liberal progressivism, and a party's power lies in its ability to adapt and represent the changing views of society accurately. Ignoring this reality can result in the continued erosion of support and a lack of influence.

While Werner's preselection may have been based on the decisions of the local branch membership, it does raise concerns about the party's commitment to reflecting the broader community's sentiments. The selection of candidates who do not represent the diversity of viewpoints within their electorates can hinder the party's credibility and disconnect them from the needs and aspirations of the people they aim to serve.

As the Liberal Party navigates the intricate political landscape in Victoria, the challenges they face highlight the need for a more inclusive and representative approach. Overcoming these hurdles will require a thorough examination of candidate selection processes and a genuine commitment to understanding and addressing the concerns of the wider electorate. Failure to do so may impede the party's ability to regain support and influence in the state and, ultimately, the federal arena.

***

JULY

SERIOUS CORRUPTION ICAC FINDINGS FOR BEREJIKLIAN AND MAGUIRE

1 July 2023

The NSW Independent Commission Against Corruption has released its long-awaited findings into the actions of former New South Wales Premier Gladys Berejiklian and former Member for Wagga Wagga, Daryl Maguire, exposing their involvement in serious corruption.

These findings come as a blow to the former premier, who had been portrayed by some as a victim of circumstance, entangled in a relationship with Maguire. The ICAC report shatters that narrative, revealing a level of corruption that goes beyond personal entanglements. It uncovers a culture of secrecy, cover-ups, and financial improprieties that undermines the integrity of New South Wales politics.

The extensive report reveals that Berejiklian breached public trust by supporting a grant to the Australian Clay Target Association—$5.5 million—and the construction of a hall for the Riverina Conservatorium of Music—$25 million. Additionally, the ICAC recommends that the public prosecutor file charges against Maguire for advancing his own financial interests through land deals and a visa scheme, which could also have ramifications for some former federal Liberal Party ministers.

After nearly two years of criticism and speculation, the release of the ICAC findings brings clarity and validates the suspicions many had about corruption within the New South Wales political landscape. The 600-page report—published in two volumes—delves into various instances of corruption, laying bare the extent of the wrongdoing.

While the ICAC did not recommend charges against Berejiklian, the report strongly criticises her inaction despite being aware of the corruption taking place. Her infamous "I don't need to know about that" recording from 2018, where Maguire is boasting of brokered deals with Chinese property developers in western Sydney, and widely circulated in the media, stands as a testament to her misconduct.

Daryl Maguire: I've been doing my books and my accounts. Counting, counting my tax refund!
Gladys Berejiklian: Good. Given the size of it, it'll take you a week to count it all.
Maguire: It's true. And the good news is William tells me we've done our deal. So hopefully, it's about half of all that's gone now.
Berejiklian: That's good—I don't need to know about that bit.
Maguire: No, you don't.
Berejiklian: Yeah.

THE MOST CORRUPT NSW PREMIER

This marks the highest level of corruption among New South Wales premiers, with Berejiklian becoming the third Liberal Party premier to have been labeled "corrupt" by the ICAC. The previous instances involved Nick Greiner, whose charges were overturned on a technicality, and Barry O'Farrell, who resigned over a failure to disclose a wine donation; however, the audacity of the corruption in this case is deeply troubling.

Berejiklian's downfall is particularly tragic, considering her inspirational rise from a young child with limited English proficiency to becoming the state's premier. However, her acceptance of corruption tarnishes her once-inspiring story, casting doubt on her future employment prospects in Australia. Potential diplomatic positions overseas may be the only viable option—and at some distant point in the future—although the public's willingness to accept someone with a proven record of corruption as a representative remains uncertain.

Critics from the Liberal Party have been quick to attack the ICAC and its findings, echoing their sentiments even before the report's release. The reduction of ICAC funding by both Berejiklian and former Premier Mike Baird adds another layer of complexity to the issue. Former Prime Minister Scott Morrison, who previously criticised the ICAC as a "kangaroo court," had even considered endorsing Berejiklian as a candidate in the 2022 federal election.

The mainstream media's portrayal of Berejiklian as a victim has also faced widespread criticism, a level of support which seemed to continue, even after ICAC found that she engaged in serious corruption, preferring to focus on her management of the COVID pandemic, even though there were serious outbreaks that occurred during her time in office, most notably, the *Ruby Princess* debacle in 2020, and a failure to lockdown early enough in June 2021.

The ICAC report includes 18 recommendations, emphasising the need for changes in New South Wales political culture and mandatory corruption training for parliamentarians. The fact that such training is necessary raises questions about the suitability of these individuals for parliamentary roles if they require instruction on identifying corruption. Wouldn't it be obvious to most people what corruption is in public office?

The pervasiveness of corruption in New South Wales politics has led to a lack of understanding and acknowledgment of its existence. However, with the ICAC findings now exposed, it is crucial for the state to address this issue head-on and work towards restoring public trust and integrity in the political system.

THE CORRUPTION IN NSW NEEDS TO END

The revelations surrounding Gladys Berejiklian's tenure mark a significant moment in New South Wales politics. It is a stark reminder that corruption is not confined to the shadows but can permeate the highest levels of power. The ICAC's thorough investigation, despite attempts to discredit it, serves as a reminder of the importance of an independent body holding those in power accountable.

The state's political culture must undergo a comprehensive overhaul to prevent future instances of corruption and ensure that those who occupy positions of authority act in the best interests of the people they serve.

The road to redemption for New South Wales politics is long, but the exposure of corruption and the ICAC's in-depth report may serve as a catalyst for change. It is a pivotal moment for the state to re-evaluate its political landscape and strive for a more transparent, accountable, and ethical governance system.

***

INSURRECTION SPARKS CONCERNS ABOUT AUSTRALIA'S INVOLVEMENT IN UKRAINE

1 July 2023

In a surprising twist of events, the leader of the Wagner paramilitary group, Yevgeny Prigozhin, orchestrated an insurrection in the Russian city of Rostov-on-Don over the weekend. This unexpected move culminated in an agreement to surrender his weapons and seek exile in Belarus, brokered by Belarusian President Alexander Lukashenko. However, concerns about Prigozhin's safety in Belarus have emerged, with speculations about the potential risks he may face even in his place of exile.

The incident has left many questioning the proximity of this event to a possible coup in Russia. While the details remain unclear, it has become a focal point in the context of the ongoing war in Ukraine, which has lasted nearly 18 months. The situation is further complicated by the uncertainty surrounding the future of the Russian leadership, raising the spectre of a conflict that could extend beyond Ukraine's borders, potentially sparking turmoil within Russia itself.

Despite the gravity of these developments, the coverage of the events in Australia has been notably limited, prompting criticism of the media's handling of such a significant international occurrence. Australians seeking information found it challenging to obtain comprehensive updates through mainstream channels, leading many to turn to social media platforms like Twitter and Reddit or international news outlets such as CNN and Al Jazeera.

The confusion surrounding the location of the incident added to the complexity, with two cities named "Rostov" causing initial ambiguity. The eventual realisation that Rostov-on-Don, situated approximately 60 kilometres from the Ukrainian border, played host to the events brought the situation closer to the epicentre of the ongoing conflict.

The clash of propaganda from various sources further complicated the narrative with Russian, Ukrainian, Prigozhin's, and Western perspectives created a web of conflicting information, making it difficult for news outlets to discern facts from propaganda. The ABC, faced with the challenge of navigating through this intricate web, seemingly chose caution in reporting until a clearer picture emerged.

International journalists stationed in Ukraine and Russia played a crucial role in providing on-the-ground insights. Russia, still carrying remnants of its historical micro-control and police-state mentality from the Soviet era, has made it challenging to obtain accurate information. The potential for an event that weakens the Putin regime or brings about a change with ramifications for the war in Ukraine and the stability of the Russian Federation has significant geopolitical implications for Europe and the world at large.

Australia, despite lacking direct political interests or influence in the region, has been impacted by the war's consequences: supply chain disruptions since the conflict began have contributed to inflation rates in Australia, and the country has extended military and financial support to Ukraine. The recent diplomatic tensions, exemplified by the shutdown of the new Russian Embassy construction in Canberra, further underline Australia's involvement in the regional turmoil.

The possibility of the conflict escalating into a global war, involving NATO and potentially the United States, raises the spectre of Australia being drawn into a larger conflict, with potential ramifications reaching a doomsday scenario and the use of nuclear weapons. As the situation unfolds, there are far-reaching consequences that may arise from the war in Ukraine and its ripple effects on global stability.

THE AUSTRALIAN MEDIA GOES MISSING

As the situation in Russia continues to unfold, the possibility of reaching its end game looms large, prompting close scrutiny from various regions and republics within the Russian Federation. The eyes of the world are on Moscow, where the future of the nation hangs in the balance. Yet, despite the gravity of these developments, Australians found themselves largely in the dark about the unfolding crisis through their domestic media.

Criticism has been directed at ABC News—which does have a 24-hour news channel—that during this critical period, it offered minimal coverage of the unfolding events. This stands in stark contrast to the channel's decision to air an extended broadcast of former U.S. President Donald Trump's remarks, including his controversial statements and conspiracy theories, earlier in the same week, hardly an issue which should rank in Australia's media interest, especially considering that much of the U.S. media had chosen to limit exposure to Trump. Additionally, the ABC published a speculative news article pondering the potential implications of Trump's presidency for Anthony Albanese in 2024—why does the ABC need to worry about a speculative event, that may not even happen and, if it does, is two years away?

The apparent prioritisation of speculative reporting over real-time global events has fueled criticism of the ABC, and the discrepancy in coverage becomes more conspicuous when considering the gravity of the situation in Russia and its potential impact on global affairs. The lack of in-depth reporting extends beyond the ABC, with News Corporation also facing accusations of providing shallow coverage of the Russian developments.

An intriguing angle to this media dynamic is the historical relationship between Rupert Murdoch and Russian President Vladimir Putin—Murdoch's entry into the Russian media market, facilitated by Putin in the early 2000s, is now being reciprocated by Murdoch, who, two decades later, seems to be reluctant to provide critical coverage of the Putin regime. While the influence of News Corporation in Australia is not as overtly pro-Putin as seen on Fox News in the U.S., this historical relationship is influencing the depth and nature of reporting on Russian events.

The question of why ABC and News Corporation, among other outlets, chose to underreport such a significant international development remains unanswered. Speculation ranges from financial considerations, such as avoiding weekend rates for journalists, to perceptions of relevance to the Australian audience. The decision to prioritise coverage of speculative events in the United States over a real-time global crisis raises questions about media priorities and responsibilities in delivering timely and crucial information to the public.

In terms of expert commentary, when the incidents in Russia were finally reported, the choice to bring in opposition spokesperson Senator Simon Birmingham rather than the foreign minister Senator Penny Wong or the Prime Minister has sparked concerns about how the mainstream media favours the Coalition, even though they are not in government. While it's acknowledged that Senator Wong may have been preoccupied with the rapidly evolving situation, the decision to feature Birmingham rather than a government official, adds to the perplexity surrounding the media's approach to the unfolding events in Russia.

POLITICAL REPRESENTATION AND BALANCE IN AUSTRALIAN REPORTING

This choice of Birmingham as the "go-to" commentator on Russia, rather than the Foreign Minister or Prime Minister has ignited discussions about media management and political representation. Whether this decision stems from poor media management by the federal government or reflects the media's inclination to offer a voice to the Coalition is a matter of debate.

Critics argue that the media's tendency to frequently feature Coalition representatives undermines the authority of the federal government. The perception that the Coalition is treated as the default government in the media landscape, even when they are in opposition, can distort the public's understanding of the political landscape. The Labor government, in turn, may find itself competing with the opposition for media time, a situation that seems counterintuitive. Why seek the perspectives of the opposition in the first instance, when they have no official capacity in representing Australia, and no ability to change any policy position? This unusual arrangement of seeking commentary from the Coalition was never extended to the Labor Party when they were in opposition, so why is it occurring so frequently now?

Leader of the opposition, Peter Dutton, was also a "go-to" person for commentary on Russia and Ukraine—rather than the Prime Minister—and while issues of international significance like the situation in Ukraine ideally warrant bipartisan support, Dutton's criticisms of the Albanese government for its handling of the Ukraine crisis and suggesting the Labor government hasn't offered enough support, have added a divisive element.

The media's willingness to run with these narratives, even when it becomes evident the former Morrison government and the current Albanese government have offered comparable levels of support to Ukraine on a pro rata basis, further adds to the frustration. The media's role in presenting balanced perspectives is crucial, and it's evident that this balance is skewed. The call for bipartisan support on critical international issues may be compromised by the media's tendency to amplify divisive narratives and provide a platform for criticism without proper context.

The issue extends beyond party politics, with questions raised about the influence of certain media outlets on the ABC—whether the ABC is influenced by News Corporation or if broader structural issues within the Australian media contribute to the perceived imbalance is a point of contention.

In the midst of a global crisis with significant geopolitical ramifications, Australians are dealing not only with the complexities of international relations but also with concerns about the objectivity and balance of their media. As the situation in Russia and Ukraine continues to evolve, the role of the media in shaping public perceptions and influencing political discourse remains a subject of scrutiny and debate.

***

A GROWING DISSATISFACTION WITH THE FEDERAL GOVERNMENT

1 July 2023

Recent opinion polls have painted a nuanced picture of the political landscape, revealing intriguing shifts in public sentiment. While the two-party preferred voting figures remain relatively stable, with Labor at 54 per cent and the Coalition at 46 per cent, a closer look at the Essential opinion poll suggests a growing concern for the federal government.

The Essential poll looks into the broader question of whether Australia is heading in the right direction. The numbers tell a story of diminishing optimism over the past year. In May 2022, 48 per cent of respondents believed the country was on the right track, while 27 per cent disagreed. Fast forward to May 2023, and the figures have undergone a notable transformation: optimism has dwindled to 41 per cent, while those expressing pessimism have risen to 38 per cent. The most recent month has seen a sharp turn, with only 33 per cent affirming Australia's positive trajectory and 47 per cent asserting the opposite.

The decline in the perception of the country's direction raises questions about the government's performance and the potential impact on voting intentions. While interpreting such data requires caution, a common trend is that dissatisfaction with the country's direction often reflects a lack of confidence in the governing party.

Despite the variability in individual viewpoints, there still appears to be a consistent trend favouring Labor over the Coalition. This indicates a broader sentiment that Labor is carrying out the task of government successfully, even if specific issues are viewed through different ideological lenses.

There are a series of factors that could be contributing to the shifting public sentiment: housing affordability, interest rate rises, cost of living pressures, and negative media coverage of the Voice to Parliament have been identified as potential catalysts, and the convergence of these issues may be eroding the patience of the electorate, with a perceptible decrease in goodwill toward the government, particularly in its handling of these key concerns.

The government's performance faces scrutiny on multiple fronts: the management of AUKUS deal, social housing investment, Stage 3 tax cuts, the continuing funding for private religious schools, and resistance to media reform and sports betting advertising regulation are cited as examples of perceived contradictions and policy missteps. While acknowledging that it's still early in the government's tenure, it is essential that the government needs learn swiftly and adapt quickly to address pressing issues.

CHALLENGES AND OPPORTUNITIES FOR THE FEDERAL GOVERNMENT

In the intricate world of politics, the power of narrative is a well-worn but essential concept. Governments, in essence, are storytellers, shaping public perception through the tales they weave. The Liberal Party, adept at this craft, has demonstrated a mastery in narrating a story, often tinged with high-level negativity and on many occasions, veering into misinformation and untruths.

One case in point is the prolonged saga of "Beazley's $10 billion black hole" that persisted for almost a decade after the Coalition won the 1996 federal election: Kim Beazley, leader of the opposition after Labor's election loss, was never Treasurer—he was finance minister and didn't have direct responsibility for the Budget—but that didn't stop the Coalition from endlessly lampooning Beazley, forcing him to retreat from discussions about the economy, even though the Labor government between 1983–96 had managed the finances relatively well.

The contrast is stark when one considers the relative silence around the trillion-dollar n national government debt left by the Coalition upon exiting office in 2022, yet the Labor government rarely mentions this massive debt.

In this political equation, there is a call for a proactive approach in crafting a robust narrative that not only counters negative portrayals but also provides a clear explanation of government actions and decisions. Treasurer Jim Chalmers, recognised as a skilled political communicator, is an underutilised political asset, and could play a central role in preparing the electorate for potential policy shifts, such as changes to Stage 3 tax cuts or adjustments to negative gearing and capital gains tax.

Ultimately, the government needs to reassert its confidence, disregarding media narratives that question its legitimacy and ignoring critics. Trust in the Cabinet's ability to make the right decisions should be encouraged, with the understanding that the electorate will render judgment at the ballot box in less than two years' time, in 2025.

NAVIGATING THE SHIFTING TIDES IN THE ELECTORATE

The aftermath of the last federal election serves as a compelling lens through which we can examine the evolving landscape of Australian politics. While the victory for the Labor Party was not a resounding endorsement, with only 32 per cent of the primary vote, it underscored a desire for change among voters. However, the Labor Party, like its Liberal counterpart, might not be fully grasping the message sent by the electorate.

A critical point is the shifting demographic, particularly among younger voters who have distanced themselves from the Coalition and increasingly turned to Labor, not directly, but through the advantage of preferential voting. This demographic trend could potentially see a further migration towards the Australian Greens in the future, but the federal government, while not currently facing an immediate threat from this shift, should consider this in its policy development and political behaviour in the future.

The critique extends to the handling of issues such as the housing Future Fund, where the Labor government is perceived to have fallen short in political communication. A more effective explanation of the fund's setup, considering budget constraints and other challenges, might have mitigated some of the issues and political problems surrounding it: instead, the Australian Greens have seized the opportunity to control the narrative on housing issues.

The broader message is clear: being in government is not just about policy development and implementation but also about controlling the political agenda. The current political vacuum, evident in discussions around the Voice to Parliament and the housing Future Fund, has allowed right-wing voices and related propagandists to fill the space.

Every political party aspires to be in government: that always has to be the end goal. However, demographic changes, coupled with evolving environmental priorities, could reshape the political landscape in the coming years. The Australian Greens, with their emphasis on environmentalism, have made notable gains, and this shift aligns with changing attitudes among voters.

The traditional parties, may need to undergo reform to remain relevant to modern Australian life and the way they present ideas, as well as the structures of political parties, might need adjustment. The evolving dynamics of Australian politics demand a keen understanding of demographic shifts and changing priorities. The cautionary message is clear: political entities must adapt and communicate effectively to address the evolving expectations of the electorate, otherwise they risk being surpassed by more attuned and responsive parties in the future.

***

NATIONAL ANTI-CORRUPTION COMMISSION FINALLY COMES TO LIFE

8 July 2023

The National Anti-Corruption Commission has finally commenced its operations, marking a significant milestone in Australia's ongoing battle against corruption. With 44 referrals already on its docket, the commission is gearing up for what promises to be an extensive and high-profile investigation, with many fingers pointing towards members of the former Morrison government.

The spectre of corruption looms large over the previous administration, with a laundry list of alleged misdeeds coming to light. The clandestine ministries under former Prime Minister Scott Morrison has raised many concerns, setting the stage for a series of controversies that have now found their way into the NACC's purview.

One of the key areas under scrutiny is the questionable land deals in Western Sydney, where the government reportedly overpaid Liberal Party donors by a staggering $27 million, for land only valued at $3 million. This financial discrepancy, if proven true, underscores a potential misuse of public funds and raises questions about the integrity of these transactions.

The controversies extend beyond financial improprieties: the dubious drought envoy reports by Barnaby Joyce, who received $675,000 for reports that remain shrouded in mystery and have never been released, add another layer to the many allegations. The forgery of documents by Angus Taylor in the Sydney City Council scandal in 2019, further muddies the waters, implicating high-profile figures in the corridors of power.

The web of accusations also entangles figures such Senators Bridget McKenzie, Michaelia Cash and Linda Reynolds, and MPs such as Alan Tudge and Stuart Robert, creating a complex list of alleged corruption that the NACC is poised to unravel, or at least look investigate, to see if any illegalities have occured. From illegal water deals to the sports rorts scandal, the commission's plate is undoubtedly full, suggesting a prolonged and intensive inquiry lies ahead.

However, as Australia welcomes the establishment of the NACC, there are apprehensions echoing the cautionary tale of the New South Wales Independent Commission Against Corruption. The ICAC faced budget cuts from successive governments, restricting its capacity to take on cases, thereby prioritising larger investigations at the expense of smaller ones. The fear is that the NACC may encounter similar challenges in subsequent years, potentially diluting its effectiveness in rooting out corruption at all levels.

Despite these concerns, there is a unanimous call for a zero-tolerance approach towards corruption within the electorate. The establishment of the NACC is seen as a long-overdue step toward ensuring accountability in Australian politics. The journey to this point has been fraught with political wrangling, with the Australian Greens first advocating for an anti-corruption commission as early as 2009. The Morrison government's promise to introduce an anti-corruption commission in December 2018 was met with skepticism, especially given the lack of substantial legislative progress until 2021, before dumping the project altogether in early 2022.

As the Labor Party championed the cause so much during the 2022 federal election, it had to ensure that delivered on this promise. The NACC's formation is therefore seen as a response to public demand for accountability, challenging the longstanding culture of unchecked political conduct.

In the broader context, the establishment of the NACC serves as a crucial deterrent against corruption, embodying a collective hope that such bodies may one day become obsolete. While the Morrison government seemed to transform the federal government into a hotbed of scandal and corruption, the NACC stands as a potential corrective force, aiming not only to expose wrongdoing but also to prevent its occurrence in the first place. The NACC has a formidable responsibility of upholding the principles of transparency and integrity in Australian politics.

NACC FACES EARLY POLITICAL CHALLENGED IN ITS QUEST FOR TRANSPARENCY

In the wake of the officially commencing its operations, inaugural Commissioner Paul Brereton has wasted no time in clarifying the commission's purpose and asserting its commitment to transparency and accountability.

> **Paul Brereton:** "This is an historic moment. First and foremost, the people of the Commonwealth are no longer prepared to tolerate practices which might once have been the subject of if not acceptance, at least acquiescence. You have clearly expressed the desire for a Commonwealth anti-corruption agency. In doing so it has enacted legislation which embodies the best practice principles for corruption commissions.

These include the ability to consider referrals from anyone the ability to commence an investigation on our own motion, a requirement for the heads of Commonwealth agencies to refer allegations of corruption to us the ability to conduct hearings to obtain evidence, including to summons witnesses to require production of documents, and to take evidence under oath or affirmation.
And should it be sought to weaponise the commission through inappropriate and unfounded referrals, I will not hesitate to use the power to make public statements if necessary, to avoid damaged reputations, and to say that the referral was inappropriate."

Despite Brereton's early warning against politicising the NACC, the commission has already found itself at the centre of political games, with Senator Linda Reynolds publicly announced her intention to refer the compensation payment made to Brittany Higgins by the federal government to the anti-corruption commission. The confidentiality typically associated with such referrals was seemingly cast aside, as Reynolds's public declaration raised concerns about the potential politicisation of the commission, with accusations that she is attempting to use the NACC for political gain.

Of course, the move also reflects the values of the modern Liberal Party, an ultra-reactionary force that seeks to dismantle anything created by their political opponents, and there have been comparisons made with the Republican Party in the United States, which serves as a stark reminder of the divisive nature of contemporary politics.

There is a growing concern that the NACC, a body meant to enhance accountability and transparency, could become a pawn in the political game. Critics fear that the Liberal Party may attempt to undermine the commission for strategic political advantage. The very institution created to combat corruption may find itself entangled in the web of political machinations.

Amidst these concerns, there is a call for a nuanced understanding of the NACC's purpose. The commission is intended to assist public servants in performing their duties more effectively by providing a confidential platform to investigate allegations of corruption. While some matters may seem corrupt on the surface, a private investigation allows for a careful examination of claims before they become public, protecting individuals from unfounded allegations that could tarnish their reputations.

As the NACC navigates its early days, the actions of political figures such as Senator Reynolds serve as a litmus test for the commission's resilience in the face of potential politicisation. Whether the NACC will fulfil its mandate as an impartial anti-corruption watchdog or succumb to the pressures of political manipulation remains to be seen. The evolving landscape underscores the challenges inherent in establishing and maintaining institutions aimed at upholding the principles of integrity and accountability in the realm of politics.

THE BEREJIKLIAN FALLOUT: POLITICAL FIGURES SEEK TO DIMINISH ANTI-CORRUPTION EFFORTS

The recent revelations from the New South Wales ICAC regarding former Premier Gladys Berejiklian offer a stark preview of the challenges the NACC may encounter in the future. The ICAC report, which labeled Berejiklian as a "seriously corrupt politician", triggered a defensive and aggressive response from high-profile figures, most notably, Peter Dutton.

Dutton's attempt to downplay the significance of the ICAC announcement by portraying Berejiklian as an innocent victim caught up in a relationship with a questionable partner is an attempt to attack the ICAC, with the insinuation that she was merely a victim of circumstance rather than a culpable actor in corrupt activities has intensified the debate over the politicisation of anti-corruption bodies.

The ICAC's findings, while not resulting in criminal charges, nonetheless delivered a damning verdict on Berejiklian's conduct. The fact that Dutton and others within the Liberal Party sought to undermine the credibility of such a reputable investigative body raises concerns about the potential erosion of public trust in these institutions.

The question arises: Is Dutton's attempt to downplay the ICAC announcement a strategic move to shield himself and his political colleagues from future scrutiny by the NACC or similar bodies? The concern is that when politicians attempt to diminish the significance of anti-corruption commissions, particularly when it pertains to their own political allies, it signals a troubling pattern that could extend to the national level.

The ICAC, known for its integrity and commitment to unearthing corruption, has served as a model for similar bodies globally. The fact that Dutton is willing to cast doubt on its pronouncements suggests a potential conflict of interest or an attempt to pre-emptively deflect attention from wrongdoing within his own political circles.

Berejiklian's case, while complex, raises fundamental questions about corruption and its manifestations. The notion that one can be "seriously corrupt" without direct personal gain may seem contradictory, but it underscores the nuanced nature of corruption. The absence of charges against Berejiklian leaves a lingering puzzle, as the official explanation emphasised the lack of material gain. However, the intricacies of her relationship and the potential for more revelations suggest that the story may not yet be fully unravelled.

As the NACC commences its operations, the Berejiklian case serves as a cautionary tale. Politicians who attempt to dismiss or undermine the findings of anti-corruption bodies risk eroding public trust in these institutions, which play a crucial role in upholding the principles of transparency and accountability. The unfolding chapters of this saga will determine not only the fate of individuals implicated but also the trajectory of Australia's fight against corruption at the highest levels of government.

***

ROBODEBT REPORT RELEASED: A DARK CHAPTER IN AUSTRALIA'S HISTORY

8 July 2023

In a significant development this week, the long-awaited Robodebt Royal Commission Report has been unveiled, adding another layer to the ongoing scrutiny of Australia's controversial debt recovery scheme. At a staggering 990 pages, the exhaustive report delves into the heart of the Robodebt program, revealing a multitude of issues, accompanied by a comprehensive set of 57 recommendations.

Of particular interest is a special "sealed section" within the report, concealing references to individuals earmarked for potential civil and criminal prosecution. The contents of this section have been forwarded to the National Anti-Corruption Commission, and until the Department of Public Prosecutions determines the possibility of charges, the identities of those implicated remain undisclosed. The sheer weight of this sealed section has sparked intense speculation and anticipation, as Australians wait to learn who might be held accountable for the injustices associated with the Robodebt scheme.

Prime Minister Anthony Albanese's response to the report underscores the gravity of the findings. He acknowledges the courage displayed by some of the most vulnerable Australians, who, in the face of injustice, hardship, and grief, played a pivotal role in exposing the flaws of the Robodebt program. The Prime Minister expressed unequivocal condemnation, labeling the scheme a "gross betrayal" and a "human tragedy". He emphasised the scheme's unlawfulness under the former Liberal government, highlighting the colossal sum of $1.8 billion in debts raised against over half a million Australians.

The report further contends that the Robodebt scheme, implemented by the Liberal Party, was not just flawed but characterised as a "crude and cruel mechanism", traumatising individuals on the mere possibility of owing money. Albanese characterised it as a costly failure of public administration, causing immeasurable harm in both human and economic terms.

The release of the report has triggered a collective sigh of relief among those affected by the Robodebt system. Families of the more than 2,000 individuals who suicided after receiving a Robodebt notification will find validation in the report's conclusions. Witnesses who testified at the Royal Commission, as well as those who tirelessly advocated against the failures of the Robodebt system, now see their efforts vindicated.

As the public grapples with the details of the report, attention turns to the sealed section and the potential ramifications for those within it. Speculation abounds about the identities of individuals, with at least three public servants and four ministers cited as potential candidates. The possibility of criminal charges looms large, and the Prime Minister's scathing remarks during a press conference suggest a government taking a strong stance against any perceived criminal activity within its ranks.

A DAMNING INDICTMENT OF COALITION GOVERNMENT MISMANAGEMENT

The report has unraveled a deeply disturbing narrative of bureaucratic mismanagement and institutionalised torment inflicted upon vulnerable Australians. The program, deemed illegal and unlawful, was exposed as a gross betrayal of trust, resulting in canceled and refunded debts totaling $1.8 billion. The Royal Commission has laid bare the extent of the harm caused by the scheme, emphasising the magnitude of the missteps and the subsequent toll on individuals.

The Robodebt system targeted citizens receiving social security or pension payments, issuing debt notices for substantial amounts, often for debts they did not owe. The victims, already dealing with financial struggles, found themselves entangled with debt collection agencies or facing court battles over baseless claims. The scale of the program's failure is emphasised by the staggering number of affected individuals—433,000 identified by the federal court, with tens of thousands more subjected to what Minister for Government Services Bill Shorten describes as a government "shakedown".

Shorten, addressing the victims of the scheme, expressed the Royal Commission's findings as a testament to the betrayal of trust, and pointedly highlighted the government's role in "gaslighting" the nation for four and a half years, fundamentally breaking the trust between citizens and their government. Victims, who were treated as guilty until proven innocent, faced the reversal of the burden of proof and were subjected to vile political tactics when they dared to complain.

The report, as articulated by Commissioner Catherine Holmes, condemns the Robodebt scheme as both crude and cruel. It underscores the lack of fairness and legality in the program, pushing individuals to feel like criminals. Commissioner Holmes is scathing in her assessment of Minister Stuart Robert, citing incompetence and cowardice, and accused Prime Minister Scott Morrison of deliberately allowing his Cabinet to be misled.

The Robodebt Royal Commission stands out as a masterclass in investigative procedures. Commissioner Holmes' thorough examination of all involved parties, her refusal to whitewash or sugar coat the findings, and the commitment to due process exemplify the importance of such inquiries. Despite political pressures and attempts to dismiss the report as a "witch hunt", the commission has delivered a damning indictment of the Robodebt scheme and those responsible for its implementation.

The report's vindication of the victims and its unflinching scrutiny of government actions underscore the critical role of Royal Commissions in holding those in power accountable and ensuring justice for those who have suffered.

CALLS FOR ETHICAL OVERHAUL

As the fallout from the Robodebt Royal Commission Report reverberates through Australian politics, the Liberal Party finds itself entangled in a complex web of deflections and political deliberations. Just as was observed in the wake of the ICAC report exposing serious corruption involving Berejiklian and Daryl Maguire, the Liberal Party appears to be attempting to shield itself from the damning findings of the Robodebt Royal Commission.

Former government minister Senator Bridget McKenzie, in a move typical of the political game, has shifted blame onto the public service, arguing that proposals brought to the Cabinet were assumed to be legal under Australian law. This attempt to redirect responsibility underscores the political dimension of the aftermath of the Royal Commission, as each party seeks to manage the narrative and mitigate the damage to its reputation.

In a similar vein, Peter Dutton, the former Minister for Defence, accuses the government of releasing the report strategically, claiming it coincides with the timing of the Fadden byelection. The Fadden byelection itself becomes a focal point in the political chess game. While it has to be acknowledged that any government will use unfavourable news against the opposition during such events, and the political impact of the Royal Commission report on the electorate would have been strong, irrespective of whenever it was released.

However, Dutton's diversionary tactics have become obvious, as he endeavours to shift the conversation away from the Robodebt scheme. Instead, he focuses on topics such as nuclear energy—the standard go-to issue for the Liberal Party whenever they need a political diversion—the Voice to

Parliament, and employing every possible distraction to avoid addressing the illegal and bordering-on-criminal nature of the Robodebt program.

The Royal Commission report serves as a final reckoning for the Liberal Party, particularly its hard-right faction that has wielded far too much influence since 2007. The report's findings, revealing the illegality of the Robodebt scheme, raise questions about the selection process that allowed figures like Scott Morrison, Stuart Robert, Christian Porter, and Alan Tudge to ascend to positions of power.

The broader call to all political parties to scrutinise their recruitment processes reflects a desire for a more ethical and accountable political landscape. The hope is to prevent individuals with questionable ethics and motivations from attaining public office, fostering a return to a political environment where merit and commitment to public service take precedence over self-interest. The Robodebt Royal Commission, in its unflinching examination, serves as a catalyst for broader reflection on the state of Australian politics and the imperative for meaningful change.

***

INTEREST RATES AT THE CENTRE OF AUSTRALIA'S POLITICAL DRAMAS

8 July 2023

In the midst of a political landscape filled with a wide range of competing issues, one topic has managed to dominate headlines and public discourse—the ever-crucial matter of interest rates. It seems as though, in the grand theatre of federal politics, the spotlight is consistently trained on this economic lever, elevating it to a status of national obsession, perpetuated by the relentless coverage of the mainstream media.

In the lead-up to the eagerly awaited announcement on interest rates, a palpable tension gripped the nation: economic and political commentators engaged in a protracted debate, offering a spectrum of predictions about whether the rates would ascend or descend—*or stay the same!*—and what repercussions these changes might hold for the Australian economy. While some preferred the prudence of waiting for an official announcement, the Reserve Bank surprised many by choosing to maintain the interest rates at 4.1 per cent.

The conduct of Reserve Bank Governor Philip Lowe during this period has also come under scrutiny, especially as his tenure faces a critical moment with the upcoming decision on his renewal in September, where his failure to raise interest rates when deemed necessary and his pre-2022 federal election claim that rates would remain untouched until 2024, have destroyed his chances of re-appointment. His actions at the time have also ignited speculation about the potential political underpinnings of the Reserve Bank's decisions.

The political arena further muddies the waters, with the Liberal Party seizing the opportunity to assert its economic prowess, where immediately following the Reserve Bank's announcement, leader of the opposition Peter Dutton attributed the decision of the Reserve Bank to leave interest rates as a result of the superior economic management of the Liberal Party, despite their absence from government for 14 months.

As the political cycle continues, the Liberal Party's claim to superior economic management is facing many challenges, with recent opinion polls indicating a shift in public perception, with the party losing its long-held image as the paragon of economic competence, especially after they left a one trillion dollar national government debt behind in May 2022. This, coupled with a historical reassessment of economic management by both Labor and conservative governments, challenges the notion that economic stewardship is the exclusive domain of any single party.

The discourse surrounding Lowe's position has taken a sharper turn, suggesting that his continued tenure may be untenable past September 2023. Speculation has arisen that the government may be biding time until a replacement can be installed, with the announcement by the government that there are two potential successors to Lowe. Criticism is also directed at Lowe's apparent detachment from mainstream Australia, notably highlighted by his suggestion that those struggling financially could alleviate their situation by renting out a room in their home or opting for cheaper groceries—a sentiment that seems out of touch with the realities faced by many, and certainly not a predicament that he would ever find himself in.

As the Labor government, now in office for just over a year, begins to navigate economic challenges, the stakes are high. The electorate usually grants a grace period for a new government to address inherited economic issues, however, the task of economic ownership now falls squarely on their shoulders, irrespective of whether the created the problems in the first instance.

NAVIGATING GLOBAL FORCES, SURPLUS SURPRISES AND POLITICAL DILEMMAS

As the nation deals with the differing economic narratives and political machinations, a broader perspective on the role of governments in steering economies comes into focus. Acknowledging the limits of governmental control over economic forces, it becomes apparent that external factors such as global events, trade disruptions, supply issues, and unforeseen crises such pandemics or international wars can exert considerable influence on the economic landscape. A downturn on the New York Stock Exchange can reverberate across the world, impacting Australian imports and exports for months on end.

Australia's economic fortunes are not isolated; the complexity of global interdependence underscores the challenge of attributing economic success or failure solely to governmental actions. While governments can nudge the economy in the right direction, they are not omnipotent controllers of every economic variable. Instead, their effectiveness lies in mitigating the impact of adverse external conditions—a task the last government, critics argue, failed to accomplish. The Reserve Bank, armed with its primary tool of interest rates, finds itself engaged with the limitations of this singular mechanism as a panacea for economic challenges.

A notable revelation adds a layer to the economic tapestry—the reassessment of the budget surplus. Initially estimated at $4.2 billion during Jim Chalmers' budget announcement in May, it has now burgeoned to a substantial $19 billion. This shift is attributed to factors such as higher commodity prices, increased corporate and personal tax revenue, and a more robust labour market. Economic commentators, particularly those traditionally aligned with conservative views, present this surplus as a testament to the fortuitous state of the "lucky country" or Chalmers just happening to land on good economic times, rather than any competence on his part.

Chris Richardson, a conservative economics commentator, claimed the surplus "an embarrassment"—words that he would never use to describe a budget surplus produced by a Coalition government—challenging the conventional wisdom that surpluses are unequivocally good. The new narrative seems to be that surpluses are always *good*, except for when they are produced by Labor governments, which for some inexplicable reason, are always *bad*. This newfound surplus, viewed by some as serendipity rather than strategic economic planning, sparked debate about its utilisation. Suggestions emerge that the surplus should be redirected toward addressing the cost of living and other societal concerns—a proposal previously absent when a Coalition government occupied the seat of power.

The Prime Minister, Anthony Albanese, has signaled a conservative response, opting to retain the surplus. Economically, this decision aligns with the imperative of curbing inflation, a delicate balancing act orchestrated by both the government and the Reserve Bank. However, from a social perspective, questions arise about alternative uses for the surplus, such as raising job seeker aid or tackling outstanding HECS student debts.

This fiscal surplus, poised to shape the political landscape over the next 12 months, introduces a nuanced dynamic. The prospect of releasing more money into the economy through Stage 3 tax cuts in 2024 complicates the government's stance on economic intervention. The argument that releasing surplus funds now would spur inflation conflicts with the potential contradiction of endorsing such a move in the future if economic conditions persist.

The economic abilities of Treasurer Jim Chalmers, which appear at this stage to be superior to those of his predecessor, Josh Frydenberg, provides a glimmer of hope amid the economic complexities. However, skepticism lingers, rooted in the history of paper surpluses and unfulfilled promises. As the nation watches attentively, the utilisation of the surplus remains as a critical test—a test that could redefine not only economic policies but also the public's trust in governmental economic stewardship after nearly a decade of mixed outcomes.

***

FALLOUT FROM ROBODEBT INTENSIFIES AMID CALLS FOR MORRISON RESIGNATION

15 July 2023

The fallout from the Robodebt Royal Commission report continues to reverberate throughout Australian politics and while media interest in the issue may have waned, the implications of the report are far from over. Calls for former Prime Minister Scott Morrison to resign from Parliament have gained momentum, with critics asserting that the blame for the Robodebt scandal—described by Federal Court judge Bernard Murphy as a "massive failure in public administration"—extends beyond Morrison alone.

The revelations in the Robodebt Royal Commission report have shed light on the widespread issues plaguing the previous Liberal–National Coalition government's automated debt recovery system. As public scrutiny intensifies, the focus has shifted to various former ministers and members of the public service who were involved in the flawed implementation of Robodebt, including Stuart Robert, Alan Tudge, Christian Porter, and potentially other Coalition Cabinet ministers.

Although Kathryn Campbell, a senior figure in the public service, has become the public face of opprobrium within this Robodebt scandal, there are likely others within the public service who will have to face the consequences of their involvement. While the push for Morrison's resignation has not only come from other opposition parties but also within the Liberal Party itself, removing Morrison from Parliament will not mark the end of the Robodebt scandal, as the issue runs deeper and wider than his individual responsibility.

While there is a growing consensus within the community that Morrison should resign, it is important to note that he is not solely to blame for the Robodebt debacle. Nevertheless, the Liberal Party appears to be using him as a scapegoat, hoping that his resignation will mitigate some of the damage ahead of the next federal election, due in 2025. Morrison's disastrous reign as prime minister continues to be a reminder of the Liberal Party's challenges. However, his resignation is not such a simple process, as it would require him to retire, resign—or face charges related to Robodebt resulting in a criminal conviction with a potential jail term of over 12 months.

The Liberal Party finds itself in a difficult position regarding Morrison's tenure. While they could disendorse him from the party, he would still remain in his seat for up to two years until the next federal election. Consequently, the party's options to hasten his departure are limited. The longer Morrison stays in Parliament, the more damage he potentially inflicts on the Liberal Party's reputation. Yet, it remains uncertain how they will manage his exit, as they lack definitive alternatives.

Considering the future prospects for Morrison, his chances of securing a lucrative post-political job appear bleak. The revelations from the Robodebt Royal Commission report, including the possibility of corruption charges, make it unlikely for him to attract prominent employment opportunities—although it could be argued that the "seriously corrupt" former NSW Premier Gladys Berejiklian is employed by Optus, so perhaps there may be an opening available there for Morrison as a sidekick? Or PwC, a consultancy firm that seemed to very open to corrupt deals with the former Coalition government?

Also, Morrison's current role as a backbencher offers him a $230,000 salary, as well as freedom from significant responsibilities, and the ability to enjoy the benefits associated with the position. Why would someone like Morrison leave politics if this is his only viable option?

THE ROBODEBT FALLOUT CONTINUES

As the fallout from the Robodebt Royal Commission report continues to unfold, the demand for accountability and justice remains at the forefront. The public's expectation for action extends beyond the resignation of Morrison from Parliament, as the full scope of responsibility and potential corruption must be thoroughly addressed. The Robodebt scandal has become a defining issue in Australian politics, and the consequences for those involved are far from over.

Morrison, of course, has dismissed the adverse findings against him, claiming that the Commission "did not understand how the government operates". If *how government operates* includes breaches of protocol, corruption, incompetence, and the implementation of an illegal and unconstitutional scheme, then perhaps it is true—the Commission didn't understand how the Morrison government operated but, then again, it's possible no one else did, including Morrison himself.

Despite the damning findings, Morrison's refusal to accept the report's conclusions holds little weight—Morrison's reputation as a liar further raises doubts about his credibility and his lack of trustworthiness extends beyond this particular issue, rendering his presence in Parliament of questionable value. History has shown that former prime ministers often contribute to the Australian community in various capacities after leaving politics. However, Morrison's leaves behind a vacuum and his prospects seem limited, offering little in terms of domestic or international contributions.

There are also rumours the Cronulla–Sutherland Sharks rugby league team—a club littered with its own scandals of drug cheating, salary cap rorting and player misbehaviour—are considering removing Morrison as their number one ticket holder. This would serve as a significant blow to his ego, considering the perks associated with the position—such as free games and access to the corporate box. The potential loss of this affiliation underscores the dwindling popularity of Morrison and highlights his struggle to find relevance outside of politics.

THE LACK OF ROBODEBT INTEREST FROM THE MAINSTREAM MEDIA

While the mainstream media did initially reported on the release of the Robodebt Royal Commission report—how could they not?—its coverage has been perfunctory and has since dwindled over the past few days. The 24-hour news cycle, driven by the constant search for new stories, does contribute to this phenomenon but it is worth noting that if a Labor government had been implicated in such an illegal scheme, the media coverage would likely have been far more extensive, especially when comparing with the Royal Commissions into trade union governance, and the Rudd government's home insulation scheme, in 2014. Both of these were instigated by the Abbott government, primarily as a political attack on Labor, and were enthusiastically promoted by a compromised and partisan conservative mainstream media. Robodebt? Not so much.

Independent media outlets and social media played a crucial role in bringing Robodebt to the public's attention—most notably, the campaign commenced by the digital rights activist Asher Wolf—with the mainstream media offering limited coverage and languishing far behind with their interest. This disparity does raises questions about media biases and their role in holding conservative governments accountable.

The blame for the Robodebt scandal should not solely rest on one or two individuals: Kathryn Campbell, is now facing scrutiny for her involvement and surely her future within the public service should be coming to an end, as if there was any further evidence required. However, it is evident that the blame game serves as a convenient tactic for those in the media and the Liberal Party to deflect responsibility. A more diligent media would have pursued a thorough investigation, exposing all those responsible.

The leader of the opposition, Peter Dutton is seeking to sweep the Robodebt disaster away from scrutiny, emphasising the need to "focus on the future". Fortunately, the newly established National Anti-Corruption Commission is also focused on the future and will be closely examining the 'sealed section' of the Robodebt Royal Commission report and potentially uncovering additional names involved.

Will Dutton's name be one of those listed? The pursuit of justice and accountability should take precedence over political posturing and while Dutton's posturing was solely focused on providing a message to take to the Fadden byelection over the weekend, this pursuit needs to follow through in interests of the public.

The Robodebt scandal highlights the systemic issues of abuse of vulnerable people in the community, and protecting those in political office, which lead to a lack of transparency and accountability. As public sentiment continues to evolve, the demand for change will become more pronounced. The National Anti-Corruption Commission and the Department of Public Prosecutions must fulfill their duties by charging those responsible for the illegal Robodebt scheme. It is essential to address the systemic flaws within governance to prevent similar instances of misconduct and ensure a more transparent and accountable government. It is must never ever be allowed to happen again.

***

THE COMPLEXITIES OF COMBATING MISINFORMATION IN POLITICS

15 July 2023

In the ever-evolving landscape of political discourse, a new battleground has emerged—one where the weapons of choice are not physical arms, but rather the dissemination of information, or more accurately, misinformation. At the forefront of this battlefield is the proposed federal government's Combating Misinformation and Disinformation Bill, currently navigating the the path of public consultation and comment.

As the Bill goes through the draft exposure stage, inviting public input, a counter-narrative has swiftly unfolded. A campaign of misinformation has been unleashed, predicably, Sky News and the News Corporation conglomerate have rallied against the Bill, ironically, weaving a range of misleading narratives that are, to echo Steve Bannon's rhetoric, "flooding the zone with shit".

Predictably, the opposition doesn't stop at media outlets; it extends to the political sphere. The Liberal Party, aligning itself with the campaign against the Bill, and beneath the surface, a complex web of alliances has come to the fore, where the very existence and success of certain entities appear intertwined with the dissemination of misinformation.

In the current political landscape, where the lines between fact and fiction blur seamlessly, it was hoped that the proposed legislation would stand as a flickering beacon attempting to pierce the fog of deception. Yet, there are questions about its efficacy: the Bill, in its current form, resembles a fragile fortress against the tidal wave of misinformation, almost as if the industry it seeks to regulate has had a hand in crafting its foundations.

The global stage offers a curious dichotomy: countries with robust legislation targeting misinformation boast a more responsible media landscape, exemplified by New Zealand, Canada, and much of Europe. On the flip side, nations lacking such regulations, including the United Kingdom, United

States, and Australia, are dealing with a media environment spiraling out of control, an environment which undermines key elements of democracy.

Amidst the irony of media giants and political entities decrying the proposed legislation, the need for some level of control is apparent. The relentless flow of misinformation through social media and mainstream channels has transformed into a proverbial sewer pipe, inundating public discourse.

However, as the battle lines are drawn, a cacophony of voices rises. Radical libertarians and staunch advocates of free speech vehemently oppose any constraints on their right to express opinions, regardless of their veracity. The push for an unrestricted freedom of speech, devoid of accountability, emanates from political quarters and media outlets alike, fostering an environment where responsibility is willingly cast aside.

The essence of free speech, a cornerstone of democratic societies, often becomes a point of contention. However, when unraveling the layers, it becomes clear that the concept is often misconstrued. While it grants individuals the liberty to criticise the government without fear of persecution, it doesn't provide a *carte blanche* for any form of expression without responsibility.

Recent events, such as the Israel Folau saga in rugby union, where he sent out offensive and provocative homophobic slogans under the guise of "religious expression," underscore the limits of free speech within private entities. The delicate balance between corporate values and individual expression comes into focus, challenging the notion that absolute freedom is the antidote to a healthy democratic discourse.

As the debate intensifies, the proposed legislation stands as a testament to the struggle to rein in the unchecked spread of misinformation. It is a battle not only against external forces but also against the very pillars of an information ecosystem that thrives on ambiguity and irresponsibility.

How effective will the battle against misinformation be?

While the need for better control over the rampant spread of falsehoods in political discourse is undeniable, skepticism arises regarding the Labor government's Bill as a panacea for the ailment plaguing our information ecosystem.

The crux of the matter lies in the Bill's seemingly feeble provisions. The powers granted to the Australian Communications and Media Authority to develop a code of conduct and industry standards raise questions about their impact. The absence of authority to remove offending material and the exclusion of election or referendum content from its purview pose significant limitations. This glaring gap implies that material disseminated during crucial democratic processes remains immune to regulation, allowing a breeding ground for racist, misleading, and blatantly false information.

In the current Voice to Parliament debate, for example, where misinformation has proliferated, the Bill's shortcomings become even more apparent. The legislation, as it stands, appears toothless, leaving one to wonder about its purpose and efficacy. If News Corporation were to adopt a strategic approach, they could give a simple nod of approval to the Labor government, followed by a return to their "business as usual" approach to publishing lies, misinformation and disinformation: that's how limited the expected impact from the proposed Bill—in its current format—appears to be.

The critical question arises: what has the Minister for Communications, Michelle Rowland, been doing over the past 14 months? The media landscape, in dire need of reform, remains seemingly untouched. The ABC needs a comprehensive overhaul to meet the demands of the digital age, as does its editorial standards, which have in decline for much of the time the Coalition has been in office, especially over the past five years since the appointment of Ita Buttrose as the Chair of the ABC. However, the proposed legislation falls short of addressing these broader issues, leaving one to question the depth and scope of the government's commitment to media reform.

While the Bill may be seen as a step in the right direction, it prompts a call for more robust measures. A constant suggestion surfaces—a Royal Commission into the media—a comprehensive and impartial examination that could pave the way for substantial reform. Concerns linger about the Labor government's seemingly cautious approach to media giants and anti-Labor activists such News Corporation. The desire to maintain a cordial relationship with influential media outlets, perhaps in the hope of favourable coverage—which is never going to come from the likes of News Corporation—remains perplexing.

In this landscape of uncertainty, the ultimate effectiveness of the proposed legislation remains an open question. Only time will unveil whether it is a mere stepping stone toward more substantial reform or a gesture to appease critics without addressing the core issues at hand. As the debate unfolds, the need for a comprehensive, far-reaching approach to media reform becomes increasingly apparent, leaving us to ponder whether the current Bill is a mere starting point or a culmination and the end of the government's efforts in this arena.

***

THE FADDEN AFTERMATH: A FAMILIAR RESULT LEAVES THE PARTIES UNCHANGED

22 July 2023

The Fadden byelection has concluded and in the world of politics, electoral events always hold some significance, even if it may not amount to much in the grand scheme of things. This particular byelection, held in Queenland's Gold Coast, is known for its conservative tendencies and its lack of major swings from one election to the next.

Unsurprisingly, the Liberal–National Party emerged victorious, with their new candidate, Cameron Caldwell, securing a comfortable 13-point margin, and the win is being touted by News Corporation as a massive success for Peter Dutton and a significant blow to the Labor Party, signaling the end of Anthony Albanese's honeymoon period as leader.

However, upon closer examination, the results appear to be nothing more than business as usual. The byelection outcome can be considered a typical stock-standard result with little excitement or change. While the *Daily Telegraph* has at least reported the election accurately on this occasion—a win to the Liberal–National Party—leaders facing political challenges often attempt to amplify any victory to appear more substantial than it actually is.

In this case, this win may help Dutton retain his position for a little longer, allowing potential challengers such as Sussan Ley or Angus Taylor more time to prepare their challenge. Conversely, Dutton will have an opportunity to stabilise his leadership within the Liberal Party, assuming the party continues to support his efforts.

This situation brings to mind the 2020 Eden–Monaro byelection, where the Labor Party narrowly won, against expectations. However, the *Daily Telegraph* sensationalised the results, claiming it was a crushing blow for Anthony Albanese, even though the party he led had just won. Such tactics are not uncommon for the conservative media, as they usually try to spin victories for the Liberal Party—and even their losses—to their advantage.

The victory for the Labor Party in Eden–Monaro stabilised Albanese's leadership, enabled him to lay a platform to start engaging the electorate against an unpopular Prime Minister, Scott Morrison, which ultimately led to victory at the 2022 federal election. While Dutton's win may not guarantee a similar trajectory for him, it serves as a reminder that even a small victory can pave the way for greater success in the future.

There have been some questions about whether the Fadden byelection result can provide any insights into the upcoming federal election. Upon analysis, however, there appears to be very little that can be inferred from it. The Australian Greens experienced a 4 per cent drop in their vote, and the Legalise Cannabis Party—in their first election appearance—managed to secure 7 per cent of the vote. Aside from these minor shifts, the overall change in voter sentiment was relatively limited, with a 2.8 per cent swing against the government.

However, byelection results often reflect the mood of the electorate on a specific day and in a particular region, making them somewhat unrepresentative of the broader Australian community. Moreover, with the next federal election not scheduled until 2025, there is ample time for political landscapes to evolve and issues to surface, rendering the byelection results less impactful in the long run.

A similar sentiment can be applied to the seat of Aston, where the Liberal Party suffered a dramatic loss in April this year. While this outcome was indicative of the political climate at the time, it cannot be seen as an absolute predictor of the future political landscape. Politics is a fluid and ever-changing arena, and events between now and the next federal election can significantly alter the political dynamics.

The Fadden byelection might have declared a winner for the Liberal–National Party, but its significance remains modest in the larger political context. A victory is a victory, no matter how small, and it can potentially lead to greater achievements down the line. Nevertheless, using byelection results as a crystal ball for future elections is a speculative exercise at best, as the political climate can undergo considerable shifts over time. As the nation looks ahead to the 2025 federal election, much is yet to unfold in the dynamic world of Australian politics.

***

THE CONFLICTS OF INTEREST IN GOVERNMENT OUTSOURCING

22 July 2023

Deloitte, one of the prominent "Big Four" consultancy firms, finds itself embroiled in controversy yet again: this time, the spotlight is on allegations of conflicts of interest and the misuse of sensitive government information acquired during its consultancies with the federal government. The unfolding scandal bears a striking resemblance to the breaches that came to light earlier this year involving another leading firm, PwC. As the revelations continue to emerge, they are mostly uncovered through the relentless efforts of Australian Green Senator Barbara Pocock and Labor Senator Deborah O'Neill, who have formed the most formidable Parliamentary tag-team since Senators Robert Ray and John Faulkner in 1990s, and forensically probed the issue in Senate estimates.

Amidst the unfolding controversy, questions have arisen about the remuneration of Deloitte's executives, particularly the Managing Partner, Scott Grimley, who reportedly earns a staggering $2.8 million per year—five times the salary of the Prime Minister. This stark contrast has sparked debates about the fairness of such high compensation, especially when compared to the salaries of essential workers like nurses, who earn significantly less, yet bear a heavier tax burden.

Senator O'Neill's persistent and probing questioning during Senate estimates has brought to light the concerns of the Australian public regarding the value generated by executives earning such high salaries. With a considerable portion of this income coming from public money, citizens are demanding greater accountability and transparency in the allocation of taxpayer funds.

In responses, Grimley maintained that he believes his compensation is a fair reflection of the responsibilities he undertakes and the value he brings to the firm. However, the discrepancy between executive earnings and the average Australian wage has ignited a national conversation about income equality and the utilisation of public funds.

Deloitte's corruptive practices have brought the wider issue of government outsourcing to the forefront and the calls for stronger legislation to address conflicts of interest and the misuse of sensitive information have gained momentum. Additionally, some have advocated for a Royal Commission to investigate the practices of government outsourcing further. Insiders from within both Deloitte and PwC have suggested that the recent revelations may only scratch the surface, with other major players in federal government outsourcing—such as EY, KPMG, Accenture, and McKinsey—potentially facing similar scrutiny.

The substantial annual outlay of at least $21 billion on government outsourcing has raised concerns about the need for more robust checks and balances to ensure that taxpayer money is spent prudently and ethically. As Deloitte faces intense scrutiny for conflicts of interest and the misuse of government information, the Australian public remains deeply invested in the outcome of Senator Pocock and Senator O'Neill's inquiries. The controversy has not only raised questions about executive remuneration but has also sparked broader discussions about the integrity of government outsourcing practices and the responsible use of public funds.

THE PRIVATE SECTOR DOES BETTER? NO, IT DOESN'T

In recent years, various governments' decisions to slash public service positions and outsource essential tasks to consulting firms have sparked debates about accountability and the effectiveness of these measures. Critics argue that while governments may have intended to seek external expertise, the results have been far from satisfactory, leading to the erosion of a once well-run public service. Additionally, concerns over the mismanagement of funds and confidential government information have further fueled the discussion.

Since the era of Malcolm Fraser's "razor gangs" and subsequent administrations, the Australian public service has undergone significant changes. With the advent of the Howard, Abbott, Turnbull, and Morrison governments, a trend of reducing the public service workforce emerged, coupled with the increasing reliance on external consulting firms. While proponents of this approach believed it would lead to cost savings and increased efficiency, skeptics argue that it has not yielded the expected outcomes.

One prominent issue raised by critics is the lack of transparency regarding the payments made to these consulting firms, with estimates suggesting that billions of dollars may have been allocated without adequate accountability.

The absence of a clear trail of funds has left many questioning the efficacy of outsourcing and its impact on the overall functioning of the government.

The public service's inability to handle critical matters has also prompted a call for reform. However, the government's response to these concerns has been met with mixed reactions. While some officials advocate for bringing certain services in-house, others warn of bureaucratic complexities and potential redundancies if internal management of external contractors is pursued. One proposed solution put forward by the government is to employ an additional 10,000 public servants to address the outsourcing dilemma and strengthen internal capabilities.

However, opponents argue that this approach may create more administrative layers without necessarily resolving the fundamental issue of outsourcing. Opposition leader, Peter Dutton, a vocal critic of increasing the public service workforce—an opposition leader who opposes everything proposed by the Labor government—seems to be defending the current outsourcing model, suggesting that it enables seamless collaboration between government and private sector entities. Nonetheless, proponents of reform, including Treasurer Jim Chalmers, need to prioritise the public interest over corporate interests.

BRINGING THE PUBLIC SERVICE BACK TO THE PUBLIC

In response to mounting pressures for change, there is a growing sentiment that certain—if not many—outsourcing functions should be brought back in-house. Proponents argue that this would restore direct accountability and facilitate better control over government affairs. However, implementing such a measure would necessitate a restructuring of senior public servants and how the public service interacts with government.

Recent developments, such as the suspension of former senior bureaucrat Kathryn Campbell without pay—and her subsequent resignation—further underscore the urgency of addressing the outsourcing issue. While this may involve difficult decisions, proponents contend that a clean-up of the public service is essential to restore public trust and ensure effective governance.

The debate over the future of outsourcing and the public service is likely to continue as the government attempts to strike the right balance between external expertise and internal control. Finding a viable solution will require thoughtful consideration and a willingness to learn from past mistakes to create a more efficient and accountable government for the Australian people.

***

2026 COMMONWEALTH GAMES CANCELLATION SPARKS CONTROVERSY

22 July 2023

Australia's deep-rooted passion for sports and its cherished gold medals are sources of national pride, whether we like it or not. However, the 2026 Commonwealth Games took a surprising turn as the Premier of Victoria, Daniel Andrews, made the decision to cancel the event, and the announcement has ignited a heated debate among sports enthusiasts, the public, policymakers, and athletes alike.

One of the primary reasons that led to the abrupt cancellation was a massive cost blowout that left authorities reeling. Originally estimated at $2.6 billion, the budget for the event had spiraled exponentially, ballooning to $6 billion, with Premier Andrews candidly acknowledging the possibility of the cost reaching a staggering $7 billion, making it a fiscal nightmare for the state's economy.

Besides the financial burden, other factors also weighed heavily on the Premier's mind. Government priorities had evolved, necessitating a re-evaluation of the significance of the Commonwealth Games in the broader context of Victoria's developmental and infrastructure goals. As the Premier asserted, directing these colossal funds into pressing regional health and housing initiatives could yield far-reaching benefits for the state's citizens, when compared to a two-week sporting event of declining interest and international relevance.

While financial considerations were undeniably pivotal, a deeper undercurrent of concern emerged from voices that transcended sports enthusiasts. The Premier's decision struck a chord with individuals who have long been critical of graft and corruption plaguing elite sports, such as instances of malfeasance in prominent sporting events like the Olympic Games and the FIFA World Cup often attributed to senior officials. Premier Andrews' candidness about the escalating costs resonated with those who value transparency and financial responsibility in governance.

However, the cancellation of the 2026 Commonwealth Games did not come without its share of detractors. Athletes, who had been eagerly preparing to compete on the international stage, expressed their dismay—perhaps the disappointment felt by these sportspeople might give them a better understanding of the challenges that were faced by the music and entertainment industry during the COVID pandemic, where large events were cancelled at the last minute and many performers in the industry did not receive any of the Jobkeeper support that was offered to so many other people working in other industries.

The Premier's decision was not made lightly. While acknowledging the heartache it may cause among athletes, he emphasised the long-term benefits of diverting resources towards pressing regional needs. The legacy of past sporting events, such as the 2000 Olympic Games in Sydney, loomed large, serving as a cautionary tale of budget overruns and limited tangible gains.

As the debate rages on, the cancellation of the 2026 Commonwealth Games has emerged as a politically polarising issue, pitting the desire for sports glory against the call for prudent fiscal governance. With the decision now set in stone, the focus shifts to the future and how the redirected resources will shape the wellbeing of Victoria's communities and residents.

MEDIA DUPLICITY TAKES CENTRE STAGE

Conservative media commentators, such as 3AW's Neil Mitchell, have been vocal about their skepticism towards hosting the Commonwealth Games, ever since the Victoria made the decision in early 2022, way before the cancellation was made, and warned against potential financial risks and expressed doubts about the event's overall financial viability:

> "I've got an idea the government won't like—cancel the Commonwealth Games—we just can't afford them. They now need to sit down with games authorities and say, as many cities have before, 'we got a problem here', find out what it would cost to get out of it. Other cities have done it. Other cities have struggled to make money. Why should this be any different in Victoria? Now the games might be a nice idea. Although I can't imagine huge crowds turning out for what is really a jumped-up school sports. But even if you accept they're a nice idea, we just can't afford them".
> Neil Mitchell, 22 May 2023.

And now that the government has done exactly what conservatives were calling for—cancelling the Commonwealth Games—they've shifted their stance and are now criticising the Andrews government for cancelling the Games and allegedly causing "reputational damage" to Australia's international image.

With the dust yet to settle, it remains uncertain how the cancellation will affect businesses in Victoria, particularly those that were anticipating an economic boost from the Games—although the Gold Coast Commonwealth Games in 2018 failed to materialise any of the great economic benefits that were promised either. And, true to form, we can expect the conservative media to seek out cafe and gym owners, among others, to highlight how this cancellation will impact their livelihoods in some unexplained way, just to place the pressure back onto the Andrews government.

THE AFTERMATH: A PARTISAN DIVIDE ALONG POLITICAL LINES

As the dust settles on the decision to cancel the 2026 Commonwealth Games, the aftermath continues to unveil a polarised response along party lines. Some view the cancellation as part of a broader campaign to oppose anything associated with Premier Andrews and the Victoria Labor government. While the bitter disappointment felt by athletes is undeniable, there are now discussions about whether this could spell the end of the Commonwealth Games altogether.

Interestingly, the decision to cancel the Games may inadvertently be doing the world a favour by prompting a re-evaluation of how major sporting events are organised, especially given the long-term negative effects of these events on local economies and communities, and the high level of corruption and graft within these organisations that often casts a shadow on the integrity of such events.

Looking at the present, the decision to redirect the substantial budget of the Games towards more pressing issues in social housing, education, and healthcare resonates with those prioritising the welfare of Victoria's citizens. While sports enthusiasts and fans may lament the lost opportunity for glory, the prospect of investing in long-lasting social benefits is a more prudent and responsible choice.

Nevertheless, the cancellation has not been without repercussions. Commercial stations, especially Seven West Media—the holders of the Commonwealth Games broadcasting rights—now face the challenge of reworking advertising strategies and budgets due to the sudden change in plans. On the other hand, questions have arisen regarding the ABC's vehement opposition, considering their reliance on sports coverage for viewership is not as significant as commercial networks.

The broader role of sports in mainstream media has also been called into question. While sports reporting occupies a considerable portion of media space, not everyone finds it relevant or engaging. The decision to prioritise local sports, housing, healthcare, and infrastructure over hosting an event for the sake of an increasingly irrelevant sporting event is becoming a topic of interest for those who believe in channelling resources where they can create tangible, long-term benefits for the community.

As Victoria moves forward, the cancellation of the Commonwealth Games will continue to be a topic of debate and reflection. The decisions made in the wake of this event could shape the state's future approach to hosting large-scale sporting events. The balance between showcasing Australia on the international stage and addressing critical domestic needs will remain a delicate consideration for policymakers and citizens alike.

While the disappointment felt by athletes is genuine, the ultimate test lies in whether Victoria will embrace this decision as a means to focus on social and economic development, or if the allure of hosting future sporting events will again tempt the state into pursuing potentially costly endeavours. The significance of this choice extends far beyond sports, resonating with broader questions of fiscal responsibility, accountability, and societal priorities. Only time will tell how this decision shapes the future landscape of Victoria and its standing on the global stage.

***

GOVERNMENT FUNDING FOR PRIVATE SCHOOLS DOUBLES, RAISING EQUITY CONCERNS

22 July 2023

In the past decade, the Australian government's financial support for private schools has surged, reaching double its previous levels, prompting concerns about the country's education equity. Among 38 countries in the Organization for Economic Co-operation and Development, Australia now ranks as one of the least equitable schooling systems. This disparity in funding distribution has not materialised overnight but is the culmination of a steady shift in the way schools are financed by federal and state authorities over the last 25 years.

The roots of this substantial increase in funding can be traced back to the policies initiated during the Howard Government in 1996. The primary motive behind these measures was to grant parents the "freedom to choose" the type of schooling they wanted for their children. Accordingly, more financial resources were allocated to private schools with the intention of making them more affordable. However, over time, this funding boost has failed to translate into accessible education, as private school fees continue to escalate, rendering them unaffordable for many families—defeating the purpose of Howard's policy and resulting in a wholesale transfer of federal funds away from public schools and towards private.

Critics argue that while parents should have the right to select the education they desire for their children, it should not be predominantly supported through public funding. Calls for reform in the distribution of public funds to the schooling system have grown louder. The current arrangement poses a significant challenge for policymakers as they grapple with the complexity of balancing the education preferences of parents with the need for a more equitable system.

One of the main challenges is the belief among aspirational parents that increased government funding for private schools will lead to improved access for their children. However, experts argue that this notion is a false promise, and the heart of the issue lies in whether private schools truly need public funding. Advocates for reform suggest that redirecting the substantial public investment from private schools to the public education system could result in meaningful improvements across the board.

The debate surrounding private school funding has persisted since the 1950s when the Menzies Government began providing local Catholic schools with funding to secure political support from the Democratic Labor Party. However, it was during John Howard's tenure that the concept of "choice" was prominently used to justify the government's increased investment in private sectors. Critics contend that the notion of choice served as a smokescreen for a deeper ideological commitment to neoliberal practices. This approach saw more public funds being channeled into private health care, aged care, early childhood education, and private schools, all under the banner of providing more choice to citizens.

The consequences of this approach have been far-reaching. The steady influx of public funds into private schools has resulted in around 40 per cent of them being overfunded by an estimated $3 billion. Despite this, private schools show no intention of relinquishing these extra funds. Instead, they have invested in lavish facilities and amenities, such as multiple swimming pools, expansive sports fields, advanced science and technology laboratories, and fleets of new school buses, while public schools struggle to meet their basic needs.

Presently, the federal government allocates a substantial $27 billion annually to education, with $10 billion going to public schools and $17 billion to private schools. Meanwhile, state and territory governments also contribute significantly, providing approximately $32 billion in total for education. However, the significant discrepancy in federal funding between public and private schools continues to raise concerns about the growing inequality in the education system.

As policymakers grapple with the complex challenge of addressing the funding disparity between public and private schools, the issue remains contentious. The underlying question persists: can Australia bridge the gap and create a more equitable education system while upholding the right of parents to choose the education they believe best suits their children's needs?

GONSKI REFORMS: A MISSED OPPORTUNITY FOR EQUITABLE EDUCATION

One key aspect that further contributed to the funding disparity between public and private schools can be traced back to the Gonski reforms, introduced in 2012 under a Labor government. The Gonski report was widely regarded in the education sector as a fair and reasonable approach to addressing funding issues. However, the reforms didn't receive the full support they deserved, and the government at the time failed to follow through with the intended changes.

The Gonski reforms aimed to create a more equitable funding model, removing political interference from the funding process. However, some critics argue that the implementation of these reforms has paradoxically exacerbated the funding discrepancy between public and private schools. The conservative Liberal–National governments that followed after September 2013, seemed to overlook the Gonski reforms, choosing instead to direct funding towards favoured institutions and political acquaintances without adequate consideration.

Furthermore, the Howard Government's introduction of funding based on socio-economic status for private schools ended up being perceived as another administrative manoeuvre to boost private school funding. While the idea was to address disparities based on students' socio-economic backgrounds, it had the unintended consequence of further favouring private schools at the expense of public schools.

One factor that has allowed conservative governments to push their education agendas more effortlessly is the lack of widespread parental involvement in the education system. The narrative around choice has tapped into the fears and concerns of parents, who understandably want the best education for their children. However, these policies have been primarily targeted at parents, not the students themselves, who ultimately bear the consequences of such decisions.

Addressing the funding imbalance is crucial, especially in regions where wealthier suburbs often have better-funded schools. While it is essential to acknowledge the challenges faced by schools in economically disadvantaged areas, it is equally vital to recognise that schools in wealthier regions should receive appropriate funding reflective of their resources and requirements.

The notion of equity in education funding doesn't mean that one school is inherently more deserving than another. Rather, it seeks to ensure that all students, regardless of their background, have equal opportunities to access quality education. This requires a re-evaluation of the funding allocation process, possibly reducing excessive funding to some private schools while redirecting resources to areas where they are most needed.

While there may be valid arguments for providing certain types of assistance to private schools, such as teacher training, the ultimate goal should be to create a system where every student, regardless of their location or circumstances, has access to the same opportunities and support.

The Gonski reforms represented a step towards a fairer funding model that aimed to bridge the gap between public and private schools. However, their full potential remains unrealised, leaving room for improvement and reform to ensure that the education system truly prioritises the needs and opportunities of every child across Australia. Only through concerted efforts to prioritise equitable education funding can the nation strive towards a more balanced and inclusive schooling system, empowering all students to reach their full potential.

***

THE CONSERVATIVE MEDIA'S ENDLESS ATTACKS ON LABOR AND THE VOICE

22 July 2023

In recent weeks, the political landscape in Australia has remained relatively stable, with opinion polls showing little deviation from their long-standing trends. However, this has not deterred the conservative media from launching relentless attacks on Prime Minister Anthony Albanese and the Labor government, suggesting that its honeymoon period has come to a close and that it is facing mounting challenges.

Despite consistent poll numbers, certain voices in the mainstream media have painted a bleak picture for the Prime Minister and Labor and, regardless of the statistical evidence, the cheer squad and supporters in the conservative media are determined to promote the notion that the Liberal Party in opposition is somehow flourishing, while the Labor government is faltering.

Opinion polls, while showing slight variations over the previous six months, have actually been leaning favourably towards the Labor government, with the Resolve poll showing a two-party preferred vote of 58.5 per cent for Labor, and 41.5 per cent for the Liberal and National parties—hardly the sign of a "massive blow" for the Labor government.

Additionally, the recent federal byelection in Queensland seat of Fadden also suggests a lack of significant change in public sentiment. Nonetheless, the conservative media remains unswayed, continuously bolstering the image of a thriving Liberal Party headed by an unflappable leader, Peter Dutton.

Critics have questioned the media's persistence—News Corporation, Seven West Media, Nine Media and, increasingly, the ABC—in presenting a skewed narrative, essentially operating as propaganda outlets for conservative politics. The perception of biased reporting has led to renewed calls for a Royal Commission into the media in Australia, with proponents of an inquiry demanding a fair and unbiased source of information in the mainstream media.

While some figures in the conservative media such as *Herald Sun* opinion writer Andrew Bolt are predicting Albanese's potential overthrow—without any evidence to support this outcome—it is important to remember former Prime Minister Kevin Rudd was removed by Caucus in 2010, even though he was in a strong electoral position and very few people suspected such a move could occur. However, the circumstances today for Albanese differ significantly from those for Rudd in the past.

It is evident that public opinion is susceptible to media influence, and concerns have been raised over potential conflicts of interest within certain media circles. Calls for greater transparency and unbiased reporting continue, with the ultimate goal of a media landscape that presents the facts fairly and separates opinion from objective information.

For now, the stable polls suggest that the Labor government continues to hold its ground, while the conservative media's fervent anti-Labor narrative seems quite divorced from political realities.

A NEGATIVE FEAR-DRIVEN CAMPAIGN OF DIVISION CONTRIBUTING TO DECREASED SUPPORT FOR THE VOICE TO PARLIAMENT

As Australia moves closer to the crucial referendum on the Voice to Parliament, the latest Newspoll opinion poll indicates a decline in support, with figures showing a decrease to 43 per cent in favour and 49 per cent against the proposal. While some critics question the reliability of Newspoll figures, it is apparent that across various polls, support for the Voice to Parliament has been falling. The trajectory of public sentiment appears to resemble that of the Republic referendum in 1999, where initial enthusiasm waned as the debate raged on.

At the time, the Republic referendum faced a similar fate, with divisions within the campaign and a vacuum of leadership that was filled gleefully by the "no" campaigners. The ongoing negative campaign by figures such as Dutton has seemingly taken its toll, combined in a lack of political control over the narrative on the part of the proponents of the Voice to Parliament, most notably, the Prime Minister.

Albanese's recent call for the "yes" campaign to "step up" has raised concern, as though he was distancing himself from the initiative, with some belief that his comments are a sign that he might not want to bear the brunt of any potential failure if the referendum does not succeed.

There are also comparisons that can be drawn between Albanese's 2022 election night commitment to the Voice to Parliament and former Prime Minister John Howard during his 1998 election victory speech, where he pledged to achieve Reconciliation with Indigenous Australians by 2001, only for Howard to never mention this again, and then actively campaign against

Indigenous interests. To be sure, while the pledges by Albanese and Howard respectively may have had similar sentiments on their respective election night victory speeches, it's unfair to suggest Albanese has left the Voice to Parliament behind to squander, in the same way Howard left Reconciliation behind.

Albanese has actively advocated for the Voice to Parliament, prepared legislation for the referendum, and publicly committed to holding it. However, critics contend that more decisive action and an unwavering commitment are required to secure the necessary public support.

The heated debate surrounding the referendum has led to the release of information pamphlets from both sides. However, there is no requirement by the Australian Electoral Commission for the published material to be factual or truthful, leading to a web of fabrication in many of the "no" campaign's arguments.

Veteran journalist Kerry O'Brien highlighted one such example, where the "no" campaign claims that the Voice to Parliament "won't help Indigenous Australians", arguing that it is unreasonable to make such definitive statements, as the potential benefits of the Voice to Parliament are rooted in providing policymakers with greater access to the wisdom and perspectives of grassroots Indigenous communities.

CHALLENGES EXIST, YET THERE IS OPTIMISM FOR THE VOICE TO PARLIAMENT REFERENDUM

The tactics employed by Warren Mundine and the "no" campaign—especially targeting those religious groups who opposed the same-sex marriage plebiscite in 2017—is politically motivated and divisive and suggestive that not only are these groups homophobic, but they are fundamentally racist as well.

Drawing parallels with the litany of broken promises throughout Australia's history—King George's edict to Captain Arthur Phillip in 1787 for the British to enter into "peaceful negotiations" with Indigenous people, only for them to be massacred and have their land stolen from them; a promise of equal rights, only for these to never be granted; former Prime Minister Bob Hawke's 1988 promise for a Treaty; Howard's promise for Reconciliation by 2001—so many promises, yet none achieved—skepticism remains among some members of the Aboriginal and Torres Strait Islander community, who have been disappointed in the past by unfulfilled commitments.

Despite the challenges and negative campaigning, there remains optimism among proponents of the Voice to Parliament. Some observers believe that a change in Liberal Party leadership, with a new leader publicly supporting the "yes" vote, could potentially sway the outcome in favour of the referendum.

However, the path to success is not without obstacles, as the issue remains contentious—by those in public life who want the Voice to Parliament to be contentious and are creating as much division as possible—and winning over those who have reservations about the referendum will require significant effort.

THE STRUGGLE TO ACHIEVE TRUE RECONCILIATION
The struggle to achieve Reconciliation and progress for Indigenous Australians has been a long and arduous journey. Past promises of treaties and Reconciliation have yet to materialise, fueling skepticism and caution. The current proposal for the Voice to Parliament represents an opportunity for a step forward, even though some argue that starting small and building momentum may be the more pragmatic approach.

Despite the challenges and the uncertain road ahead, there remains hope that Australians will ultimately make the right decision when it comes to the referendum. While some fear a potential loss through lack of effort or divisive campaigning, others are optimistic that the Australian public will see the value in this initiative, embracing the opportunity to move towards a more inclusive and equitable society.

As the referendum approaches, the Australian public faces a critical decision. The fate of the Voice to Parliament initiative hangs in the balance, with both proponents and opponents making their cases. With the stakes high and the potential for positive change significant, Australians will be tasked with navigating through the sea of information and rhetoric to make an informed decision that aligns with the values and future they envision for their nation. The coming months will reveal whether history will repeat itself and continue with its long list of broken promises or whether this time, the nation will embrace the opportunity for progress and Reconciliation.

The significance of this referendum cannot be understated. The eyes of the nation are on this historic moment, waiting to see if the call for change and recognition will be answered with a resounding "yes".

***

DUTTON UNDER FIRE OVER OFFSHORE PROCESSING CORRUPTION ALLEGATIONS

29 July 2023

The Leader of the Opposition, Peter Dutton, finds himself embroiled in a scandal involving offshore processing contracts in Nauru and questions are being raised about Dutton's knowledge of dealings with a corrupt businessman who was convicted of corruption and bribery in 2020.

The controversy traces back to Dutton's tenure as the Minister for Home Affairs and a senior member of the Coalition government when the Australian Federal Police briefed Dutton on an investigation into businessman Mozammill Bhojani's corruption and bribery allegations in 2018. Despite this, the Department of Home Affairs proceeded to enter into new contracts with the Bohjani's company Radiance International, one month later and the company continued to be paid until May 2022, even after Bhojani's conviction.

Dutton must provide answers as to why the Australian government at the time continued to engage in contracts with a corrupt businessman. Calls for accountability have intensified, and there have been calls for Dutton to step down temporarily during the investigation. If found innocent, he return to his position; if he is not, he should then face further investigation and possible legal proceedings.

The public's frustration over such dubious dealings by politicians is reaching a tipping point. Dutton's leadership within the Liberal Party has also come into question, as he seems unable to garner the support needed to secure votes within the electorate—any dissatisfaction with the Labor government's handling of cost of living issues has not translated into a shift towards the Liberal Party, with opinion polls indicating any broader public disillusionment with the federal government is shifting over to independents and smaller political parties.

The Department of Home Affairs, created in 2017 and headed by Dutton at this time, has also come under further scrutiny. Critics argue that the amalgamation of various departments under one banner has resulted in a chaotic and poorly run organisation and Dutton's leadership style of the department, often characterised by a stereotypical Bjelke–Petersen Queensland Police mentality, has been criticised for prioritising appearances over practical results. Essentially, the Department of Home Affairs was a creation to continue Dutton's political ambitions to one day become prime minister, one which is unlikely to be ever achieved.

CALLS FOR ROYAL COMMISSION INTENSIFY

This scandal has also cast a shadow over the entire immigration and offshore detention system. The Australian Greens have called for a Royal Commission to investigate not just this specific issue but also the cruel and barbaric treatment of asylum seekers and the allocation of government funds within the system—as well as the possible links that several corporate entities have with the Liberal Party, raising suspicions of potential financial gains for some senior Coalition members.

Concerns about the financial dealings and connections of certain entities—such as Paladin, Canstruct, Radiance International—involved in the offshore processing contracts have also emerged, with strong ties to the Liberal Party and individuals on the ground in Nauru and Manus Island in Papua New Guinea. The conditions in these detention facilities were described as "rickety", poorly constructed, and understaffed, leaving many wondering where the large sums of money allocated to these projects ultimately went.

How can a company with assets of $8—in the case of Canstruct—be awarded $1.6 billion in government contracts, without any experience in offshore detention services? Or $423 million to Paladin, a little-known security provider which was registered in a beach shack on Kangaroo Island and postal address located in Singapore? The cost of this contract was estimated to be $1,600 *per person, per day*, excluding food or welfare services. That is an astronomical amount.

FUNNELLING PROFITS TO COALITION MINISTERS?

A recent parliamentary inquiry exposed the proposed structure by the Synergy 360 lobbying firm, potentially enabling former Coalition Minister Stuart Robert to profit from government contracts. Robert has denied these allegations—which is what he'd be expected to say—but material that is provided to parliamentary inquiries usually has substance and some credibility must be attributed to such claims. This development has further heightened suspicions surrounding financial dealings within the former Coalition government.

While the link between Synergy 360 and Stuart Robert—or to the Liberal Party—is yet to be proven, will there be other allegations made of legal structures that were created by Paladin or Canstruct, primarily to benefit other Coalition MPs and Ministers? Or a slush fund for other political purposes?

This has raised questions about the true extent of corruption within the ranks of the former Coalition government, and the vast sums of money involved point to a deeper systemic issue that has the potential to further erode public trust in the political system.

It also provides some pointers to why the Coalition delayed the establishment of a national anti-corruption commission—it was promised by former Prime Minister Scott Morrison in 2018, and never came to fruition under his government—with many now speculating that the reluctance to introduce such a commission was an attempt to shield themselves from future scrutiny.

It is clear that accountability and transparency within the offshore detention system is urgently needed. As the calls for Royal Commission by the Australian Greens become louder, there needs to be an in-depth investigation into these alleged corrupt practices and financial connections.

A properly conducted and clearly defined Royal Commission could serve the public interest by providing comprehensive answers and holding those responsible accountable, without the need for a government to become embroiled in political games. The Royal Commission into the Robodebt Scheme was an excellent example of this: clearly defined, professionally managed, and letting the facts speak for themselves.

Although the most senior public servant responsible for the Robodebt Scheme has resigned—Kathryn Campbell—questions persist about whether justice will be fully served and whether all parties involved will be held accountable; for example, Scott Morrison, Stuart Robert, Alan Tudge and Christian Porter. The public demands transparency and assurances that all individuals involved will face the consequences of their actions, regardless of their position.

But, still, it did show the public interest being served by a well-defined Royal Commission, and the Albanese government should follow this up with a clearly defined investigation into the offshore immigration detention system.

In the aftermath of this scandal, it is evident that sweeping reforms are necessary to address systemic loopholes and corruption, not only within offshore immigration detention, but all of government activity—which of course, is the rationale behind the newly-created National Anti-Corruption Commission.

Dutton's reputation and political future hang in the balance as the public demands answers and calls for accountability intensify. The extent of the corruption and its impact on Australia's political climate will undoubtedly be subjects of intense public debate in the coming weeks.

***

AUSTRALIA'S FIRST WELLBEING BUDGET: A PARADIGM SHIFT

29 July 2023

In a groundbreaking move, Treasurer Jim Chalmers has unveiled Australia's first-ever wellbeing budget, officially known as the Measuring What Matters: National Wellbeing Framework. This innovative approach to budgeting aims to bridge the gap between financial prosperity and the social wellbeing of the Australian community, prioritising the needs of real people over abstract fiscal concepts.

Chalmers emphasised that budgeting should not merely revolve around numbers and economic indicators like budget surpluses or deficits. Instead, it should encompass a comprehensive assessment of how financial decisions made by the government impact the lives of citizens and the nation as a whole.

"The traditional measures are important, but they don't give the full picture," Chalmers said. "The government's primary focus is addressing inflation and laying the foundations for future growth, but it is important that we simultaneously work on better aligning our economic and social goals in our communities and right across the country."

The newly introduced Wellbeing Framework intends to serve as a measuring tool that draws together all aspects of government activities, guiding policies and spending towards promoting the wellbeing of the people. Chalmers further expressed that such a shift is necessary to assess the social costs of achieving budget surpluses and to ensure that the benefits are equitably distributed among the population.

However, the Framework has not been without its critics, with detractors primarily coming from conservative media outlets such as News Corporation, Nine Media and Seven West Media. Critics have been quick to pinpoint minor flaws in the report, magnifying these issues in an attempt to undermine the initiative. Nevertheless, Chalmers has defended the Framework, suggesting that social scientists have been effectively measuring similar indicators for decades, and it is high time the government takes notice of their findings.

The Wellbeing Framework is examines 50 key indicators, ranging from life expectancy and job satisfaction, to health outcomes, mental health, environmental issues, financial stress, and safety. Several countries, including Scotland, New Zealand, Finland, Wales, Germany, Iceland, and Canada, have already implemented wellbeing budgets successfully. The positive impact of these initiatives on their respective societies serves as evidence that such a shift in budgeting can be effective.

Former Treasurer Josh Frydenberg dismissed and ridiculed the wellbeing concept in 2019—offensively alluding to ashrams, incense, and lewd commentary about 'yoga positions'—but alternative approaches are necessary to ensure the wellbeing of the nation, rather than solely focusing on crude statistical measurements that focus primarily on budget surpluses and deficits. The success of the Wellbeing Framework lies in its ability to account for the social consequences of financial decisions, paving the way for a more holistic and sustainable economy.

The media's reception of the Wellbeing Framework has been mixed. While some media outlets lauded the initiative as a crucial step forward, others have resorted to criticism, displaying a lack of understanding and, at times, resorting to baseless and childish attacks, which simply support their anti-Labor narrative, rather than looking at the merits of alternative—and better—ways of ensuring the finances of the federal government are working towards the wellbeing of the community, and a more comprehensive evaluation of social, cultural, and political impacts on the people that make up an economy.

Conservative opposition parties, particularly the Liberal and National parties, have also been quick to criticise the Wellbeing Framework. However, given their delivery of poor budget outcomes between 2013–2022, their attacks have been shallow and lacking in substance. Former Treasurer Joe Hockey's 2014 budget faced significant backlash and almost ground the economy to a halt, while Scott Morrison's subsequent budgets also caused economic difficulties.

Moreover, the recent budgets presented by Josh Frydenberg, which centred on significant cost-cutting measures, failed to garner enough support for passage, and saw the economy heading towards recession in late 2019, with only the onset of the COVID pandemic stopping his reputation as a financial manager deteriorating even further.

It's evident that these critics from the opposition want to avoid a focus on social and cultural impacts because it adds another level of scrutiny to their budget proposals. They question the need for additional considerations beyond traditional economic measurements, suggesting that these new perspectives may not reflect well on their budgetary decisions.

THE PRIMARY FUNCTIONS OF A WELLBEING ECONOMY

However, proponents of wellbeing budgets and the new economic thinking it embodies, such as economist Professor Mariana Mazzucato and Chief Executive Officer at VicHealth, Dr. Sandro Demaio, stress the importance of incorporating human factors into budgetary decisions. They advocate for a reorientation of economic activities around health and wellbeing, emphasising the need to create fiscal space for comprehensive health measures. Mazzucato further encourages forging symbiotic relationships between public and private actors, working together to achieve common goals.

Demaio highlights three fundamental aspects of a wellbeing economy approach: long-term planning, equal value to social, health, and environmental markers of success, and prioritisation of essential areas like housing, education, social and employment issues, and preventative health. These perspectives argue for a more inclusive and equitable economic model, prioritising the wellbeing of all citizens and future generations.

Despite the support from economists and experts, some members of the mainstream media remain hesitant to embrace these new ideas fully. They often gravitate towards conventional political figures and conservative ideologies. Critics argue that the media's reliance on these voices fails to present a more diverse and informed discussion on the potential benefits of a Wellbeing Budget.

The debates surrounding the Wellbeing Budget reflect Australia's broader crossroads when it comes to economic, political, environmental, and social reforms. As the country continues to grapple with the ongoing effects of the COVID-19 pandemic, the opportunity for governments to implement progressive approaches to problem-solving becomes paramount.

In contrast, the opposition's approach has been uninspiring, obstructing progress without presenting viable alternatives. The lack of a clear and defined purpose for the opposition has raised concerns among the public, who expect constructive contributions to the national debate on critical issues.

As the discussions evolve, the Wellbeing Budget and the broader new economic thinking behind it remain points of contention and hope for the future. While opposition parties continue to resist, many experts and citizens call for a more inclusive and compassionate economic model that benefits all members of society.

Australia's path towards reform will require innovative ideas and a willingness to challenge established norms. Whether the Wellbeing Framework becomes a permanent fixture or not, it has undoubtedly opened the door to broader discussions about the nation's future and the wellbeing of its people.

The success of the Wellbeing Framework will depend on how well it is embraced and implemented over the next few years. However, it may revolutionise budgeting practices and serve as a model for other countries looking to create more inclusive and people-centric economies.

***

AUGUST

MORRISON'S ROBODEBT DENIAL FACES FIERCE CRITICISM

5 August 2023

The Australian Parliament came alive with renewed activity last week, with many critical issues vying for attention. While housing, education, and Reconciliation initiatives are crucial, it's the spectre from the past that refuses to fade into obscurity: the sinister Robodebt scheme and the damning Royal Commission report.

The Housing Australia Future Fund and the progress towards Reconciliation through an amplified Voice to Parliament are undoubtedly pressing matters. However, they seem overshadowed by the shadows of Coalition government program that wreaked havoc on countless lives. The Robodebt debacle, a scheme designed to supposedly claw back social security overpayments, has resurfaced with a vengeance as the aftermath of the Royal Commission report unfolds.

In a striking display of audacity, the former Prime Minister, Scott Morrison, brazenly dismissed the Commission's damning findings against him. The report meticulously detailed the unintended suffering inflicted on individuals and their families yet, Morrison staunchly asserts that he bears no responsibility, denouncing the Commission's conclusions as "disproportionate, incorrect, and unsubstantiated".

There are chilling echoes of Morrison's rhetoric in the divisive tactics employed by former U.S. President Donald Trump, a style of politics that we thought we might have left behind. Morrison's claims that he is a victim of political targeting also ignited a war of words with Minister for Government Services, Bill Shorten, who vehemently countered that the real victims are those whose lives were lost and trust eroded due to the unlawful scheme, not Morrison, who he labelled "a bottomless well of self-pity with not a drop of mercy for all of the real victims of Robodebt".

Shorten's impassioned response, laced with anger and frustration, drove home the enormity of the pain inflicted by the Robodebt scheme, emphasising that those who suffered were not politicians such as Morrison protected by parliamentary privilege, but everyday Australians stripped of their dignity and livelihoods. The Royal Commission, hailed as one of the most comprehensive and exhaustive in modern times, wielded its authority to reveal the truth behind the former government's actions.

However, Morrison's attempts to belittle the Commission's legitimacy have sparked a fierce criticisms from other quarters. His attempts to disentangle himself from the scheme's web of consequences, insisting that he is not accountable for its repercussions, made him look foolish. Morrison's evasion of responsibility is emblematic of the broader political trend that existing during the Liberal–National Coalitions time in office between 2013–22, echoing the public's frustration with politicians who evade accountability at every turn.

In the court of public opinion, Morrison's defence stands—labelled by Shorten as the "Morrisonian Doctrine" of lies and mistruths—on shaky ground. Comparing the Royal Commission's rigour to that of landmark inquiries such as the banking Royal Commission, or the investigation into child sexual abuse in religious institutions, the implications of this report may lead to fundamental reforms in Australia's political landscape. Yet, the former Prime Minister's refusal to accept his role in the debacle remains a symbol of his obstinacy.

IGNORANCE OF THE ROBODEBT FACTS

How can Morrison be so ignorant of the facts? The Robodebt scheme followed a painstakingly and forensically detailed examination by the Commission, encompassing thorough investigations and testimonies, bringing to light the extent of the suffering endured by countless individuals and their families due to the flawed scheme.

The voices of witnesses, often lost in the political manoeuvring from the Coalition at the time, and a mainstream media which showed a noticeable reluctance to engage deeply with the issue, found a platform through independent media outlets, which initially were instigated through the work of information activist, Asher Wolf.

The proceedings, though, were not lost on the public. The transparency and accountability displayed by the Royal Commission stood in stark contrast to Morrison's response, which were purely attempts to sidestep his own culpability and the former Prime Minister's insistent denial of the Commission's findings raises serious questions about the nature of accountability in the political landscape.

As Morrison endeavours to distance himself from the Robodebt debacle, suspicions have grown regarding his motivations, possibly a pre-emptive measure in preparation for potential appearances at the National Anti-Corruption Commission, where his actions could face further scrutiny.

Other former Ministers, such as Alan Tudge and Christian Porter, who were also under scrutiny due to their involvement in the Robodebt scheme, could also face investigation by the National Anti Corruption Commission, despite their assertions that they were not named within the special "sealed section" of the Royal Commission report. However, despite these assertions from former Ministers, the aftermath of the Robodebt report underscores the complexity of the situation and the need for thorough investigations to reveal the complete truth.

In the midst of this political storm, the public demands answers. Morrison's dismissive demeanour during Shorten's accusations, coupled with his apparent lack of remorse, has left many astounded, with Morrison laughing in parliament while Shorten's comments were being made—surely not the best response to make when considered the lives forever altered by the effects of the Robodebt scheme.

One question still lingers: can a nation truly move forward when its leaders refuse to face the past? The urgency for accountability will intensify as survivors and affected families demand justice through potential class action lawsuits. The previous government's efforts to whitewash the debacle could also be challenged by a legal reckoning that transcends the confines of political privilege.

The question of Morrison's political future also looms large, with his already-damaged reputation tarnished further by his insolent response to the Commission's report. His reluctance to accept accountability is at odds with a public that demands transparency and responsibility from their leaders. As the nation grapples with the aftermath of this ordeal, one thing is certain: the debate over political accountability has only just begun, and the waves of reform it ushers in are likely to reverberate for years to come.

***

CALLS INTENSIFY FOR A ROYAL COMMISSION INTO IMMIGRATION DETENTION

5 August 2023

While all eyes have been on former Prime Minister Scott Morrison and his inept defence for his actions in the Robodebt scheme, more pressure has been mounting on the current leader of the Liberal Party, Peter Dutton. The latest public demands for accountability have led to renewed calls for a Royal Commission into immigration detention practices, an issue that has stirred outcry and ignited a heated debate within federal parliament.

The impetus for this renewed push for a Royal Commission stems from a series of revelations that have surfaced over the past weeks that the Home Affairs Department, under the purview of Peter Dutton, entered into significant contracts with a businessman who was under investigation for allegations of corruption and bribery. This revelation, combined with comments made by Dutton himself, has only exacerbated the controversy surrounding his tenure and actions during his time in office.

During a recent exchange, Dutton asserted: "as Minister I had no involvement whatsoever in relation to the contract negotiations, the execution of the agreements". He also emphasised that the procurement arrangements in place during his tenure were consistent with those of his predecessors and maintained that he was not privy to any briefing related to the matter and had no memory of receiving such information.

These assertions, however, have not gone unchallenged. The Australian Federal Police has refuted Dutton's claim, asserting that a meeting between him and the law enforcement agency *did* indeed occur. The discrepancy in statements has further fueled suspicions and intensified the demand for a thorough investigation.

In response to growing public concern, the federal Labor government has taken initial steps by initiating an independent inquiry into the contracts involving the businessman in question. However, critics argue that this step may not suffice, given the gravity of the allegations and the broader issues at play within the immigration detention system.

This controversy has reignited calls for a Royal Commission into immigration detention practices. Advocates argue that such a commission would provide an avenue for an impartial, thorough examination of the matter, uncovering the truth behind the alleged corrupt practices and ensuring transparency within the system.

However, the question of whether a Royal Commission will be established remains contentious. Some believe that the government should gather all relevant information before announcing such a commission, in order to avoid unnecessary expenditures and bureaucratic delays. Furthermore, there is a perception that the many parts of the electorate are not invested in pursuing a fair and transparent immigration detention system and asylum seekers, potentially creating a complex political problem for the Albanese government.

The potential implications of a Royal Commission extend beyond addressing the immediate controversy. It could also create political opportunities for conservative opposition parties—especially the Liberal Party—who have always leveraged anti-asylum seeker rhetoric to gain an advantage. As a result, the decision to establish a Royal Commission into the immigration detention system is a complex and delicate one, with political, ethical, and practical considerations at play.

IMMIGRATION AS THE POLITICAL PLAY TOOL FOR CONSERVATIVES

The issue of immigration detention and treatment of refugees has long been a source of easy political capital for conservative parties, manoeuvring to find a stance that resonates with their respective voter bases. A comparison of records reveals a nuanced dynamic; Labor's position arguably reflects a marginally better track record in handling refugee and asylum seeker issues in some instances. However, the broader trend suggests that the Liberal Party, particularly since John Howard's tenure between 1996–2007, has been more prone to adopting a hardline approach and milking every opportunity to gain advantage from the more racist parts of the electorate.

The core question remains: what are Australia's obligations in the 21st century, over 70 years after the establishment of the 1951 *Refugee Convention*? Many argue that these obligations endure, grounded in the principle of protecting those seeking refuge from persecution. However, the underlying moral imperative to treat refugees fairly and humanely has often been overshadowed by political considerations—especially when looking at Australia's treatment of asylum seekers and genuine refugees in Nauru and

Manus Island—but there is a growing sentiment that it is time to reassert this moral compass.

The call for a Royal Commission has gained traction, with various political figures and parties demanding an impartial and comprehensive investigation into the matter. Senator Nick McKim from the Australian Greens emphasised the gravity of the allegations, stating that "highly credible and extremely serious allegations of systemic corruption" require the scrutiny that only a Royal Commission can provide.

Zoe Daniel, the independent member for Goldstein, added her voice to these concerns, highlighting the need for a broader independent inquiry into offshore processing contracts that continued despite warnings about the businessman's investigation. The Prime Minister, Anthony Albanese, has refrained from directly mentioning a Royal Commission but underscored the responsibility of Dutton to explain the expenditure of taxpayer money.

The potential for a Royal Commission hinges on many factors, encompassing both political calculations and public interest. Establishing a Royal Commission requires a delicate balance between political benefit and addressing genuine concerns. However, the urgency to address the lack of transparency and accountability within the immigration detention system has heightened the pressure on the government.

The issue extends beyond Dutton, with broader systemic questions about immigration detention practices in Australia. Critics argue that billions of dollars have been spent without proper accountability, necessitating an in-depth investigation to shed light on the allocation of resources and the treatment of those within the system.

The political fallout and ethical implications of the situation are far-reaching. The public's demand for transparency and accountability underscores a growing expectation for integrity within the political sphere. The potential long-term consequences for Peter Dutton's political career are uncertain, but the mounting controversies are undoubtedly eroding his standing within the opposition, a position which is possibly too low to be resurrected.

The pressure on Dutton will continue to mount, as will the calls for the Albanese government to hold a high-profile investigation as soon as possible. The enduring calls for a Royal Commission underscore the public's deep-seated concerns about transparency, accountability, and fairness within the immigration detention system. It is evident that while the debate might ebb and flow in the short term, there needs to be a critical spotlight cast on the functioning of the nation's institutions and the conduct of its political leaders.

***

GREAT BARRIER REEF IN DANGER: AUSTRALIA'S ENVIRONMENTAL EFFORTS ATTACKED

5 August 2023

Amid growing concerns over the fate of the world's most iconic coral ecosystem, the Great Barrier Reef, the United Nations Educational, Scientific and Cultural Organization (UNESCO) has announced a surprising decision to defer its verdict on listing the reef as 'in danger' for another year. This announcement comes as a stark contrast to its previous stance, highlighting a shift in the Australian government's approach towards reef preservation over the past year.

The announcement, although met with cautious optimism by environmentalists, raises questions about the extent of Australia's commitment to safeguarding this natural wonder in the face of mounting climate threats. The reef's health has been significantly impacted by rising ocean temperatures and coral bleaching events, which are increasingly attributed to global climate change.

The Minister for the Environment, Tanya Plibersek, underscored the efforts of the Australian government in an attempt to justify UNESCO's decision. "The actions of our government have changed," Plibersek stated. "We've worked very closely with UNESCO and the Queensland Government, investing $1.2 billion in additional funding to protect the reef and addressing issues such as water quality, fisheries management, and the impact of marine pollution."

One of the pivotal factors contributing to this shift is the Australian government's renewed focus on climate change. The move towards renewable energy and the commitment to legislating a pathway to net-zero greenhouse emissions have been highlighted as significant differentiators by UNESCO. The minister emphasised that these measures are crucial in combating the impacts of climate change, which threaten the very survival of coral reefs across the globe.

However, critics argue that the Australian government's efforts, while commendable on some fronts, remain insufficient in the grand scheme of reef preservation. Despite the rhetoric of progress, the federal Labor government has faced criticism for granting approvals to new coal mines and thermal coal projects. Most notably, the controversial Isaac River Mine project and a recent thermal coal mine approval in Queensland have raised concerns about the government's genuine dedication to curbing carbon emissions.

Environmental activists emphasise that even with a shift in messaging, Australia's actions on the ground are far from comprehensive. While an emphasis on renewable energy and greenhouse gas reduction is indeed a step in the right direction, the persistent approval of fossil fuel projects contradicts these goals. The delicate balance between economic interests and environmental stewardship continues to challenge the government's credibility on the global stage.

As the world grapples with the devastating impacts of climate change, the recent news of July marking the hottest month on record and escalating temperatures in the eastern states of Australia further underscore the urgency of the situation. Experts assert that the reef's vulnerability to warming waters and coral bleaching is far from abating, making the case for immediate and meaningful action even more imperative.

While UNESCO's decision to delay the Great Barrier Reef's endangered listing reflects some positive strides by the Australian government, the underlying question remains: Are these measures enough? Environmentalists and experts argue that while progress is evident, Australia must go beyond incremental changes and adopt more substantial and long-term strategies to truly protect this irreplaceable natural treasure for generations to come.

AUSTRALIA'S CLIMATE CROSSROADS: BALANCING URGENCY AND REALPOLITIK

As the world record July heat continues to cast a spotlight on the pressing climate crisis, Australia finds itself grappling with a complex juggling act—one that involves not only mitigating environmental degradation but also navigating the intricate web of political and economic interests. With rising temperatures, unprecedented fires, and a changing climate landscape, the nation stands at a critical juncture, requiring tough decisions that have long-term consequences.

Heatwaves and fires: July's record-breaking heat has shattered previous temperature thresholds, with experts reporting unprecedented levels of heat discomfort. In Iran, the Persian Gulf International Airport's alarming heat index of 66.7 degrees Celsius serves as a chilling reminder of the perilous conditions humanity faces due to unchecked climate change. Australia, too, is feeling the heat, with rising temperatures and intensifying bushfires painting a grim picture for the coming months. The past scars of the devastating bushfire season of 2019/20 remain fresh, casting a shadow of anxiety over communities across the country.

UNESCO's Great Barrier Reef debate: The ongoing discourse surrounding the Great Barrier Reef's endangered status further underscores the high stakes of Australia's climate dilemma. UNESCO's delayed decision on listing the reef as endangered highlights the Australian government's efforts to address concerns about coral reef deterioration. Nevertheless, critics argue that the peril facing the reef is not diminished by diplomatic manoeuvrings—it's a global environmental concern that transcends political discourse.

Labor's balancing act: The Labor government faces a delicate balancing act between championing environmental responsibility and ensuring the livelihoods of workers in industries that contribute to emissions. While environmentalists demand urgent action to curb carbon emissions, the complexities of transitioning away from fossil fuels demand careful planning and execution. Critics suggest that Labor's efforts have been promising but lack the decisive impact needed to match the scale of the challenge.

Mismatched state and federal agendas: Australia's climate strategy remains fragmented, with states pursuing varying agendas in coal and gas projects that often contradict national emission reduction goals. The disjointed approach, with states and federal government acting independently, raises concerns about a lack of co-ordinated action towards a shared goal.

Climate fatigue and delayed response: The urgency of addressing climate change is undeniable, yet the gap between rhetoric and action continues to widen. Observers argue that successive governments' limited measures, often framed as a compromise between environmental concerns and economic realities, have fallen short of the transformation required to avert the worst impacts of global warming. Critics assert that the incremental pace of change fails to acknowledge the immediacy of the threat.

Australia's climate debate mirrors the global struggle between economic interests and environmental imperatives. The heightened reality of hotter temperatures, more frequent fires, and changing ecosystems amplifies the urgency for decisive action. The challenge is not only for governments but also for individuals, corporations, and civil society to align their practices with the demands of the planet.

As political leaders grapple with the complexity of climate change, scientists' warnings resonate. The recurring 'wake up calls'—from record-breaking temperatures to environmental catastrophes—serve as stark reminders that the world cannot afford to ignore the evidence any longer.

Australia's choice, like that of nations worldwide, is to heed these warnings and embrace the transformative actions needed to safeguard the planet's future, or to risk being remembered as the generation that knew the crisis but failed to act. The path forward lies in finding common ground between competing interests and making choices that prioritise the health of the planet over short-term gains.

***

DIVISIVE POLITICS: DUTTON'S FEAR AND LOATHING ON THE VOICE TO PARLIAMENT

12 August 2023

In a political issue marked by increasing polarisation, opposition leader Peter Dutton is attempting to recalibrate his leadership of the Liberal Party by engaging in an increasing racist campaign to vehemently oppose the Voice to Parliament. This move has raised concerns about the tactics employed to undermine a significant step towards Indigenous reconciliation and empowerment and Dutton's actions not only threaten to deepen divisions within the nation but also shed light on his personal ambitions and the tactics he is willing to employ to achieve them.

The issue gained further traction following the Garma Festival in Arnhem Land, a significant Indigenous cultural event presented annually. The festival showcased a spirit of goodwill and unity, but Dutton's absence spoke volumes about his stance on Indigenous matters. Prime Minister Anthony Albanese's suggestion for Dutton to attend the festival was met with refusal, underscoring the growing divide within the political landscape.

Albanese's invitation highlighted the significance of the Voice to Parliament, a progressive proposal aimed at addressing historical inequities and fostering greater representation for First Nations people in Australia. However, Dutton's refusal to engage constructively with Indigenous communities underscores a troubling pattern of avoiding dialogue and perpetuating fear.

Dutton's engagement with media outlets known for their conservative leanings, such as Ray Hadley's shock-jock show on 2GB, further indicates a preference for divisive tactics over inclusive discourse. The absence of direct communication with Indigenous communities and the electorate suggests a willingness to stoke the flames of discontent while avoiding accountability.

The opposition leader's strategy becomes even clearer in the context of the ongoing campaign against the Voice to Parliament and his narrative revolves around sowing seeds of doubt, using fear, and appealing to divisive sentiments. His opposition hinges on insinuations that the Voice to Parliament proposal would empower only a select group of hitherto unknown Indigenous 'elites', thereby ignoring the broader benefits for marginalised Indigenous communities.

The underlying motives for Dutton's stance become evident when viewed through the prism of his own leadership ambitions. With the spectre of the next federal election looming, Dutton appears to be capitalising on divisive tactics to secure his political foothold. However, this approach raises questions about the kind of leadership Australians deserve.

Dutton's aversion to the Voice to Parliament reflects a broader trend within the conservative political landscape. Employing the familiar playbook of sowing chaos and blaming others for the ensuing division, Dutton's approach appears more focused on self-preservation than addressing the complex challenges faced by Indigenous communities.

This divisive strategy is not without its critics. Observers argue that Dutton's tactics rely on fear-mongering and misinformation. By focusing on issues like treaties and the Indigenous Voice, Dutton redirects attention from economic concerns and the cost of living, exploiting public anxieties to maintain his political relevance.

Dutton's resistance on this occasion is not an isolated incident; it's part of a larger pattern of utilising fear as a political tool, as well as hostility to Indigenous issues—his opposition hinges on notions of white 'loss' and resentment, tapping into fears of dispossession and change. This approach draws comparisons to past instances—in 1997, former Prime Minister John Howard claimed during negotiations on the Wik legislation that 78 per cent of 'backyards' were vulnerable to native title claims—where similar tactics were used to stoke division and maintain the status quo.

In contrast, proponents of the Voice to Parliament believe that this initiative represents a step towards Reconciliation and empowerment of First Nations people. Critics of Dutton's strategy argue that it perpetuates a politics of fear and negativity, sidestepping the constructive dialogue required for meaningful progress. As the opposition leader doubles down on his stance, the divide between those advocating for inclusivity and those appealing to fear continues to widen.

COALITION'S POLITICAL GAMESMANSHIP UNDERMINES THE NATIONAL INTEREST AND INDIGENOUS RIGHTS

In a recent revelation by the *Australian Financial Review*, a disturbing pattern of political subterfuge within the Liberal Party has come to light, suggesting that the party's primary motivation behind their opposition to the Voice to Parliament proposal is not only to quash a vital initiative for First Nations people but to also gain a political upper hand, further highlighting their disregard for the national interest.

In the Senate, Senator Penny Wong astutely pointed out that figures such as Dutton are perpetuating the legacy of former Prime Minister Scott Morrison, consistently prioritising their political agenda over the broader interests of the country and the sentiment expressed by a Liberal Party MP that victory in the upcoming election hinges on defeating the Voice to Parliament underscores this unscrupulous strategy.

The Coalition's approach reeks of political nihilism, exploiting a matter of public significance—the Voice to Parliament—as a mere pawn in their quest for power. Their meanderings are not only a blow to the aspirations of First Nations people seeking a meaningful platform but also a testament to the Liberal Party's willingness to exploit any issue, no matter how crucial, for their own political gains.

The focus isn't on the merits of this proposal or its potential to address historical injustices; rather, it's a strategic attempt to undermine Prime Minister Albanese. This brand of political opportunism is not only a disservice to the electorate but a grave disservice to the spirit of democracy itself.

Moreover, the commentary on Dutton's ambitions for the prime ministership is a stark reminder of his divisive history. Dutton, a political figure whose legacy seems rooted in negativity, has consistently demonstrated a propensity for discord whether in government or opposition: walking out of the Apology to the Stolen Generations in 2008; his attempts to sway the result of the 2018 Victoria election with his 'African gangs' narrative; his decision to overturn the dual Indigenous naming of army bases while he was Minister for Defense.

His controversial decisions, including overlooking community safety programs in Indigenous communities while serving as Minister for Home Affairs, are emblematic of a leadership style that thrives on chaos.

Critically, this narrative also highlights the vital role of media in upholding democratic values. The lack of stringent scrutiny and accountability from the mainstream media has allowed politicians like Dutton to persist with their self-serving agendas unchecked, thereby perpetuating the erosion of public trust.

As the political landscape continues to evolve, the discourse must shift towards genuine national interests and progressive reforms rather than short-term political victories. The Liberal Party's calculated moves demonstrate a disregard for the greater good, mirroring global trends of populism and misinformation that ultimately undermine the foundations of a just and equitable society.

Within this context, the Labor government needs to eschew 'politics of politeness' in favour of assertiveness is a plea for substantive change. The message resonates with a need for realignment toward policies that reflect centrist Australia and transcend the corrosive influences of divisive politics.

In hindsight, the Labor government's delay in pushing for a referendum on the Voice to Parliament into the end of 2023 was a mistake, as it allowed room for misinformation campaigns orchestrated by vested interests. This serves as a cautionary tale of missed opportunities and the importance of seizing the momentum when the public sentiment is most favourable, which would have been the case soon after the Labor government was elected in May 2023.

UNMASKING THE COALITION'S TACTICS

The underhanded tactics employed by the Liberal and National parties during parliamentary question time have extended this narrative of manipulation, misinformation, and opportunism, and provocative questions from figures such as Dutton and deputy leader Sussan Ley have laid bare a strategic ploy to hijack valuable parliamentary time and create the illusion of inordinate focus on the Voice to Parliament initiative. So why is Albanese taking on these questions with the importance that they do not deserve?

Albanese's inclination to provide comprehensive answers to seemingly absurd questions has inadvertently played into the Liberal Party hands, allowing them to craft a narrative that he is excessively engrossed in the Voice to Parliament, even though it's the Liberal Party itself that is obsessed. This tactic serves a dual purpose: firstly, to divert attention from the urgency of rights of First Nations people and constitutional reform, and secondly, to cast Albanese as preoccupied to a fault, thereby painting a picture of unbalanced priorities.

The recurring mention of a 'conspiracy theory' surrounding the length of the Uluru Statement from the Heart is a classic case of political smoke and mirrors. The Coalition's attempt to delegitimise the statement by insinuating that it is longer than it actually is seeks to undermine the credibility of Indigenous voices—as if whether a document is either one page or 26 pages is really a public debate worth having—and reveals the desperation behind the Coalition's efforts to fabricate discord where there is none.

However, these machinations transcend mere parliamentary tactics. They expose a larger pattern of behaviour that extends back years, all the way back to 1996 with the election of the Howard government, who was elected on the promise of national harmony, only to spend the next 11 years in office creating as much chaos and division as possible, a legacy that still remains with the Liberal Party. The Coalition's history of divisive strategies, stoking xenophobia, and exploiting societal fault lines for political gain is a stark reminder that their priorities lie more in retaining power than in serving the nation.

The reluctance of the Coalition to support the Voice to Parliament resonates with their larger pattern of resistance to change. Rather than embracing meaningful reform, the Coalition seems locked in a time capsule, clinging to the Howard-era conservatism. This refusal to evolve and address the needs of a changing Australia may ultimately prove detrimental to their political future.

The challenge now for the Labor government, as well as for all Australians, is to demand transparency, accountability, and genuine commitment to the public interest. The Coalition's gambit to manipulate parliamentary discourse, evade real issues, and exploit divisions should serve as a wakeup call to the electorate.

The responsibility lies with citizens to demand better from their elected representatives and to reject the corrosive brand of politics that prioritises personal ambition over the collective wellbeing of the nation. However, this task is difficult with a compliant mainstream media which is always happy to work in unison with the Coalition in stoking and perpetuating these fears, as is currently being displayed in their magnification and amplification of every small matter that could offer some benefit and improvement for the life of First Nations people.

In the face of these tactics, it is paramount that the Australian people remain vigilant, recognising that the nation's future hinges on leaders who prioritise the public good over short-term gains. The battle for the soul of Australian democracy is ongoing, and it is imperative that it is fought with unwavering determination, fact-based discourse, and a commitment to a better and more just future.

Ultimately, Dutton's refusal to engage with Indigenous communities and his rejection of the Voice to Parliament reflects a regressive approach to politics that prioritises his personal ambitions over the wellbeing of the nation. Australians deserve leaders who are willing to embrace unity, engage in informed dialogue, and work towards a more inclusive future. As the debate continues, the question remains whether Dutton's divisive tactics will prevail or whether Australia will opt for a path of reconciliation, progress, and hope.

***

THE TROUBLING SAGA OF THE LEHRMANN TRIAL

12 August 2023

In a perplexing turn of events, the report from the Board of Inquiry into the Criminal Justice System—specifically into the trial of Bruce Lehrmann, accused of an alleged rape at Australian Parliament House in 2019—has been unveiled. However, far from providing a sense of closure, the report has ignited a wave of criticism directed at the judiciary and handling of the case by the Australian Federal Police. This trial's narrative is a poignant reminder of systemic failures within the criminal justice system and the undeniable need for transparency and accountability, especially when it comes to sexual violence perpetrated against women.

The unraveling of the trial of Lehrmann began in October 2022, when jury misconduct led to its abrupt termination. The ensuing inquiry, commissioned by the ACT government and led by Walter Sofronoff KC, was entrusted with examining the trial's mishandling. The findings are distressing: a cascade of mishaps involving Liberal Party ministers, the Australian Federal Police, and the maltreatment of the complainant in the trial, Brittany Higgins. The report's release raises grave concerns about the legitimacy and fairness of the judicial process.

Prominent legal commentators, including Geoffrey Watson, former counsel assisting to the NSW Independent Commission Against Corruption and a director of the Centre for Public Integrity, have not minced words in condemning the report's perceived targeting of ACT public prosecutor Shane Drumgold, who subsequently resigned. "The language used against Drumgold is severe," Watson said. "It reads to me like an effort to wreck Drumgold, his reputation and his career [and] it has probably had that effect".

The report's alleged bias has ignited suspicions that the investigation's integrity has been compromised and the notion that the head of the inquiry maintained a continuous dialogue with journalists, culminating in the delivery of the final report to a senior News Corporation journalist,

Janet Albrechtsen, before being presented to the ACT government, further undermines the process's credibility.

The entire sequence of events surrounding the Lehrmann trial constitutes an extraordinary chapter in Australian political history, characterised by a cloak of secrecy and apparent cover-ups. Questions loom large: what are the motives behind these actions? Is it a mere sequence of unfortunate events or a concerted effort to suppress the truth? Who is being protected, and why? While the principle of the presumption of innocence is paramount, it does not grant *carte blanche* for obscuring evidence, tampering with tapes, or pursuing defamation suits against the media.

Critics highlight the disconcerting manner in which individuals have been shielded from accountability. An apparently inept, incompetent and unknown 23-year-old, who was facing disciplinary action resulting from ministerial dissatisfaction, is being afforded the protection that few people ever receive—certainly not Brittany Higgins—and this presents a baffling paradox. The Lehrmann case and subsequent inquiry has also caused the wreckage of multiple careers, begging the question of whether such devastation was warranted or an orchestrated attempt to deflect attention from more profound issues—perhaps a cover-up to ensure that Scott Morrison's 2019 election campaign wasn't derailed, an election that he went on to win?

Comparisons are drawn to historical cases such as the Sydney Hilton Hotel bombing incident in 1978, where so many conspiracies were floated, and blame was apportioned to the Ananda Marga sect (and others), and there was a wide range of manipulative narratives applied to distort the truth and what had actually occurred.

Yet, the Lehrmann trial appears to defy comprehension, and the legal and political incompetence, coupled with perceived corruption of the legal process, has cast a shadow over the foundational pillars of the justice system in the ACT. How could one case have so many errors and mistakes, and involve so many levels of incompetence, including in the subsequent inquiry?

The defendant's inconspicuous status on the political stage raises questions about the motivation behind the apparent protection afforded to him. While the principle of presumption of innocence must be upheld, the ACT Public Prosecutor's assertion that of the 12 jurors, 11 were prepared to convict, presents a further puzzle. Of course, in Australia's legal system, cases of this nature must reach a unanimous verdict—so, according to law, Lehrmann is innocent; he has also maintained his innocence and no findings have been made against him.

The innocent verdict notwithstanding, the stench of a cover-up lingers, fuelling suspicions of concealed motives involving higher powers.

The involvement of the Liberal Party and the Australian Federal Police in this quagmire further taints the waters. The erosion of public trust in the Australian Federal Police raises concerns about systemic integrity, demanding urgent reforms and investigations. Beyond the Lehrmann trial, the broader issues of accountability, transparency, and trust in the criminal justice system must be urgently addressed.

THE COMPLEX POLITICAL WEB SURROUNDING THE AUSTRALIAN FEDERAL POLICE

As the pieces of the puzzle surrounding the Lehrmann trial continue to emerge, scrutiny falls heavily on the Australian Federal Police and the entire framework that surrounds it. While the formation of the Federal Police was rooted in noble intentions in 1917, namely to protect the office of the Prime Minister, its recent actions have cast a shadow of doubt on its integrity and motivations.

With accusations of improper dealings between the Australian Federal Police and major consulting firms such as PwC that have drained taxpayer funds, calls for its dismantling or thorough restructuring grow louder. The toxic culture within its ranks and its disturbing alignment with influential entities raise concerns about the true nature of its operations.

A particularly distressing aspect of the Lehrmann trial saga is the disparate treatment of the accused and the complainant, Brittany Higgins. The grave injustices committed against her and the subsequent preferential treatment of the accused highlight the deeply rooted issues within the Australian Federal Police and the overall culture within Parliament House. It is a stark reminder that the preservation of the office should not come at the expense of justice, fairness, and accountability.

The conduct of Sofronoff KC has also complicated matters. Briefing journalists during the inquiry not only raises ethical concerns but also lends credence to suspicions that transparency and impartiality were sacrificed. Out of all the journalists that Sofronoff could have leaked his inquiry report to, he chooses Albrechtsen from News Corporation. With a history of undermining Brittany Higgins' credibility, Albrechtsen's role in the narrative adds another layer of complexity. The seeming intention to vilify Higgins and tarnish the reputation of key individuals further erodes trust in the transparency of the investigation process.

As the tangled web of the Lehrmann trial continues to unravel, a cloud of uncertainty hangs over the Australian Federal Police and the Canberra police force. The need for urgent reforms, transparency, and accountability has never been more pressing. The calls for a fresh start—perhaps involving overseas recruitment and the removal of compromised senior management, gain traction as the system's secrecy and flaws become more apparent.

The currents of change are palpable, driven by a growing public demand for transparency and fairness. Whether a mere government initiative or a more profound shift in societal expectations, one thing is clear: the status quo is no longer tenable. For Australia to regain its trust in the justice system and reclaim its reputation, the shadowy corners must be illuminated, and the foundations of transparency and accountability must be fortified.

The Lehrmann rape trial and its aftermath expose a distressing saga of incompetence, manipulation, and apparent corruption within the Australian judiciary and police. The veil of secrecy surrounding the trial and its subsequent inquiry reflects a dire need for transparency, accountability, and sweeping reforms. Only by addressing these systemic failures head-on can Australia hope to restore faith in its justice system and prevent such episodes from tarnishing its history in the future.

***

RENEWED PUSH FOR NUCLEAR ENERGY SPARKS A NEW EMPTY DEBATE

19 August 2023

The National Party's persistent and irrational advocacy for nuclear energy in Australia has once again ignited a heated debate, prompting yet another round of discussions on the feasibility and viability of such a move. Critics argue that while the party has consistently raised the issue during its time in Opposition—primarily as a diversion and smokescreen from other issues—it has failed to follow through when in government, raising strong doubts about its motivations.

National Party leader, David Littleproud emphasised the need for "commonsense solutions and political leadership" in addressing Australia's energy challenges, urging collaboration across party lines and exploration of innovative avenues, including small-scale modular nuclear reactors—which is an unproven and hazardous technology, despite what Littleproud says.

Historically, nuclear energy in Australia has been met with resistance for a range of political, technological and financial reasons. Reports dating back to the 1950s have consistently raised doubts about the viability of nuclear energy as an industry in the country, and various industry figures and government reports have highlighted the substantial costs and unfeasibility of establishing nuclear power stations. While proponents have periodically championed nuclear energy, its potential remains unfulfilled due to economic, environmental and technical challenges.

Furthermore, the National Party's fluctuating stance on nuclear energy raises questions about its motivations. Their renewed interest in nuclear energy seems to be driven by a desire to create political leverage and diversion, and support their vested interests in the mining sector, rather than a genuine solution to the nation's energy needs. Advocates for renewable energy emphasise that Australia's energy future lies in sustainable sources such as wind, solar, and hydro power, along with re-evaluating the generous long-term gas contracts the Howard government made to China, Japan and South Korea, and not within nuclear energy.

In a world experiencing more extreme weather patterns and shifting seasons, the call for a comprehensive and responsible energy strategy becomes more urgent. As discussions unfold, it remains to be seen whether the National Party's renewed push for nuclear energy—an area that they never push when they are actually in government—will lead to meaningful policy change or continue to be mired in political rhetoric.

POLITICAL OPPORTUNISM AND THE IDEOLOGICAL DIVIDE

The ongoing debate over nuclear energy in Australia has been characterised by political opportunism and a deep ideological divide, and it's clear that the Liberal–National Coalition's repeated mention of nuclear power functions is a tactical political strategy rather than a genuine policy proposal.

In the context of their propensity to talk about energy solutions from opposition, it is essential to scrutinise the Coalition's track record on energy policy when they were in government. When the Coalition left office in 2022, it left behind an energy market plagued by uncertainty and a lack of clear policy direction. The inability to reach a consensus on energy policy, exemplified by the National Energy Guarantee disagreement during Malcolm Turnbull's tenure, has led to higher energy costs for consumers and an underwhelming performance in being able to extract fair and equitable prices from energy exports.

The Coalition's has little credibility on national energy policy and while its current push for nuclear energy is partially an attempt to make itself seem relevant, its policy implementation in government has often fallen short and it is this inconsistency that raises scepticism about the party's ability to create effective and forward-thinking policies in the national interest.

Moreover, the debate over nuclear energy is closely tied to events within the political landscape, with conservative politicians often resurrect the issue of nuclear power when faced with political challenges. Liberal Party leader Peter Dutton talked up the prospects of nuclear power in August last year, primarily because he'd been outplayed politically on the climate change legislation the federal government introduced last year. Dutton also attempted to bring nuclear energy into the national debate several months, at the time the report from the Royal Commission into the Robodebt scheme was released, a report which was highly critical of the Coalition's administration of the scheme.

The broader energy debate also underscores a divide between political parties. The push for renewable energy, often championed by the Labor Party and the Australian Greens, contrasts with the conservative Coalition's focus on nuclear energy and continued support for fossil fuels. While some conservative voices advocate for "green coal", critics point out the lack of proven technology and the potential environmental and financial costs associated with such an approach. While the Labor Party's commitment to fossil fuel industries and its acceptance of political donations from this sector also raises questions about its political motivations, at least they are making a push towards renewable energy and legislating key emissions reduction targets.

As the political landscape evolves and public sentiment shifts toward more sustainable energy solutions, the Coalition's reliance on the nuclear energy debate as a scapegoat for other issues becomes increasingly apparent. The changing times may necessitate a re-evaluation of the party's energy policies, focusing on solutions that align with current environmental concerns and economic realities.

THE PRICE OF ENERGY: COMPARING VISIONS FOR AUSTRALIA'S ENERGY FUTURE

As the debate over nuclear energy in Australia continues, questions about the cost of various energy sources and the motivations behind policy choices have come to the forefront. The Coalition's emphasis on non-renewable energy sources, including fossil fuels and nuclear power, has raised concerns among critics who seek to explore the economic viability and environmental impact of these options.

While some speculate that the Coalition's support for these industries stems from their economic advantages, the numbers paint a different picture. Despite recent increases in the cost of renewable technologies, such as wind and solar, a joint report by the CSIRO and the Australian Energy Market Operator indicates that these sources remain the most affordable forms of energy. With further adoption and technological advancements, wind and solar are projected to become even more cost-effective in the coming years.

Comparing the capital costs per kilowatt, the disparity becomes evident. Nuclear energy stands at approximately $US7,000 per kilowatt, while wind power comes in at $1,700 per kilowatt and solar at $1,300 per kilowatt. For reference, coal power is around $4,000 per kilowatt, and coal with carbon sequestration technology, a method the Coalition usually promotes as a solution to greenhouse emissions control, costs around $6,500 per kilowatt—approaching the cost of nuclear energy. These figures, albeit in US dollars, highlight the considerable cost discrepancy between nuclear power and renewable alternatives.

The Coalition's continued emphasis on non-renewable industries might be driven by a desire to maintain political differentiation with their opponents, but most of this is catering to fossil fuel interests and donors, as it's patently evident that it's not based on a desire to obtain the cheapest and most efficient form of energy, or to provide cost-benefits to the public. The debate extends to both sides of the political spectrum, with the Labor government also navigating the balance between economic interests and environmental concerns. While they too have ties to industry supporters, at least they have demonstrated a greater commitment to promoting renewable energy solutions and making a tangible difference.

In recent years, discussions on energy have grown increasingly polarised, with intellectual discourse giving way to political name-calling and oversimplified arguments. This polarisation often obscures the complexity of the nuclear energy debate.

There have been many investigations into the viability of nuclear energy in Australia since the 1950s and not one has recommended that it is an industry that should proceed on a scale that is currently being called for by the Coalition. If nuclear is the solution that leaders such as Dutton and Littleproud proclaim, why is it absent as an energy source in Australia after 70 years of debate? The simple answer is: it's not a viable industry and has been overtaken by renewable energy sources which are far more effective and cost-efficient.

Certainly, let there be a public debate about the merits or otherwise of nuclear energy—yet again—but it too often descends into political opportunism and leads to more time-wasting and public distraction.

The future of Australia's energy landscape remains uncertain. As technological advancements continue and the costs of renewable energy sources decline, the nation faces critical decisions that will shape its economic, environmental, and political trajectory. While the Coalition's stance on non-renewable energy sources persists, the broader shift towards sustainable solutions indicates that the path forward lies in embracing the changing energy paradigm.

As the ongoing debates unfold, the hope is that the nation ultimately finds itself on the right side of history, contributing to a greener and more prosperous future.

***

THE REACTIONARY CPAC BIGOTS AND BANDITS HIJACK THE NATIONAL AGENDA

26 August 2023

In a world where political ideologies seem to traverse borders more freely than ever before, the latest cavalcade of conservative harlequinade took centre stage in Sydney. As the Conservative Political Action Group (CPAC) presented its annual conference with its usual fare of soiled and sad brand of divisiveness, it's important to ponder the implications of importing an American-style conservative agenda to an Australian political landscape that is more receptive to a unique blend of progressive policies and traditional values, rather than reactionary bandits who are only too happy to hijack the national agenda for their own self-serving interests.

The timing of CPAC's Australian foray couldn't have been more poignant, coinciding with the National Labor conference—an event that typically garners attention for its focus on workers' rights and social justice. The stark contrast between these two gatherings highlighted the ideological divide that has become increasingly pronounced in Australian politics.

CPAC, an American-born event, has in recent years expanded its horizons beyond the borders of its home country. Its Australian incarnation, however, has sparked controversy, with critics arguing that the imported agenda doesn't align with the nuanced socio-political climate of the nation. CPAC promotes itself as "a values-based organisation that espouses the best of Howard, Reagan and Thatcher", but its values are more aligned to creating division, creating conflict, punching down on people, and manufacturing divisive issues that simply don't exist in the community.

At the heart of the opposition to CPAC's presence is a concern about the conference's alignment with certain issues that have long stirred debate. The denial of climate change, a fervent embrace of extreme libertarianism, racism, and opposition to the Voice to Parliament all feature prominently on CPAC's agenda, all of which are out of step with the majority of Australians who tend to favour policies that promote environmental stewardship, social equality, and recognition of the rights for First Nations people.

The conference has also raised eyebrows for its lack of intellectual rigor, with many instances of misinformation and sensationalism that have emanated from not just this conference, but CPAC events from the past. In an era where the importance of expertise and factual accuracy is more important than ever before, the conference's cavalier approach to facts and the disparagement of experts have left many questioning its credibility and integrity.

For example, the prominent right-wing "shock-jock" media figure, Alan Jones, kick-started this rhetoric by claiming: "They feed into the propaganda taught in the classroom. It feeds into the propaganda of kids. They put kitty litter in girls' toilets, because some girls want to be cats. I mean, you can't who is who has opened their mouth on a single sentence about any of this, where we have indoctrination rather than education."

Perhaps no-one has opened their mouths about this because none of it actually happened. And this is what this fringe group of so-called conservatives is reduced to: debates about kitty litter in girls' toilets, because this is what is important to them.

The roster of CPAC speakers, which included a mix of former politicians and right-leaning personalities, also suggests a high level of irrelevance. Senator Jacinta Nampijinpa Price received 3 per cent of the vote of the last federal election; Pauline Hanson received 0.8 per cent of the vote in Queensland; Senator Alex Antic received even less at the 2019 federal election—just 0.06 per cent of the vote, or 687 of the 1.1 million votes cast in South Australia. Warren Mundine was first rejected by the Labor Party, and rejected by the electorate as a Liberal Party candidate in the 2022 federal election.

Then there's other former politicians who have long retired from politics, or rejected by the electorate: Barnaby Joyce, pantomime retail populist politician; Amanda Stoker, rejected by the voters of Queensland; Tony Abbott, rejected as Prime Minister by his own party and the voters in the seat of Warringah; John Anderson, out of politics since 2007; Bronwyn Bishop, a political has-been. And on top of this, there's the Australian Christian Lobby, and the Institute of Public Affairs.

Many of these figures hold views that are extreme and on the fringe, and have little relationship with mainstream Australian values.

However, the debate surrounding CPAC's presence in Australia isn't confined to its ideological differences alone. Of course, a healthy democracy thrives on a diversity of viewpoints, and while the conference may represent a minority perspective, it is crucial for robust political discourse to encompass a range of opinions. This sentiment underlines the broader challenge of striking a balance between preserving freedom of expression and preventing the spread of misinformation or divisive rhetoric.

In a world where populist movements and polarised politics are on the rise, CPAC's brand of conservatism is unlikely to find a home in Australia, and the future of conservatism—if there is one—needs thoughtful engagement and an appreciation for empirical evidence, rather than outright hostility and abuse of people and the issues that it doesn't approve of.

A DESIRE TO HUMILIATE PEOPLE IS AN UNACCEPTABLE BRAND OF POLITICS

Aside from the many fringe issues that were adopted by CPAC, it's also a brand that is based on offensiveness, humiliation and belittling people and marginalised groups. The lowlight was the closing address by the hoax comedian Rodney Marks, who appeared as "Dr Chaim Tsibos", a fictitious United Nations diplomat.

Marks' jokes, laden with innuendos and racially insensitive remarks, commencing with a welcome to "traditional rent seekers" and mocking Indigenous Australians, to the howls of laughter from the audience, epitomised the propagation of derogatory stereotypes and the normalisation of offensive content in this context.

What is the point of this humour? What kind of people gain enjoyment from this brand of humour? Why is it necessary for CPAC to humiliate the people who have been historically marginalised and abused by the white political system since 1788? Why are these types of conservatives so happy to promote the disease of racism that most of the world is trying hard to eradicate?

The incident involving Marks is not isolated, but rather emblematic of a broader debate about the values espoused by CPAC and their compatibility with Australian principles. The event's alignment with certain extreme viewpoints and its promotion of divisive rhetoric has no place within Australian society: it's a racist agenda that represents an outdated and exclusionary version of conservatism that stands at odds with the nation's progressive direction.

However, amidst the controversy, there are those within the conservative ranks who are challenging the narrative. Senior Liberal figures such as Senator Andrew Bragg and NSW MP Matt Kean have distanced themselves from CPAC's agenda, emphasising that it does not reflect the true spirit of conservatism or the Liberal Party's values—although this message is at odds at the high number of current and former Coalition MPs who attended the conference—but it is this internal division that highlights the difficulties for moderate Liberals and the efforts to redefine themselves in a changing world.

TRYING TO ACHIEVE POLITICAL SUCCESS THROUGH IGNORANCE

Beyond the conference's ideological struggle, another contentious issue emerged at a Liberal Party rally organised in Perth by Senator Michaelia Cash, who ramped up the rallying cry of "don't know: vote no" against the Voice to Parliament—no surprises here: it was, after all, Senator Cash who organised the preference deal with the racist One Nation in the lead-up to the 2017 WA election.

Of course, this conservative brand of politics needs to appeal to the ignorance of the electorate if it is to achieve its political goals. But it's counterproductive, undermines the democratic process, and a focus on emotional appeals rather than substantive discussions echoed broader concerns about the role of misinformation in contemporary political discourse.

An informed world is not the friend of the modern Liberal Party, so it can't do the hard work of trying to appeal to the electorate with the facts of the day—that is the road to political oblivion—so, as it was for CPAC, it needs to fan the flames of racism, bigotry, ignorance and misinformation, and show a paucity of intellect, if it is to survive.

As CPAC and its associated events continue to stoke debates about Australia's political future, it remains uncertain whether their brand of conservatism will resonate with the changing demographics and values of the nation. The controversies surrounding the conference's content and messaging underscore the need for a nuanced understanding of conservatism that is both reflective of historical values and adaptable to a diverse and evolving society.

In a world marked by the proliferation of misinformation and the intensification of political polarisation, there will be more events such CPAC which will attempt to shape public discourse in a destructive manner, events which are devoid of respectful dialogue and critical thinking, and nor can they contribute to the greater good of society.

As the dust settles on CPAC's controversial conference in Australia, the broader conversation about the intersection of global ideologies and local values will continue. Whether the imported conservatism of CPAC can resonate with a nation known for its pragmatism and commitment to progress remains to be seen. The clash between these contrasting worldviews serves as a reminder that, in an age of increasing interconnectedness, the preservation of national identity, decency and values remains a complex and delicate endeavour.

***

THE DISPARITY OF CORPORATE PROFITS AND WORKER EXPLOITATION IN AUSTRALIA

26 August 2023

In the current reporting period, the Australian corporate landscape has been ablaze with soaring profits. The Commonwealth Bank's staggering $10.2 billion profit; Coles' $1.1 billion profit; Woolworths' $1.6 billion; and the Qantas $2.5 billion record profit, highlight a string of massive financial outcomes. Such buoyant results, however, emerge amidst a backdrop of stagnant wages and heightened cost of living pressures. The juxtaposition of record corporate profits with the struggles of the everyday worker raises important questions about equity and social responsibility within Australia's economic framework.

At first glance, the surge in corporate profits might seem like a promising sign of economic prosperity; after all, healthy corporate growth often signifies a robust and thriving economy. However, a closer examination reveals a stark reality: the benefits of this prosperity are not evenly shared among the population. The assertion that a "healthy corporate sector is the sign of a healthy economy" must be supplemented with an analysis of how these profits are distributed and how they contribute to the overall wellbeing of society.

While these profits undeniably lead to gains for shareholders, the majority of Australians do not possess such investments. Roughly 51 per cent of the population does not own shares, emphasising the point that these financial rewards are concentrated in the hands of a relatively small segment of society. This concentration of wealth and power within a privileged few raises ethical concerns about the broader implications for social cohesion and economic inclusivity.

A more disconcerting connection emerges when one considers the contrast between these astronomical corporate profits and the long-standing issue of stagnant wages. Over the past decade, Australian workers have faced limited wage growth, leaving many struggling to keep up with the rising cost of living. This underlying disparity between soaring corporate profits and stagnant wages is reflective of a damaging corporate culture that prioritises shareholders and executives over the workforce that sustains these profitable enterprises.

The call for greater social responsibility from corporations is heightened by the increasingly visible connection between stagnating wages and burgeoning profits. The notion of introducing a 'super profit tax' of between 20–40 per cent pushed by unions reflects an attempt to reclaim a portion of these extraordinary earnings for the broader society. While corporations often emphasise their philanthropic endeavours—such as Andrew Forrest at mining giant Fortescue Metals Group—the disparity between their immense profits and the limited nature of their social contributions raises important questions about the true extent of their commitment to social welfare.

As corporate profits continue to climb to record heights, it is crucial to critically assess their impact on Australia's economic and social fabric. The current scenario paints a picture of inequality and disconnect between the financial elites and the workforce that enables their prosperity. There needs to be a more equitable distribution of corporate gains, as well as the urgency for increased corporate social responsibility.

THE TIN EAR OF THE BUSINESS SECTOR

In the face of mounting evidence that the current state of corporate profits is perpetuating inequality, it is imperative to reconsider the existing tax system and its relationship with both individuals and large corporations. Rather than treating taxes as a form of theft—a view commonly espoused by the libertarian right—it is time to reshape this narrative into one that recognises the shared responsibility of all stakeholders, including corporations, in contributing to the welfare of the broader society.

The suggestion that corporate taxes should be lowered during a period of surging profits overlooks the fundamental principle of fairness. The call from the CEO of the Business Council of Australia Jennifer Westacott to lower corporate taxes is not aligned with the present need for equitable wealth distribution. Now is not the time for leniency; instead, it is an opportune moment to harness the unprecedented prosperity of big businesses and channel some of that prosperity back into the community. Hospitals, schools, infrastructure, and various social services rely on public funding, a significant portion of which could be drawn from the abundant profits generated by these corporations.

While the government's move to initiate a task force under the Australian Competition and Consumer Commission to scrutinise competition in key sectors is a step in the right direction, it is essential to acknowledge that more comprehensive reforms are required to shift the balance of power in favour of the community over corporate interests. The ongoing evolution of the economy necessitates proactive and adaptive strategies that address future challenges while also addressing current disparities.

The recently released intergenerational report by Treasurer Jim Chalmers highlights the long-term demographic and economic shifts that Australia will face in the coming decades. While an aging population and changing demographics pose significant challenges, the report's implications extend beyond demographics alone. Technological advancements, shifts in workforce dynamics, and evolving social structures will demand a forward-thinking approach that considers the needs and aspirations of future generations.

While Prime Minister Anthony Albanese recently advocated for long-term governance and slower reform, rather than implementing impactful changes in the short-term, the urgency of the present cannot be ignored. The famous adage by John Maynard Keynes, "in the long run, we are all dead," underscores the importance of finding a balance between visionary long-term planning and responsive short-term action. Striking this equilibrium is a challenge, yet it's essential to ensure that immediate issues are not sacrificed at the altar of deferred reforms.

The current corporate profits narrative in Australia raises pressing questions about equity, social responsibility, and the future economic landscape. Reconfiguring the tax system to ensure fair contributions from corporations, as well as the utilisation of profits to bolster public services, is essential for addressing the widening gap between corporate prosperity and worker wellbeing.

The ongoing transformation of the economy underscores the need for adaptable, forward-thinking reforms that balance long-term aspirations with immediate needs. The complexities of governance and political dynamics further emphasise the necessity for innovative solutions that prioritise the welfare of the nation over partisan concerns. As Australia navigates the intersection of corporate profits, worker rights, and economic evolution, it is crucial to envision a future that benefits all, rather than a privileged few.

***

SEPTEMBER

THE HI-VIZ CORPORATE APPEASEMENT: POLITICS, AND CORPORATE INFLUENCE

2 September 2023

In an era marked by growing public skepticism toward political leadership and increasing concerns about the influence of corporate interests on government decisions, a recent choice by Prime Minister Anthony Albanese has reignited the discourse surrounding the intertwining of politics and business.

The focal point: it might seem like a trivial matter, but it was the Albanese's choice of attire during a visit to Karratha, where he made a announcement regarding Australia's dependence on the mining sector, particularly emphasising the critical minerals sector encompassing resources like lithium and nickel. While the essence of the announcement may have been a matter of national importance, it was the emblem on his clothing that set off a cascade of criticisms and raised fundamental questions about the nexus of power and corporate influence in contemporary politics.

The symbolism behind the Prime Minister's attire is both apparent and disconcerting. Albanese's decision to don a high-visibility vest emblazoned with the Rio Tinto logo sent a stark message—one that suggested a troubling proximity between the highest office of government and corporate interests. It is a message that resonates far beyond the initial visual impact; it underscores the blurred lines between political authority and private sector persuasion. This act encapsulates a broader issue in modern politics, where the perceptions of events often hold as much sway as the actual intentions behind them.

This instance is not an isolated one: it is part of a larger pattern of politicians, including the previous Prime Minister Scott Morrison, engaging in symbolic dress-ups and donning attire prominently featuring the logos of mining companies. These gestures, while dismissed as harmless or trivial by supporters, cannot be ignored or brushed aside. They collectively reflect an ongoing trend where corporate interests appear to be encroaching further into the domain of governmental authority.

It is crucial to recognise the importance of maintaining a clear demarcation between corporate interests and government decisions. A robust separation between the two is essential to ensure that policies and regulations are crafted in the best interest of the citizens and the nation, not by the agendas of powerful entities.

The presence of the Rio Tinto logo on the Prime Minister's vest also goes beyond mere optics; it raises concerns about ethical considerations. Rio Tinto, a multinational mining corporation, has been embroiled in controversies, most notably for its destruction of Aboriginal rock art dating back thousands of years in the Juukan Gorge in 2020—a grievous act that speaks to a disregard for cultural heritage and human rights. By wearing attire associated with such a company, the Prime Minister inadvertently or otherwise sends a message that may be perceived as an endorsement of this behaviour. It is a stark reminder that in politics, perception often shapes public opinion more than the actual intentions of those in power.

In addition to these concerns, the broader issue of multinational mining companies exploiting Australia's mineral resources with relatively minimal contributions to the national treasury warrants attention. The Australian government, as outlined in the Constitution, holds ownership of these resources on behalf of the public, yet foreign companies have historically reaped substantial profits with comparatively little financial obligation to the nation. This situation raises questions about equity and fiscal responsibility, issues that should be of paramount importance to any government.

THE SYMBOLISM OF ALBANESE'S VISIT TO WESTERN AUSTRALIA

The intricacies of political symbolism and its impact on public perception was also profoundly evident in the context of Albanese's visit to Western Australia. This journey, ostensibly for a special cabinet meeting in Perth–Boorloo, was strategically positioned as a means to solidify the Labor Party's stronghold in the state. Western Australia, a resource-rich region with a powerful mining industry, is a vital battleground for political influence. In state politics, the Labor government maintains a commanding presence, holding 53 of the 59 seats, while at the federal level, it secured nine out of the 15 seats, aided by a significant 10.5 per cent swing towards the party during the 2022 federal election.

The significance of this trip cannot be overstated. It underscores the symbiotic relationship between politics and industry, especially in a state so heavily reliant on the mining sector. But the trip also adds to the perception that politicians, in this case, the Prime Minister, are beholden to corporate interests, potentially influencing their decision-making in favour of these companies.

The public perception of politicians as being in the pocket of powerful corporations has long been a contentious issue in politics. Such perceptions have often fueled cynicism and mistrust among voters, undermining the integrity of the democratic process. It is a perception that all political parties, not just Labor, should strive to dispel. In an era where political trust is increasingly fragile, politicians should be cautious about giving the impression of subservience to corporate entities.

Moreover, it is essential to recognise the significant financial contributions made by corporations such as Rio Tinto to political processes in Australia. While these donations might not flow directly to political parties, they find their way to influential third-party entities like the Minerals Council of Australia and the Business Council of Australia.

In recent years, Rio Tinto alone has contributed approximately $4.6 million, while other mining giants like BHP and Glencore have also made substantial donations, resulting in a staggering $137 million influx of funds from the mining industry over the past two decades. These contributions raise legitimate concerns about the undue influence of big business on political decisions, a problem that has plagued democratic systems around the world.

BEYOND OPTICS: LEADERSHIP AND ACCOUNTABILITY

The Prime Minister's visit to Karratha aligning his office with the Rio Tinto logo extends beyond the immediate optics and touches on critical aspects of political leadership, campaign financing, and the role of the media in holding leaders accountable.

While we can't expect the Prime Minister of the day to denounce a corporation's environmental or human rights record while they are making a public announced on their site—there is a time and a place for this—the public does expects its leaders to act in the best interests of the nation, which includes protecting the environment and respecting human rights.

There is also controversy surrounding the delayed release of the climate crisis report by the federal government and this delay also underscores the importance of transparency and accountability in governance. The public deserves access to information that can impact their wellbeing and the environment, especially when there is a link between environmental damage and mining companies such as Rio Tinto. Delaying the release of such a report raises suspicions about political motivations and the prioritisation of short-term interests over the long-term health of the planet.

A solution to that problem of government links with business and financial donations would be a ban on donations and fully publicly-funded elections, which would reduce the undue influence of big business on the political process. Publicly-funded elections can help level the playing field, ensure transparency, and minimise the perception that politicians are beholden to their financial backers. While there may be concerns about the impact on associated think tanks and interest groups, the priority should be to safeguard the integrity of the democratic process.

Moreover, a vigilant media should be doing far more in holding leaders accountable. Media outlets should not shy away from questioning and critiquing the actions of political leaders, regardless of their party affiliation, as the media plays a crucial role in providing information, fostering public debate, and ensuring that leaders are answerable to the electorate. However, this is unlikely when the dominant owners of Australia media—Kerry Stokes and Rupert Murdoch—also hold substantial mining and resources, and an neutered ABC which seems to have forgotten that there was a change in government in 2022, and is still pandering to the political interests of the Liberal Party.

It is essential to recognise that constructive criticism of political leaders does not imply that everything a government does is inherently bad and acknowledging positive actions and praising good governance is equally important. The Albanese government has achieved much during its 15 months in government, and is a marked improvement on the behaviours and performances of the Morrison government. However, during periods when concerns about governance are pronounced, criticism can serve as a valuable check on power and a catalyst for improvement: this is the case for the Albanese government, as it is for all governments: no administration is going to be perfect, but the goal is to make governments less imperfect and seek improvements wherever possible.

MEDIA REFORM UNLIKELY TO OCCUR WITH ASSOCIATIONS WITH TYCOONS AND PROPRIETORS

While much focus was placed on Albanese's visit to Karratha, there are other events and circumstances causing concern, particularly the launch of Severn West Media's new studios in the inner-Sydney suburb of Eveleigh, and his association with corporate figures, underscore the complex interplay between politics, media, and corporate interests in Australia. These instances raise crucial questions about the feasibility of achieving media reform, the ethical implications of political associations, and the alignment of political leaders with their ideological roots.

The convergence of political leaders such as Albanese and NSW Premier Chris Minns, and business magnates like Kerry Stokes at media events can be seen as emblematic of the close-knit relationships that often exist within influential circles. Such interactions can cast a shadow over the prospects of media reform, as the intertwining of political and media interests can create an environment where change becomes increasingly difficult. The perception of collusion between politicians and media tycoons further erodes public trust in the ability of the government to act independently and in the public interest.

The government's recent support for Qantas and the decisions protecting domestic airline routes raise concerns about the criteria and motivations behind government decisions. The lack of transparency in the denial of extra flights for Qatar Airways, juxtaposed with the apparent benefits provided to Qantas, fuels suspicions of favouritism and corporate influence in government decision-making. The perception of special privileges granted to Qantas, particularly in light of the provision of a Chairman's Lounge VIP pass to the Prime Minister's son, underscores the importance of maintaining public trust and dispelling any perceptions of impropriety.

The alignment of Albanese with corporate interests and his apparent departure from the principles of the Socialist Left faction within the Labor Party—the faction that Albanese originated from and used to move up the ranks of the party—also is concerning. While the complexities of governance often necessitate compromise and negotiation, leaders should strive to uphold the values and policies they have passionately advocated for throughout their political careers. The disappointment expressed by some segments of the electorate reflects the challenge of maintaining ideological consistency in the face of political realities.

The dynamics surrounding Albanese's engagements with corporate interests highlight the intricate web of political, media, and corporate relationships in contemporary Australia. While supporters have argued that "it's just a hi-viz shirt" and suggested that there is enough criticism from conservative media interests such as News Corporation and why should smaller independent and progressive media outlets add to the noise, it's more than "just a hi-viz shirt". It's *far* more than that.

These events call into question the feasibility of long-overdue media reforms and actions that are in the public interest, the perception of political associations, and the alignment of leaders with their ideological foundations. While the challenges of governance are undeniable, leaders must navigate them with a commitment to transparency, accountability, and the values they have long championed. Only by doing so can they hope to earn and maintain the trust of the electorate and uphold the principles that underpin their political ideologies.

***

THE VOICE IS A BATTLE FOR AUSTRALIA'S SOUL BUT HOW WILL IT END?

2 September 2023

The Voice to Parliament referendum has been set for October 14, 2023. This referendum proposal, which has been in the pipeline for nearly a decade, evolved from a unified and bipartisan starting point and has morphed into a conservative-led contentious and polarising issue within the nation's political landscape. At its core, this referendum is not just a vote on a legislative change; it's a litmus test for Australia's stance on race relations and just how serious it about the pathway towards Reconciliation.

Put simply, the "Yes" campaign appeals to a positive and better future, not just First Nations people, but for the country as a whole. On the other hand, the "No" campaign appeals to a myopic inward-looking past, a historical attribute that we wished had been pushed to a far-distant time, but has been easily retrieved by a hate-led Liberal Party and mainstream media that is based on fear, insecurity and, in many cases, outright racism.

How is it that a relatively small and insignificant amendment to the Constitution—and a largely immaterial change for so many people in Australia but could provide great symbolic and practical change for First Nations people—has been whipped up into an irrational media-driven frenzy of racism and hate?

It's an easy answer: mainstream Australia has great difficulties shedding its racist past and, despite the success of the Mabo decision in 1992, the great white experiment of *terra nullius* still continues up to this day, a concept that many seem to be resentful for giving up for fear of losing their ill-gotten gains acquired during two key dates: 1788: the original invasion; and 1901: the date the conquest was officially signed-off into one of the most racist and exclusionary Constitutions devised by a team of old, white, bearded men, who had no intention of including anyone of colour, especially the First Nations people.

Initially, the concept of a Voice to Parliament enjoyed bipartisan backing in its inception in 2015, when it was presented to then Prime Minister Malcolm Turnbull, and supported by then Leader of the Opposition, Bill Shorten. Both sides of the political aisle recognised the importance of addressing the concerns of Indigenous communities and advancing Reconciliation efforts. However, the narrative surrounding this proposal took a sharp turn when certain elements within the conservative faction of the Liberal Party decided to exploit the Voice to Parliament for political gain. What began as a shared commitment to progress soon devolved into a divisive issue driven by political opportunism and, as we have seen historically, whatever actions are adopted by the Liberal Party, are soon followed and supported by the mainstream media.

For many Australians, particularly those of First Nations heritage, this referendum carries profound significance. It signifies more than just a checkbox on a Reconciliation "to-do" list. It is a chance for Australia to take meaningful steps toward addressing the historical injustices faced by Indigenous communities. While it may not fully meet all expectations, the referendum represents a blend of powerful symbolism and a substantial stride toward practical solutions.

The significance of this referendum extends beyond its legislative implications. It presents a challenge to the broader Australian community—a challenge to reflect on their commitment to Reconciliation. Over the past few decades, words advocating for Reconciliation have been spoken frequently, but the extent of genuine commitment has often been questioned. How many businesses and organisations create Reconciliation Action Plans, but then leave them withering behind, gathering dust in the corporate board rooms? The referendum provides an opportunity to demonstrate whether these sentiments will be translated into action.

However, the outcome of the referendum remains uncertain, with some individuals expressing skepticism about its success. While it won't achieve the remarkable 90 per cent support garnered by the 1967 referendum, it is essential to acknowledge the factors influencing public sentiment, and the role of political leaders cannot be overlooked in shaping public opinion.

The Leader of the Opposition Peter Dutton's stance on the referendum exemplifies the intersection of pure political opportunism and a lack of principle. His choice to prioritise political expediency over the "right thing to do" has fuelled doubts about the referendum's prospects. Instead of embracing the proposal as a bipartisan initiative and expressing the Liberal Party's commitment to its core principles, Dutton's approach has been marked by political calculation.

Moreover, this referendum has not escaped the broader trend of right-wing extremism influencing Australian politics. The takeover of the Victorian Liberal Party by an extreme right Pentecostal faction illustrates the impact of radical ideologies on political decision-making. Dutton's alignment with these elements reflects a growing trend of political pandering and ideological compromises.

At its core, the referendum debate reveals a disturbing undercurrent in conservative Australian politics, where winning elections is pursued at any cost, even if it means sacrificing principles and causing damage to the social fabric of the community.

In the face of these political challenges, the Australian electorate is left to grapple with the implications of their vote. It is not merely a question of supporting a legislative change but also a consideration of the broader consequences for the nation's political landscape. In this crucial moment, the responsibility rests with both politicians and citizens to contemplate the values and principles that underpin their decisions.

The Voice to Parliament referendum in Australia is not just a vote on a legislative proposal. It represents a critical juncture in the nation's history, where political opportunism clashes with the imperative for Reconciliation. The referendum tests the commitment of Australians to addressing historical injustices and offers an opportunity to bridge the gap between words and actions. The outcome remains uncertain, but the implications for Australia's political landscape are profound, underscoring the need for thoughtful consideration and principled decision-making.

THE HISTORICAL FIRST NATION STRUGGLE FOR JUSTICE IN AUSTRALIA

The road to Reconciliation in Australia has always been a challenging journey, marked by resistance and reluctance to address the historical injustices endured by Indigenous peoples. Throughout history, initiatives aimed at returning rights, land, and dignity to First Nations communities have faced formidable obstacles: the *Land Rights Act* of 1976 to the Mabo decision in 1992; the creation of the Native Title Tribunal; the National Apology to the Stolen Generation in 2008; all were met with significant resistance and each historical step towards justice has been met with fierce opposition and skepticism. Even attempts to repatriate culturally significant artifacts, such Yagan's head from England, have faced resistance.

The Voice to Parliament referendum is no exception to this pattern. While Prime Minister Anthony Albanese's words have echoed a message of unity, opportunity, and Reconciliation, there remain significant challenges on the horizon. The promise of "a more unified, reconciled Australia with greater opportunities for all" is a compelling vision, but it is not without its detractors.

Current opinion polls suggesting a surge in support for the "No" campaign remind us of the divisive nature of this issue.

Opposition to the referendum is fueled by powerful conservative interests, whose tactics often rely on misinformation and misrepresentation. At times, this opposition reveals an underlying strain of racism, and it appears to be motivated by a nihilistic desire to obstruct progress for the sake of obstruction, with racist rhetoric and unfounded claims clouding the debate, diverting attention from the core issues.

Dutton's recent claim that the ballot is "being rigged" due to the distinction between ticks and crosses by the Australian Electoral Commission, is a prime example of the misinformation campaign surrounding the referendum. Such baseless allegations undermine trust in public institutions, and this divisive rhetoric mirrors a troubling global trend, reminiscent of tactics employed by former U.S. President Donald Trump. While Dutton's actions may be seen as a poor imitation of Trump, they reflect the unsettling state of affairs within the Liberal Party.

The challenges posed by these tactics highlight the critical need for informed and thoughtful discussions among the Australian populace. Conversations within workplaces, sports clubs, faith communities, and among family and friends are essential for countering misinformation and promoting a clear understanding of the referendum's purpose and significance.

The history of Indigenous rights and reconciliation in Australia has been fraught with resistance and struggle. The Voice to Parliament referendum represents another pivotal moment in this ongoing journey, offering the promise of a more unified and reconciled nation. However, the path forward is not without its challenges, including a well-funded opposition fueled by misinformation and, at times, racism. The responsibility now falls on the Australian people to engage in meaningful conversations and make informed decisions that reflect the values of unity, justice, and progress. Only through such engagement can the nation hope to overcome the obstacles and achieve the promise of a more inclusive and reconciled Australia.

WHAT COMES FIRST: THE VOICE OR THE TREATY?

One of the central arguments by some Indigenous advocates against the Voice to Parliament proposal is the notion that it should come *after* the establishment of a Treaty, a subsequent step in the Reconciliation process, rather than a precursor. This viewpoint acknowledges the intertwined nature of these initiatives and the difficulty of achieving a Treaty without the foundational support of the Voice. It's a complex, chicken-and-egg scenario, where the order of implementation remains contentious.

But very few in the "No" campaign are proposing a Treaty: if they are so vehemently opposed to the simple proposition of the Voice to Parliament, it's highly unlikely that they would support the steps that are considered to be more complex, such as a Treaty. And for conservative politicians, more complexity just provides a greater option for political opportunism and race baiting.

The lengthy process leading up to this referendum has, understandably, generated frustration. Indigenous communities and their allies have waited for 122 years for meaningful change since Federation in 1901, and the prospect of another decade or so before a Treaty is realised is understandably disheartening. However, embracing the Voice to Parliament now brings the nation closer to the eventual Treaty, preventing further delays that could extend for decades beyond.

While governments often lose referenda—36 of the proposed 44 questions since Federation have been defeated—the historical precedent indicates that an unsuccessful referendum outcome does not necessarily lead to an electoral defeat. Nevertheless, predicting the political fallout of this particular referendum remains challenging. The divisive nature of the campaign and the persistence of the "No" campaign's tactics make it difficult to foresee the ultimate impact on the upcoming election.

In this context, the figure of Peter Dutton emerges as a central and controversial figure and his approach to the referendum debate has been marked by racism and a failure to demonstrate leadership. While divisive strategies have found support in the past, there is a growing sense that such tactics are losing favour within the broader community. The referendum outcome will be a litmus test of whether these divisive strategies still resonate with voters.

THE ONE ELDER STRATEGY

Additionally, the Liberal Party's adoption of the "one Elder strategy", where individual MPs claim to have consulted with one Indigenous leader who opposes the Voice to Parliament, raises questions about the depth of community engagement and the diversity of perspectives within Indigenous communities.

One particularly striking example occurred on the ABC's *Q+A*, where the Liberal MP Aaron Violi asserted that an Indigenous leader in his electorate is opposed the Voice to Parliament and, as a result, he was also going to advocate for a "No" vote. We don't know who this Elder is—Violi claimed that if he was named, he would suffer a backlash from his community—we don't know in which circumstances these comments were made: was it a community forum; was it a meeting in Violi's office; was it an impromptu meeting in a café or on a street walk?

We don't know the answers to any of these questions, yet Violi's assertion creates doubt and flies in the face of the evidence that around 80 per cent of First Nations communities support the Voice to Parliament proposal. Such strategies risk oversimplifying a complex issue and ignoring the varied opinions within Indigenous communities. Should MPs base their decisions after consulting with just one person? Anecdotes, rather than evidence?

It also raises questions about the role of the mainstream media in these circumstances. Violi should have been interjected by the host of *Q+A*, and told in no uncertain terms, that because he couldn't verify his story and wasn't prepared to name who this Elder is, that it shouldn't be used to push a political line: it's one of the key tenets of professional journalism—unnamed and unverified sources cannot be taken to be truthful, and his commentary should have been closed down. But such are the standards that exist at the ABC, who in general, seem to be fueling the public scepticism towards the Voice to Parliament, purely because it's been presented by a Labor government.

As the referendum campaign intensifies over the next six weeks, it is likely that the "No" campaign will continue to employ similar tactics—statements based on the experiences of one unnamed individual, disingenuous commentary, and even outright lies.

WE ALL LOSE UNDER A "NO" CAMPAIGN DRIVEN BY FEAR AND DIVISION

Regardless of the referendum's outcome, it is unlikely to significantly alter Peter Dutton's political standing. His divisive and polarising approach has garnered both fervent opposition and indifference. If the referendum were to result in a "No" vote, it would be a narrow one, and unlikely to transform Dutton's image or attract newfound support. The public perception of Dutton is deeply entrenched, and this referendum alone is unlikely to substantially alter his political fortunes.

Looking beyond the referendum, the changing landscape of Australian politics and society comes into focus. While there are still elements of racism within the country, they no longer hold the same sway as in previous decades. The voices of those espousing racist views may be growing louder, but their influence is diminishing. Australia has made significant strides in combating racism, although there is still work to be done. The end of the era represented by figures such as Dutton appears imminent, as their divisive tactics find fewer receptive ears in a more inclusive and enlightened Australia.

As we approach October 14, the future of the Voice to Parliament referendum remains uncertain. But what is clear is that the nation is watching—and the international community—and the choice made on that day will reverberate through Australia's history.

It is a testament to the resilience and determination of First Nations people and their allies, who continue to push for a more inclusive and equitable Australia. Irrespective of what happens on October 14, and despite the antics of the destructive and demeaning "No" campaign, Reconciliation in Australia will continue: it's too important to give up just because of a group of conservative and nihilist Liberal Party MPs who are just too far gone down the rabbit warren to know any better.

And it's also essential to remember that the day after the referendum, Australia will still exist as stolen land and there are large tracts of territory that have never been handed back to the original owners. It is the land of First Nations people: always has been; always will be. That will never change.

***

THE CHANGING INDUSTRIAL LANDSCAPE FOR GIG ECONOMY WORKERS

9 September 2023

The return of Parliament to Canberra last week has brought industrial relations, particularly the conditions and rights of gig economy workers, to the forefront of the political agenda in Australia. The discussions centre around the need for significant changes to existing legislation in order to provide gig economy workers with enhanced job security, improved wages, and safer working environments. These proposed amendments also encompass critical provisions for ensuring equal pay for equal work and the criminalisation of wage theft. Additionally, there is a focus on establishing minimum standards for penalty rates, superannuation, and insurance, as well as regulating the process of deactivation, whereby employees can be removed from gig platforms without justification.

These proposed changes appear to be a reasonable response to the challenges faced by gig economy workers, and it's difficult to understand why there would be any resistance to these changes. Many of these workers are engaged within platforms operated by massive multinational corporations such as Uber, which have reaped substantial profits while providing low pay and substandard working conditions to their employees. In this context, it becomes imperative to reassess the role of work, emphasising fair compensation for the tasks performed rather than enabling big business players to exploit the labour market.

Nevertheless, the reaction to these proposed reforms has not been universally positive. Employer groups, notably the Australian Chamber of Commerce and Industry, have launched an expensive advertising campaign against the idea of equal pay for equal work, arguing—without any logic—that these reforms could harm businesses, as if commerce should be placed at a far greater level than human life.

Liberal Party leader Peter Dutton has criticised the legislation, suggesting that it primarily serves the interests of organised labour and "the unions" (*memo to Dutton: the Labor Party was created in 1891 to advocate for the agenda of union*) but this is to be expected: his role is to disagree with everything the Labor government proposes, in some forlorn hope that this will somehow improve his electoral appeal.

The concept of "fair pay for fair work" and efforts to improve working conditions for a demographic that has endured subpar conditions for far too long, should be an issue that could garner bipartisan support, if we lived in a normal world and the politics of Australia was populated with sane and reasonable people. However, we don't live in a normal world: contemporary politics often reflects a deeply divided landscape where finding common ground is increasingly elusive except, of course, when it concerns salary increases for politicians: there will always be bipartisan support for this matter.

A WORKERS' PARADISE LOST

It is somewhat astonishing to reflect upon the evolution of Australia's industrial relations landscape. In the early twentieth century, Australia was renowned as a "worker's paradise", boasting a robust system of wage regulation and workers' rights. This system effectively ensured the equitable distribution of wealth, thanks to fair labour practices and a thriving goods and services sector. Wages were commensurate with the tasks performed, and this arrangement was widely accepted by governments, business, workers and the community.

In the earlier parts of Australian Federation, the Court of Arbitration played a pivotal role in this system by allowing unions to make ambitious claims, even if they were never expected to be fully granted. This practice spared the court from the administrative burden of handling numerous minor claims. Interestingly, over time, some of these ambitious claims began to be met as a result of natural economic processes such as inflation and changes in the cost of living.

However, this paradigm began to shift with successive governments, kicked-started by the Hawke government's Accord process in the 1980s, and more notably during the Howard era after 1996. Since then, the discourse on wages and workers' rights has taken a precarious turn, with wages stagnating for many workers and highly skilled professions being chronically underpaid while other managerial sectors receive overcompensation. This complex web of issues has created a challenging environment for workers reliant on a fixed wage.

As the Labor government takes action to address the evolving industrial relations landscape, it is important to acknowledge that progress may need to accelerate to meet the urgent needs of gig economy and labour-hire workers.

The political process takes time to turn, but decisive and positive steps must be taken to rectify the current imbalance in worker rights and compensation.

These debates surrounding industrial relations changes for gig economy workers in Australia reflect the broader challenges of reconciling the interests of workers, businesses, and political agendas. While the path forward may be fraught with contention, addressing the issues faced by gig economy workers is a step toward creating a more equitable and just labour market in Australia. The complexities of this endeavour underscore the need for careful deliberation and swift, decisive action to ensure that all Australians can enjoy fair compensation, job security, and safe working conditions in the rapidly evolving world of work.

THE IMPERATIVE FOR CHANGE: ADDRESSING WORKER EXPLOITATION

The proposed workplace law changes are seemingly uncomplicated and are needed to recalibrate the discrepancies and disadvantages for workers that have crept into the gig economy sector. Yet, there is strong opposition the Liberal and National parties, as well as from influential business interests. While it is acknowledged that there must be a balance between business and worker interests, many argue that this balance has tilted too far in favour of business for far too long.

One critical aspect of this debate is the nature of the businesses involved. Gig economy platforms like Uber, Menulog, Hungry Panda, and Airtasker have built their business models on the exploitation of workers and the erosion of workers' rights and conditions, and follows on from the expansion of large corporations in recent decades, whose success has been built on the back of this exploitation. While the technological disruption and innovation evident through these platforms has been a historical feature human progress and social change, these models are leveraging technology to the detriment of workers, and in a way that has never occurred before.

The call for change is straightforward: to rectify these imbalances in the industrial relations landscape. The proposed changes aim to ensure that workers are fairly compensated, have job security, and work in safe conditions, addressing key concerns about underpayment and precarious employment.

The Minister for Industrial Relations, Tony Burke, ridiculed questions from business groups about costs associated with these reforms by suggesting that "underpaying people is cheaper. Slavery is probably cheaper too… there is some modest pass through here, we are talking about some of the lowest paid people in Australia. And if that means there's a tiny bit extra that you pay when your pizza arrives to your door, and they're more likely to be safe on the roads getting there, it's a pretty small price to pay."

Business groups have argued that higher labour costs may result in higher prices for consumers, but the human cost of their gig economy practices is undeniable. Workers, often among the lowest paid in Australia, bear the brunt of these cost-saving measures. Burke's commentary emphasises that the true cost of these practices extends beyond the immediate financial transaction, as the safety and wellbeing of workers are also at stake.

The financial impact of these reforms will result in an estimated $500 million per year allocated to labour-hire workers and approximately $400 million for gig economy workers. From a worker's perspective, these additional funds represent a vital improvement in their livelihoods, helping them to meet their basic needs and maintain a decent standard of living.

The opposition to these changes from business leaders and the Liberal Party, underscores the deep divisions in the ongoing discourse on industrial relations. But what is their alternative? Slavery? Even then, it's doubtful conservatives would be satisfied with a serf-styled arrangement or, if wages were reduced to $2 per day that African workers receive, a view supported by Gina Rinehart in 2012: she'd argue that even $2 per day will send businesses broke, and the need to reduce them even further.

The historical perspective provided by Karl Marx and Adam Smith reminds us that wages are not merely expenses for businesses but also investments in the workforce. A well-compensated and secure workforce can be more productive and contribute positively to a nation's economic growth. The failure of business leaders and the Liberal Party to recognise this fundamental economic principle underscores the current challenges facing the industrial relations landscape in Australia.

COMPETING INTERESTS AND IDEOLOGIES

The debates and discussions surrounding gig economy workers and industrial relations changes in Australia reveal a complex landscape marked by competing interests and ideologies. On one side, business and employer groups, as well as the Liberal and National parties, often stand in opposition to labour-related reforms proposed by a Labor government and supported by the unions.

Their perspective, rooted in the basic accountants' idea of labour as a commodity to be exploited for minimal cost, is overly simplistic and underscores their resistance to any measures that seek to enhance worker rights and wellbeing. This uncompromising stance, which seemingly disregards even the most basic principles of fairness and dignity, raises important questions about the ethical dimensions of modern employment practices.

However, it is essential to recognise that the government plays a crucial role in shaping and regulating the labour market to ensure that it functions in the best interests of all citizens. Even Friedrich Hayek, the doyen for conservative economists and supporters, acknowledged the necessity of government intervention when free markets produce unfavourable economic outcomes, particularly for the working poor. This perspective emphasises the responsibility of government to address market failures and protect the most vulnerable members of society.

There are many deeply problematic practices of gig economy companies and this situation offers an insight into the future of work, if these practices are left to proliferate. While there are some individuals who find fulfillment in such work arrangements, the prevalent issues of low wages, precarious employment, and dangerous working conditions cannot be ignored.

The call for regulation in this context is not an attempt to stifle innovation or hamper business growth. Rather, it is an acknowledgment that certain practices have reached a point where they are detrimental to the wellbeing of workers and the broader community. Regulation, when well-balanced and carefully implemented, can help address these issues without stifling economic progress.

In the end, the evolving landscape of industrial relations in Australia underscores the importance of finding a middle ground, where the rights and interests of workers are safeguarded while allowing businesses to thrive. Achieving this balance is a complex task, as it involves reconciling competing perspectives and ideologies. However, it is a challenge that must be embraced, as the wellbeing of workers, the fairness of our society, and the sustainability of our economy all depend on finding equitable solutions in the face of evolving labour practices and the gig economy.

There needs to be a more nuanced and balanced approach to industrial relations to ensure that Australia can continue to prosper as an advanced and civilised economy, but it's an approach that an uncivilised business community and Liberal Party is not prepared to consider, preferring a world that resides in the law of the jungle.

***

FEAR OF CHANGE: A STALLING FORCE IN AUSTRALIAN POLITICS

9 September 2023

Australia, a nation supposedly known for its free and adventurous spirit, its boldness and bravery in the face of challenges, presents a perplexing paradox when it comes to political change. While the rhetoric and caricature of the "land down under" extols the virtues of a dynamic and fearless society, its political landscape often appears as the opposite. Why is this lack of courage so prevalent in Australian politics, especially when the inertia it creates can be so easily exploited by deeply conservative forces?

The fear of change in Australia manifests in various arenas, from referendums to debates on industrial relations, and is often characterised by a pervasive belief pushed forward by conservatives that any alteration to the status quo will result in catastrophic consequences. Despite the recurrent nature of these alarmist campaigns, the doomsday scenarios have never materialised. Yet, this fear-mongering cycle continues, aided and abetted by a compliant mainstream media, perpetuating political gridlock and stifling progress.

One of the enigmatic aspects of Australian politics is the stark contrast between the cliché of nation's adventurous spirit and its reluctance to embrace change, particularly on issues related to Indigenous rights and constitutional reform. Understanding the origins of this fear requires examining historical, cultural, and political factors that have shaped the nation's psyche.

The roots of this fear of change could be traced back to the formation of Australia's Constitution in 1901, or even further beyond, with the fear of the outsiders ever since invasion of the continent in 1788. The ease with which frenzies can be whipped up around constitutional amendments points to a fundamental issue in the nation's foundational document. The Republic referendum of 1999 serves as an illustrative case, where the fear of change overshadowed any rational discourse, ultimately leading to the proposal's defeat. Could it be that this fear is grounded in a broader anxiety about

Australia itself, a continent that was stolen and now faces the potential of being reclaimed by First Nations people, even if it is on a very miniscule level?

Another significant factor contributing to this fear of change is the enduring legacy of conservatism, particularly the brand of conservatism that gained prominence under the Howard Government in 1996, which has left an indelible stain and stench on Australian politics, even when governments of a different political stripe take the reins. In the 2007 federal election campaign, Kevin Rudd, felt the need to portray himself—and the Labor Party—as 'fiscal and social conservatives'; likewise for Anthony Albanese in 2022, who adopted a 'cautious and careful' leadership persona, and this behaviour of centrist or even marginally left-of-centre leaders exemplifies this enduring influence. This quasi-bipartisan conservatism has limited the scope for radical change, even when such change is urgently needed to address contemporary challenges.

The asymmetry in the way political parties present themselves exacerbates this issue. While Labor leaders often find it necessary to adopt conservative stances to appeal to a broad electorate, we are never ever going to see Liberal Party leaders announce a radical socialist agenda to counteract this conservatism. This one-sided political dynamic further reinforces the cautious and conservative approach that hampers significant change in Australia.

This fear of change is a pervasive force in Australian politics, inhibiting progress on critical issues such as Indigenous rights and constitutional reform. Rooted in historical, cultural, and political factors, this fear is compounded by a legacy of conservatism that transcends party lines. Understanding this phenomenon is crucial for the nation to move forward and embrace necessary changes in an ever-evolving world.

THE COMBATIVE NATURE OF AUSTRALIAN POLITICS AND ITS IMPLICATIONS

This fear of change is not limited to specific issues such as the Voice to Parliament or constitutional reform; it permeates the entire political landscape. Australia's political sphere is characterised by a unique combative nature, which often impedes the progress of important policy initiatives. This combative atmosphere, coupled with conservative forces, further contributes to the inertia in Australian politics.

The adversarial nature of Australian politics makes it challenging to achieve meaningful policy reforms. Unlike some other democracies where cooperation and consensus-building are valued, Australian politics often devolves into a battleground, where conservative opposition parties act as if they are a 'government in exile'. Even when they are out of power, the conservative Liberal Party maintains significant influence, supported by media and business sectors known for their cautious and conventional views.

Australia's self-perception as a bold and brave nation, derived from its sporting achievements and military history, contrasts with the political climate. While Australians take pride in their national identity as fearless adventurers (albeit a trait that never seems to be inclusive of Indigenous political warriors and heroes such as Pemulwuy, Yagan or Jandamarra), political campaigns tend to appeal to anxieties and prejudices rather than their better nature. The divisive nature of campaigns, as seen in the same-sex marriage debate of 2017 and the current Voice to Parliament debate, exploits these fears and insecurities, making it easier for conservative forces to sway public opinion.

Moreover, the phenomenon of the "tall poppy syndrome" prevails in Australia, where anything that deviates from the mainstream is often met with resistance. This mentality, while intended to maintain equality and prevent arrogance, can stifle innovation and progress, even when these changes are in the best interest of the broader society.

Negative campaigning is another aspect of Australian politics that exacerbates the fear of change. Campaigns that focus on the fear of missing out or the fear of the unknown are often used to manipulate public sentiment. An example is the infamous "Don't know; Vote no" slogan—such an inane and ignorant, albeit powerful, tactic—which tapped into fears and uncertainties during the same-sex marriage debate. This kind of messaging can easily sway public opinion and create a hostile environment for progressive change.

Australia is facing many social, economic, and political challenges that require significant reforms. However, the pervasive fear of change and the combative nature of politics have left the nation in a state of inertia, as if the populace are prisoners trapped in Plato's cave, seeing their own shadows on the wall for the first time and being too frightened to act.

Contrary to the popular myth of Australia as a young, free-spirited nation, it has often played it safe, especially at the federal level, with a history of conservative governments dominating the political landscape. Nevertheless, there have been moments when Australia has risen to the occasion and embraced change in the past, so why is it not doing it now?

BREAKING THE STALEMATE: A CALL FOR COURAGEOUS LEADERSHIP AND COMMON SENSE

A more recent example of this lack of courage relates to the Australian Greens' proposal to legalise cannabis. Despite substantial public support—around 78 per cent, according to opinion polls—and potential economic benefits, the immediate rejection of the proposal by the Labor government reflects the prevailing resistance to positive social reforms.

While this is only one minor part of social reform, where are the courageous leaders who can navigate the political landscape with empathy, compassion, and common sense to bring about the much-needed positive social and political change?

The reluctance to embrace positive social reforms, such as the legalisation of cannabis—or the reluctance to establishment of an anti-poverty commission (*for goodness sake!*), highlights the prevailing fear of change in Australian politics. The question arises: What is the root cause of this fear? Is it the apprehension of negative media headlines, religious and conservative backlash, or perhaps the influence of powerful interest groups like the Christian lobby?

These examples underscore the challenges in breaking through the political inertia. Even in states where one party holds a significant majority, like Western Australia where the Labor government holds 53 of 59 seats in the lower house, and has control of the legislative council, misrepresentation and resistance from opposing parties can hinder meaningful change.

The Liberal Party in Western Australia only holds two seats, and is not even the official opposition, but it managed to create an outrage about recent changes to Aboriginal cultural heritage laws. The result: the laws were repealed soon after they were introduced. It becomes evident that courage, leadership, and a genuine commitment to progress are essential components in overcoming these barriers.

Australia needs leaders who are unafraid to take calculated risks, challenge the status quo, and engage in constructive dialogue on critical issues. That's their job: otherwise, why make the huge effort of getting in parliament, and then getting into government, and then wilt at the first sight of resistance? This is how the conservatives win, and it's almost as though they don't need to sit on the government benches to be in power and control the political agenda.

This is a significant obstacle in Australian politics, leading to political stagnation and missed opportunities for positive social and political reform. To break free from this stalemate, Australia needs leaders who are unafraid to challenge the status quo, engage in evidence-based policymaking, and prioritise the wellbeing of their citizens.

It is time for courageous leadership, empathy, and common sense to guide the nation toward a future characterised by progress, compassion, and inclusivity. Only then can Australia overcome its fear of change and address the pressing challenges of the twenty-first century.

***

UNRAVELLING CONTROVERSY AND MISINFORMATION ON THE VOICE

16 September 2023

Australia is currently at a crossroads with the impending Voice to Parliament referendum, a crucial moment in the nation's democratic journey. With the writs for this referendum already issued, the legal formalities are in place following the Prime Minister Anthony Albanese's announcement of the referendum date a few weeks ago. However, despite not receiving the usual media frenzy and attention associated with general elections in the country, the issues surrounding it have ignited a storm of controversy and misinformation pushed through by "No" campaigners—including the Leader of the Opposition, Peter Dutton—in their quest to deny a positive initiative for First Nations and an attempt to inflict political damage on the Labor government.

The referendum process, in practice, closely mirrors that of a general election, with voters expected to participate in a similar manner. However, the real crux of the matter lies in the unfolding campaign, which has followed a contentious turn, ever since Dutton decided to engage maliciously in this campaign, use it as a political opportunity, rather than an opportunity to unite the country in a historic moment, and decide that he wouldn't support it and, therefore, campaign against it.

In recent weeks, the spotlight has shifted to the dissemination of misinformation originating from the "No" campaign, a misinformation campaign which has raised significant concerns about the integrity of the democratic process in Australia.

The "No" campaign has—among other nefarious activities—resorted to using phone banking centres that are actively calling random voters and spreading a web of falsehoods about the potential consequences if the Voice to Parliament referendum were to succeed. These misleading claims have taken various forms, including suggestions that the referendum's success would lead to the abolition of Australia Day, Anzac Day, demands for compensation and reparations to First Nations people, the possibility of "backyards being stolen", and a push for a Treaty, even though no such plan is on the agenda. Strikingly, much of this misinformation has found resonance with some members of the community, illustrating the complexity of public sentiment on Indigenous issues. Notably, many of the talking points employed by the "No" campaign have found their way into the rhetoric of Liberal Party politicians, adding political weight to the campaign of misinformation.

Constitutionally, the Voice to Parliament needs to have flexibility in the way that it is interpreted by both Parliament, and the High Court—if it is to ever reach that stage—so it can provide legal solutions in the future, without being constrained by interpretations from the past: otherwise, we'd need to hold a referendum every time a circumstance changes, or be rushing to the High Court to interpret whatever the actions of Parliament might be, when it's up to the Parliament to decide.

The legal intentions of the Voice to Parliament are clear and indubitable, as outlined by the Solicitor–General Stephen Donaghue in his advice to the Prime Minister in April. But the "No" campaign has ignored this advice and sown the seeds of fear and apprehension, suggesting a *de facto* veto role over [*insert fear campaign of choice here*], and claiming that the entire legal and parliamentary system will collapse. Only the absence of a "the end is nigh" placard campaign has saved the "No" campaign from complete ridicule but, even then, a receptive audience is always at hand for even the most disingenuous strategy.

The Voice to Parliament is simple: a mechanism to provide an Indigenous perspective on decision-making—but even still, leaving it up to the government of the day to decide whether to accept that perspective or not. It couldn't be any clearer, but the evolving narrative from the "No" campaign suggests that its influence could extend far beyond Indigenous issues, impacting the lives of all Australians. In recent weeks, the fear-mongering campaign against the Voice to Parliament has intensified, coinciding with the approaching referendum date of 14 October. Outlandish and ludicrous claims are now being propagated with increasing frequency, making it difficult to predict where this campaign of misinformation will ultimately lead.

What is behind this increasingly maniacal, lunatic and ridiculous campaign, one that is scraping the absolute bottom of the credibility barrel, laced with a healthy dose of racism and ignorance? It is evident that the "No" campaign is experiencing a sense of panic and urgency. Despite opinion polls suggesting the "Yes" vote is falling in public support, is the situation more precarious for the "No" side than it appears to be?

The "Yes" has faced its own challenges, including a lack of initial inspiration and strategic missteps, and unable to fully comprehend that once the Liberal–National Coalition made the decision not to support the referendum, that the entire strategy of the campaign would need to be rewired and reconfigured. Or perhaps, they also underestimated how vicious, how racist and how opportunist the Coalition was going to be, once they decided that their opposition was not going to be based on values or an ethical appreciation of what was at stake but, rather, an attack on the Labor government and scoring a political victory against the Prime Minister.

But why would we expect any different from the Liberal Party? They exacerbate racial tensions wherever possible for political gain, whether it's amplifying the Tampa incident from 2001 and the associated "children overboard" saga; "African gangs" in Melbourne in 2018; walking out of the Apology to the Stolen Generation—as Dutton did in 2008; failing to act on the *Bringing Them Home* report from 1997.

As the referendum date approaches, it is imperative for Australians to critically evaluate the issues at hand, separating fact from fiction. The referendum's outcome will have far-reaching benefits, and it is essential that voters make informed decisions based on accurate information and a genuine understanding of the Voice to Parliament proposal. But it's hard to do, when the bad-faith actors within the Coalition—almost all of them—have no interest in achieving positive outcomes, and only have the sole intention of scoring political points.

THE DESPERATION OF THE "NO" CAMPAIGN: LIES, MISINFORMATION AND THE POLITICS OF POLARISATION

What is striking about this campaign of misinformation is the persistence with which it is propagated. When confronted with accusations of pushing falsehoods, the "No" campaign does not retreat but instead seizes the opportunity to amplify its misinformation further. Such behaviour deviates significantly from the norms of rational discourse and suggests that the stakes for the Liberal Party are extraordinarily high, and it appears that the party genuinely believes that its political survival hinges on defeating the Voice to Parliament. This belief, however, raises an unsettling question: If the cause they champion is so strong, why resort to a campaign grounded in lies, fabrications, and misinformation?

The answer: it's got nothing to do with the issue in question and is a political strategy imported directly from the United States, particularly from the playbook of the Republican Party. This strategy, which prioritises obstruction and disinformation over substantive policy discussions, has roots dating back to figures like President Ronald Reagan in the 1980s, former

Speaker of the House of Representative, Newt Gingrich in the 1990s, and further refined in recent years by politicians such as US Senate leader, Mitch McConnell. The essence of this approach is simple: Say "no" to everything, regardless of its merits, spread falsehoods, and mislead the public. And it doesn't matter what the prize is for winning; it's all about the winning.

However, what makes this strategy concerning is its detachment from the real-world consequences of political decisions. For these reactionary conservatives, winning is the end in itself, irrespective of the harm caused by their policies. It becomes a victory in an ethereal sense, disconnected from the tangible impact on people's lives and this approach invariably leads to poor governance, where politicians who excel in opposition find themselves ill-equipped to govern effectively once they assume power. Figures like Tony Abbott in Australia and Donald Trump in the United States, who championed disruptive agendas and divisive rhetoric, struggled to achieve meaningful accomplishments during their tenures in office.

Now, Peter Dutton and the Liberal Party in Australia are following a similar playbook, employing tactics that prioritise lies and misinformation over constructive policy proposals. *It's all about the winning!*

The consequences of such a strategy are clear: If Australia did have the misfortune of Dutton ever becoming Prime Minister, his government would likely find itself adrift, lacking the ability to address the real challenges facing the nation. When a political platform relies on falsehoods to survive, the public quickly discerns the lack of substance behind it, as exemplified by Scott Morrison's loss at the 2022 federal election, where the lies were so plentiful, it was difficult to notice the truth, on those rare occasions when it did arise.

A more prudent strategy for the Liberal Party on the Voice to Parliament would have been to approach the referendum as an issue transcending political divides. They could have pledged support for the Voice to Parliament while vowing to improve and refine its implementation. Instead, their obstinacy and relentless campaign of misinformation have solidified the perception that they stand against progress and Reconciliation. If the referendum is to fail, they would be remembered as the obstructionists who prevented Australia from taking a meaningful step toward true Reconciliation, inclusivity and understanding.

In the end, the Liberal Party's strategy may have put them in a "lose–lose" position, and their reliance on American billionaires and political advisors with questionable intentions has further undermined their credibility. In its current makeup, it is doubtful that the party can contribute constructively to the nation's future. Their time in government between 2013–22 is instructive, and it would be repeated again in the future, should they ever return to government in their current form: A legacy of division, misinformation, and missed opportunities, leaving the task of repairing the damage to future governments.

THE VOICE TO PARLIAMENT REFERENDUM AND THE PATH FORWARD

The Voice to Parliament referendum in Australia has emerged as a unique and contentious chapter in the nation's political landscape. It should have been an opportunity to unite the country but, instead, is languishing as an event that has been hijacked and demolished by conservative forces, led by Peter Dutton and the Coalition.

Whether or not the referendum is successful or not, is not the point. It's evident that race issues are always bubbling under the surface and like a dormant virus, can always be activated when the diseased minds of conservative members of parliament see an opportunity that can be exploited for political gain. Certainly, this is a sign of a dysfunctional Liberal Party but as bad as this situation is, it's not the most significant problem.

The real problem is this: When the first opinion polls in August 2022 after the Prime Minister released the draft wording of the Voice to Parliament referendum question—way before any campaign details were even released—35 per cent of those people polled, said they would vote "No" anyway. *35 per cent.* This was before the Coalition even considered whether to support the referendum or not, and way before the vile "No" campaign began to activate its strategy of lies and misinformation. This is the real problem; unprompted, 35 per cent of the electorate said they would vote against the Voice to Parliament, even though there were no details available.

It is evident that the "No" campaign was always going to resort to extreme and unreasonable tactics but still, this departure from reasoned debate raises questions about the sincerity of their cause and the motivations behind their campaign. The strategy of pushing misinformation and using divisive tactics is reminiscent of political strategies imported from the United States, where political polarisation has been exacerbated in recent years. The consequences of such an approach can be damaging, as evidenced by the lacklustre records of politicians who prioritise obstruction and disinformation over substantive governance.

Moreover, the "No" campaign's tactics appear to have outflanked the government, catching them off guard. Could there have been a better way? Probably. All of this is in hindsight but it highlights the need for clear and effective communication strategies from political leaders, especially during critical moments such as referendums.

During the week, Victoria Premier Daniel Andrews provided straightforward and succinct message emphasising the importance of listening, better outcomes, and recognition of the oldest continuous culture. It was clear and serves as a model for political leaders, not just on the Voice to Parliament, but all political communications. Clearer communications from the outset for the Voice to Parliament would have been far better but, perhaps, given the level of racism that mainstream Australia generally reserves for Indigenous Australia, it's quite possible that even the most perfect of perfect political campaigns would still have arrived at the same point where we are right now.

It's clear that the Liberal Party is using the Voice to Parliament referendum as a testing ground for its negative messaging and misinformation campaign in readiness for the 2025 federal election. That the Liberal Party exists in its current form is a bad outcome for Australia but, this is who they are, and not much is going to change in the short-term period.

However, it is a profound opportunity for Australia to take a meaningful step toward inclusivity, understanding, and Reconciliation. Indigenous voices have consistently called for the recognition of their unique perspective, and the referendum represents a chance to heed these calls and forge a more equitable future.

The lead-up to the Voice to Parliament referendum in Australia has brought to the fore issues of misinformation, political polarisation, and vile communication strategies in the country's political landscape.

It didn't need to be like this. The Liberal Party decided that they wanted to be on the wrong side of history, and that's for them and their membership to face up to and decide whether they want to remain in the doldrums and exist as an esoteric and out-of-date debating club on par with conservative university politics, or become a meaningful party that can offer the Australian community something far more substantial in the future.

Regardless of the referendum's outcome, the path forward should involve constructive engagement, listening to Indigenous voices, and fostering a deeper understanding of Australia's rich cultural diversity. It is through such measures that Australia can build a more equitable and inclusive society, moving beyond the divisive conservative tactics that have marked this chapter in its political history.

***

THE END OF INTEGRITY: POLITICAL JOURNALISM IN AUSTRALIA

16 September 2023

The role of journalists within the Australian media has become a subject of intense scrutiny and debate in recent times, and a troubling trend has emerged within the mainstream media landscape, one that raises fundamental questions about the core responsibilities of journalists.

This trend is characterised by a distressing habit among journalists and media outlets to uncritically amplify the statements and actions emanating from conservative interests, in business circles, and in politics, most notably from the perspective of the Liberal–National Coalition, even though they are currently not in government. Consequently, this not only shapes the news agenda but also raises serious concerns about the quality and integrity of political journalism in Australia.

Peter Dutton, as the Leader of the Opposition, stands at the forefront of this media phenomenon. It is not uncommon to witness his statements and declarations receiving extensive coverage, even when their newsworthiness is questionable, and their accuracy is in doubt or completely wrong, as it was when Dutton claimed 60 per cent of Canada's energy requirements are powered by nuclear power plants (*wrong: it's actually 14 per cent*) and this incorrect figure was then widely reported in the media.

This peculiar emphasis on opposition voices creates a stark contrast with the traditional role of the media, where journalists are expected to act as watchdogs, scrutinise the government and opposition alike. Instead, what we observe today is an unsettling shift in the balance of media coverage, with opposition Shadow Ministers often being elevated to a status nearly equivalent to that of their government counterparts.

The unbalanced treatment of opposition leaders versus government officials becomes all the more evident when we recall the media's behaviour during the nine years between 2013–22, when the Labor Party was in opposition. In those years, the media did not place the opposition on a pedestal or grant them an undue level of attention—this is not a matter of opinion: why else would the media run with the narrative during the 2022 federal election campaign of *"who is Anthony Albanese, and why do we know so little about him"*? No one could ever ask "who is Peter Dutton" today, because everything he says appears in the media every single day of the week.

This striking contrast underscores a concerning shift in journalistic practices, where the Liberal–National Coalition—in opposition—has come to enjoy an unusual level of media exposure and influence.

Moreover, the failure to critically evaluate the statements and actions of the Leader of the Opposition has led to a disturbing decline in the quality of political journalism. Some mainstream journalists have rationalised their role as mere conveyors of politicians' statements, arguing that their job is to reflect and repeat what politicians say. However, this perspective neglects the fundamental role of journalists as watchdogs, responsible for exercising judgment and discernment in determining what is truly newsworthy, notable, and relevant to the public interest.

In essence, journalists are meant to be the gatekeepers of truth and accountability, rather than passive conduits for political narratives. Their responsibility is to hold those in power accountable, seek the truth, and expose falsehoods whenever they are encountered. Unfortunately, the prevailing trend in Australian political journalism appears to be one of repetition and amplification of political rhetoric, regardless of its veracity. This raises concerns that journalists have become instruments of political manipulation, rather than the guardians of an informed and engaged citizenry.

It could be argued that the Labor government is too busy for media engagement on such a significant level, and this perhaps justifies this journalistic imbalance. While it is plausible that the government may be occupied with the numerous responsibilities of state, it is equally plausible that the media's preference for sensationalism and controversy, often at the expense of reasoned government officials, plays a significant role in this dynamic.

The media landscape, which now includes even previously respected institutions like the ABC, prioritise the sensational over the substantive. This preference for controversy and demonstrably false claims has contributed to a disheartening media environment where reasoned members of the government struggle to gain the attention that we'd normally expect to see from a national government. Rather than challenging these figures of misinformation, the media seems content to give a platform to sensationalism, further exacerbating the deterioration of political journalism.

This situation is not unique to Australia; it reflects a broader trend in media culture, where the prevailing practice is to let political figures speak without challenge or correction. The media appears to have adopted a passive stance, allowing individuals like Peter Dutton, Sussan Ley, Michaelia Cash, James Paterson, and Barnaby Joyce to make unverified claims without rigorous follow-up questions or fact-checking. This departure from investigative journalism undermines the crucial role of the media in fostering transparency, accountability, and public discourse.

The best journalism is characterised by a commitment to questioning, scrutinising, and seeking the truth. As a widely circulated meme aptly puts it, when one party claims it's raining while the other asserts it's not, the journalist's responsibility is not to quote both parties but to look out the window and ascertain the actual weather conditions. The current state of political journalism in Australia falls short of this ideal. While there are undoubtedly dedicated journalists who adhere to these principles, their voices often struggle to gain the same prominence as those who prioritise sensationalism over substance.

THE DETERIORATION OF SUBSTANCE AND CONTEXT

The erosion of journalistic integrity within Australian political reporting becomes more evident when we examine recent cases that highlight the media's penchant for amplifying sensationalism over substance. Two such cases stand out, one involving Prime Minister Scott Morrison and the other featuring Senator James Paterson.

In the first case, Scott Morrison's briefing to an ABC journalist regarding a visit to China by Prime Minister Anthony Albanese, and meeting with Chinese President Xi Jinping was presented in a manner that demanded critical scrutiny. The story appeared on the ABC website, almost as a media release straight from Morrison's PR team:

> "Morrison has warned that his successor should not be too keen to accept an invitation to China"...
> "One opposition MP who listened to the former leader's speech inside Parliament House told the ABC it was generally well received by Liberal and National party members" ...
> "He was warning us about [President] Xi and his regime—urging us to hold the line, and not follow Labor's approach," the MP said.
> "Scott told us he continued to be proud at how his government stood up to China and that other countries followed our lead" ...
> "His comments on Russia were made with reference to the contemporary actions of Chinese banks in supporting the Russian economy, effectively undermining Western sanctions," one Liberal MP said.

There are "unnamed sources"—which is journalism code for "I made this up", and for all we know, the unnamed Liberal MP could actually be Scott Morrison himself.

This showed a complete lack of discernment on the part of the journalist and the subsequent editorial decision to present the story without adequate context or verification. Morrison's statements were relayed without the necessary probing questions: Why was he sharing this story now? What were his motives? Could these claims be corroborated independently?

It is essential to emphasise that while the former prime minister's words may carry inherent newsworthiness due to his position, the manner in which they were reported left much to be desired. The absence of these critical questions, coupled with the prominent coverage, suggested a failure in journalistic discernment. The story appeared more as a vehicle for self-promotion by Morrison and a means to embarrass the Albanese government on an issue where bipartisan support should have been paramount. This episode underscores the pressing need for journalists to exercise a more vigilant and probing approach to their reporting, focusing not just on the what but also the why and the how behind political narratives.

In the second case involving Senator James Paterson, the media's treatment of his statements exemplifies another concerning trend. Paterson's suggestion that parliamentary staff should undergo security vetting was presented as headline news without sufficient context or counterarguments. This might be a good idea but shouldn't we hear from the government first? The absence of a government response or expert analysis further contributed to the distortion of the story. The mere fact that Paterson is a member of the opposition should have prompted a more critical examination of his proposal, rather than presenting it uncritically.

This unfiltered amplification of opposition voices by the media perpetuates a distorted perception of the political landscape. An uninformed observer could easily mistake the opposition's statements for government policy or perceive Senator Paterson as a key government figure when, in reality, he holds a different role. This failure to provide adequate context and balance in political reporting contributes to a skewed public perception of the political discourse, further undermining the media's role as an impartial and informative watchdog.

These cases underscore a deeper issue within Australian political journalism—one characterised by a conservative framing of news that requires reform. The culture of journalism and political reporting appears to be in need of a significant shift. While politicians and their behaviour are often scrutinised for necessary change, the same level of introspection and transformation must extend to the realm of media and journalism.

It is essential to acknowledge that the Australian media landscape has seldom seen the emergence of a newspaper with the stature and influence of renowned international publications like the *New York Times* or *The Times* of London. Despite the dedication and hard work of journalists, the Australian media has often been marred by a tendency to intersperse excellent stories with trivial content, celebrity gossip, or seemingly inconsequential articles.

This trend is not unique to a particular publication but rather seems endemic to the broader media culture. While journalists may wholeheartedly believe in the significance of their work, the prevailing environment occasionally demands a balance between substantive journalism and more commercially appealing content.

The current state of Australian political journalism raises profound concerns about the role of the media in a thriving democracy. Recent cases demonstrate the media's failure to provide adequate context, discernment, and balance in its reporting, with a clear tendency to prioritise sensationalism over substance and provide favour to conservative interests.

To address these issues, it is imperative that not only politicians but also journalists and media outlets undertake a critical evaluation of their practices and embrace a more informed, responsible, and balanced approach to political reporting.

THE IMPERATIVE FOR MEDIA REFORM IN AUSTRALIA

In examining the state of political journalism in Australia, it becomes evident that the challenges facing the media landscape are multifaceted and deeply entrenched. The cases discussed in this essay underscore the pressing need for reform and a renewed commitment to journalistic integrity and professionalism. While the Labor government has emerged victorious in the 2022 federal election, it is clear that they face a different kind of challenge when it comes to managing the media landscape.

One of the key issues confronting the Labor government is the relentless onslaught of opposition narratives that often drown out their message to the electorate. The opposition's dominance of the airwaves and the media landscape with what can only be described as "meaningless garbage" presents a significant obstacle to effective communication. This predicament is not novel; history attests that Labor governments have long contended with a media environment that tends to disadvantage them.

The call for media reform in Australia is not a new one, and it resonates with increasing urgency. The goal is not for the government to exert control over the media, mirroring authoritarian regimes such as China, North Korea and China, but rather to foster a fairer, more professional, and equitable media environment. Such reforms would serve the public interest by ensuring that citizens have access to accurate, well-balanced, and informative reporting.

The failure to address media reform perpetuates an environment where centre-left governments struggle to gain a fair hearing, where two or three positive stories are overwhelmed by a deluge of negative coverage. It is incumbent upon the Labor government to recognise that striving for *faux* balance in an inherently imbalanced media landscape may not be the most effective approach. Instead, confronting the systemic issues and pursuing meaningful reforms would not only benefit the current government but also pave the way for a more transparent and informed political discourse for future governments of all persuasions.

Media reform, long overdue, should be a priority, and the Labor government's reluctance to address this issue remains perplexing. By advocating for and implementing comprehensive media reforms, Australia can aspire to a media environment that fosters a more informed citizenry, supports robust democratic processes, and ensures a fair and equitable platform for all political voices.

***

CLIMATE CHANGE AND EXTREME WEATHER WARNINGS: A CALL FOR URGENT ACTION

23 September 2023

In the midst of spring, Sydney recently experienced an unusual and unsettling phenomenon: five consecutive days of 35-degree heat. This unseasonal weather has left residents puzzled and concerned, as it defies the typical climate patterns of the region. While such temperatures might be expected in the height of summer—and only just—this occurrence in September is a clear sign of the changing climate in Australia.

The memory of the devastating bushfire season of 2019/20 still haunts us. It was a period when the country witnessed half of its territory engulfed in bushfires, and severe weather events wreaked havoc in every state and territory. This catastrophe led to widespread suffering and loss, leaving scars that are far from healed. Now, there are ominous predictions that the upcoming summer season could rival the horrors of that fateful year.

The warning bells have been sounded, not just by weather experts but also by the Premier of NSW, Chris Minns, who has urged communities to brace themselves for extreme heat in the coming summer. However, such warnings are only meaningful if they are accompanied by substantial support and concrete action provided by federal, state and territory governments. What are the lessons that have been learnt from the last extreme bushfire season?

The Australian government's commitment to reducing greenhouse gas emissions by 43 per cent by 2030 is a step in the right direction. But with each passing day, the urgency of the climate crisis becomes more apparent. The transition from fossil fuels to renewable energy sources is imperative, but it must happen at a pace that matches the urgency of the situation.

What's even more concerning is the reluctance of many media outlets—and the conservative side of politics—to explicitly connect these extreme weather events to global warming. Despite the overwhelming scientific consensus, some media sources remain hesitant, often due to ties their media proprietors—

Rupert Murdoch and Kerry Stokes—have with oil, gas, and coal producers. This hesitation impedes public understanding and action on climate change.

Across the world, in northern America, Europe, south-east Asia and Africa, we have witnessed catastrophic fires, floods, and earthquakes tied to climate change. Yet, it's perplexing that some media outlets, particularly those influenced by fossil fuel interests, fail to acknowledge the obvious correlation between these events and global warming. The planet is setting new records every year, and it's not the kind of record-breaking anyone should celebrate.

As we look to the future, political compromise is no longer an option. Climate change is not an issue where competing interests can be balanced to everyone's satisfaction. If we fail to act decisively, there will be no winners, no matter one's political affiliation or economic interests. The very existence of our planet is at stake.

While optimism may be scarce, the need for action is abundantly clear. A change of government at the 2022 federal election offered some hope, but there needs to be faster action and unequivocal commitment to address climate change. The time for action is now, for the sake of our planet, the wellbeing of future generations, and all the ecosystems that depend on a stable climate.

THE CHALLENGE OF SHORT-TERM INTERESTS AND POLITICAL GRIDLOCK

It appears that the prevailing theme in addressing climate change is the prioritisation of short-term political interests over the imperative of long-term action. Regrettably, this is not a challenge unique to Australia. Around the world, major nations seem reluctant to take the climate crisis seriously, primarily because they are both the biggest contributors to the problem and the ones with the most to lose, including economic powerhouses like China, the United States, most of Europe, and indeed, Australia.

While it is true that some efforts are being made, they still fall short of what is required to combat climate change effectively. The warning signals have been flashing for decades, dating back to the 1960s, and each passing decade—the '70s, '80s, '90s and beyond—has brought a fresh call for urgent action, but more often than not, these calls have transformed into nothing more than empty promises. The consequences of inaction are now glaringly evident in the form of bushfires and floods in Australia, as well as similar disasters across the globe.

In Australia, legislative changes have been incremental and piecemeal. The commitment to reduce greenhouse gas emissions by 43 per cent is certainly an improvement compared to the non-binding 26 per cent that was proposed by the Liberal Party in 2022. However, the Australian Greens advocate for a reduction of at least 78 per cent, possibly even as high as 90 per cent, which is more in line with what is needed to curb climate change. The current pace of action does not match the urgency of the situation.

To effect real change, it may be necessary to establish a *supra*-governmental body with the authority to halt certain activities. For instance, a body with the power to curtail certain forms of mining or resource extraction that are contributing to environmental degradation. The concept of carbon credits, though initially well-intentioned, has failed in practice, often resulted in the trading of emissions rather than a true reduction.

Another significant challenge lies in the longevity of legislation. Climate policies and initiatives are often at the mercy of changing governments. For instance, the carbon pricing scheme implemented by the Gillard government in 2012 effectively reduced emissions during its brief existence, but it was abandoned by the Abbott government in 2013, resulting in an increase in emissions. This illustrates the disruptive influence of politics on climate action.

One potential solution might involve implementing legislation with long-term effects that are difficult to reverse, regardless of changes in government. Over time, such measures could become embedded in society, making it politically challenging for future administrations to dismantle them. A case in point is unleaded petrol, which has remained in place for over three decades, despite past attempts to reintroduce leaded petrol.

The crux of the issue lies in the very nature of our democratic system, which often makes it difficult to make difficult decisions. Elected officials are understandably hesitant to support policies that might jeopardise their political careers. Addressing this challenge requires a more informed and engaged citizenry. Achieving this involves improving education and media, ensuring that people understand the critical issues at stake. Currently, distractions such as celebrity news and sports often take precedence, allowing those in power to operate with impunity.

In essence, addressing climate change requires a profound shift in priorities and a willingness to make difficult, long-term decisions that transcend political cycles. It necessitates a more informed and engaged public that holds leaders accountable for their actions on this critical issue.

THE URGENT NEED FOR ACTION AND GLOBAL COOPERATION

The recurring pattern of inaction on climate change is a cause for great concern. Calamities like wildfires, floods, and extreme weather events elicit temporary calls for action, but these calls often result in small, incremental changes that ultimately fail to address the magnitude of the problem. It's a cycle that repeats itself, with governments, regardless of their political affiliations, demonstrating a lack of serious commitment to tackling climate change. This, despite the fact that climate change ranks among the most critical international security issues.

The unfortunate polarisation of climate change as a 'left-versus-right' issue further exacerbates the problem. Conservative governments often deny the urgency of climate change, while centre-left governments, at best, take incremental steps toward mitigation. The reality, however, is that the challenge transcends partisan politics. It is a global issue that requires a collective and decisive response.

This lack of meaningful action extends beyond Australia; it is a global phenomenon. Very few governments worldwide have enacted comprehensive climate change measures commensurate with the scale of the challenge. Climate conferences like COP (Conference of the Parties) meetings are held regularly, with each new gathering offering a glimmer of hope for progress. The upcoming COP Convention on Climate Change in Dubai promises to introduce a global stocktake of emissions, energy transition, and climate finance to be revisited every two years. However, such incremental steps are not sufficient in the face of a rapidly escalating climate crisis.

In Australia, the debate over issues like the closure of the Liddell power station and the expansion of coal mining continues. This indecision and reliance on traditional practices hinder meaningful progress and the fear of legal challenges and political fallout discourages bold action. But the truth is, we have run out of any leeway and room to move. We can no longer afford to delay or defer responsibility to future generations or governments.

The timeline for addressing climate change has become alarmingly compressed. The modest goal of 43 per cent reductions in emissions is no longer adequate. To avert catastrophic consequences, we must aim far higher for reductions of 60–90 per cent. While achieving 100 per cent reductions—or net zero—may seem like an insurmountable challenge, it's imperative that we explore every avenue, even radical reforms in mining technology, to pursue this goal.

The urgency of the situation cannot be overstated. We are on borrowed time, and every passing day inches us closer to irreversible environmental damage. It's time for principled politicians at both the federal and state levels to rise to the occasion. It's time for global cooperation that transcends politics, borders, and vested interests.

We find ourselves at a pivotal moment in human history. Climate change is not a distant threat; it is *here*, it is *now*, and it demands our immediate and sustained attention. The path ahead is challenging, but it is not insurmountable. It requires decisive action, innovative solutions, and the political will to prioritise the future of our planet over short-term interests. We must remember that the consequences of inaction affect us all, regardless of political affiliation or geographical location. The time for action is now, and the collective efforts of individuals, communities, and nations hold the key to a more sustainable and resilient future.

***

THE MANIACAL DEBATE OVER NUCLEAR ENERGY IN AUSTRALIA

23 September 2023

In the realm of Australian politics, the topic of nuclear energy resurfaces with a predictable regularity, akin to the changing of the seasons. It's a discussion that often emerges when the Liberal Party finds itself grappling with political quandaries or crises, prompting us to question the motives behind this persistent revival.

As if we need any reminding, the recurring reports and studies commissioned over the past sixty years have uniformly concluded that nuclear energy is economically unviable for Australia, most recently, the 2019 report commissioned by Angus Taylor, who served as the Minister for Energy at the time. These comprehensive assessments have consistently pointed out the impracticality of nuclear energy from an economic standpoint. However, the Liberal Party's persistence in advocating for nuclear power appears less rooted in a genuine desire to establish a nuclear industry and more in its utility as a political wedge issue, particularly when the party finds itself in the opposition. Curiously, despite being in power for substantial periods since 1996—20 years—the Liberal–National Coalition has never made a substantial push to overturn the ban on nuclear energy.

Furthermore, nuclear energy is a contentious subject in Australian politics, much like the divide between left-and-right on climate change and energy policy worldwide. The conservative right often champions nuclear and fossil fuel energy, while the progressive left advocates for renewable energy sources. This ideological schism fuels the ongoing debate over nuclear energy in Australia, further highlighting its political nature.

One recurring element in the nuclear energy discourse is the concept of small modular reactors (SMRs). The Liberal Party, and sometimes the National Party—occasionally in unison!—periodically reintroduce this topic into the public sphere. It is a circular argument that resurfaces like clockwork, despite the lack of substantial progress or change in circumstances. Even media outlets such as the ABC contribute to this cyclical discussion, sometimes repeating similar panels and discussions with familiar faces. They did this recently with an episode of *Q+A*, which was almost a replay of an episode just two months earlier, featuring the same guest, William Shackel, a 17-year-old nuclear activist whom the media seems to be promoting as Australia's answer to Sweden's Greta Thunberg—albeit from the opposite side of the ideological divide.

The constantly rekindled and recycled debate surrounding nuclear energy in Australia reveals a complex interplay of political motivations and policy considerations. While proponents argue for its economic benefits and potential role in achieving net-zero emissions, opponents emphasise the consistent conclusions of reports, emphasising the impracticality of nuclear energy on economic, environmental, and political grounds. The cyclic nature of this debate ignores the reams of comprehensive, evidence-based assessment of nuclear energy's feasibility and its malalignment with Australia's energy and environmental goals.

THE COMPLEXITY OF THE NUCLEAR ENERGY DEBATE

As is the case on many campaigns supported and promoted by conservative interests, the ongoing debate surrounding nuclear energy in Australia is marked by a considerable degree of misinformation and misdirection. One common misconception is that the ban on nuclear energy in Australia— legislated by the Howard government in 1998—equates to a ban on assessing its cost. This oversimplification disregards the fact that multiple government reports since the 1960s have included detailed cost assessments for nuclear energy. The Switkowski report into uranium and nuclear industries from 2006, in particular, stands out as the most comprehensive examination of nuclear energy's costings, conclusively demonstrating its unviability.

In the midst of this debate, the involvement of young individuals in politics and energy discussions—such as William Shackel—is commendable. However, being so misguided and forcing the transformation of opinion into fact is dangerous. It is essential to ensure that such participation is based on a well-informed understanding of the complexities of the issue. The notion that lifting the ban on nuclear energy is solely about obtaining cost assessments is a tactic to mislead, as costings have been available for years, and there is nothing in any legislation that precludes any corporation or government entity to obtain costings. This debate requires a more comprehensive examination of the economic, environmental, and safety implications associated with nuclear power.

Critics often argue that renewable energy sources, such as solar panels and wind turbines, pose their own set of challenges, including disposal when they reach their use-by date. In reality, these technologies are recyclable, much like many other modern technologies. Moreover, proponents of nuclear energy sometimes assert that it is the cleanest and cheapest form of energy, which warrants its immediate adoption. However, these claims do not align with the available evidence. Nuclear energy is not the cheapest option, nor the "cleanest", or else it would have gained widespread use within Australia long ago.

One of the more contentious aspects of the nuclear energy debate revolves around the disposal of radioactive waste and the risk of meltdowns. While the probability of a meltdown is statistically low, the catastrophic consequences when such events do occur are a source of great concern. Historically, there have been four major nuclear meltdowns—Fukushima in 2011, Chernobyl in 1986, Three Mile Island in 1979, and the lesser-known SL-1 accident in Idaho in 1961, with each causing long-lasting environmental and health consequences. The management of nuclear waste also presents a daunting challenge, as it remains hazardous for tens of thousands of years. Incidents like Fukushima serve as stark reminders of the risks associated with nuclear power, and they underscore the need for absolute foolproof safety measures, which are difficult and costly to guarantee.

Moreover, the lengthy construction timelines of nuclear reactors, typically spanning a decade or more, do not address immediate energy needs or climate change concerns. In contrast, renewable energy sources can be deployed more quickly and are increasingly cost-effective.

The nuclear energy debate in Australia is far from straightforward. It is a complex issue that requires careful consideration of economic, environmental, and safety factors. Misconceptions and oversimplifications can hinder meaningful discourse, and the past experiences of nuclear disasters serve as a sobering reminder of the high stakes involved. As the debate continues, it is imperative that all perspectives are considered, and that evidence-based decision-making prevails to ensure a sustainable and secure energy future for Australia.

THE UNYIELDING CHALLENGE OF NUCLEAR ENERGY IN AUSTRALIA

Cost, politics, and the enduring question of economic viability loom large in the ongoing discourse surrounding nuclear energy in Australia. Indeed, cost remains one of the most formidable barriers to the adoption of nuclear power in the country. Even nuclear scientists acknowledge that while advancements have made nuclear energy safer than it was decades ago, the sheer economic burden makes it an impractical choice in Australia.

This sentiment is echoed by experts such as Warwick McKibben, a conservative economist and former Reserve Bank board member who contributed to the Switkowski inquiry into nuclear energy. McKibben's assertion is clear: nuclear energy would have been marginally viable in 2006—when the Switkowski report was released—and has become wholly uncompetitive when compared to the rapid advancements in renewable energies in 2023.

The proponents of nuclear energy often overlook a crucial aspect of the equation—the perspective of energy companies and the practicality of their investments. Energy providers are not swayed by political rhetoric or impassioned arguments on television programs such as *Q+A*, or whether political leaders such as Peter Dutton wish to use nuclear energy as a political wedging strategy. They are, first and foremost, driven by the bottom line and the potential for profitable returns on their investments. At present, the case for nuclear power in Australia does not align with their financial objectives, as there are more cost-effective and less risky alternatives readily available.

In essence, the Liberal Party's recurrent emphasis on nuclear energy appears to be more of a political tactic than a genuine commitment to the industry's development. Their track record, spanning 20 of the past 27 years in government, demonstrates a lack of tangible action in this regard. It begs the question of whether this is merely political posturing, a way to create a point of difference leading up to the next federal election, or a deliberate distraction from other pressing issues. The broader industry and business community, characterised by pragmatic and profit-driven decision-makers, are unlikely to be swayed by these antics in the political playground.

While the proponents of nuclear energy may temporarily capture the attention of some supporters and undecided individuals, the ultimate feasibility of such a venture remains questionable. The economic impracticality of nuclear power in the current energy landscape, coupled with the evident political motivations of some proponents, casts doubt on the likelihood of substantial progress in this arena. While the discussion persists, the hard-nosed realities of economics and the pressing need for sustainable and cost-effective energy solutions are likely to steer Australia's energy trajectory in other, more practical directions.

***

RUPERT AND THE EMPIRE: A LEGACY OF NEGATIVE INFLUENCE AND BAD BEHAVIOUR

30 September 2023

Rupert Murdoch's recent decision to step down as the chairman of Fox News and News Corporation, passing the torch to his son, Lachlan Murdoch, marks a significant moment in the ongoing saga of the Murdoch media empire. However, this transition is far from the end of Rupert Murdoch's enduring influence and leaves an uncertain future not only for News Corporation but also for the broader media landscape in Australia.

Over the years, Rupert Murdoch has wielded immense power and influence, stretching across three continents and significantly shaping the political and media landscapes in Australia, Britain, and the United States. Despite the gradual decline of mainstream media's power, it remains a formidable force that continues to impact political narratives and public opinion.

Murdoch's legacy is a complex one, marked by a slew of controversies and allegations. While he has garnered praise from many sycophantic political leaders and media figures for his "passion and principles", his actions have come under deep scrutiny in the past, most notably, the Leveson inquiry in the UK in 2011, which revealed allegations of criminal behaviour within his media empire.

Critics argue that Murdoch has frequently acted in bad faith, employing his media outlets to propagate misinformation and pro-conservative propaganda. His public support—through his media networks—for figures such as Russian President, Vladimir Putin, and his influential role in Donald Trump's 2016 election victory have also drawn sharp criticism. Moreover, his media outlets have played a role in promoting the unsubstantiated claim that the 2020 US election was stolen, which ultimately contributed to the shocking events of the Capitol Hill riots in early 2021. Is this the *passion and principles* his misguided supporters are applauding?

Many voices, such as Australians for a Murdoch Royal Commission and former Prime Ministers such as Kevin Rudd and Malcolm Turnbull, have called for Murdoch to face legal consequences for his actions, suggesting that his media licenses should have been revoked based on these previous actions, particularly in his home country, Australia. Yet, Rupert Murdoch has largely remained unscathed by the consequences of his actions, and at the age of 92, it seems increasingly unlikely that he *will* be held accountable.

Beyond media ownership, Murdoch has exerted significant influence on the political landscapes of Australia, Britain, and the United States. His support for politicians like Boris Johnson and Theresa May in the UK, as well as Donald Trump in the US, has played a role in shaping these countries' political narratives.

Critics argue that Murdoch's media outlets have been instrumental in perpetuating the status quo, making it challenging for significant policy changes, such as gun law reform in the United States, to gain traction and his newspapers and television shows tend to echo the same themes and arguments to other parts of the world, with localised variations.

Interestingly, in the media markets where Murdoch's media outlets do not have a strong presence, such as Canada, New Zealand, and mainland Europe, there is often a more diverse and balanced media landscape. Even in Italy, where the media tycoon Silvio Berlusconi had a similar polarising effect on politics and media, there were enough counterbalances to offset their white-dominated, one-sided and conservative perspectives.

It is tempting to speculate about the eventual end of Murdoch's influence. Still, as long as Rupert Murdoch remains active in the media landscape, he is unlikely to relinquish his grip easily, even if it is as 'Chairman Emeritus', whatever that might represent. The rise of Lachlan Murdoch, while not without its challenges, seems to be a continuation of the Murdoch dynasty's presence in the media world.

Rupert Murdoch's legacy is one characterised by a complex interplay of power, influence, and controversy. His media empire has left a negative mark on the political and media landscapes of multiple countries, and its impact continues to reverberate through the world of media and politics. As the baton is passed to the next generation, the future of the Murdoch empire remains uncertain, but one thing is certain: Rupert Murdoch's influence is far from over, and needs to be counteracted and reduced wherever possible.

THE ONGOING INFLUENCE AND CONTROVERSIES OF THE MURDOCH EMPIRE

The future of News Corporation and its impact on the media and political landscapes remains uncertain and Lachlan Murdoch's role and the direction he will take in Australia, the US, and the UK are questions that have yet to be fully answered. The Murdoch empire, with its right-wing media outlets such as Fox News and Sky News "after dark", has often been criticised for its sensationalist and over-the-top approach, blurring the line between news and entertainment.

While for many people, these outlets are primarily for freak-show amusement or a perverse form of "infotainment" and many viewers can see through the rhetoric, it is undeniable that they wield significant influence. They have the ability to sway public opinion and radicalise certain segments of the population and it is this influence has led to concerns about the potential erosion of democracy and the spread of conspiracy theories, which can have real-world consequences, as evidenced by the Capitol Hill riots.

The business model employed by News Corporation and Fox News involves magnifying particular news stories to create outrage. When such stories are lacking, they are often manufactured to maintain viewership and readership. But is such a great business model? This approach can be lucrative, but it also comes with significant risks. For example, pushing the narrative of the "stolen election" following the 2020 US election resulted in a $US797 million defamation case against News Corporation by Dominion Voting Systems. There is also the looming threat of the Smartmatic case, which could lead to even more substantial financial repercussions: two lawsuits at a possible cost of over $US2 billion. How is this a business model that can sustain the company in the long term?

Rupert Murdoch should have faced consequences for his actions long ago. The phone hacking scandals of 2011, which led to the closure of News of the World publication, should have resulted in a criminal trial for Murdoch. However, he managed to evade serious consequences by offering apologies and promises to clean up the company's act, suggesting "it was the most humble day of my life". At the Leveson Inquiry, James Murdoch proclaimed "these actions do not live up to the standards that our company aspires to, and it is our determination to both put things right, make sure these things don't happen again, and to be the company that we've always aspired to be".

If anything, since the Leveson Inquiry in 2011 and since those weasel-words were uttered by both James and Rupert Murdoch, the behaviour of News Corporation has become significantly worse. In hindsight, those promises were hollow, as News Corporation and Fox News have continued to operate with lower journalistic standards and, instead of improving and a *determination to both put things right, make sure these things don't happen again*, the media empire has become more unhinged, contributing to the polarisation of political discourse.

One notable aspect of Rupert Murdoch's influence is the fear that many politicians have of him. Even though some politicians have publicly clashed with him, there is often a reluctance to take decisive action against him. This influence extends beyond individual politicians and permeates the media landscape in Australia. Many media outlets such as the ABC, Seven West Media and Nine Media now feel the need to compete with the Murdoch model, compromising journalistic integrity in the process.

The rise of independent media outlets has provided an alternative to the Murdoch-dominated landscape, offering diverse perspectives and challenging the status quo. However, Murdoch's influence still casts a long shadow over the media industry in Australia and beyond.

As for the future under Lachlan Murdoch, it remains to be seen whether he will chart a different course or follow in his father's footsteps. Rupert Murdoch's historical precedent, taking over the empire when his own father passed away, showed that he was not always considered the best fit at the time. Lachlan, in contrast, has the advantage of having his father as a mentor and advisor, which could shape the direction of News Corporation and, potentially, in a very negative way.

The true impact of Lachlan Murdoch's leadership will likely remain uncertain until Rupert Murdoch either passes away or becomes too incapacitated to continue his involvement. Regardless of the outcome, the Murdoch empire's influence, controversies, and complex legacy are unlikely to fade into obscurity anytime soon. The ongoing saga of the Murdoch empire will continue to be a subject of interest for historians, media analysts, and psychologists, as it raises questions about the intersection of media, politics, and power.

THE UNCERTAIN FUTURE OF THE MURDOCH EMPIRE

Part of the uncertainty of the Murdoch empire arises from the internal dynamics within the Murdoch family, as well as Lachlan Murdoch's own business track record—the failure of One.Tel in the 1990s and 2000s being the most significant—and his political leanings.

One of the challenges Lachlan Murdoch faces is the shadow of his own family name. He will not only be contending with the expectations and pressures associated with inheriting a media empire but also the comparisons to his father, Rupert Murdoch, who has been a dominant figure in the media landscape for decades. Rupert's reputation as a shrewd businessman, a charismatic leader, and a formidable media mogul has set a high bar for Lachlan to meet.

Rumours of Lachlan Murdoch's right-wing and fanatical approach to using media for political motivations have always raised concerns. However, it is important to remember that these claims remain speculative, and Lachlan's true intentions and direction will only become evident over time and, for as long as Rupert Murdoch is alive, his presence will continue to influence the empire, making it challenging to gauge the extent of any potential changes.

The saying that 'the first generation builds the empire, the second generation consolidates, and the third generation destroys' has often been cited in discussions about family-owned enterprises. In the case of Rupert Murdoch, it appears he may be oscillating between the phases of consolidation and potential destruction of the empire and the mounting defamation cases and diminishing influence the mainstream media in general, suggests that the Murdoch empire is already be in decline.

However, the fate of News Corporation will not solely depend on the Murdoch family dynamics. External factors such as evolving media landscapes, regulatory changes, and shifts in audience preferences will also play significant roles in shaping its future. The media industry is in a state of flux, with digital platforms and independent media outlets gaining prominence.

Comparisons to other dynasties, such as the Fairfax and Packer dynasty in Australia, or the Vanderbilt and Hearst empires in the United States, provide some insight into the potential trajectory of the Murdoch empire. These families saw their wealth and influence diminish in the third generation, suggesting that a similar fate may await News Corporation. While it is worth noting that each dynasty is unique, the fate of the Murdoch empire does remains uncertain: it could diminish completely, as was the case with Kerry Packer's Australian Consolidated Press; or it could morph into a *supra* behemoth, even greater than its current global reach. It's unlikely.

Rupert Murdoch faced skepticism when he took over the News Limited business after the death of his father, Keith Murdoch, in 1952, and yet he went on to become a transformative figure in the media world. There are doubts over Lachlan Murdoch, but it has to be remembered that his father faced the same doubts, albeit at a much younger age.

There will continue to be a range of internal and external influences: the dynamics within the Murdoch family, the evolving media landscape, and Lachlan's own decisions will all play crucial roles in shaping the direction of News Corporation. A crucial first business decision of nominating former Prime Minister Tony Abbott to the board of Fox Corporation does not bode well. Abbott has no business experience and skill and, while he was the Prime Minister of Australia, he is a totemic culture war warrior who only has an interest in divisive and polemical outcomes, as was evident during his prime ministership between 2013–15.

This is the wrong direction: if Lachlan Murdoch wanted to show the business community that he is a leader with business acumen and wanting to change the direction of News Corporation and, to echo the words of James Murdoch from 2011, to show *determination to both put things right, make sure these things don't happen again,* this is not the right decision.

Whether the empire continues to thrive, undergoes transformation, or faces decline will be a topic of ongoing speculation and analysis in the ever-changing world of media and politics. It's early days, but a day-one decision to install Abbott onto the board of Fox Corporation could also indicate that Lachlan Murdoch is oblivious to the fact that he could fast-tracking the demise of News Corporation. And if that is the result, wouldn't that be a sight to behold.

***

DANIEL ANDREWS: A LEGACY OF LEADERSHIP AND MAINSTREAM MEDIA MADNESS

30 September 2023

Daniel Andrews, the 48th Premier of Victoria, has stepped down after serving the state for an impressive nine years. In his resignation announcement, he reflected on his time in office, highlighting his dedication to doing "what's right, not just what's popular". Andrews' political journey was marked by significant electoral victories and a contentious relationship with both the mainstream media and his political detractors, notably populated by conspiracy theorists and extremists.

Andrews' tenure as Premier was noteworthy for several reasons. He managed to secure three consecutive election victories in 2014, 2018, and 2022. The 2022 election, in particular, stands out as a significant achievement, given the perception that the entire media industry in Melbourne was against him. Despite the odds, he not only retained power in 2022 but increased his majority—56 seats in a parliament of 88—defying expectations, although the expectations of a dent in this majority—or even a defeat—were solely magnified by the media, without any evidence to support their claims that Andrews was facing a political demise.

Throughout his nine years in office, Andrews faced numerous political challenges and accumulated his fair share of detractors, as is to be expected for a political leader in office for such an extended period of time. However, his enduring popularity, with a consistent approval rating of over 60 per cent, in addition to a landslide victory in 2018 and a consolidating win in 2022, suggests that he was far from the divisive figure many in the media portrayed him to be.

The mainstream media tried to play a crucial role in shaping negative public perceptions of Daniel Andrews, as it does for any prominent political leader who is from the centre-left or non-conservative persuasion. The 2022 election campaign saw widespread and unfounded criticism of Andrews in many media outlets, including *The Herald Sun*, *The Age*, the ABC, and multiple television channels and raises important questions about the influence of media bias on electoral outcomes and the electorate's ability to discern fact from opinion, although the electoral results suggest the negative and relentless media campaign against Andrews didn't have an effect. If that's the case, why does the media expend so much maniacal energy on a fruitless exercise, quite often humiliating themselves and the profession of journalism?

Critics often pointed to the state's substantial debt during Andrews' leadership, even though once all the key economic factors and indicators are assessed, it's not too dissimilar to debt levels and management in other states and territories across Australia. Still, it's essential to acknowledge that this debt was primarily allocated to fund much-needed infrastructure projects, leading to Melbourne's transformation into a more liveable and prosperous city—according to the Economist Group, Melbourne was ranked either the most liveable, or second most liveable city in the world between 2014–23, and ranked third at the time of Andrews' departure. While concerns about debt are valid, the purpose and results of the spending must also be considered.

One of the most significant challenges Andrews faced during his tenure was managing the COVID-19 pandemic. His efforts were not without their difficulties, including the early outbreak linked to the *Ruby Princess* cruise ship in 2020, an outbreak primarily caused by the NSW Government, and ongoing issues with the management of the pandemic and implementation of lockdowns. However, it is essential to contextualise his pandemic response in comparison to other states, particularly New South Wales. In hindsight, the inconsistent and poorly thought-through management in New South Wales, along with a perceived lack of competence from senior ministers, including NSW health minister Brad Hazzard, underscored the complexity of pandemic decision-making.

Despite the hurdles and controversies magnified by the mainstream media, Andrews' leadership was characterised by his commitment to good policy over political expediency. He was unafraid to make unpopular decisions when he believed they were necessary for the greater good of the community. This approach resonated with the public, as evidenced by his consistent approval ratings and electoral victories.

GOVERNANCE AND POLICY INITIATIVES

Andrews' tenure as Premier was marked by a series of significant policy initiatives and social reforms. His leadership has seen the implementation of progressive programs, including public housing initiatives, voluntary euthanasia legislation, measures to combat domestic violence, universal childcare, and a comprehensive approach to negotiating a treaty with First

Nations people. Additionally, Victoria consistently held some of the lowest unemployment rates in Australia, reflecting the government's successful economic management.

One key area of contention surrounding Andrews' leadership is the state's level of public debt. Critics have often portrayed Victoria as economically mismanaged, citing high levels of debt as evidence. However, a closer examination of the numbers reveals a more nuanced picture. Victoria's current public sector debt stands at $139 billion, while New South Wales, carries a debt of $135 billion. Of course, Victoria does have a smaller population—6.6 million, compared to 8.1 million in New South Wales, so the per capita debt does show a significant difference, with Victoria's per capita debt at $21,000 compared to $17,000 in New South Wales.

However, it is essential to acknowledge that Victoria provided substantial income support during the early stages of the COVID-19 pandemic, contributing to its debt levels. This support was necessary due to delays in vaccine distribution and income support from the federal government, particularly during the critical early months of the pandemic, delays that were instigated by the Morrison government primarily to cause political damage to the Victoria government, and favour the Berejiklian government in New South Wales. Despite these challenges, Victoria remains in a favourable position to manage its debt in the long run.

Comparing Victoria's economic situation to that of New South Wales reveals striking similarities in debt management into the future, yet the media often focuses more on Victoria's financial challenges. This discrepancy in media coverage raises questions about the portrayal of Andrews' government and how unfairly it was targeted by many sections of the media, most notably News Corporation and the ABC, a practice that continued up to the time that Andrews resigned, with most of the media reports glowingly and enthusiastically announcing his departure, as if he was a despised political leader in the mold of Romanian dictator Nicolae Ceaușescu or Zimbabwe's Robert Mugabe.

If in the eyes of the mainstream media that Andrews was such a terrible and awful leader, why do so many people want to live in Victoria? Melbourne's fast-growing population is a testament to the appeal of living in Victoria, as more people choose to move there than to any other Australian state. This population growth reflects the government's effective governance and its ability to provide a high quality of life to its residents.

Despite these achievements, the mainstream media's portrayal of Andrews and his government has often been highly critical. The media's role in shaping public opinion is significant, and the negative narratives surrounding

Andrews raise questions about the media's objectivity and its responsibility to provide balanced reporting.

Andrews' legacy as Premier of Victoria is characterised by effective governance and a commitment to progressive policies. However, his tenure has also been marked by relentless media scrutiny and negative portrayals. While opinions about his leadership may vary, it is clear that Victoria has thrived under his leadership, and the media's influence on public perception warrants further examination.

MEDIA INFLUENCE, AND THE FUTURE

The media's portrayal of Andrews and his government was often highly critical and unprofessional, with some outlets engaged in pure click-bait sensationalism and pro-conservative bias. His handling of the COVID-19 pandemic was a case in point, with daily press conferences becoming platforms for what often seemed like pointless or conspiratorial questions, especially from *The Herald Sun*, and then replicated by others in the media.

On the ABC's *Insiders* program, the panellists—and the host—were in unison when it was suggested that Andrews avoided scrutiny, by bypassing the mainstream media and conversing with the electorate through social media—even though many journalists in the mainstream media diminish the role of social media and claim that it had a negligible effect of electoral outcomes, and falsely asserted that he was reluctant to appear in the media and, when he did, he rarely provided the answers they were looking for.

Again, this defies the evidence: just like every other political leader across Australia during the early parts of the COVID-19 pandemic, Andrews appeared in daily press conferences until every question was asked and answered—even the more ridiculous questions from News Corporation journalists—and his media conferences would typically run for up to 90 minutes. How can journalists assert that Andrews "avoided scrutiny", when he offered as much time as possible to the media of all persuasions? And if they now deem that it wasn't enough, how can Andrews be blamed for the time wasted by inane and insane 'gotcha' questions asked by News Corporation journalists, which essentially were a public nuisance and health hazard?

As hard as they tried, the mainstream media couldn't land any political blows on Andrews or the Victoria Labor government and now that he has left at a time of his own choosing, they're behaving like jilted lovers after a messy divorce, and having their juvenile tantrums over fractures and fissures that they primarily created. And just like the jilted lover, they're telling everyone within earshot how bad he was and trying to get everyone to side with their side of the story. *It really is embarrassing.*

Now that Andrews has resigned from office, the future of Victoria is in the hands of Jacinta Allan, the new Premier, and she inherits a legacy of mostly positive results but also some challenges. While it's unlikely that she will face the same level of visceral hate from the media, the bar has been set high, and she must contend with the weight of expectations.

Even still, while a Caucus meeting was going through the formalities of appointing Allan as the new leader, journalists from the ABC and News Corporation were claiming that there were now ructions within the Labor Party: a challenger to Allan had been found, Andrews had lost his temper and a 'shouting match' ensued, and asserted the transition to a new leader would be a long-drawn-out drama which would take months to resolve and cause major damage to the Labor government.

As it happened, the Caucus meeting was actually a tame and sedate affair; there was no shouting, Allan was appointed the new leader of the Victoria Labor Party and, therefore, the Premier of Victoria. The meeting was over within half an hour: so much for the "months" this would take to resolve and the major damage that was being agitated by key journalists from the ABC Melbourne, Richard Willingham and Bridget Rollason. *They got it all wrong.* But, as is the case for most journalists from the mainstream media, there are no consequences and certainly none of the scrutiny they were demanding of Daniel Andrews.

Looking ahead, the next Victorian election is not due until November 2026, providing Allan with time to solidify her position and implement her vision for the state. It is crucial for the media to approach her leadership with professionalism and objectivity, focusing on the policies and outcomes rather than sensationalism or personal bias.

Andrews' legacy is one of effective governance, progressive policies, and resilience in the face of relentless media scrutiny. While opinions on his leadership may vary, his legacy as one of Victoria's better premiers is undeniable. His ability to withstand the electoral challenges speaks to his political acumen and his commitment to good governance. As time passes, history may come to view him as one of the most effective premiers not only in Victoria but also in the broader context of Australian political history. And this is despite what the mainstream media wanted the electorate to believe. As usual, *they got it all wrong.*

***

OCTOBER

THE FINAL WEEK OF THE VOICE CAMPAIGN: WHAT WILL THE RESULT SAY ABOUT US?

7 October 2023

The Voice to Parliament referendum is a crucial moment in Australian history, with voting now open until 6pm on 14 October, when the polling booths close. The referendum is significant as it seeks to address the long-standing issue of Indigenous representation and recognition within the Australian political landscape. However, as is often the case in referendums, it has been marred by a familiar pattern of fear, division and misinformation, primarily from the "no" campaign and the Liberal Party. This tactic of sowing fear and confusion is not unique to this referendum but has been a recurring theme in Australian politics, where the fear-mongering and misinformation campaigns are designed to manipulate public opinion and create uncertainty, making it challenging for voters to make informed decisions and governments wishing to implement positive social change.

Recent opinion polls suggest a slight swing back towards the "yes" vote in this late stage, though the "no" campaign still leads and is likely to defeat the proposal. However, the real votes cast in the referendum will ultimately determine the outcome, and there is much ground to cover before the final votes are counted on 14 October. The referendum's simplicity—just the one question with just a "yes" or "no" choice—might suggest a straightforward process, but the political landscape is far from simple.

The combination of political opportunism, a right-wing nihilist Liberal Party, with its leader perceived as having little to offer—but acting as though he has nothing to lose—has created a volatile mix. This mix has contributed to the divisive nature of the campaign and has left many Australians disillusioned with the entire process. Both campaigns, the "yes" and the "no," have been criticised for their shortcomings, making it difficult for voters to discern the relevance and truth amidst the noise. But whose fault is this?

One alarming trend in this referendum is the spread of lies from the "no" campaign being repeated as facts. When challenged, those propagating these falsehoods dismiss credible sources as "fake news", or suggesting that there are sinister and ulterior motivations, or the government and Indigenous people have "something to hide". This erosion of trust in reliable information sources further complicates the decision-making process for voters.

Despite the challenges and divisions, it is our hope that common sense and empathy will prevail, and Australians will make an informed decision that reflects the nation's commitment to justice and Reconciliation.

SUPPORT AND CHALLENGES IN THE VOICE TO PARLIAMENT REFERENDUM

While the Voice to Parliament referendum has faced its fair share of challenges and misinformation, there have also been notable expressions of support from various quarters, shedding light on the complexities and nuances surrounding this crucial issue.

One encouraging development is the growing number of individuals and public figures voicing their support for the "yes" campaign. Nathan Cleary, the captain of the premiership-winning Penrith Panthers and a prominent figure in the rugby league sports community, posted a video advocating for a "yes" vote, emphasising the importance of Indigenous voices and representation. Such endorsements from respected figures can have a significant influence on public opinion and contribute to raising awareness about the referendum's significance.

However, despite these positive endorsements, the "no" campaign, backed by the Liberal Party and other conservative forces, continues to promote fear, division, and confusion and their divisive rhetoric threatens to undermine the national discourse on Indigenous representation and recognition. It is essential to critically examine some of the arguments put forth by the "no" campaign and their implications.

One key moment in this debate was the exchange between Liberal Party federal MP Dan Tehan and "yes" campaigner and Indigenous lawyer, Noel Pearson, on the ABC's *Q+A* program. Tehan's argument seemed to revolve around the idea that power already exists within the Senate, and the government's numbers in the Senate determine its actions.

However, Pearson pointed out that the heart of the issue is not the power within the Senate but the constitutional provision itself. He emphasised that the referendum aims to grant the parliament the explicit power to make laws concerning Indigenous matters, a power currently absent in the constitution.

Pearson's response highlighted a critical distinction between constitutional power and legislative power. While the referendum deals with constitutional change, the details of legislation and its implementation would be the responsibility of the parliament—as it has always been—but an issue that was totally overlooked by Tehan. This clarification is vital to understanding the scope and impact of the referendum: Tehan is a member of parliament but was happy to show to the public, his ignorance of the political system he is supposedly a part of.

The "no" campaign has not limited itself to substantive arguments alone. It has also resorted to basic diversions include calls for more audits of funding for Indigenous programs and the propagation of various conspiracies, tactics which primarily serve to distract from the central issue and create confusion among voters.

Moreover, the controversy surrounding the colour purple, used by the "yes" campaign, adds another layer of complexity to the discourse. The Australian Electoral Commission's objection to the colour purple due to its resemblance to their own branding colour has sparked allegations of cheating and trickery from News Corporation news outlets, providing further distractions from genuine debate on Indigenous representation.

In this charged atmosphere, it is crucial to remember the core issue at hand—the need for Indigenous recognition and representation within the Australian political landscape. The debate should focus on the merits and implications of the proposed constitutional change rather than becoming mired in distractions and misinformation.

INDIGENOUS RECOGNITION AND THE BIG DIVERSION

The referendum has seen the use of divisive tactics and misinformation by political leaders, particularly from the "no" campaign. One notable example is leader of the opposition Peter Dutton's suggestion that Indigenous recognition *could* be made but should come with the caveat of recognising migrants as well, a proposition that has nothing to do with the Voice to Parliament, and no one is asking for.

This tactic, typically used by former prime minister Scott Morrison, attempts to sound inclusive while simultaneously downplaying the significance of recognising Indigenous Australians, in a form of 'sympathy and concern trolling' to seem genuine in his concern but acting with great disingenuity. It also creates a false division by implying that acknowledging one group somehow diminishes the importance of acknowledging others.

Moreover, Dutton's claim that Alan Joyce, the former CEO of Qantas, had the power to veto the referendum question is a blatant falsehood. This assertion not only spreads misinformation but also raises questions about how such a scenario would even be possible: where is the proof for such act, and why wasn't it asked for by the media? It highlights the role of the mainstream media in amplifying false claims without critical analysis. Journalists have a responsibility to fact-check and critically evaluate statements made by political leaders before reporting them.

The low standards of journalism in Australia have allowed political leaders to make unfounded claims that are then uncritically reported and further magnified. This lack of scrutiny has been a significant problem in the referendum campaign, as it allows misinformation to circulate and distort the public discourse.

In contrast to these divisive tactics and misinformation, the Uluru Statement from the Heart presents a genuine and concise call for Reconciliation. While some may attempt to muddy the waters with distractions and falsehoods, the Uluru Statement remains a clear and succinct one-page statement representing the aspirations of Indigenous Australians for recognition and self-determination on the matters which directly relate to them.

REFLECTIONS AND THE PATH FORWARD

In this final week of campaigning for the Voice to Parliament referendum, there is a sense of trepidation not only about the outcome but how vicious the "no" campaign will become in the final days. Throughout this campaign, it has been hard not to draw parallels with the Republic referendum of 1999, which also faced its share of fear and confusion. There are striking similarities, but also key differences that shed light on the current state of affairs.

In his 1998 election victory speech, John Howard promised a referendum on the republic but, as someone who is a staunch monarchist, he did his best to sabotage the process and there was a failure within the electorate to seize the opportunity when it arose. In his 2022 election victory speech, Anthony Albanese also promised a referendum, advocating for a Voice to Parliament, the difference being that Albanese was a believer his proposal: Howard was a cynic who despised the idea of a republic but offered it as a scrap to the moderates within the Liberal Party and enabled him to walk on boths side of the left and right camps of the party.

One pivotal moment during the 1999 Republic referendum was the rejection of the direct-election of the president, despite popular support of around 80 per cent for it. Similarly, with the Voice to Parliament, there have been suggestions that a two-step process—first legislating the Voice to Parliament and then proposing a referendum in five-to-ten years to alter the Constitution, might have been more effective.

However, it's crucial to recognise that the Liberal Party's obstructionist approach, regardless of the proposal, hampers progress: if the Labor government proposed Indigenous recognition in the Constitution, the Liberal Party would have opposed that, despite what they are saying now. If the Voice to Parliament was legislated, they would work to denigrate that as well, and unleash the current opponents, Jacinta Price and Warren

Mundine, to add their high level of misinformation and negativity: this is the Liberal Party of Peter Dutton—"no" to everything proposed by a Labor government.

Dutton's attempt to create doubt around the referendum's process and continuous false claims demonstrates a lack of vision and a tendency toward small-minded tactics. Such approaches may yield short-term political gains—a likely defeat of the referendum—but fail to inspire confidence in the long-term, which, in politics, always has to the be an election victory. The evidence in every opinion poll since May 2022 suggests that the Liberal Party is not getting any closer in being able to win the next federal election, due in 2025.

Ultimately, the outcome of the referendum won't be known until the polling booths close at 6pm on 14 October, but the fate of Peter Dutton's political career is uncertain. However, regardless of the result, the real issue at hand is the future of Australia as a nation committed to justice, Reconciliation, and Indigenous representation. A "yes" vote is a step towards healing historical injustices and forging a more inclusive future: a "no" vote risks perpetuating division and alienation and offers a template for how future elections and referenda will be played out.

In the end, the Voice to Parliament referendum is not just about political meanderings or electoral victories; it is about shaping the future of a nation and its commitment to recognising the rights and aspirations of Indigenous Australians. Dutton and his conservative bedfellows are a minor irritant and will end being an insubstantial footnote in Australia's political history: like all the irritants who have preceded him in federal politics, it's all he deserves.

Truth, Treaty, Reconciliation will continue, regardless of whether the referendum is lost: Dutton has decided he's not a part of this process, but at least he won't be in public life long enough to express his regret for not supporting the Voice to Parliament because he 'didn't grasp the significance of the moment', as he explained in 2022 for walking out of the 2008 Apology to the Stolen Generations.

As citizens, it is our collective responsibility to make an informed choice, one that reflects our values and the kind of society we want to build. Regardless of the outcome, the journey towards Reconciliation and justice must and will continue, and political leaders should prioritise a vision that transcends petty politics and truly reflects the aspirations of the Australian people.

***

THE DISABILITY ROYAL COMMISSION: A VITAL CALL FOR REFORM

7 October 2023

The Royal Commission into Violence, Abuse, Neglect, and Exploitation of People with Disability is a crucial inquiry that aims to address the deep-seated issues surrounding the treatment of people with disabilities in Australia. Initiated in April 2019 in response to widespread reports of maltreatment, this Royal Commission represents a significant step towards rectifying injustices and ensuring a more inclusive society for all Australians. While it may not have garnered as much media attention as the Robodebt Royal Commission, its importance is undeniable, and it offers a glimmer of hope for those advocating for the rights and wellbeing of people with disabilities.

The Royal Commission was established to delve into the distressing accounts of violence, abuse, neglect, and exploitation faced by individuals with disabilities, highlighting the systemic failures that perpetuated these issues. The report that emerged from this comprehensive investigation presented a broad spectrum of recommendations intended to rectify these problems. These recommendations encompass changes to laws, policies, structures, and practices, with the ultimate goal of fostering a more inclusive and just society. As Bill Shorten, the Minister for Government Services, remarked, "We understand that this nation can and should do better." The report exposed the harrowing reality of the experiences of many in the disability sector, pushing for swift and substantive action.

One of the report's pivotal recommendations is the introduction of a disability rights Act, an idea passionately supported by Australian Greens Senator Jordan Steele-John. Such legislation would provide a comprehensive framework to uphold the rights of disabled individuals, as articulated under the United Nations Convention on the Rights of Persons with Disabilities. What makes this proposed act all-encompassing is its intention to cover both public and private services, creating a holistic approach to protecting and promoting the rights of people with disabilities. This Act would also serve as the foundation for establishing a disability commission, which would enable individuals to file complaints related to ableism, segregation, or abuse. These complaints would then be investigated, and consequences enforced.

The critical role of a disability rights Act and the associated commission cannot be overstated. People with disabilities have long endured violence and abuse, but the Royal Commission provided a national mechanism to address these issues. By instituting the disability rights Act and maintaining this mechanism for complaints and redress, Australia takes a significant step toward ensuring the rights and wellbeing of individuals with disabilities are upheld and protected. This Act, when enacted, would signify Australia's commitment to a more inclusive, just, and equitable society, where people with disabilities can live their lives with dignity and without fear.

Despite Australia's self-perception as an inclusive and just society, its track record on addressing the concerns of people with disabilities—or many other marginalised group—is far from perfect. This calls for immediate attention and action, and it should be a matter of bipartisan support, and a process which would reinforce the nation's commitment to securing a fair go for all Australians, with special emphasis on those with disabilities. This is not only an ethical imperative but also a testament to the nation's dedication to upholding human rights and fostering inclusivity.

AUSTRALIA'S FAILURE TO PROTECT A VULNERABLE GROUP IN SOCIETY

The distressing reality of the Disability Royal Commission is a painful testament to the systemic neglect and maltreatment of some of the most vulnerable members of society. The release of the report has laid bare a grim truth: Australia's system has failed those who needed it most, individuals with disabilities who should have been provided with the support and care necessary to function optimally in society.

The report's findings are indeed disheartening, and they reinforce the urgency of the situation. Even though not all details of the report have been thoroughly reviewed, the glimpses that have been shared in media summaries are deeply upsetting. People who rely on society's support to lead fulfilling lives are being systematically mistreated, abused, and denied their basic rights. The report stands as a stark reminder of the profound responsibility that society holds in safeguarding the rights and wellbeing of its most marginalised members.

Bill Shorten deserves credit for acknowledging the report's findings and expressing his commitment to implementing its recommendations. The fact that there are 223 recommendations within the report is both a testament to its comprehensiveness and an indication of the enormity of the task at hand. It's important to acknowledge that rectifying the systemic issues and failures revealed by the Royal Commission will be a long-term endeavour, one that may extend beyond Shorten's tenure as a government minister. But the urgency of the matter dictates that we must begin the process of reform without delay.

The Royal Commission was commissioned by the former Liberal–National Coalition government, making it clear that this issue should transcends political divides. However, the many recommendations included in the report are only the first step. To bring about meaningful change, ongoing support from ministers and advocates within the political system is crucial. The responsibility for implementing these changes does not rest solely with the government, but it necessitates a cross-party effort to ensure that the recommendations are effectively put into action.

The disappointing political response from the opposition, particularly from the Shadow Minister for Social Services, Michael Sukkar—who primarily played political point-scoring games by ignoring the content of the Commission's report and focusing on the $527 million funding provided by the Coalition when they were in government—emphasises the need for a united and non-partisan approach to addressing the issues raised by the Royal Commission. The wellbeing and rights of people with disabilities should be above politics, and there should be a shared commitment to making necessary changes.

The Disability Royal Commission is a stark reminder of the need for a profound and urgent transformation in how society treats and supports individuals with disabilities. The comprehensive report and its 223 recommendations offer a roadmap to rectify systemic issues and provide a more inclusive, just, and empathetic society.

To achieve these changes, it is crucial that political leaders set aside their differences and work together to ensure the wellbeing and rights of people with disabilities are safeguarded, as should have been the case all along. It's time to make these long-overdue reforms a reality and offer equity to all Australians, regardless of their abilities or disabilities.

***

THE VOICE: MISSED OPPORTUNITIES, RACISM, AND POLITICAL OPPORTUNISM

14 October 2023

The Voice to Parliament referendum in Australia has concluded, with 39.4 per cent supporting the proposed Constitutional amendment and 60.6 per cent opposing it. It's a significant loss for a proposal which was meant to recognise First Nations people in the Constitution, create a permanent Voice to Parliament and continue the pathway towards Reconciliation. Instead, the defeat has confirmed Australia as an insular small-minded nation that is susceptible to fear campaigns, fearful of change and happy to see itself as a mixture of "little-Britain" and pre-1990 apartheid South Africa.

One of the most striking aspects of the Voice to Parliament referendum was the poor quality of the campaign, which was marred by misinformation, disinformation and political opportunism. While it is important to note that the referendum's outcome was not a simple reflection of the political divide between the Labor Party and the Liberal–National Coalition parties, there are lessons that will be learned by all sides of politics.

The campaign for constitutional recognition of Indigenous Australians was a cause championed by the Labor government—initiated by the Indigenous community through the Uluru Statement from the Heart, and with bipartisan political support in 2017—but the "No" campaign effectively capitalised on fear and uncertainty, exploiting misinformation and playing on the doubts of many voters.

The Liberal Party's negative role in this campaign was also significant. It is lamentable that they resorted to spreading misinformation and untruths—and left unchecked by many media outlets—believing that such tactics used in a federal election will lead them back into government, but there's very little evidence that that will end of being the case. All the former Liberal Party seats identified as "teal independents"—Warringah, Goldstein, Curtin, Kooyong, Mackellar, Wentworth, North Sydney—ignored the messaging from the Liberal Party and voted in favour of the Voice to Parliament, indicating that these seats are unlikely to flow back to the Liberal Party at the next election.

It's obvious that the leader of the Liberal Party, Peter Dutton, sought to use this referendum to boost his own credentials and standing in the electorate but, while he might have won this battle—at huge cost to the Indigenous community—there is nothing to suggest this will have any influence on the next election. Of the 36 previous defeated referenda questions that have been sponsored by the government, on 33 occasions, those governments have gone on to win the next federal election.

Dutton is a divisive character who has shown no inclination to unite the nation, protect the body politic or display leadership qualities that appeal to many people within the community. This was an opportunity to show leadership, but his performance has been lacking and unlikely to sway many voters in the additional 19 seats the Liberal Party need to win at the next election, if they wish to form government. Dutton is too toxic, too dour, he is viewed as a racist figure, and doesn't hold the gravitas or intellect to gain a sufficient following. But, enough about the white leaders: this referendum was meant to be about Indigenous people, but ended up being an ideological culture war battle drummed up by the racist right-wing media.

The Voice to Parliament referendum was not just another administrative change to the Constitution; it was about addressing important social issues and rectifying historical injustices. The referendum's failure reflects deeper issues within Australian society and it demonstrates a reluctance to embrace change, vulnerability to scare campaigns, and the presence of strong racist undercurrents.

Australia's historical issues with racism are well-documented. The country's treatment of Indigenous people and the policies of the past, such as the Stolen Generations, highlight a painful history of discrimination and oppression. The referendum results echo the fact that these issues are far from resolved, as many Australians remain hesitant to support measures aimed at addressing these historical wrongs.

The parallel between the 1999 Republic referendum and previous unsuccessful referenda in the Australian context, such as the 1988 inquiries, is undeniably conspicuous. In each instance, a confluence of elements including fear-mongering campaigns, a prevailing distrust of political authorities, aversion to change, and the propagation of disinformation played a critical role. This apprehension of change, when intertwined with the entrenched belief in the immutability of the Constitution, has consistently hindered progress on various fronts.

The 1988 referenda posed inquiries regarding fixed-term parliamentary tenures, a guarantee of equitable electoral processes, the inclusion of references to local government, and the assurance of fundamental rights and freedoms. Astonishingly, all of these proposals met resounding defeat in a campaign spearheaded by the then-novice Member of Parliament, Peter Reith, with the intent of inflicting "political damage" on the Prime Minister at the time, Bob Hawke.

The pertinent question arises: Have we collectively relinquished our critical faculties to such an extent that we are susceptible to vacuous fear campaigns promulgated by opportunistic politicians, even when the subject matter we are rejecting serves the public interest? One cannot help but ponder how anyone in sound judgment would cast their vote against enshrining guarantees of "free and fair elections" or safeguarding "rights and freedoms" within the Constitution. Is it not the bedrock of the Australian identity to be grounded in principles of being "young and free", or is this just another convenient illusion that appears in gold sporting events?

There is a disconcerting dissonance within the body politic and the electorate when modest and straightforward propositions are defeated by ambitious politicians who exploit referenda opportunities to bolster their own profiles, all while the public remains largely in the dark about these contrived spectacles.

The nation's timidity was glaringly evident in its reluctance to award itself the privilege of free and equitable elections in 1988, or to grant itself additional rights. All this, merely because a vested-interest political leader in a well-tailored suit, armed with a megaphone, persuaded the populace that such reforms were against their best interests. *How did we become so susceptible to such manipulation?*

In 1999, a similar timidity was displayed when the prospect of becoming a fully independent nation with its own head of state was deemed too daunting to pursue. *How did we become so insecure about our own future?*

Fast-forward to 2023, a proposition of fundamental import for non-Indigenous Australians—albeit profoundly significant for the Indigenous community—has been defeated, all at the behest of a white Liberal Party leader; a black man who only seems to represent himself—Warren Mundine—and his accomplice in this pantomime act, Senator Jacinta Price. They all played a pivotal role in framing the referendum as "divisive", even as they themselves fanned the flames of division. The public, once again, succumbed to this narrative, not necessarily because they believed their words, but perhaps because they were presented with words that they wanted to hear: "if you don't know, vote no". *How did we evolve into a nation so bereft of enlightenment and still plagued by the disease of racism?*

The Voice to Parliament referendum, though unsuccessful, has shed light on the challenges Australia faces in addressing its historical racism and effecting meaningful constitutional change. The campaign's misinformation and political manipulation are glaring issues that demand scrutiny. The referendum's outcome is a reflection of the broader societal issues that persist in Australia, emphasising the need for ongoing efforts to combat racism and promote understanding and reconciliation within the nation.

A HISTORICAL PERSPECTIVE AND THE WAY FORWARD
The Voice to Parliament referendum not only reflects contemporary challenges but also unveils a deeper historical struggle with racism in Australia. It is essential to recognise that the referendum campaign has highlighted the need to usher in a new era of politics in Australia. A sensible and productive political debate is vital for the country's progress. This transformation involves not only the behaviour of politicians but also the media's role. Until Australia has ethical, principled politicians and responsible media outlets, the nation will continue to face challenges.

The referendum has also revealed the myth of Australia's self-image as an important international player on the world stage, when, essentially, it still behaves as a remote colony of Britain or a "deputy sheriff" of the United States. This self-perception has kept the nation stuck in a certain mindset: a colonial outpost so afraid of change, even when it's in its best interests. Australia must evolve beyond this limited perspective, recognising its unique identity as a sovereign nation, with a unique Indigenous culture which is keeps wishing to repress. Continuing to adopt a subordinate role in international relations inhibits Australia's potential to be a global leader in addressing important issues, such as Indigenous rights.

Australia has been historically divided on Indigenous issues, and this division persists today: there's no other way to read this referendum result. However, it falls upon political leaders to bridge this divide, not exacerbate it. Prime Minister Anthony Albanese's efforts to reduce this division have been commendable, but he could have been more assertive. In contrast, figures like Dutton and National Party leader David Littleproud have contributed to increasing this division, primarily because they are leaders of small mind and cannot see the merit in anything, unless there is some political benefit to their electoral stocks.

THE LIMITATIONS OF THE CONSTITUTIONAL PROCESS
The outcome of the referendum also underscores the limitations of the constitutional process. Australia's Constitution, while a foundational document, has its imperfections and limitations. However, this referendum experience has demonstrated that tampering with the Constitution can be a complex and arduous process, often fraught with obstacles and divisions.

Perhaps the Constitution should be left as a historical artifact, varnished and hung in a *ye olde world* Australian museum, an outdated relic of the past. While the Constitution is a well-constructed and crafted legal document, a document that was created in 1900 and is virtually unchangeable when it comes to dealing with the modern world in 2023, is perhaps not worth the paper that it's written on.

Australia remains the only colonised country in the world that does not officially recognise its Indigenous heritage in its Constitution. This constitutional silence on this issue is a reflection of the nation's historical apprehension and reluctance to confront its past and forge a better future. The referendum's outcome, as well as the divisive campaign leading up to it, underscore the immense challenges that lie ahead in addressing this historical omission.

The Voice to Parliament referendum has brought to the forefront a myriad of issues affecting Australia, from racism and division to political manipulation and the limitations of constitutional reform. This historic vote should be seen as an opportunity for reflection and reform, a catalyst for change rather than a symbol of failure.

As Australia grapples with its complex history and the ongoing struggle for Indigenous recognition and Reconciliation, it is crucial for political leaders, media organisations, and the broader public to embrace a more enlightened, principled, and inclusive vision of the nation. In this journey towards a more unified and equitable Australia, the lessons of this referendum should not be forgotten, but rather serve as a source of inspiration and motivation to address the nation's deepest wounds and create a more just and inclusive future.

***

THE NEW WAR ON GAZA: A HISTORICAL CONTEXT AND RECENT ESCALATION

14 October 2023

The Israel–Palestine conflict has long been a source of tension and violence in the Middle East and recent events, such as the attacks by Hamas militants and Israeli military retaliation, have reignited this long-standing conflict. These events, which have garnered condemnation from various parts of the Western world, particularly in Australia, highlight the urgency of addressing this issue.

The actions of Hamas, the central Palestinian political organisation with a history of militancy, where their attacks resulted in the deaths of over 1,200 people just on the other side of the border of the Gaza Strip, sparked outrage and condemnation. In response, the Israeli military launched a counteroffensive into Gaza, leading to even more casualties, almost 2,000. This cycle of violence has been a recurring theme in the Israeli–Palestinian conflict, with each side blaming the other for initiating hostilities, which then leads to other attacks and counter-offenses.

The timing of these events, as observed in previous conflicts, is often linked to political events and developments in Israel. Previous wars in 2008, 2014, and 2021 coincided with general elections and other key political events within the country, which had nothing to do with Palestine, but were primarily used by prime ministers such as Ehud Olmert and Benjamin Netanyahu to show their "tough-on-Palestine" credentials, a proven vote-winner in Israeli elections. In this instance, the push for a coalition government by Netanyahu that included "annexation and dispossession" plans for the Gaza strip only added to the tensions. The Israeli military had actually received a warning from Egyptian intelligence about an imminent attack on 7 October, emphasising the complex intelligence and political dynamics at play—the state of Israel possesses the most sophisticated missile alert systems in the world, and comprehensive surveillance over Gaza and, at this stage, it is quite unclear how Hamas managed to bypass this complex network and break its barriers.

Did Netanyahu want this attack to occur? It certainly helped achieve his political goals, as the coalition that he had been desperately trying to form since November 2022, was finally agreed to and signed, several days after the Hamas attacks.

A notable aspect of this ongoing conflict is the disproportionate casualty figures between the two sides, which is rarely featured within the western media. From 2008 up until September 2023, 6,407 Palestinians have been killed and over 152,000 injured, while 308 Israelis were killed and 6,307 injured, resulting in a ratio of approximately 20 to 1. This stark imbalance in casualties underscores the humanitarian crisis and the need for a balanced approach to resolving the conflict.

It is essential to recognise that the Israeli–Palestinian conflict is deeply rooted in historical, political, and territorial issues, making it a multifaceted challenge, along with the interference and influence over many years by large external powers: Britain, United States, the Soviet Union, and the manipulation of vassal states in the region. The perpetuation of this conflict is closely tied to political interests in all these countries and the manipulation of these events for political gain and international efforts have often exacerbated and prolonged conflict and deterred any potential for achieving a lasting resolution.

It is crucial to distinguish criticism of governments and movements from prejudice against people but this distinction is rarely applied within western media outlets. Criticising the actions of Hamas or the Israeli government should not imply a sweeping condemnation of the entire Palestinian or Israeli population. The conflict is not a black-and-white issue, and understanding its nuances is crucial for any meaningful resolution. The recent escalation underscores the urgency of addressing this long-standing and intractable conflict.

INTERNATIONAL RESPONSES AND THE PLIGHT OF PALESTINIANS

Australia, like many other countries, has historically shown solidarity with nations facing crises and attacks, and while it's not unexpected, the federal government has expressed support for Israel's "right to defend itself", as it has done in previous conflicts but this stance does not adequately address the complex realities on the ground, and largely ignores the experiences from the Palestinian perspective.

The statement by Australian Foreign Minister Senator Penny Wong highlights the predictable nature of the government's position: She recognises the apparent nature of the attacks and the security challenges Israel faces;

there is a clear acknowledgment of the devastating loss of life and the attacks on civilians, reflecting the grim reality of the situation; the government's call for the release of hostages and its support for Israel's right to self-defence. These are all consistent with past positions taken by the federal government.

However, the concern lies in the double standard in Australia's foreign policy. While Australia has swiftly expressed solidarity with Israel during times of crisis, the same level of support or sympathy is rarely extended to the people of Palestine. Public buildings, including the Sydney Opera House, have been floodlit with the colours of Ukraine; of France; and now the blue and white of Israel, to show solidarity with the suffering of those countries. But why do we never see the black, white, green and red of the Palestinian flag when their peoples suffer the consequences of terror attacks and indiscriminate wars governed by corrupted Israeli prime ministers?

The Australian government's approach to this conflict lacks balance. When Israel initiates or responds to attacks with military force, the prevailing narrative often emphasises its "right to self-defence". However, such leniency is not typically extended to Palestinians, especially those living in Gaza, which is often described as the largest open-air prison in the world.

Gaza, a densely populated area of 365 square kilometres, is home to over two million people, who are facing severe restrictions on their movement due to Israeli naval and land blockades. This situation is classified as an "occupied territory" by the United Nations, and the collective punishment by the Israeli military—a clear war crime according to Common Article 33 of the Geneva Conventions—has exacerbated the humanitarian crisis.

The international community, including Australia, must consider the long-term consequences of this approach. Continuing to subject the people of Gaza to such dire living conditions only serves to deepen the roots of the conflict and fosters a sense of desperation and hopelessness among the population, which can contribute to further radicalisation and violence.

In the interest of achieving a peaceful resolution, Australia and the broader international community should certainly advocate for restraint on both sides and the protection of civilian lives. While recognising Israel's right to self-defence is important—as it is for any country—it should be equally vital to advocate for a fair and just resolution to the Israeli–Palestinian conflict. This entails addressing the legitimate aspirations of the Palestinian people, scaling back the incursions of Palestinian lands by Israeli settlers in the West Bank, and acknowledging the historical context and complexities of the conflict.

MEDIA REPRESENTATION AND ADVOCACY FOR A BALANCED VIEW

The media's role in shaping public perceptions of the Israeli–Palestinian conflict cannot be underestimated. The way news is framed, the narratives that are emphasised, and the voices that are heard all have a profound impact on how the public understands this complex and protracted conflict. It is essential to critically assess how media coverage and advocacy shape the discourse and influence public opinion.

One notable aspect of media representation is the difference in attention given to humanising the suffering on both sides. The spotlight often falls on Israeli victims, their names, and stories, while Palestinian casualties rarely receive the same level of coverage. *Israeli victims have names: Palestinian victims remain anonymous*. It's the basic rule of warfare—dehumanising the enemy makes it easier to eliminate them—and the western media has chosen who the enemy is, and quite clearly.

The exchange between the Australian Broadcasting Corporation's Sarah Ferguson and Mustafa Barghouti, the Secretary General of the Palestinian national initiative, underscores this issue:

> **Sarah Ferguson:** "No one is disputing that all lives are of equal value, and we understand where you are coming from. But I would like your *human response* to the events that we have seen over the past few days that have been reported by media the world over."
>
> **Mustafa Barghouti:** "I totally do not accept, and I refuse taking any child hostage. Do you want me to name to you, the 140 children who were killed in Gaza by Israeli airstrikes? Do you want me to tell you—*let me answer*—do you want me to tell you that I was shot by a sniper while I was treating an injured person with two gunshots and I'm still carrying these gunshots in my back. I am not going to talk about this ... let's look at the causes of this. The main cause of everything horrible that is happening to Palestinians and Israelis is the continuation of illegal Israeli occupation of Palestinian land."

When asked for a "human response", it is usually Palestinians who are expected to provide it, while the same empathy is rarely sought from Israeli officials. *No one is disputing that all lives are of equal value*. Yes, they are. Every western media outlet questions this value and always places the value of Israeli lives far above Palestinian lives. It's been obvious for many years.

This imbalance in media portrayal not only perpetuates a one-sided perspective but also fuels resentment and frustration among Palestinians. Such disparities in the portrayal of suffering can deepen the divide between the two communities and hinder the prospects for peace.

Another concerning aspect is the selective reporting of extremist rhetoric. While the media highlighted offensive chants by some Palestinian protestors at the steps of the Sydney Opera House, it is essential to acknowledge that extreme views can be found on all sides of the conflict, including on the Israeli side. The failure to consistently address inflammatory statements made by Israeli individuals or politicians leads to a skewed perception of the situation.

Furthermore, the lack of scrutiny when extremist statements are made by Israeli officials perpetuates an environment where moderation and balanced dialogue are stifled. The Israeli Defense Minister's reference to Palestinians as "animals" is one such example. The failure to challenge such rhetoric can contribute to the dehumanisation of Palestinians, making it easier to justify harsh and punitive actions against them.

Critics often accuse those who highlight these disparities of engaging in "whataboutism" and of simplifying the complexities of the conflict. However, this criticism can be seen as a way to avoid addressing these issues directly. Instead, it is crucial to acknowledge the ongoing humanitarian crisis, disproportionate casualty figures, and the long-standing issues that underpin this conflict. The mistreatment of any population and the suppression of human rights should be a cause for concern, irrespective of the geopolitical context.

The media plays a significant role in shaping public perceptions of the Israeli–Palestinian conflict and the coverage should aim for a balanced and nuanced view, which includes the humanisation of all victims and holds all parties accountable for their actions and rhetoric. A more comprehensive and fair portrayal of the conflict is essential for fostering understanding and, ultimately, for finding a just and lasting solution to this protracted and deeply entrenched issue.

THE ROLE OF POLITICAL COMMENTARY AND DIPLOMACY

The Australian political landscape, like those of other nations, has witnessed a spectrum of opinions regarding the Israeli–Palestinian conflict and such a multifaceted and deeply entrenched issue demands a nuanced approach from politicians and political commentators. However, recent statements from Australian political figures have drawn criticism for potentially exacerbating tensions and oversimplifying the situation.

Former Prime Minister John Howard's assertion that the Labor government "did not do enough to condemn" Hamas attacks and comments from Deputy Liberal Party leader Sussan Ley regarding the need for the government "to do more"—without ever articulating what this could be—exemplify the challenge of discussing a highly sensitive and multifaceted issue. The political point-scoring during a crisis can undermine diplomatic efforts and hinder Australia's role in the international community.

Liberal Party leader Peter Dutton's suggestion that Prime Minister Anthony Albanese was "condoning anti-Semitism" and calls for the release of national security details add another layer of complexity to the discourse, which were purely designed to undermine the Australian government. Why do conservative political figures always seek politicisation of national security and foreign policy issues? Foreign policy should be approached with seriousness and sensitivity, avoiding the politicisation of intelligence briefings and diplomatic matters.

The Australian political system generally adheres to the convention that opposition parties should refrain from overt criticism of foreign policy, particularly during international crises. Foreign policy decisions are often based on intricate international relationships, treaties, and strategic interests, which are not readily influenced by domestic political posturing. Instead, a bipartisan approach that puts national interests ahead of political advantage is essential in foreign policy matters.

If there is going to a push that "now is not the time for whataboutism" and to provide more balance perspectives—which essentially is another way of shutting down debate—it should also be acknowledged that now is also not the time for political point-scoring by conservative opportunists such as Dutton and Ley. Opposition parties have a role to play in holding the government to account, but during foreign policy crises, their approach should prioritise national interests and international diplomacy over partisan politics.

The Israeli–Palestinian conflict remains a highly complex and contentious issue with deep historical roots. International responses, including media representation, diplomatic engagement, and political commentary, play a significant role in shaping perceptions of the conflict and influencing potential pathways to peace.

While the conflict persists, it is imperative for all parties, including the international community and foreign governments, to exercise restraint and to support efforts for a just and lasting resolution. The delicate nature of this conflict requires careful and balanced diplomacy, and any political commentary should prioritise national interests and the wellbeing of all affected communities. A thorough understanding of the complexities and nuances of this conflict is essential for charting a path toward a peaceful and equitable resolution.

***

REFLECTIONS ON THE DEFEAT OF THE VOICE TO PARLIAMENT REFERENDUM

21 October 2023

The recent defeat of the Voice to Parliament referendum in Australia, with 39 per cent in favour and 61 per cent against, signifies a missed opportunity for advancing Indigenous rights and Reconciliation and this outcome is particularly disheartening for Indigenous communities and their supporters, who had hoped for a different result.

Prime Minister Anthony Albanese's response to the referendum's failure demonstrates the government's commitment to Reconciliation, despite the setback, where he acknowledged the challenges faced in the journey towards Reconciliation, emphasising that the issues the referendum aimed to address persist. The federal government remains dedicated to these objectives, and the failure of this particular referendum does not mark the end of efforts to bring about change. Albanese's speech reflected a message of hope, unity, and a continuing commitment to improving the position of First Australians.

Indigenous Affairs Minister Linda Burney's response also highlighted the disappointment felt by many; however, she emphasised resilience, the ongoing pursuit of Reconciliation, and the need for better outcomes for Indigenous communities and the importance of engaging with Indigenous Australians to identify practical solutions for future generations.

Despite the disappointment, the defeat of the referendum serves as a catalyst for analysing its causes and implications. The referendum's rejection perpetuates Australia's status as the only colonised country without constitutional recognition of its First Nations people, a fact that will likely remain a topic of debate and discussion for years to come.

Various factors contributed to the referendum's defeat: Inherent racism, though often passive, certainly played a role in influencing the "No" vote. Conservative political affiliations, with the Liberal and National parties choosing not to support the referendum, also had a significant impact. Additionally, disinformation campaigns and the spread of false information likely swayed public opinion. The media's role in disseminating information and shaping public opinion was instrumental in the outcome, which raises concerns about the ethics and integrity of media outlets in informing the public on critical issues.

The failure of the Voice to Parliament referendum underscores the ongoing challenges Australia faces in its quest for Reconciliation. While the outcome is disappointing, it serves as a call to action for those who want to see positive social change in the nation. The analysis of the referendum's defeat should prompt continued efforts to address systemic racism, foster political unity, and promote responsible and unbiased journalism. Despite this setback, Australia must remain committed to closing the gap and striving for a more equitable and just society, especially for its First Nations people. The referendum's defeat does not mark the end of the road to Reconciliation but, rather, a reminder of the long journey ahead.

THE IMPLICATIONS OF THE REFERENDUM'S FAILURE IN AUSTRALIA

The difficulties surrounding the Voice to Parliament referendum go beyond the immediate factors that led to its defeat. It highlights the broader challenges of achieving constitutional change in Australia and the referendum's failure underscores the immense hurdles that any proposed constitutional amendment must overcome, making constitutional change an almost impossible endeavour.

Constitutional change is indeed a complex and laborious process in Australia, and this is not necessarily a negative feature of the system—the Australian Constitution is designed to be stable and to protect fundamental principles and rights. However, the challenge lies in striking the right balance between preserving these foundational principles and adapting the Constitution to address contemporary issues, such as recognition of First Nations people—New Zealand is mentioned in the Constitution as a possible future state of Australia. Why is New Zealand recognised in the Constitution—a fully independent nation with no likelihood or intention of becoming a part of the federation of Australia—while the First Nations people are not? This is an anachronism that needs to be resolved.

The rejection of the Voice to Parliament referendum by the Liberal–National Coalition exemplifies the difficulty of achieving constitutional change without bipartisan support and this lack of consensus on an issue as significant as Indigenous recognition raises questions about the willingness of certain political factions to prioritise national unity and Reconciliation over partisan interests.

The referendum's defeat also highlights the role of negative political tactics and disinformation campaigns in influencing public opinion, and these negative forces in the country easily magnify and manipulate political and social issues, making them seem much more contentious than they actually are. In this context, it's crucial to consider the impact of media, misinformation, and the tactics employed during political campaigns on the outcomes of referendums.

The fact that the "Yes" campaign appeared to resonate more with university-educated urban populations suggests a need for a more inclusive and effective outreach strategy. If this observation is accurate—provided by Kos Samaras from the political consultancy firm RedBridge—it underscores the importance of reaching a broader cross-section of the population in future attempts to effect constitutional change.

Looking ahead, it is reasonable to consider the potential consequences of the referendum's failure, as it may be a long time before another referendum is proposed on any issue, especially those related to Indigenous recognition. Will this defeat also place a handbrake on other issues of constitutional reform, such as the Australian republic?

The Voice to Parliament referendum's failure serves as a stark reminder of the complexities of constitutional change in Australia. It emphasises the need for broader consensus, effective outreach, and a vigilant approach to combat misinformation in future campaigns, whether it be a referendum, or a general election. The referendum's defeat is more than just a setback for Indigenous recognition; it raises questions about the state of the country's political landscape and its ability to embrace change.

LACK OF EMPATHY IN THE AFTERMATH

The aftermath of the Voice to Parliament referendum defeat has revealed a disheartening lack of empathy from some quarters of the "No" campaign, even in the face of victory. Reports of celebrations in Queensland, with prominent figures like Gina Reinhardt in attendance, contrast sharply with the sombre response from Indigenous leaders.

Why are they celebrating? What is there to celebrate?

Indigenous leaders sought to hold a week of silence and lower the Indigenous flag to half-mast at public buildings to reflect upon this loss. However, conservative forces and sections of the media criticised this gesture, labeling it as an "affront to democracy". This response highlights the polarised nature of Indigenous and the lack of understanding of those deeply affected by the referendum's outcome.

The Indigenous community, along with the many "Yes" voters and campaign supporters, is left with a sense of disappointment and frustration. The criticism they face for expressing their grief and disappointment is, in many ways, a heartless from the conservatives in Australia and reveals a prevailing sentiment that it is not sufficient to defeat one's opponents in political battles; they must be annihilated as well. It is a harsh and unsympathetic response to the emotional and historical significance of this referendum for Indigenous communities.

The sentiments expressed by Indigenous author Melissa Lukashenko, who suggested that "white Australia doesn't want to give blackfellas anything, even when it's nothing" highlight a pervasive issue. The referendum's defeat reinforces a broader pattern of systemic neglect and denial of Indigenous rights and aspirations.

And it is this denial that was prevalent with many from the "No" campaign. Liberal Party leader Peter Dutton said that he would hold a second referendum to offer Indigenous recognition only, rather than a Voice to Parliament: he has since backtracked on this, suggesting that Australian's are "over" referendums and won't want to see another one "for some time" to come.

Warren Mundine, who suggested Treaty would be best achieved through a "No" result, has also backtracked on this. Dutton and Mundine lied—no surprises—but this questions the sincerity of their positions and their commitment to achieving meaningful change for Indigenous people.

In the aftermath of the referendum, it's evident that the "No" campaign's strategies and deceptive claims throughout the campaign have left a lingering bitterness and animosity. Their use of misleading slogans, allegations of rigged votes, and a lack of transparency in their messaging have eroded trust. If they were so convinced of the merits of their case, why did they resort to outright lies and misinformation? Where is the courage in their convictions? The simple answer is that there was none. Dutton engaged in divisive politics to appeal to the conservative base, the privileged and wealthy, the propertied class, and the captains of industry who benefit from a divided nation and wish to maintain the status quo.

What about Mundine and Jacinta Price? It's likely that they will soon receive their proverbial "30 pieces of silver" for their services to these captains of industry. With their previous work seemingly completed, Price appears to be moving on to her next divisive point: launching a wholesale attack on transgender people.

The connection between this and her role as a Senator for the Northern Territory remains unclear but surely there'll be a cap in hand for these services rendered—after all, when the Howard government created the Northern Territory National Emergency Response in 2007, the saying went around: 'whenever there's an intervention in the NT, there's always a Price to pay". And this has gained some more traction recently, with the revelations published at the Kangaroo Court of Australia, of a $12 million funding scam, where the mother of Jacinta Price, Bess Price, works.

LESSONS FROM DEFEAT

Following the defeat of the Voice to Parliament referendum, several critical lessons and considerations have emerged for both the government and the broader Australian society. The failure of the referendum underscores the importance of securing bipartisan support for any substantial issue presented in a referendum.

Another significant issue that emerged during the campaign was the gradual nature of the proposed change. While the media and the "No" campaign exaggerated the significance of the Voice to Parliament, some voters questioned its relevance, especially since the government of the day could choose to disregard the recommendations put forth by the Voice.

While a Labor government might be receptive to these recommendations, it is likely that a future Coalition government could persistently overlook and dismiss anything proposed by the Voice to Parliament. In such a scenario, one might wonder about the purpose of this consultative group, as any government—whether Labor or Coalition—could simply disregard their recommendations. They might be heard but ultimately ignored. Should the referendum question have aimed for more than just establishing a consultative body?

This is a question that will remain unanswered, but it is worth noting that no one from the "No" campaign was suggesting that more should be offered to Indigenous communities. In fact, doing so might have exacerbated divisions. However, should everything desired by the Indigenous community have been included on the table? This might have encompassed a treaty, a truth-telling process, a full Reconciliation process, reserved seats in Parliament, and reparations.

While such proposals might also have encountered challenges in garnering public support, given the vocal opposition the modest Voice to Parliament faced, they could have contributed to a more comprehensive discussion of Indigenous rights and recognition in Australia.

The Voice to Parliament referendum's defeat serves as a powerful reminder of the complexities and challenges in addressing Indigenous rights and reconciliation in Australia. It emphasises the need for political unity, clarity, and comprehensive engagement with the public on these critical issues.

The campaign's aftermath also calls for an examination of Australia's image on the world stage and the imperative to address the consequences of this defeat, both domestically and internationally. Ultimately, the referendum's failure should serve as a catalyst for change and a call to action to address the pressing issues of Indigenous recognition and reconciliation in the country.

***

IS IT THE END OF THE ROAD FOR RECONCILIATION IN AUSTRALIA?

21 October 2023

The recent rejection of the proposal for the Voice to Parliament in Australia has raised profound questions about the future of Reconciliation in the country. Whether the result of the referendum was a "yes" or a "no", it was anticipated that the process of reconciliation would continue, regardless of the outcome. However, the resounding "no" vote has cast a pall over the prospects of Reconciliation, leading to a sentiment within the Indigenous community that Reconciliation is, in fact, dead. In order to gain a deeper understanding of this perspective, it is essential to analyse the statements made by prominent Indigenous figures, Marcia Langton and Lloyd Walker, and to consider the broader context in which these developments are occurring.

Langton, a respected Indigenous academic and advocate, expressed a deep sense of disappointment in the wake of the referendum's failure, seeing it as a missed opportunity for Australia to formally recognise Indigenous people in the Constitution and to provide them with an advisory body to Parliament, a body which would have been instrumental in addressing the myriad disadvantages faced by Indigenous communities. The rejection of this proposal, in her view, reflects a failure on the part of the majority of Australians to overcome their colonial biases and recognise the existence and rights of Indigenous Australians. Langton also criticised the "No" campaign for poisoning public opinion against this proposition and against Indigenous Australia.

Walker, another Indigenous leader, acknowledged the efforts made to push the proposal forward, particularly by Prime Minister Albanese, but he recognises the difficulties that lay ahead for the Reconciliation process. He also highlighted the fact that while the "no" vote represented a significant percentage, there remained a substantial portion of the population that supported the proposal, suggesting that progress had been made, even if it was not enough to secure a victory.

The rejection of the Voice to Parliament has exposed the inherent challenges in the Reconciliation process in Australia where, historically, Reconciliation has been driven and defined by the non-Indigenous community, leaving Indigenous peoples with little agency in shaping the terms and conditions of Reconciliation.

This referendum offered a unique opportunity for Indigenous people to express what they wanted in the Reconciliation process, but the resounding rejection by the Australian electorate symbolises a harsh reality—a reality that Indigenous communities had asked for something meaningful and significant to them, and received nothing. The result highlights the significant divide between the broader Australian population and the Indigenous communities, further complicating the path toward Reconciliation.

The outcome has left a sense of disillusionment within the Indigenous community, with some believing that Reconciliation is now "dead". The rejection of the proposal for a Voice to Parliament underscores the difficulties and challenges that continue to impede the reconciliation process. However, it is important to acknowledge voices like Lloyd Walker's, which hold onto hope and believe that while it may be difficult, Reconciliation is not impossible.

The rejection of the proposal has also led to a shift in the Indigenous community's perspective, with some realising that even an inadequate step like the Voice to Parliament was at least a step in the right direction. The path forward remains uncertain, and the Indigenous community will undoubtedly play a pivotal role in determining how Reconciliation evolves in the years to come.

RESHAPING RECONCILIATION: STATE-LEVEL TREATY AND TRUTH TELLING

While there is a strong belief within the Indigenous community that a federal Treaty is the best avenue for Reconciliation, the current landscape—following the defeat of a very modest and minor Constitutional amendment—suggests that the Treaty process may be more viable at the state and territory levels. This notion is supported by the fact that several states, such as Victoria, Queensland, and Western Australia, have already commenced their treaty processes. South Australia, too, is in the process of setting up its own Voice to Parliament, indicating a commitment to addressing Indigenous issues and concerns.

One of the striking aspects of these state-level treaty initiatives is that they do not require referendums, and governments at the state and territory levels have proactively initiated these processes, demonstrating a more flexible approach to addressing Indigenous issues compared to the federal government. Notably, the Queensland Liberal–National Party's decision to withdraw support for the treaty process after the referendum results highlights the shifting landscape and the challenges that lie ahead for reconciliation.

Moreover, the historical context surrounding the establishment of Colony of New South Wales on Invasion Day in 1788 has introduced legal complexities to the Treaty process. While there are some discussions about Treaty in New South Wales, the Premier, Chris Minns has announced that nothing will be progressed in this field until after the 2027 NSW election. But should any Treaty be first established in New South Wales, as it was this colony that instigated the annexation and theft of Indigenous land 235 years ago?

The Australian Constitution includes a provision for the acquisition of property by the Commonwealth on just terms, outlined in Section 51. However, this provision is complicated by the fact that the land upon which Australia was federated in 1901 had already been stolen from Indigenous peoples for 113 years. Negotiating a treaty for New South Wales would entail addressing the dispossession and land theft that occurred in the colony's early history, making it a legal and historical quagmire that demands resolution.

Nevertheless, the Treaty process, whether at the state or federal level, appears to be an inevitable and essential step toward Reconciliation. It is becoming increasingly clear that Indigenous communities are asserting their right to shape the terms of Reconciliation and to secure recognition and justice for past wrongs. The rejection of the Voice to Parliament proposal at the federal level has underscored the urgency of these issues and the need for an evolving approach to reconciliation.

There is also the concept of "truth telling," another critical component of Reconciliation. Truth telling, as outlined in the Uluru Statement from the Heart, involves recognising the truth of Australia's history since colonisation and formally acknowledging the injustices, violence, and suffering that Indigenous communities have endured.

While some may resist confronting this history, truth telling is a fundamental step in the healing process and in bridging the divisions of the past. Historical documents, accounts of frontier wars, and the origins of place names all contribute to this process, but there is a need for a formal truth-telling commission to make these accounts official and to facilitate a broader understanding of Australia's history. How did Slaughterhouse Creek in New South Wales get its name? Or Murdering Gully in Victoria? Both were scenes of massacres of Indigenous people—around 50 people near Moree in 1838, and around 40 near Camperdown in 1839. How many people are aware of these histories?

However, as with the Treaty process, truth telling does not require a constitutional referendum to initiate. It can be set in motion without the need for a nation-wide vote, offering a more flexible and immediate avenue for addressing historical injustices.

The emergence of state-level Treaty processes and truth-telling initiatives indicates a shifting landscape and a growing commitment to addressing Indigenous issues and historical injustices. The future of Reconciliation in Australia will likely involve a combination of local, state, and federal efforts to recognise the truth of the past, negotiate treaties, and foster a deeper sense of unity and justice in the nation.

To effectively advance this agenda, it is crucial for governments to demonstrate their sincerity, engage with Indigenous communities, and address the concerns of the broader population to create a more inclusive path forward.

CHARTING A NEW COURSE: STRATEGIES FOR ADVANCING RECONCILIATION IN AUSTRALIA

One of the central themes in the aftermath of the referendum is the need for governments and advocates to adapt their approaches. While the Voice to Parliament proposal had a target on its back from the moment Anthony Albanese announced it on election night in May 2022, the Treaty process in states like Victoria demonstrates that governments can take proactive steps to address Indigenous issues without the need for a referendum. The quiet progress made in Victoria, in particular, serves as an example of how governments can move forward with projects without excessive fanfare, ensuring that they align with the Reconciliation agenda.

One of the core points emphasised by the "No" campaign was the presence of 11 federal members of parliament and Senators, leading to their question of why there is a need for a Voice to Parliament. Their arguments can, in turn, be used against these opponents: if that's their argument, then governments should proceed to utilise these MPs and Senators and establish an Indigenous working group equipped with the necessary resources, funding, and support needed to advocate effectively. How could these opponents then disagree with this approach, considering it aligns with what they've essentially called for?

The rejection of the Voice to Parliament—as difficult as this is for many in the Indigenous community and "Yes" campaigners to accept—should not be viewed as an insurmountable setback but rather as a call to adapt and innovate. Indigenous communities, like many other marginalised groups, often face resistance to change and are subjected to stereotypes and biases. In this context, to achieve goals and agendas, Indigenous advocates can work strategically, laying low when necessary and seeking opportunities to make changes in ways that may not attract widespread attention but do get the job done.

Moreover, Reconciliation should not be a one-sided effort and solely on the terms of non-Indigenous Australians, and there needs to be a confrontation of their own biases and engagement in open dialogues to foster a sense of unity and shared responsibility. It is a challenging path, but Reconciliation demands a willingness to confront historical injustices and embrace the diversity that enriches the nation. This involves a collective introspection that transcends the divisions of the past.

In hindsight, the campaign for the Voice to Parliament referendum faced several challenges. The timing of announcing the referendum and setting the date allowed misleading information to take root, while the messaging lacked the simplicity and resonance that could have appealed to a broader audience.

Looking forward, there may not be another referendum on Indigenous recognition for several decades. In the meantime, it is vital to analyse the failures and lessons from this campaign and apply them to future efforts. Australia is a diverse and evolving nation, and the path to Reconciliation will require ongoing adaptation, innovative strategies, and collaboration between all segments of society.

The rejection of the Voice to Parliament proposal is undoubtedly a setback, but it is not the end of the Reconciliation journey in Australia—or, at least, it shouldn't be. Governments, advocates, and the broader population must adapt and find new ways to advance the Reconciliation agenda. By embracing creative solutions, utilising the Indigenous voices already in Parliament, and promoting unity and shared responsibility, Australia can continue the path toward Reconciliation and justice for Indigenous communities. The challenges are formidable—as they always have been—but they are not insurmountable, and the quest for Reconciliation remains a shared commitment.

***

POST-REFERENDUM: BATTLING THE SHADOWS OF MISINFORMATION IN THE MEDIA

21 October 2023

In the aftermath of the Voice to Parliament referendum, a momentous event in Australia's recent political history, the absence of key figures from the public discourse is noted with some relief by many. Prominent figures like Warren Mundine and Jacinta Price, well-known for their vocal stance against the referendum, have momentarily exited the spotlight. Even the leader of the opposition, Peter Dutton, has seen his platform diminished following the referendum, however, amid this short-lived tranquility, there looms a sense of inevitability that the fiery rhetoric of misinformation will return.

The aftermath of the referendum has exposed a troubling aspect of the Australian media landscape. Almost immediately after the polls closed, mainstream media outlets began scrutinising the veracity of claims made by the 'no' campaign, unveiling a disturbing underbelly of falsehoods, misinformation, and disinformation. But where were these voices during the campaign? Would it not be more fruitful for these outlets to outline the misinformation during a campaign—when it matters—not afterwards, when it can't affect a single vote?

During the referendum campaign, lies and misinformation were rampant and the legitimacy of the proposed model for change—essentially, a simple change—was the subject of contention. Divisions that were promoted by Indigenous 'no' campaigners—primarily Mundine and Price—further muddied the waters. Price, a notable campaigner against the reforms, garnered attention for her controversial statements. She presented as a relatively young Indigenous woman challenging the prevailing narrative, asserting that colonisation had not negatively impacted Aboriginal people. This assertion—patently false according to historical accounts and scholarly research—stirred debate and confusion among non-Indigenous Australians.

It is vital to acknowledge that misinformation doesn't spread in a vacuum; it thrives in an environment where it can find fertile ground. Many of statements publicly offered by Price and Mundine, though false, resonated with some parts of the electorate because they catered to a desire to believe in a harmonious, non-racist Australia. These assertions, grounded in misinformation, contributed to the wider misinformation gap and a distorted public discourse.

The blame for the referendum's outcome cannot be placed solely on the shoulders of misinformation, but it undoubtedly played a substantial role. Misinformation capitalises on gaps in public understanding, which was evident in the confusion over the difference between constitutional and legislative changes. Moreover, many Australians have limited personal interaction with First Nations people, forming their perceptions primarily through clichéd and usually negative media portrayals. These perceptions can be heavily influenced by biased or misleading media narratives, further enabling misinformation to take root.

Western Sydney, in particular, stood out as a region where misinformation had a pronounced impact. False narratives, such as the fear of losing one's home or the perception that the reforms would grant special privileges, were pervasive. Yet, it is essential to consider the responsibility of those on the 'no' side in addressing these inaccuracies. Did they have a moral obligation to counter such misinformation? This question was posed to many leaders of the 'no' campaign but was usually met with indifference and creating a smoke screen to obfuscate the real issues.

In the wake of this referendum, the Australian public is left to grapple with not just the outcome but the unsettling presence of misinformation within the mainstream media. The stage is set for a deeper examination of the role media plays in shaping public opinion and whether it has a responsibility to dispel misinformation rather than allowing it to thrive unchallenged.

FALLING SHORT: AUSTRALIAN MEDIA'S ROLE IN PROPAGATING MISINFORMATION

Some media outlets—such as SBS and NITV—have consistently called out the falsehoods and misrepresentations that plagued the campaign. However, the same cannot be said for some of the more prominent media organisations in Australia.

The ABC and Nine Media have come under scrutiny for their handling of the misinformation. Critics argue that, rather than diligently fact-checking and providing the necessary context, these outlets either published the information verbatim from the 'no' campaign or regurgitated the misinformation without adequate context. Such practices not only failed to fulfill the media's fundamental duty to inform the public accurately but also inadvertently—or in some cases, deliberately—lent credibility to false claims.

News Corporation, long criticised for its sensationalism and bias, has frequently been labeled a "factory of misinformation". This reputation makes it unsurprising that it continued to disseminate harmful narratives and misinformation during the campaign. The lack of integrity in reporting perpetuates a cycle of mistrust and division.

The entire blame for the success of the 'no' campaign can't be placed upon the media's shoulders. It's important to acknowledge that, even before this referendum began, the consensus on Indigenous issues like the Voice to Parliament, Treaty, and truth-telling was far from unanimous, as is to be expected within a functioning democratic system. The 'no' campaign effectively seized on pre-existing doubts and prejudices, framing them as reasons to oppose the reforms. In such a climate, the role of the media was pivotal, and its failure to fulfill its professional responsibilities is concerning.

Almost all the nonsensical claims made by the 'no' campaign could easily be debunked, especially the far-fetched assertions from the fringes of the movement.

The 'no' campaign presented a bewildering array of unfounded claims, from baseless fears of losing personal housing titles to bizarre notions of United Nations mandates and QAnon-fed conspiracies. Many of these claims targeted elite Indigenous figures and allegations of newly-created secretive Voice to Parliament offices in Canberra—and many other parts of Australia—with no verifiable existence. A responsible and principled press should have swiftly debunked these absurdities, leaving the 'no' campaign with no fertile ground for their falsehoods. The absence of such rigorous fact-checking allowed these claims to fester and influenced the public discourse significantly.

A well-informed media, upholding its professional standards, could have challenged the 'no' campaign from the outset, rather than waiting until the referendum had concluded. Such rigorous journalism might have pressured the 'no' campaign to articulate fact-based, data-driven arguments, which, if they existed, would have been the best counterpoint to the proposed changes.

Instead, the result is a nation now perceived internationally as being in a similar situation to a pre-apartheid South Africa—a comparison that Australians might find troubling but, essentially, is a situation that exists in many parts of Australia. The media's failure to fulfill its watchdog role and act as a safeguard against misinformation not only jeopardised the integrity of the referendum but also the standing of Australia on the world stage.

A LACK OF COMMITMENT TO TRUTH, ACCURACY AND RESPONSIBILITY

The central role of the media in a functioning democracy is to hold truth and accuracy in the highest regard, to be a vigilant watchdog against misinformation, and to scrutinise the narratives presented to the public. Yet, it seems that during the Voice of Parliament campaign, many media outlets fell short of this essential duty.

The media's coverage of the referendum campaign was characterised by sensationalism and a propensity to amplify misinformation and lies rather than scrutinising them. Figures like Warren Mundine, Jacinta Price, and Peter Dutton occupied an inordinate amount of space in the media landscape, and it was almost as if they were not only campaign spokespeople for the 'no' side but also for the 'yes' side, given their omnipresence. In contrast, the 'yes' campaign did not seem as concentrated within the media, featuring a broader array of voices and perspectives.

Mundine and Price made many outrageous and unverified claims throughout the campaign yet, their statements, which often lacked factual basis, were reported extensively. These figures became the focal points of media coverage, often overshadowing the wider and more substantive discussions of the proposed reforms. While it is crucial to ensure diverse voices are heard in a democratic society, it is equally vital that media outlets exercise discernment in who they amplify.

Certainly, the 'yes' campaign did receive extensive media coverage, but the media's predilection for sensational narratives, such as the suggestion that colonisation was beneficial for Indigenous people or that they "have never had it better", worked against the 'yes' campaign. It is a predicament in which the media often prioritises clickbait and shocking headlines over nuanced, informative, and balanced reporting. The media, by focusing on the most extreme claims, marginalises the reasoned and factual arguments presented by proponents of reform. This approach might garner higher viewership or readership in the short term, but it can ultimately compromise the integrity of journalism.

In light of these issues, there is a call for a re-evaluation of the media landscape, as well as substantial reform in how the media presents news and political analysis. The media should not serve as a platform for figures whose claims are not grounded in facts, rather, it should prioritise and reward good journalism. The role of the media should be to present accurate, fact-based information and to foster constructive dialogue in a society, rather than perpetuating misinformation.

MEDIA BALANCE VS. RESPONSIBLE REPORTING: THE DILEMMA OF CONTEMPORARY JOURNALISM

Laura Tingle's criticism of the ABC's approach to news coverage, with its apparent emphasis on achieving "balanced and equal perspectives" rather than focusing on sound reporting, has drawn attention to a significant dilemma in contemporary journalism. The pursuit of "balance" should not equate to the indiscriminate allotment of equal time or platforms to two diametrically opposed arguments. It is an erroneous notion that giving space to both experts and individuals espousing baseless claims contributes to informed public discourse.

Indeed, granting equal time to experts and non-expert propagators of falsehoods only serves to confuse the audience and undermines the very essence of journalism. Tingle outlined the situation where the ABC provided its journalists with time sheets during the campaign to track the balance of their guests and articles. This bureaucracy has the potential to stifle the media's accountability to the public, turning it into an instrument of political demands from the Coalition—even though they are no longer in government—rather than a vehicle for robust, unbiased information.

As a public broadcaster—which exists primarily to serve the public—the ABC has to perform in a far better and professional manner but how will improvements be achieved? The recent appointment of two ABC board members, both seemingly lacking direct broadcasting experience, has raised questions about the merit-based process behind such selections. While the Minister for Communications, Michelle Rowland, asserts that merit-based considerations were central to these appointments, the public remains in the dark regarding the other candidates and the reasons for these specific choices. These developments add to the growing concern about the media's independence and integrity.

To address the challenges within the media landscape, it's imperative to clear out the entire board of the ABC—including these recent appointments—and start afresh. The media, especially a public broadcaster, should be accountable to the public, not to any particular political party or government.

If Australia seeks to be a global leader in various domains, including its media landscape, it must prioritise responsible and independent journalism. The media should serve as a safeguard against misinformation and sensationalism rather than a platform for figures who disseminate falsehoods.

It is essential that media outlets, political leaders, and the public, in general, rally against the perpetuation of a media landscape dominated by sensationalism and falsehoods. The Voice of Parliament campaign, while a significant moment, will eventually fade into the annals of Australia's history as new issues take its place in the public discourse. The imperative is to ensure that responsible journalism and fact-based arguments take precedence in shaping the narratives of the future. This means holding the media accountable and demanding a high standard of political responsibility.

In the end, it's time for a collective pushback against sensationalism and misinformation, not just in media but in the broader political landscape, with a commitment to a more informed, engaged, and responsible public discourse that truly serves the interests of all Australians.

***

TRUTH IN POLITICAL ADVERTISING: GOOD FOR DEMOCRACY?

28 October 2023

The federal government's intention to introduce truth in political advertising laws is a development that has been long overdue, given the significant implications of deceptive political messaging on democratic processes in Australia. Recent surveys have highlighted the overwhelming support for such legislation, with nearly 90 per cent of the electorate advocating for its implementation. This level of public endorsement underscores the urgency and necessity of these laws in the current political landscape.

One crucial aspect to consider is the existing legal framework surrounding advertising, which deems it an offense to disseminate false information in all forms of other advertising. It is a common-sense extension to apply these principles to political advertising, where misinformation can have dire consequences for the electorate. Deceptive practices have had a tangible impact on recent elections, as exemplified by the franking credits and negative gearing scare campaign in 2019 and these campaigns were marked by their misleading nature and demonstrated how the absence of stringent regulations allows falsehoods to flourish.

The recent Voice of Parliament referendum served as a wake-up call for the government, prompting it to consider the need for truth in political advertising legislation. This referendum, which aimed to establish an Indigenous Voice to Parliament and constitutional recognition, faced fierce opposition characterised by a campaign riddled with falsehoods—the fact that this referendum became a catalyst for government action speaks to the severity of the issue and the potential harm that deceptive political advertising can inflict on the democratic process.

However, not everyone is in favour of these proposed laws, with groups such as the conservative Advanced Australia and the Liberal Party have openly expressed their opposition to truth in political advertising legislation. Their resistance raises questions about their motivations and intentions as it suggests they rely on misleading or false information to advance their political goals and that, without this tool of misinformation available to them, they will have a diminished chance of electoral success in future elections.

Despite the opposition—which flies in the face of the public's desire to have this kind of legislation in place—it is essential to acknowledge that truth in political advertising legislation represents a significant step toward enhancing the quality of political discourse in Australia and reducing the spread of misinformation. These laws have the potential to set a higher standard for political campaigns and hold politicians accountable for the veracity of their claims and, in a democratic system that thrives on informed and engaged citizens, the necessity of accurate information cannot be overstated.

While the exact provisions of the legislation are yet to be revealed, the very concept of holding politicians accountable for their statements should be encouraged. The effectiveness and fairness of any such legislation will become clearer when it is put into practice but the challenge lies in striking the right balance between regulating political advertising to ensure honesty and transparency while upholding the principles of free speech and open debate.

In this era of digital misinformation and the spread of fake news, addressing the problem of false political advertising is critical. However, it should be noted that addressing political misinformation is not solely the responsibility of legislation. Media outlets and political campaigns themselves should also act ethically and responsibly to ensure that misinformation does not gain traction. The public's trust in political discourse and the integrity of the democratic process are at stake, and it is incumbent upon all stakeholders to work toward more accurate and honest political advertising.

OPPOSITION TO NEW LAWS REFLECTS A FEAR OF ACCOUNTABILITY

Opposition to the proposed truth in political advertising legislation is apparent, even before the legislation has been formally proposed. Those who stand in opposition are motivated by a desire to maintain the status quo, where they can capitalise on creating outrage, waging imaginary culture wars, and disseminating disinformation with relative impunity. And who benefits from the status quo? It's the current Liberal Party, One Nation, and figures like Pauline Hanson, Advance Australia: it's also their benefactors in the media, News Corporation and Sky News, whose business model is based on lies and misinformation. These entities are the primary beneficiaries of the ability to spread misinformation and falsehoods for political gain.

For politicians and political movements whose viability hinges on the freedom to distort the truth, the prospect of having to adhere to standards of accuracy and honesty in their political advertising is naturally unattractive.

It raises questions about the nature of their political movement and its principles: if a political entity relies on the spread of disinformation and the unrestricted use of lies as a strategy, where is the integrity and legitimacy of their objectives? Why resort to misinformation if their values cannot stand the test of veracity within the electorate?

The concerns raised by opponents of truth in political advertising often revolve around the potential for this legislation to restrict free speech and stifle legitimate political discourse. However, it's essential to recognise that the aim is not to silence political expression but to ensure that political communication is grounded in facts and truth. Truth in political advertising legislation doesn't seek to curtail the robust exchange of ideas; rather, it seeks to curb the harmful practice of spreading falsehoods for political gain.

Skeptics also point out that politicians might find ways to bypass or subvert such legislation by increasing their media appearances and utilising journalists who are willing to report their statements as fact, even if they are misleading. While this may be a legitimate concern, it doesn't diminish the importance of having clear regulations in place. The existence of alternative methods for politicians to pursue their agendas does not negate the need for oversight in political advertising.

Moreover, the effectiveness of truth in political advertising legislation may not be all-encompassing, and it may not eradicate misinformation entirely. It is a challenge to strike a balance between accountability and protecting genuine misunderstandings, where individuals may not be intentionally lying but rather misinformed or mistaken. The legislation should aim to differentiate between wilful deception and inadvertent misinformation, drawing upon the legal standard for perjury as a guide.

One significant apprehension regarding the forthcoming legislation is that it might be diluted with numerous caveats and narrow definitions of what constitutes a lie, thereby undermining its purpose. It's crucial that the legislation is robust and clear, leaving minimal room for interpretation or exploitation and any such watering down of the legislation could render it ineffectual and fail to address the root problem of dishonest political advertising.

It is worth noting that support for truth in political advertising legislation is expected to come from minor parties and independent politicians, who often find themselves at a disadvantage when competing against well-established parties that have the resources and inclination to engage in misleading advertising. The legislative process will undoubtedly be a test of the government's commitment to transparency and accountability in political discourse, and its outcome will shape the future of political campaigning in Australia. Until the legislation is officially introduced and its specifics are disclosed, the precise impact and effectiveness of these proposed laws remain to be seen. The journey toward ensuring truth and transparency in political advertising will be a nuanced and challenging one, but one that is pivotal for the health of Australia's democratic system.

GOVERNMENT'S CAUTIOUS APPROACH HINDERS TIMELY REFORMS

The cautious approach taken by Prime Minister Anthony Albanese in addressing key issues has, in some instances, hamstrung the government's ability to enact important reforms in a timely manner. While the government has made notable progress on various fronts within the first six months of its term, such as the establishment of the National Anti Corruption Commission, the issue of truth in political advertising should have been fast-tracked as a top priority immediately after securing victory in May 2022.

The fact that a parliamentary committee was set up to investigate this matter in August 2022 is a step in the right direction, however, it's concerning that it took nearly a year for the committee to complete its report. The complexity of the issues at hand is understood, but a year for the committee process seems excessive, especially given the urgency of addressing the problem of deceptive political advertising. The delay in getting the legislation up and running only further extends the timeline for potential reform.

This delay has already had consequences in the Voice to Parliament referendum, and while it's unclear if having truth in political advertising laws in place would have made a difference in the final result, it's evident that the government will need to have such legislation enacted before the next federal election to ensure that such a campaign based on misinformation is never repeated.

One of the primary considerations is the delicate balance between protecting freedom of speech, political information, and political thought, and ensuring the integrity of the political process. While freedom of speech is a cornerstone of democratic societies, it should not be misused to deceive or manipulate the electorate. The legislation must navigate this fine line while accounting for potential unintended consequences.

Determining what constitutes a lie in political advertising is another intricate issue. The legislation will need clear guidelines for assessment and a framework to determine who will be responsible for assessing whether a statement qualifies as a lie or not. Additionally, there should be a well-defined set of sanctions for those who violate the truth in political advertising laws. The legislation must be robust and carry substantial consequences for breaches to be effective.

Moreover, this legislation should not be a mere symbolic gesture or "feel-good" policy; it should be a powerful tool to maintain the integrity of the political process. Even if the courts become involved in adjudicating disputes arising from the legislation, it is crucial that the laws themselves are strong and clear.

The potential for false imputations and deceptive claims to be used as political weapons is a real concern, as has been seen in the past. The need to prevent such actions and to uphold the ethical standards of political campaigns is a driving force behind the push for truth in political advertising legislation and by holding politicians accountable for their statements and campaign claims, the hope is to create a more transparent and truthful electoral process.

In addition to legislation concerning truth in political advertising, there is an opportunity to consider broader reforms in how election campaigns are conducted and how individuals are selected for preselection in political parties.

In 2007, Scott Morrison spread lies and rumours about the successful candidate in the Cook preselection battle, Michael Towke, who was subsequently disendorsed by the NSW branch of the Liberal Party, with Morrison being installed in his place. Could these unfair practices also be included within the process of electoral reform?

While parties have their unique procedures for preselection, there is a need for overarching standards that ensure preselections are conducted honestly and ethically. This would not necessarily dictate to parties how they preselect, but rather establish a fair and consistent set of guidelines that all parties must adhere to.

The issue of truth in political advertising is a complex one, but it is one that requires swift and decisive action. The government's approach to this legislation will set the tone for how electoral campaigns are conducted and how politicians are held accountable for their statements. A comprehensive and well-crafted set of laws can bring much-needed transparency and truth to Australian politics, safeguarding the democratic process and the public's right to accurate information in political discourse. The next election must be held before May 2025, and the time for meaningful reform is now.

LEGISLATION FOR DIGITAL AGE PRESENTS A CHALLENGE

The debate surrounding truth in political advertising is not a new one; it has been a topic of discussion for over 20 years. However, over the past three to four years, it has gained significant momentum, reflecting the growing concern about deceptive political messaging. Interestingly, Australia had truth in political advertising laws in the past, albeit briefly. In 1983, just after being elected, the Hawke government amended the *Commonwealth Electoral Act* to make it illegal to publish anything that could deceive or mislead a voter. This legislation applied to everyone, not just members of parliament and political parties, and violations at the time could result in a $1,000 fine (valued at around $4,000 in 2023) or a six-month jail term.

Regrettably, this legislation was repealed before the 1984 election, with the justification that it was "unworkable". However, 40 years later, the environment has changed drastically. In the past, political campaigns were primarily limited to television, radio, and newspapers but, today, with the advent of the internet and social media, political news and advertising have taken on a multifaceted and pervasive nature. This expanded reach has created numerous opportunities for the dissemination of myths, truth, and misinformation.

It is essential to recognise that politics, to some extent, has always involved the art of manipulating the truth, but in recent years, this practice has grown increasingly extreme. Politicians, like Scott Morrison and Peter Dutton, have at times resorted to telling glaring and outrageous lies, which end up being duly reported by the media, without any context or counterbalance. While truth in political advertising laws may not entirely eliminate this behaviour, they can serve as a deterrent and impose a constraint on some of the other avenues for spreading misinformation.

The best that can realistically expect from such legislation is a slowing down of the spread of misinformation rather than a complete cessation, as political campaigns have adapted to exploit the inherent vagueness and ambiguity of whispers and rumours, as exemplified by the recent Voice to Parliament referendum. Truth in political advertising laws can help create mechanisms to counter such tactics, making it more difficult for political entities to amplify falsehoods and baseless rumours.

It's a step toward a more informed and honest political discourse, one that safeguards the integrity of the democratic process and empowers citizens to make well-informed decisions. As the legislative process unfolds and the laws take shape—hopefully in time for the next federal election—the impact on Australian politics and democracy will become increasingly evident, hopefully enhancing the transparency and credibility of the political arena.

***

WHO SPEAKS UP FOR PALESTINIAN IN THE UNENDING CYCLE OF VIOLENCE?

28 October 2023

Amidst the relentless cycle of violence and destruction that has gripped the Palestinian territories, the latest eruption of hostilities in the Gaza Strip has once again cast a grim shadow over the prospects for peace in the region. The conflict, though rooted in decades of historical animosities, has recently taken a turn for the worse, leaving both Palestinian and Israeli populations grappling with the consequences of a crisis that shows no signs of abating.

The predictability of this grim pattern is one of the most disheartening aspects of the ongoing conflict. As the latest round of hostilities escalates, observers have come to expect the same series of events to unfold. Israel, in response to perceived threats, launches harsh retaliatory measures, often involving airstrikes and military incursions into Gaza. These actions invariably result in the loss of innocent Palestinian lives, with civilians bearing the brunt of the violence. Meanwhile, the international community, represented by the United Nations and most Western governments, responds with strongly worded statements urging restraint while reaffirming Israel's right to self-defence. The United States, in particular, usually offers its "thoughts and prayers" but substantive action remains elusive.

The consequences of this unending cycle are not limited to one side of the conflict but it's obvious that's one side which bears the brunt of the pain and suffering. While the Palestinian people endure unimaginable suffering and despair, Israel, in its quest for self-preservation, finds itself mired in actions that have been widely criticised as illegal and inhumane. The occupation of the West Bank, the construction of settlements, and the ongoing encroachments into Palestinian territories are all deemed violations of international law. Yet, despite global condemnations, these practices persist.

The narrative of "self-defence", repeatedly invoked by Israel, has been stretched to its limits. How can the killing of over 8,000 civilians, mostly women and children, be an act of "self-defence"? The conflict has long ceased to be a matter of self-preservation, transforming into a multifaceted crisis that encompasses indiscriminate bombing, the targeting of hospitals, collective punishment, and what amounts to ethnic cleansing. The world watches, often unwilling to do anything, as these grave violations unfold.

In this unfolding tragedy, the glaring question remains: who speaks up for the Palestinian people? While criticism must also be directed towards Palestinian groups such as Hamas involved in the conflict, it is essential to recognise that they operate in a complex and deeply entrenched environment. The situation defies easy solutions and presents multifaceted challenges. Palestinian leaders and representatives are always asked to condemn the actions of Hamas, which they rightfully do. But why are Israeli leaders never asked to condemn the actions of the Israeli military? Why are they never asked to condemn the ethnic cleansing carried out by their own military? Their actions are likely to be identified as war crimes. Why are their actions never condemned in the Western media?

Within Israel, there exists a significant segment of the population that vehemently opposes these actions and yearns for a just and lasting resolution. Why do we never hear from the Israelis who strongly oppose this military action against Gaza?

The arrival of international troops and military support in the region from the United States, Australia, and other countries raises concerns about the effectiveness of external intervention in such a deeply rooted conflict. Will the deployment of troops yield tangible results or merely perpetuate the cycle of violence?

Ultimately, this crisis underscores that retaliations and counteractions will never arrive at a military or political solution. Civilians in Gaza are caught in a precarious and volatile situation, cut off from basic necessities like electricity, water, and food. It is a situation that demands an urgent and equitable resolution. The criticisms voiced here are not a judgment of entire citizenries but are aimed at the political organisations perpetuating this cycle of violence: the Israel military and Hamas.

As the crisis in Gaza continues to escalate, the world watches on, hoping that amidst the chaos and destruction, there might still be some hope for dialogue and a pathway forward, however unlikely that outcome might be.

ISRAELI GOVERNMENT'S CONFRONTATIONAL STANCE IN SPARKS OUTRAGE AND INTERNATIONAL CONCERN

As the crisis in Gaza continues to worsen, and as the conflict escalates, the Israeli government's actions are coming under further scrutiny and the rhetoric emanating from the Israeli government has deepened concerns about the trajectory of the crisis. The government's behaviour, resembles that of a rogue state, and its recent statement about "teaching the UN a lesson" has sparked outrage and unease.

It's worth noting that such confrontational language, akin to what one might expect from leaders like Vladimir Putin, is hardly characteristic of Western democracies. In a stark departure from diplomatic norms, this statement came in response to a speech by the Secretary General of the United Nations, António Guterres, who voiced deep concern about the dire situation in the Middle East, particularly in Gaza. Guterres expressed worry over clear violations of international humanitarian law in Gaza and unequivocally emphasised that no party to an armed conflict is above international humanitarian law.

Guterres's measured speech called for an immediate humanitarian ceasefire, emphasising the cessation of the collective punishment of the Palestinian people and the ongoing violence. His words were a plea for the international community to recognise the suffering of the Palestinian people, who have endured decades of occupation, territorial losses, economic stifling, displacement, and the destruction of their homes.

However, the Israeli military continues its relentless bombing campaign, resulting in over 8,000 innocent Palestinian casualties. The government's subsequent declaration to "teach the UN a lesson" in the face of international criticism has only added fuel to an already incendiary situation. This confrontational stance is a matter of grave concern, especially when the world is witnessing the immense human cost of the conflict.

It is essential to clarify that criticism is directed at the Israeli government, its military, and hardline elements within the country, particularly those who draw inspiration from extremist religious doctrines. Just as Hamas does not represent all Palestinian people—there are other political entities in the Palestinian territories—the actions of the Israeli government and military do not reflect the perspectives of all Israeli citizens. There exists a significant portion of the Israeli population, as well as Jewish communities around the world, who are horrified by the Israeli government's actions and seek a different path toward peace and stability.

The repercussions of this crisis extend far beyond the borders of the Israeli–Palestinian conflict. The continued violence and turmoil jeopardise the security and stability of the entire Middle East region. It's a situation of immense complexity and depth, and despite the immense challenges, hope remains that the international community can help defuse the situation.

While world leaders, including President Joe Biden, have expressed criticism and concerns about the Israeli government's actions, it is apparent that the situation may deteriorate before any semblance of improvement emerges. What is paramount is the hope that a resolution can be found that minimises harm to innocent victims and paves the way for a more peaceful and secure Middle East. The current crisis demands an immediate re-evaluation of strategies and a concerted effort to prevent further suffering on all sides.

AUSTRALIAN POLITICAL FIGURES TREATING A COMPLEX ISRAEL–PALESTINE CONFLICT AS JUST ANOTHER OPPORTUNITY

As the conflict in Gaza rages on, it's crucial to recognise the far-reaching implications and how they resonate even in countries far removed from the immediate theatre of conflict. The war may be centred around Gaza, but its political reverberations are being felt across the globe, including in Australia and recent statements and actions by Australian political figures underscore the complexity of the issue and the potential impact on domestic politics.

One such instance that drew significant attention was when the leader of the opposition, Peter Dutton, suggested that Prime Minister Anthony Albanese should visit Israel while *en route* to meet President Biden in the United States. It was unclear what the Prime Minister's visit to Israel would achieve, but Dutton decided to push this agenda, cause trouble for the Labor government and create the perception that Albanese had failed to act—what he failed to act on wasn't articulated by Dutton but given the state of Australia's mainstream media, it never needs to be articulated: it creates news copy and a point of attack on the Albanese government.

Dutton's opportunistic suggestion and the ensuing debate highlighted the delicate and nuanced nature of the Israel–Palestine conflict. It is a matter that defies easy solutions, and while passionate voices on both sides advocate for their perspectives, the complexity of the situation remains.

The government minister Ed Husic, spoke out on behalf of Palestine, emphasising the collective punishment faced by Palestinians and the obligation of governments, particularly the Israeli government, to adhere to international law. His words reflected a growing concern about the disproportionate use of force and the impact on innocent lives.

Senator Fatima Payman also made a passionate speech in the Senate, condemning the killing of innocent civilians on both sides and calling for an immediate ceasefire. Her remarks highlighted the need for the international community to take a clear stand and push for a peaceful resolution to the crisis.

All these comments add to the plurality of debate in a diverse Australian community—and who doesn't want a hostile war to end for the sake of all sides—but for the modern Liberal Party, every issue presents as a political opportunity to attack the Labor government, irrespective of how delicate an international issue might be.

The Deputy Liberal Party leader Sussan Ley, sought to focus on the points of difference and announced as loudly as possible that the Labor government was "divided" over Palestine and the entire party was fracturing over the issue. And, of course, the media duly responded where an interview with a hyperbolic Ley on the friendly outlet of Sky News, became magnified and amplified: who's got time for nuance when we can listen to the words of Sussan Ley, which were uttered purely for political reasons? Labor is divided, obviously: *Sussan Ley said so and, therefore, it must be true.*

The question of sending the Australian Prime Minister to the Middle East raises an important consideration. While diplomatic efforts are essential, it's uncertain how such a visit would contribute to resolving the deeply entrenched conflict. Following Dutton's foolish suggestion, should the leaders of every country now visit Israel?

As the crisis evolves, the priority should remain on diplomatic solutions, as sending troops might escalate the situation further. However, the realities of international relations and the complexities of the conflict often mean that wishes and moral considerations take a backseat to political and strategic priorities.

While the Israel–Palestine conflict remains a highly intricate and emotionally charged issue with significant global implications, how long can the international community stand by, watch on and witness one of the most one-sided conflicts in history?

What is the tipping point for the international community when it decides that enough is enough? Is it 10,000 civilian deaths in Gaza? Is it 20,000? Twelve of Gaza's 35 hospitals cannot be used because of damage from bombing or lack of fuel and electricity. Will the international community act when the last remaining hospital switches off its lights? At least 221 schools and 180,000 dwellings have been damaged and destroyed over the past three weeks. Is 500 schools the tipping point? Or 500,000 dwellings destroyed?

While Australia, like many other countries, grapples with how to respond and engage with this crisis, the primary goal should be a resolution that minimises the suffering of innocent civilians on both sides. But the current destruction of Gaza cannot continue. The political discourse surrounding the conflict requires careful consideration and a commitment to engaging in constructive dialogue that paves the way for a just and lasting solution. At the moment, that seems a long way off.

***

NOVEMBER

THE WORLD SITS IDLY BY AS GAZA BURNS

4 November 2023

The United Nations held a critical vote during the week, with a focus on the ongoing Gaza conflict, calling for a ceasefire and a humanitarian truce. The numbers were comprehensively in favour of the ceasefire, as 120 countries voiced their support for the resolution, emphasising the global demand for an end to the violence. However, there was a surprising and controversial twist in this international response, as 14 countries voted against the resolution, including the United States and Israel.

It's bewildering to imagine a nation opposing a ceasefire, especially when the conflict's grim human toll has captured the world's attention. Gaza has faced daily and indiscriminate bombing of dwellings, hospitals, schools, universities and shopping precincts for almost a month, resulting in thousands of deaths. What else would be needed to support a call for ceasefire?

This stark division in the vote revealed a complex web of international relations, with certain countries choosing to align themselves with the United States. The reasons for such alignment ranged from historical favours to the pursuit of future diplomatic advantages.

For example, Croatia, which cast its vote in favour of the United States: this is viewed as a "thank-you" gesture for the U.S. support during their quest for independence in 1991. This historical camaraderie influenced Croatia's decision to stand with the United States and similar motivations can be attributed to other nations keen on securing favourable arrangements with the United States in the future.

While 120 countries supported the call for a ceasefire, 45 countries abstained from voting altogether, raising questions about their stance on the issue. One of those countries was Australia, which claimed that it refrained from supporting the resolution because it did not explicitly condemn the actions of Hamas. Do they need to go onto the streets of Gaza and ask the Palestinian families of those who have died to also condemn the actions of Hamas before they could support the resolution? What is Australia's limit of tolerance to the wanton destruction, ethnic cleansing and genocide that's happening in right front of our eyes?

This decision, however, underscores a broader and more difficult aspect of international diplomacy at the United Nations. For Australia, a country with its own interests and global diplomatic considerations, such a choice was made in an effort to avoid offending powerful allies and retain a delicate balance, rather than any human rights issues.

The non-binding nature of the United Nations resolution also raises questions about its practical impact and in the realm of international law, even if it were a binding resolution, enforcing it can be a daunting task. However, resolutions like these serve as opportunities for nations to express their positions on crucial global issues, making it a platform for countries to state their stance for the world to see, and built on further action.

In this case, the resolution was an unequivocal call to halt the destruction in the Gaza Strip. Countries such as France, New Zealand, Norway, and Slovenia voted in favour of the resolution, demonstrating a significant alignment with the resolution's objectives. It's essential to emphasise that this was not a scenario where "third world" countries were ganging up on Israel; rather, it was a global consensus urging an end to the hostilities.

Australia's abstention in the vote, however, has raised concerns and controversy domestically and the decision to refrain from taking a clear stance on the issue was perceived by many as a failure to express solidarity with those affected by the conflict. It is crucial to note that the Gaza conflict has been characterised by humanitarian crises, and the world has watched with growing concern as the violence continues to escalate.

Furthermore, the conflict's nature, with its heavy civilian toll—over 10,000 Palestinians, mainly women and children, have been killed in Israel's retaliation to the events of 14 October, where 1,400 Israelis were killed by Hamas—has led to strong condemnations against the Netanyahu government.

As a diverse and multicultural nation, Australia must tread carefully to avoid stirring anti-Jewish or anti-Muslim sentiments. A call for a ceasefire may not have radically altered Australia's domestic landscape, but it would have conveyed a message of compassion and concern for the people residing within its borders, regardless of their cultural or religious backgrounds.

Australia's abstention was a passive stance, leading to criticism that it lacked decisiveness and assertiveness in the global arena. Australia's decision to abstain from the United Nations resolution on the Gaza conflict raises questions about the nation's foreign policy priorities, its commitment to humanitarian values, and its role on the international stage. The move has sparked debate and disappointment from those within the electorate, who expected a more principled and proactive approach from their government, including the Prime Minister and the Minister for Foreign Affairs.

AUSTRALIA'S ABSTENTION AND ITS GLOBAL MIDDLE-POWER POSITION

A non-binding United Nations resolution may not appear as a decisive step in resolving a pressing and deadly conflict like the one in Gaza. However, it lays the foundation for future international diplomacy and action, offering a glimmer of hope in what is a grim scenario. With 193 member states in the United Nations, a diverse range of geopolitical interests must be considered when addressing global issues, including conflicts like the one in Gaza.

The purpose of such resolutions is to set the stage for further diplomatic efforts, which might encompass a broad spectrum of actions. These actions could involve lobbying for peace, implementing a UN peacekeeping force, or establishing a UN protectorate. However, these measures remain distant prospects, contingent on international support and cooperation, primarily from influential players like the United States.

The immediate and primary goal of this United Nations resolution was to halt the relentless targeting of civilians in the Gaza Strip by the Israel military, an issue that required immediate attention and international consensus. The abstention by Australia in the vote, though, reflects the intricate web of global relations that Australia finds itself entangled in due to security alliances like AUKUS and its historical alignment with the United States.

Australia's decision to abstain in the vote highlights the complexities and constraints it faces on the global stage. While Australia's abstention might seem like an independent decision—the U.S. voted against the resolution, whereas Australia abstained—but a closer look at the background commentary and statements made by Australian envoys at the United Nations reveals a different story.

In reality, Australia's choice to abstain appears to be a less assertive, less committed position in the eyes of the international community and is in contrast to the crucial role Australia played in the creation of the United Nations in 1945, where figures such as Herb Evatt—who became the president of the UN—John Curtin, and Francis Forde played important roles in establishing the organisation, with the vision of providing smaller countries around the world a meaningful voice in international affairs.

However, nearly eight decades later, the global landscape has shifted significantly, and Australia's ability to independently influence major world issues has dwindled. Despite its role in creating the United Nations and the ideals of providing a voice for smaller nations, Australia now finds itself struggling to assert its independent stance on the international stage.

In retrospect, a "yes" vote in favour of the United Nations resolution would have increased Australia's international standing and potentially improved its relations with countries other than the United States. While Australia's commitment to its alliances and its global partners is crucial, the abstention has exposed the nation to criticism and has raised questions about its place as an independent participant on the world stage. The consequences of this decision are likely to ripple through Australia's foreign policy and diplomatic relations, making it interesting to observe how the nation will navigate its global role moving forward.

AUSTRALIA'S ALIGNMENT WITH THE UNITED STATES AND ITS COMPLEX TIES

The question of what special favours Australia secures by consistently aligning itself with the United States is a pertinent one, and it harks back to the days when Australia was often referred to as the "deputy sheriff" during the era of former Prime Minister John Howard. However, it is essential to scrutinise whether this alignment truly serves Australia's interests, especially when considering specific cases.

An illustrative case in point is the ongoing matter of Julian Assange, the Australian citizen who remains incarcerated in Belmarsh Prison in London, facing extradition to the United States on charges widely perceived as politically motivated. Prime Minister Anthony Albanese has met with President Joe Biden on multiple occasions to discuss the release of Assange, emphasising that "enough is enough" and that the case has dragged on for "far too long", yet this plea has seemingly fallen on deaf ears.

Despite the diplomatic rhetoric and repeated assurances, the situation remains unresolved, with Assange's legal plight continuing to drag on. Biden's position, emphasising the separation between politics and the judiciary, suggests a reluctance to intervene in Assange's case, causing frustration among those advocating for his release. Given Australia's consistent alignment with the United States, one would expect some reciprocal goodwill or diplomatic support, especially in securing the release of one its own citizens facing a potential extradition. But, it is yet to happen.

Australia's cooperation with the United States extends beyond political rhetoric. The recently formed AUKUS alliance, which the Albanese government inherited from the Liberal–National Coalition, underscores the nation's alignment with its powerful ally. However, the reasons for such unwavering loyalty and co-operation are not always clear, considering the apparent lack of *quid pro quo* when it comes to crucial matters such as Julian Assange's fate.

In the broader context of the Israeli–Palestinian conflict, Australia's foreign policy choices are being scrutinised closely. The recent letter of condemnation of Hamas and unequivocal support for the Israel government, signed by six former Australian prime ministers, has raised further concerns and ignited debate. The letter, signed by John Howard, Kevin Rudd, Julia Gillard, Tony Abbott, Malcolm Turnbull, and Scott Morrison, expressed support for Israel and its lauded its "promise" of avoiding civilian casualties, surely a naïve level of support, considering that over 10,000 Palestinian civilians have been killed, which raises the question of what measures the Israeli military have been taken to avoid civilian casualties, with such a high level of death and severe injuries.

Paul Keating, the only former prime minister who refrained from signing the letter, articulated concerns about its sharp and biased tone, advocating for a more balanced approach. This division within Australia's political leadership—even if it former Prime Ministers—highlights the complexities of its approach to the Israeli–Palestinian conflict.

Moreover, the media discourse in Australia concerning the conflict is another point of contention and the narrative in the Australian media leans strongly towards the interests of the Israeli government. Palestinian representatives, when given a platform, are often pressed to condemn the actions of Hamas, while Israeli counterparts are seldom asked to address the actions of the Israeli military or the issue of ethnic cleansing in Gaza.

In light of these observations, Australia's diplomatic and political stance in international conflicts, particularly in the context of its alignment with the United States and the Israeli–Palestinian conflict, remains a subject of intense debate and scrutiny.

COMPLEX DIPLOMATIC AND DOMESTIC DYNAMICS IN AUSTRALIA'S STANCE ON THE ISRAELI–PALESTINIAN CONFLICT

As the Israeli–Palestinian conflict continues to unfold, it is increasingly evident that diplomatic challenges and domestic debates are mounting globally. Egypt, for instance, has condemned the recent bombings and attacks, expressing its concern over the escalating violence. Furthermore, several South American countries have taken the unprecedented step of severing their diplomatic ties with Israel. These reactions underscore the gravity of the situation and the need for the international community to address the crisis urgently.

However, when examining Australia's position, the response appears one-sided, with limited room for nuanced or reasoned discussion. Senator Penny Wong's call for Israel to heed the international community's pleas for a ceasefire was met with harsh criticism from the Liberal Party and from Israel lobbyists in Australia, illustrating the polarised nature of the discourse.

Senator Wong's warning that the international community will not tolerate ongoing civilian casualties in Gaza, while echoing global sentiments, was also met with similar resistance and the line between supporting a different countries diplomatically and expressing humanitarian concerns becomes blurred in such a polarised context, leaving Australian politicians navigating a difficult political terrain.

Another contentious issue arose when the Canterbury–Bankstown Council decided to fly the Palestinian flag, in solidarity with the people of Palestine. This move was met with significant local support, particularly in the federal minister Tony Burke's constituency in the seat of Watson. In response to this decision, Burke defended the council's choice, highlighting the importance of recognising Palestinian lives lost in the ongoing conflict.

Burke's impassioned defence resonated with many in his electorate, where the tragic consequences of the conflict are felt acutely. The decision to fly the Palestinian flag was seen as an act of solidarity and acknowledgment of the Palestinian people's grief and suffering. While the question of whether local councils should engage in international politics is a separate debate, Burke's support for his constituents received wide approval.

However, the reaction from some quarters, including Sky News, News Corporation, the Liberal Party, and pro-Israeli lobbying groups, was predictably negative. This polarisation underscores the lack of space for constructive and balanced discussions on the Israeli-Palestinian conflict within Australia. The struggle to find a middle ground hinders the identification of the core problem and the application of a suitable solution.

In essence, the Israeli–Palestinian conflict remains a contentious and polarised subject in Australia, mirroring global debates. While there are no easy solutions to such a deeply rooted and historically charged conflict, the lack of room for nuance and reasoned discourse in Australian politics poses a challenge to finding a path toward a more balanced and constructive approach to the issue.

Representatives like Burke, who advocate for their constituents' interests and concerns, play a crucial role in shaping Australia's response to the Israeli–Palestinian conflict. The complexities and sensitivities of the issue demand careful consideration and balanced perspectives to navigate the domestic and international landscapes effectively.

The Israeli–Palestinian conflict presents a multifaceted challenge for Australia, with repercussions on both diplomatic relations and domestic politics. The ongoing debate highlights the need for constructive dialogue, diplomatic measures, and nuanced discussions to help address the crisis and bring about a meaningful resolution to the conflict. The destruction of Gaza and the continuing acts of ethnic cleansing are not the solution, and the actions by the Israel military and the Netanyahu government must be stopped now.

***

MEDIA BIAS IN AUSTRALIA AND THE FUTILE BALANCING ACT

4 November 2023

Concerns have been mounting regarding the performance of the Australian mainstream media and its commitment to balanced and unbiased reporting. Rather than addressing these concerns head-on, the media landscape in Australia is persistently tilting towards right-wing conservative interests, exacerbating the slow descent of legacy media into irrelevance. What is more alarming is the fact that there seems to be no indication that this trend will reverse anytime soon.

One prominent example of this situation has developed at the public broadcaster, the ABC, where several weeks ago, it was revealed that the ABC's approach to "balance" is the aim to provide equal time to "both sides" of a debate. While, on the surface, this may sound like a fair practice, it also means equal time for experts and non-experts alike, a humanitarian and a charlatan, a voice of reason with the voice of the irrationalist. While it might appear to be "good television"—and even then, that's not so clear—the public is left frustrated, less informed, especially when they're provided with expert information, muddied with uninformed and misguided opinion.

Another issue for the media lies in its inability to reflect upon its own behaviour and adapt to a changing landscape, and it continues to behave like a closed shop, seemingly oblivious to its waning relevance. This issue was brought to the forefront when ABC journalist Leigh Sales presented the Andrew Olle Memorial Lecture, an annual lecture on the role and future of the media. While Sales is just one journalist within the industry—and the point is not to focus on the one figure within the media—the lecture exemplified many of the problems plaguing the media as a whole. Surprisingly, a significant portion of the lecture's time was dedicated to an anecdote about incorrectly parking in ABC Chair Ita Buttrose's car park space at the ABC, followed by a hagiography of Ita Buttrose, which reinforced an impression of the industry being "matey" and incestuous.

Sales defended the media's general performances by emphasising the journalists' shared commitment, inclination and "bias" towards a "cracking story", where journalists are driven by the pursuit of a great story, regardless of political affiliations or social media backlash. However, this ultimately leads to a focus on sensationalism and competition between journalists for chasing "the scoop", and often overshadows the need for responsible journalism and public interest.

The media's fixation on the "cracking story" over public interest stories reveals a broader problem within the Australian media landscape. The media, especially mainstream outlets, appear to be too introspective, failing to adequately address the concerns and interests of the wider public. While Sales acknowledged valid points during the Andrew Olle lecture, the overarching bias towards sensationalism and competition overshadows the need for balanced and informative reporting.

The consequences of this media bias are starkly evident. Traditional newspapers are struggling, often serving as tools to attack the government or promote the opposition, rather than fulfilling their primary function of informing the public. This decline in trust and relevance of the mainstream media is a cause for concern, particularly because an informed and engaged citizenry is a cornerstone of democracy.

As the mainstream media's influence wanes, there is a risk that a shrewd government may circumvent traditional media channels, further limiting access to critical information. Smaller independent media outlets may have a role to play in filling this gap, but their capacity to do so remains uncertain. There is an unspoken need within the Australian populace for a robust, impartial, and influential media presence, but, regrettably, this need remains unmet.

Comparing the quality of journalism in international media outlets, such as Al Jazeera, the *New York Times*, and the international *Guardian*, reveals a stark contrast. These outlets are often lauded for their in-depth reporting and commitment to providing diverse perspectives. In contrast to some Australian media, they prioritise news over agendas, seeking to inform rather than persuade. In the midst of these challenges and shortcomings in the Australian media landscape, it is essential to examine how media bias impacts public perception, democracy, and the role of the media as a whole.

THE SHIFT TOWARDS "INFOTAINMENT" MEANS THE PURSUIT OF QUALITY NEWS GOES MISSING

As the Australian mainstream media continues to struggle with its issues of bias and relevance, an alarming transformation has taken place. The news landscape has shifted from a primary focus on informing the public to one that increasingly prioritises entertainment and engagement. The consequence? An audience that is switching off from traditional news sources in search of more meaningful and informative content.

It's important to recognise that nobody is advocating for dull and monotonous news delivery, as a dynamic and engaging presentation of the news is crucial to keep the audience's attention. However, the problem lies in the content itself and the quality of news reporting. The line between news and commercial interests has become increasingly blurred, leading to a decline in the substance and credibility of the stories being presented.

Many audiences are seeking genuine news reports, not just entertaining anecdotes or sensationalised narratives. This shift in viewer preferences is evident in the growing number of Australians turning to alternative news sources. Many are now looking to international outlets like CNN, BBC, and Al Jazeera, particularly for their coverage of international events such as the Palestine conflict. The internet has made it easier than ever to access diverse and high-quality news from around the world and, with this increased competition, it's unclear why local news haven't improved their depth of quality to match the alternatives that are available to their audiences.

The primary driver behind this shift is the perception that legacy media outlets in Australia offer a limited perspective and lack the depth and diversity of reporting that viewers seek. If traditional media wishes to regain its audience and regain their trust, it must recognise the need for substantive and unbiased news coverage. Quality should take precedence over sensationalism or "cracking yarns," as they are often referred to in the industry.

The term "cracking yarns" holds a special place in Australian culture as tales of adventure and intrigue, often woven with exaggerations for dramatic effect. While these stories have their place in entertainment and folklore, they should not be part of a serious news bulletin. There is a clear distinction between sharing fascinating stories and responsible journalism and audiences are increasingly aware of this distinction and demands news that provides them with a deep understanding of current events, not just entertainment.

A fundamental shift has occurred in the way Australians view their news outlets. The era when the 7PM ABC News was considered the "gold standard" for television news and factual information is fading into memory. What was once a reliable source for straightforward reporting has now evolved into a mixture of lifestyle features, entertainment highlights, and sports coverage, with the occasional nod to government actions. The emphasis on balance, while essential, sometimes results in the presentation of views that do not necessarily contribute to informed public discourse.

For instance, the practice of inviting government and opposition spokespeople, even when one party's representative is not well-versed on the topic, has raised concerns about the media's role in shaping public perception. An infamous example was the appearance of renowned physicist Brian Cox on the ABC's *Q+A*, where he was paired with the climate change skeptic, Senator Malcolm Roberts, to provide "balance". The ensuing interaction did little to advance the audience's understanding of the subject matter and instead led to frustration among viewers.

As Australians increasingly turn to alternative sources for their news, the mainstream media faces a formidable challenge. Regaining public trust and rebuilding their reputation as reliable news providers will require a return to the core principles of journalism: accuracy, impartiality, and a commitment to delivering the unvarnished truth.

IMBALANCED COVERAGE AND ITS IMPACT ON AUDIENCE TRUST

One of the prevailing issues in Australian media, particularly at the ABC, is the notion of balance. While the idea of balance in journalism is a fundamental principle, there is a growing concern that it has been taken to an extreme. The media, especially the public broadcaster, appears to have replaced the quest for high-quality reporting with an obsession for equal time given to government and opposition representatives.

This recent shift in "balanced" media coverage at the ABC can be traced back to May 2022, following the Labor Party's election victory. Since then, a more unusual approach to balance has emerged, where Labor government spokespeople and Liberal–National opposition figures are granted equal time, irrespective of what the issues are, and the result is a distortion of the role and responsibilities of these two groups. Government ministers and opposition leaders are not in equal positions; their roles and responsibilities are radically different.

This emphasis on equal time for both sides of the political spectrum seems to be unique to the Australian media landscape—and, of course, is never a balance afforded to the Labor Party when they sit in opposition—and stands in stark contrast to international news coverage. In many countries, the focus remains firmly on the government of the day, with opposition leaders receiving limited coverage, generally reserved for addressing key issues or crises—this is not so much to drown out an opposition, but is an approach that reflects the reality that it is the government that is responsible for making decisions and governing the nation. The Labor Party *is* the government, and holds 78 seats in parliament; the Liberal and National parties are *not* the government, and hold 58 seats. These political entities are not in equal positions, so why they are given equal media coverage?

The consequences of this skewed focus are evident in the decline of audience engagement with key programs such as *Q+A*, ABC *Insiders* and *7.30*. Audiences appear to have grown weary of the constant conflict-driven reporting and the overrepresentation of opposition viewpoints. The perception of one-sided conservative support by mainstream media outlets has led viewers to seek alternative sources for their news and political information.

Audiences have been gradually disengaging from legacy media for some time, but it seems that the media industry has been slow to recognise the extent of the problem. This downward spiral may continue unless significant changes are implemented.

The issue of balance, in essence, lies in the very concept of what constitutes good journalism. University-educated and cadetship journalists should be well-versed in the importance of rigorous research and balanced reporting, where historical evidence informs the story. The best instances are when shows such as *Q+A* feature panels of experts with diverse perspectives and specialties, fostering a rich and educational discussion.

On the other hand, the worst instances are when individuals with no expertise or qualifications in the subject matter are invited to speak, diminishing the quality of the conversation and failing to provide valuable insights. This approach is emblematic of the media's need to prioritise informed, expert opinions over entertainment value.

Efforts to address these concerns are seemingly underway, including changes to the ABC board and culture within the ABC. But the public broadcaster is just one media outlet. However, beyond structural changes, there is a growing call to acknowledge and promote journalists who consistently deliver high-quality work. Listening to those who excel in their craft may be the path to regain trust and recover audience engagement.

MEDIA'S ROLE IN SHAPING POLITICAL DISCOURSE AND CONSEQUENCES

The challenges facing Australian media are not confined to a single outlet but permeate the entire mainstream and legacy media landscape. The pervasive tendency to prioritise the idea of "balance" over the pursuit of equality in news coverage has far-reaching consequences. It not only erodes public discourse but also has a profound impact on the political climate.

The phenomenon of the "cracking story" or the "yarn" is not unique to Australia and has played a significant role in shaping political landscapes in other parts of the world. This approach gave rise to leaders like Donald Trump in the United States, Boris Johnson in the United Kingdom, and Scott Morrison in Australia. These are politicians who have capitalised on the media's penchant for sensationalism and entertainment, often at the expense of substantive and critical reporting.

The media's complicity in enabling these "crackpot populist politicians" reflects a deeply entrenched issue in journalism. There is a disturbing tendency to amplify sensationalism and sensational figures for the sake of higher ratings, viewership, and readership. This focus on what generates immediate attention rather than what informs the public contributes to the decay in public discourse.

The consequences of this decay are profound and extend into the political sphere. A media that prioritises entertainment over information inadvertently encourages political leaders to manipulate their messages and prioritise showmanship over substance. Such leaders can employ this strategy to enact policies that are not in the public's best interest.

This distortion of priorities within the media has fueled calls to reduce government scrutiny and regulation. While some advocate for less government intervention for a wide range of reasons related to freedom of the media, it is essential to recognise that a strong and independent media serves as a crucial check on power. When the media prioritises public interest and critical analysis over sensationalism, it becomes a powerful force for accountability.

A strong media should indeed be something to be feared, not by the people, but political leaders and those in power. It should be the guardian of truth, holding leaders accountable, and safeguarding the public's right to be informed. Unfortunately, in Australia, not enough people recognise the crucial role the media should play and often fail to appreciate the importance of a strong and independent media in maintaining a healthy democracy.

The media landscape in Australia is facing a significant crisis, driven by a preference for sensationalism and entertainment over informative, balanced reporting. The consequences of this trend reach beyond media outlets; they impact public discourse and political decision-making. It is imperative for media organisations to re-evaluate their priorities, emphasise substantive reporting, and encourage critical analysis. Only through these changes can the media regain the trust and engagement of the Australian public and fulfill its vital role in a healthy democracy.

***

SPECULATION GROWS OVER PROSPECTS OF A MINORITY GOVERNMENT

4 November 2023

There is mounting speculation that the next federal election, scheduled for May 2025 at the latest, could result in a minority government, and this speculation has gained some traction from statements put out by former independent member for New England, Tony Windsor, who suggested it's a strong possibility because of the prominence of good quality independent members of parliament, and a belief that the major political parties are being bogged down in "incremental fear".

Windsor's assertion is based on the trend over recent elections, where a growing number of independent candidates have been making inroads, securing the favour of voters who are disillusioned with the major parties' polarisation and constant politicking—this shift in voter sentiment suggests that a minority government is not only plausible but increasingly likely.

In examining the political landscape, it is crucial to consider the historical context: Australian political history reveals that first-time governments often encounter electoral difficulties during their first term, a pattern seen in the experiences of the Whitlam, Hawke, Howard, and the Rudd–Gillard and Abbott–Turnbull administrations.

One key factor contributing to the prospect of a minority government is the presence of a diverse crossbench in the federal Parliament—currently, there are 17 members on the crossbench, representing a variety of independent and minor parties. These crossbenchers—if they can eventually hold the balance of power after the next election—can wield high influence and play crucial roles in determining the direction of government policy, and it is also their presence that puts the Liberal–National Coalition at a significant disadvantage in securing a majority at the next election.

It is improbable for the Coalition to make major gains in the coming election. Certain seats, once considered strongholds for the party, such as Wentworth, Kooyong, and North Sydney, have seen a significant erosion of support, with independent candidates finding success in these areas, effectively reducing the prospects for the Coalition to reclaim these seats. This changing political landscape underscores the need for the major parties—Labor, Liberal and National—to adapt to the changing and evolving preferences of voters.

The emergence of strong, community-focused independent candidates and potential shifts in voter sentiment could also pose challenges for the Labor Party as well. While safe Labor seats have traditionally been secure, the pressure to better represent constituents is mounting, and the prospect of a 'teal' movement away from the Labor Party is not outside the realm of possibility, although it is a factor that has so far affected the Liberal Party.

Ultimately, the growing discourse around the likelihood of a minority government in Australia raises questions about the future of the nation's political landscape. The prospect of a minority government should be seen as an opportunity for the major parties to reflect on their policies and priorities, rather than a cause for concern. The last period of minority government between 2010–13 saw positive outcomes as far as legislative output was concerned, albeit with self-inflicted divisions within the Labor government and an opportunist Liberal Party that sought to create as much conflict as possible. However, the lessons learned from that experience could be crucial in shaping the nation's political trajectory in the coming years.

In the wake of these speculations, the Australian political arena is poised for a period of significant transformation. Whether these predictions of permanent minority governments materialise remains uncertain—remembering that the first decade of federal politics was dominated by the "three elevens", where political allegiances changed frequently, before navigating towards the current two-party process—but they offer a glimpse into the evolving dynamics of Australian democracy as the country approaches the next federal election.

DEMOGRAPHIC SHIFTS AND THE CHALLENGE FOR TRADITIONAL PARTIES

The growing prospect of a minority government in Australia is underpinned by a complex web of factors, one of the most significant being demographic changes within the electorate, and this evolving landscape, particularly the emergence of younger voters who display distinct voting patterns, is reshaping the country's political dynamics.

It is evident that younger voters, as a cohort, are less inclined to stick to traditional party loyalties and area showing a preference for parties and candidates that align with their progressive values, in areas such as climate change, environmental protection, housing affordability and, more recently, international issues such as the war in Gaza.

As these voters find themselves dissatisfied with the performance of established parties, they are starting to explore other options on the central-left spectrum—they might not be inherently more politically sophisticated or radical than their older counterparts, they are increasingly motivated by specific policy areas that resonate with their priorities, and are not wedded to a specific party.

This shift has significant implications for both major and minor parties. The Labor government, if it's perceived as not doing enough on these issues that matter to these voters or if they are perceived as being too cautious, may risk losing their support to other progressive alternatives, such as the Australian Greens or independent candidates who do offer different approaches to key challenges.

On the other hand, the Liberal Party, already grappling with the challenge of winning 18 additional seats to secure the next election, faces an even more formidable task given the ideological distance between itself and these progressive voters and gaining this amount of seats appears to be an exceedingly steep hill to climb.

Another issue for consideration is that first-term independent members usually benefit from the phenomenon of the "sophomore effect", where these members—or any new member of parliament—spend their initial term consolidating their seats and often increase their vote in the subsequent election, due to more recognition within the community and the benefit of incumbency. The early performance of first-term independent members indicates that there may be no compelling reasons to vote them out at this stage, reinforcing their electoral strength.

In contrast to traditional party dynamics, many of these independent members appear focused on representing their electorates and addressing the concerns of their constituents rather than pursuing ministerial positions or further political ambitions. This dedication to their electorates and the absence of careerist ambitions presents a unique challenge for the major parties, which have historically relied on a different approach to politics.

The loss of seats such as Wentworth, Kooyong, North Sydney, Mackellar, Goldstein, Curtin and Warringah in recent elections, coupled with the rise of these independent members, signals a major shift in the political landscape. It is increasingly plausible that these seats may remain out of reach for the Liberal Party for an extended period, potentially redefining both the party's future and the shape of the Australian political spectrum.

While electoral outcomes are always uncertain and can be influenced by a range of factors, it is clear that the growing presence and popularity of independent members, as well as the changing preferences of younger voters, are reshaping the Australian political arena.

CHALLENGES AND STRATEGIES FOR THE LABOR GOVERNMENT

The federal Labor government is not oblivious to the multifaceted challenges it faces, particularly the issues related to the crossbench, the decline in support for major parties, and the historical trend of first-term governments losing votes and seats at their second election. As history demonstrates, first-time governments have seen electoral setbacks in 1974, 1984, 1998, 2010, and 2016. However, the key distinguishing factor for the current Albanese government is the absence of a substantial electoral buffer to absorb these potential losses—those governments that suffered swings against them and a loss of seats all arrived into office through landslide victories and could withstand these setbacks. Although there is a large buffer between Labor and the Liberal–National Coalition—caused by the existence of a large crossbench—the Albanese government has a 78–73 margin in the lower house, meaning that a loss of three seats at the next election will result in a minority government.

During the final full year before the next election—2024—the Labor government is undoubtedly aware of the need to address these challenges proactively. To maintain its electoral position, the government will need to identify compelling issues to focus on. In 1997, the first-term Howard government was meandering, heading towards defeat at the subsequent election, before Prime Minister John Howard decided to campaign on the Goods and Services Tax, even though he specifically ruled out such a tax prior to the 1996 federal election. This campaign gave the Coalition a focal points, and they went on to narrowly win the 1998 election. Will the Labor government also be seeking a major issue to focus their attention on?

One issue that may take centre stage in their campaign is the Stage 3 tax cuts, even though they have already been legislated. The government's political strategy may involve full implementation of the Stage 3 tax cuts, despite their reservations—it may seem counterintuitive, given that there are many centre-left economists who oppose the Stage 3 tax cuts, as well as many on the Labor side of politics, but the political reality is that very few in the electorate decide to vote against tax cuts when it comes to the privacy of the ballot box.

If the Labor government is facing political difficulties in the early part of the 2024, could they switch to vaudeville and create a massive campaign based on the Stage 3 tax cuts, even though they were fiercely opposed to them when they were first proposed by the Coalition in 2018? Stranger things have happened in politics in the past—for example, Prime Minister Paul Keating winning the 1993 election on the back of an anti-GST campaign, even though he proposed his own version of a GST in 1985—so it's a prospect that shouldn't be dismissed so easily.

On other matters, the government's cautious approach, while possibly informed by a desire for stability, raises questions about its capacity for bold, audacious leadership. History has shown that leaders who were audacious and unafraid of confronting challenges, like Gough Whitlam and Bob Hawke, have achieved significant success. Conversely, leaders who were more cautious, such as Kevin Rudd or Julia Gillard, often found themselves outmanoeuvred by their own party.

In this context, and while it might be too late for this current parliamentary term, it is worth reflecting on the idea that governments should treat their first term as an opportunity to accomplish as much as possible. The prevailing sentiment is that governments should not squander their time fumbling around, hoping for re-election, but rather focus on proactive and meaningful policy changes that align with their ideals, even if full implementation is not always possible. This perspective highlights the importance of taking a principled stance and delivering on promises, not only to secure re-election but also to make meaningful progress in addressing the issues that matter to the Australian people.

THE BENEFITS AND POTENTIAL OF MINORITY GOVERNMENTS

The prospect of a minority government after the next federal election has sparked a wider conversation about the merits of such a process of governance. While the effectiveness of minority governments largely depends on the composition of the crossbench and who actually holds the balance of power, it can bring about more robust decision-making and ultimately yield better legislation, policies, and outcomes.

Minority governments can serve as a check on major parties, forcing them to make necessary but often unpopular decisions and this dynamic can be seen as a safeguard against complacency or the pursuit of purely partisan agendas. While this could lead to political gridlock, it can also compel parties to engage in more meaningful negotiations and compromises: that's what the essence of democracy is.

History offers many examples of minority governments in Australia that have achieved notable successes—the period between 1991–95 in New South Wales, marked by a minority government, witnessed significant and much-needed reforms. Similarly, the Gillard government between 2010 and 2013, during its time as a minority government, was characterised by a high level of productivity and legislative output.

Prime Minister Gillard, as the leader of a minority government, demonstrated her skills as a negotiator, successfully navigating the complex landscape of crossbench politics. These eras show the potential for minority governments to operate effectively and enact substantial policy changes, even when faced with challenging circumstances.

Australia has had only two minority governments in the past 82 years—during 1940–43 and 2010–13—but the current political climate, as well the existence of a large crossbench ensuring a greater mathematical probably, suggests that minority governments might become a more regular feature in federal politics. The ultimate impact of such a shift will depend on the composition of the crossbench and its ability to hold major parties accountable and drive positive policy outcomes.

In a political landscape often marked by partisan divides and inertia, the emergence of minority governments can offer an avenue for fresh perspectives, effective negotiation, and meaningful policy reform. The experiences of countries like Italy, which have seen numerous changes in government—69 different governments since 1945—but have continued to function and thrive, demonstrate that embracing a dynamic political landscape, even if it means occasional shifts in the status quo, can be a path to progress and improved governance.

As Australia approaches the next federal election, the possibility of a minority government should be viewed not as a disruption but as an opportunity to foster a more collaborative and effective approach to governance, one that prioritises the needs and aspirations of the Australian people. This can only be a positive outcome for the country.

***

REBUILDING BRIDGES: ALBANESE'S CHINA VISIT MARKS A TURNING POINT

11 November 2023

The Prime Minister Anthony Albanese's recent visit to China signals the closure of one diplomatic chapter, and marks a significant turning point in the recent tumultuous relationship between Australia and its largest trading partner. The success of the trip is underscored by the stabilisation of relations, a contrast to the strains imposed by the rhetoric and actions of former Prime Minister Scott Morrison and ex-Defence Minister Peter Dutton.

The origins of the strained ties can be traced back to 2018 and the Turnbull government's decision to ban Huawei from participating in the development of Australia's 5G infrastructure—while that move had its justifications on security grounds, it fueled anti-China sentiments that lingered, only to be exacerbated by the accusatory stance adopted by Morrison and Dutton in 2020, who pointed fingers at China for the outbreak of COVID-19. These actions not only strained diplomatic ties but resulted in retaliatory tariffs and sanctions imposed by China on Australian exports.

However, as the dust settles from this diplomatic storm, it is evident that the Albanese government has made significant steps in repairing the damage inflicted upon Australia–China relations: many tariffs and sanctions have now been lifted, laying the groundwork for a more co-operative future.

The complexity of the Australia–China relationship is not lost in the broader context of global politics, and balancing economic interests with human rights concerns and geopolitical considerations is an intricate act that requires diplomatic skill. The repercussions of the strained relationship were not limited to the diplomatic front; the economic toll was substantial. The Morrison government's provocative stance resulted in sanctions that cost the Australian export market approximately $20 billion annually and the lingering effects of these actions serve as a reminder that belligerent and ideologically-driven diplomacy does have tangible economic consequences.

The resolution of these trade issues was unlikely under the Coalition government: diplomatically, the Chinese government has a long memory and it wanted to inflict as much economic and political damage on the former Morrison government for its role in humiliating China on the international stage. The change of federal government in May 2022 did, however, pave the way for a recalibration of diplomatic efforts, marking a departure from the confrontational approach of the past.

AUSTRALIA–CHINA RELATIONS AMID POLITICAL DIVIDES AND HISTORICAL BIASES

The intricate relationship between Australia and China continues to unfold against the backdrop of complex geopolitical considerations, trade interests, and, notably, human rights concerns. While acknowledging the human rights issues in China—from Tibet and the treatment of Uighur people, to the situation in Hong Kong—the approach taken during Albanese's visit suggests that these concerns may not take centre stage in any future dialogue, especially when considering Australia's own human rights issues, exemplified by the failure of the Voice of Parliament referendum, which has undermined its credibility to lecture other countries about their human rights records on the international stage.

The political divide in Australia also influences the tone and tenor of engagement with China. The historical alignment between the Labor Party and China, dating back to Gough Whitlam's landmark visit in 1972, contrasts with the more strained relationships during periods of Liberal Party governance. Labor, when in power, manages the China relationship well, while the Liberal Party struggles to shed historical biases and racist undertones, notably those rooted in Menzies-era "yellow peril" rhetoric.

The Liberal Party's recent hostility towards China, marked by inflammatory rhetoric and accusations, raises questions about the sincerity of its engagement. The ongoing reference to "Airbus Albo" and the attempt to paint Albanese as ineffectual in solving the problems inherited from the previous government is immature rhetoric and indicative of a lack of substantive policy alternatives. The emphasis on Albanese's travel history, juxtaposed against his predecessors—both Tony Abbott and Scott Morrison travelled more often in their first 18 months in office—serves to expose what is perceived as a double standard in the both the Liberal Party and the mainstream media.

Albanese and the foreign minister Senator Penny Wong, have shown that it is possible to be critical in international affairs, act in one's national interest, and still maintain a diplomatic and constructive relationship. The example of former Prime Minister Bob Hawke's actions in 1989, where he protected Chinese students living in Australia during the Tiananmen Square massacre, while maintaining positive relations with China, serves as a case in point. The underlying message is clear: effective foreign policy requires nuance, pragmatism, and an acknowledgment of the interconnectedness of national interests and global dynamics.

THE MEDIA'S COLLECTIVE AMNESIA

While there have been a few media reports which have acknowledged the damage caused by the Coalition government, and the efforts to repair the Australia–China relationship initiated by the Albanese government, the broader media landscape has overlooked the role of Morrison and Dutton, deflecting responsibility from the previous government's actions.

The media's framing of Albanese's trip was primarily from the perspective of the Coalition government, with the ABC stating that the Coalition has set a "high bar" of expectations regarding the China visit—but why is the opinion of the Coalition relevant? They are not the current government: and in any case, they created these problems in the Australia–China relationship. Why does the media seek their opinions, when they have no credibility on this issue?

In their quest to embarrass the Labor government, there was a collusion between Seven West Media and the ABC in framing questions to Albanese about "trust" in President Xi Jinping, in what can be best described as conflict-based "clickbait journalism":

> **Mark Riley (Seven West Media):** "Are you convinced that you can trust President Xi?"
> **Prime Minister Anthony Albanese:** "I'm convinced that we're building a relationship that's constructive one way or we're able to talk with each other directly. And in the discussions that I have had with him, the formal discussion, but the other discussions as well. They have been positive and respectful.
> **David Speers (ABC):** "Just further to Mark's question, trust. Do you trust him?
> **Albanese:** "Well, I have, we have different political systems. But the engagement that I've had with China with President Xi had been positive. They had been constructive. He has never said anything to me that has not been done. And that's a positive way that you have to start off dealing with people."

Despite Albanese's nuanced response—which is essential in the field of diplomacy, especially when given in the host nation—the media framed it as Albanese "falling short" of confirming trust in Xi Jinping. Of course, the media should ask questions of any international relationship Australia has in the world. But, the media doesn't have the right to verbal a political leader when they don't hear the words that fit into their own political agendas.

Why was it more important to frame up Albanese in negative light—and incorrectly—when they could have addressed the actions and statements of key figures such as Peter Dutton, who played a significant role in damaging the Australia–China relationship?

Why didn't the media challenge Dutton—or Morrison—about their past statements about needing to "prepare for war" with China or their accusations regarding the origins of the COVID-19 pandemic? If the media truly seeks conflict-based journalism, they should hold accountable those responsible for straining diplomatic relations. Making Dutton accountable for his actions would be a more substantive and responsible approach to journalism, rather than generating negative headlines for political leaders who are not aligned to the politics of these conservative journalists or their proprietors.

By avoiding the difficult questions or making political leaders accountable for their past actions—while having a preference for attacking Labor leaders and governments—journalists from the mainstream media are behaving more like propaganda outlets rather than serving as independent sources of information.

There's no question that immense damage was caused by the Morrison and Abbott governments to the Australia–China relationship, who were directed by their ideological interests, rather than the national interest. But the media's responses to the positive outcomes by the Albanese government in repairing this damage, and their negative portrayals of this, suggest they have no interest in arresting their downward spiral into irrelevance, or improving their levels of trust with the news-consuming audiences and the public.

***

HIGH COURT RULING SPARKS CONCERNS OVER COMMITMENT TO HUMAN RIGHTS

18 November 2023

The return of Prime Minister Anthony Albanese to Australia marked the end of his state visits to China and Tuvalu, offering some respite from the incessant chatter from conservative commentators about "Airbus Albo™" and other commentary about him spending "too much time" overseas, and not enough on domestic issues. On his return, the first major topic addressed in Parliament was the fallout from a High Court decision declaring that a Rohingya asylum seeker held in indefinite immigration detention was unlawful held the far-reaching consequence of this ruling was the recognition that *all* indefinite detentions of asylum seekers were also unlawful, resulting the immediate release of 81 people.

This legal development pushed the political landscape into familiar territory surrounding the politics of asylum seekers, drawing the Liberal Party into the fray with their characteristic megaphone diplomacy. The opposition's narrative often moves towards overplayed pantomime, portraying such situations as a "threat to national security", a recurring theme that is designed to challenge the credibility of the Labor government. Nevertheless, the core issue should revolve around the fundamental principles of justice—no government should have the authority to detain individuals indefinitely—and the imperative to apply the law judiciously.

This High Court decision overturned a previous ruling from 2004, which had deemed the indefinite detention of asylum seekers was lawful. Responding quickly to the legal vacuum created by the ruling, the government hastily pushed through legislation to address the newly released group of stateless individuals: however, given the historical politicisation of asylum seeker matters in Australia since at least 1998, concerns loom over the potential introduction of new, equally draconian laws in response.

A central aspect of a healthy and functioning democracy lies in how it treats its most vulnerable members but there have to be doubts about

Australia's claim to be a champion of human rights, as the issues of due process in detention seems to have fallen by the wayside. Detainees, some languishing in confinement for well over a decade, challenge the foundational principles of justice. While a reasonable argument can be made for some form of detention during the processing of asylum seekers to ensure health and domestic security, prolonged, uncharged, and untried detentions are untenable and contradict many of the United Nations conventions that Australia is a signatory to.

The federal government's hurried legislation attempts to grapple with the dilemma of stateless individuals, yet the fear remains that it might lead to the imposition of new draconian measures that will again be challenged in the High Court. The broader question raised by this issue is whether Australia's commitment to human rights is faltering, as the nation comes to grips with the moral and legal dimensions of immigration detention.

COMPLEX LEGAL CHALLENGES FOR REFUGEES AND ASYLUM SEEKERS

The release of individuals classified as stateless, following this High Court ruling against indefinite immigration detention, has brought to light a range of complex legal circumstances. Some in this group have failed Australia's "character test" in their asylum applications, and a minority have committed serious criminal offences in their homelands. However, it remains a foundational tenet of Australian law that, with only a few exceptional cases, individuals cannot be incarcerated indefinitely without trial and without due legal process.

The High Court's 2004 ruling initially justified the indefinite detention of stateless individuals, which was extended to all asylum seekers, including those deemed to be genuine refugees. Advocates for refugees have long contested this system, pointing to the draconian and inhumane conditions endured by asylum seekers on Nauru and Manus Island and it is a recent legal development that marks a significant departure from Australia's approach to immigration detention.

While the reasoning behind the High Court decision is yet to be revealed, the lack of information hasn't deterred the leader of the opposition, Peter Dutton, from employing his usual tactics of fear and loathing. Dutton has been quick to paint the released individuals as "hardcore criminals" and "potential terrorists", leveraging this narrative to criticise the Labor government. Other Liberal Party MPs, seizing the opportunity, have also amplified the rhetoric, linking asylum seekers to broader issues such as anti-Semitism, the Voice to Parliament and other issues related to immigration and border security.

Despite the absence of evidence supporting these claims, the political agenda set by Dutton continues to shape public perception. The Labor government, seemingly without an effective political response, continues to be accused of fostering division and compromising community safety, even though it is the words of Dutton that are creating this social division. The political quagmire surrounding asylum seekers is not new; the Labor government did introduce mandatory detention in 1992, unwittingly providing the Coalition with a potent political weapon, ever since it first ventured into this issue in 1998, headed by the Minister for Immigration at the time, Philip Ruddock.

Over the past 25 years, the Liberal Party has skillfully capitalised on asylum seeker issues, reaping political rewards from incidents such as the *MV Tampa* affair in 2001 and the events of 9/11 in New York. In contrast, the Labor Party has struggled to formulate a coherent political strategy to address the complexities of asylum and refugee policies: surely after 25 years, they would have realised that these are the "bread and butter" issues of Liberal Party politics, and should have been able to develop a strategy to deal with the issues. Instead, they have often resorted to crafting legislation that appears tough on refugees in an attempt to deflect public scrutiny but, quite often, end up creating more political problems for them, and devalue their attempts to position themselves as the political party that takes human rights seriously.

The refugee crisis is not abating, and the challenges are evolving. Environmental refugees, potential geopolitical conflicts, and natural disasters are factors that could contribute to increased displacement. The notion that Australia might be flooded by millions of refugees is a rhetoric that is often overstated, without evidence, and usually exploited by populist right-wing politicians, such as Dutton and One Nation's Pauline Hanson. However, many refugees are driven by the urgency of seeking sanctuary, and are more likely to settle in the first available country rather than navigating the considerable distance to Australia.

Despite claims that Australia is seen as an "easy destination" with promises of free housing and cars, the reality, has been rather a provision of all *mod cons*, a prolonged and uncomfortable detention, in some cases, up to 16 years. The hope now is that the government does not respond to these developments by enacting even more stringent laws, exacerbating the already challenging situation faced by asylum seekers and refugees. This situation demands a nuanced and more humanitarian approach, a task that seems to be elusive for Australian policymakers unable to deal with the enduring complexities of immigration and asylum policies.

A CLASH OF POLITICAL NARRATIVES AND LEGAL IMPERATIVES

The persistent stance of Dutton and the Liberal Party on immigration detention issues is cynical and predictably unwavering, even in the face of a High Court ruling challenging their long-held practices. Dutton's narrative has taken yet another predictable turn, now suggesting that Prime Minister Albanese should have refrained from attending the APEC meeting until the immigration detention issue is resolved.

Minister for Home Affairs Clare O'Neil, has sought to provide clarity on the government's response. O'Neil addressed the parliament during the week, shedding light on the High Court's decision and emphasising the constitutional basis of the ruling.

> **Clare O'Neil:** "I want to address a number of falsehoods that have been raised by the opposition in this debate. And the first is one that I've heard directly from the leader of the opposition. And what he has come out today is something just frankly and very directly is incredibly stupid. He has come out today and said, 'Oh, don't worry about the Constitution, just pass a law to put them all back into tension'.
> I just want to remind the Leader of the Opposition—who has been here for 22 years—that he knows, and I know, that the Australian Constitution and a full court decision of the High Court cannot just be overturned by a decision of this chamber. That is not the political system in which we operate. I know it and he knows it."

O'Neil underscored the separation of powers in Australia's system and stressed that ministers, like anyone else, are obligated to abide by the law of the land. She unequivocally stated that the government has no choice but to comply with the High Court's directive to release individuals from immigration detention: this is the constitutional system that Australia operates under.

The parliamentary discussion that continued during the week, highlights the complexity and legal constraints surrounding the government's response to the High Court decision. It underscores the clash between political narratives and legal imperatives, further fueling the ongoing debate over the treatment of asylum seekers and the government's adherence to the rule of law. Government are compelled to navigate a delicate balance between its established policies, legal obligations, and public perception, and the Liberal Party's pandering to base political interests undermines Australia's entire legal system and the separation of the judiciary and the political system.

SEEKING A BALANCED APPROACH TO LEGISLATION AND HUMANITARIAN VALUES

Despite the clarifications from Minister O'Neil, it appears evident that the Liberal Party remains committed to playing politics with the immigration detention issue. The government, in turn, faces the challenge of fighting back politically while seeking agendas that are compatible with Labor values, as well as attempting to de-escalate the political tensions surrounding the matter, which always favour conservative politics, and usually ramped by conservative media interests.

Fundamentally, addressing this situation requires adhering to basic principles—both in policy and in law. The government must articulate a commitment to applying the rule of law, establishing clear rules on the duration of asylum seekers' detention, and outlining the criteria for achieving particular visa statuses. These measures align with basic human rights principles, which were lacking in the previous legislation administered by the Liberal–National Coalition.

Addressing the broader perspective on refugees and asylum seekers, there is a recognition that while the ultimate goal of a refugee is to return home—once it is safe for them to do so—it also has to be understood that this situation is impossible, even when the conditions in their home country improve politically. No one should ever be returned to the country they have escaped from, usually from oppressive political and social situations.

As the debates continue and legislative solutions are sought, the federal government faces the formidable task of reconciling legal imperatives, balancing community concerns, and committing to the humanitarian aspects of asylum and refugee policies. Achieving this delicate balance will be crucial in shaping a more just and compassionate approach to immigration issues in Australia which, for far too long, have been lacking.

***

THE ESCALATING CONFLICT IN GAZA AND THE INTERNATIONAL OUTCRY

18 November 2023

The conflict in Gaza continues with devastating consequences, with the Israeli military intensifying its bombing campaign, resulting in a rising death toll among civilians—over 13,000, which includes over 5,000 children and over 3,500 women—and the forced displacement of 1.7 million Palestinians from their homes. International pressure on the Israeli government to halt its military actions and seek a resolution has grown, to what is now being referred to as the "second Nakba".

"Nakba" refers to the catastrophic events of 1948 when 700,000 Palestinians were violently expelled from Palestine, marking a major historical turning point in the Middle East region, while it could be argued that the continuous displacement and ethnic cleansing endured by Palestinians over the past 75 years constitutes an ongoing Nakba, an unsettling reality that has never truly ceased. The public's increasing awareness of the situation in Gaza and a better understanding of the historical context has fueled global public outrage—if not by governments—against the Netanyahu government and the actions of the Israeli military.

Despite growing international calls for a ceasefire, closer to home, the Australian government remains steadfast in its support for Israel's "right to defend itself", refusing to advocate for a cessation of hostilities. The parliamentary debate on the matter reached a boiling point, featuring a confrontational exchange between the Leader of the Opposition, Peter Dutton, and Prime Minister Anthony Albanese.

Dutton, who seems more intent on scoring political points than expressing genuine concern, invoked historical parallels between the current situation in Gaza and the horrors witnessed during the Second World War and urged the Prime Minister to stand united with the Jewish community—even though this is exactly what Albanese had done—accusing him of a lack of solidarity and a divisive approach. Albanese, on the other hand, accused Dutton of overreach, condemning his attempts to weaponise anti-Semitism for political gain. This clash in Parliament reflects a broader polarisation, with political leaders grappling with the challenge of fostering unity in the face of deep social divisions, especially when the conservative side of politics insists on politicising the events in Gaza for its own political benefit.

This division in Australian politics is exemplified by Dutton's attempts to exploit fears and inflame tensions for advantage. The issue at hand, which essentially is to stop the loss of innocent lives in the first instance and push back the Israel military, is further complicated by the spread of misinformation. Reports, such as the debunked claim of a list of Palestinian operatives found in a Gazan hospital basement—which turned out to be a wall calendar—contribute to the complexity of discerning truth in the midst of conflict.

Both sides of the conflict—the Israel government and Hamas—find themselves lacking in widespread popular support: the Likud Party in Israel is deeply unpopular, as is Prime Minister Benjamin Netanyahu, and average polls during 2022 and 2023 show political support for Hamas at just 34 per cent. The nature of war, with its array of unverified claims and the unfortunate toll on non-combatants, underscores the urgency for a ceasefire. However, the international response, including the abstention of countries such as Australia and Canada in crucial votes at the United Nations, remains a point of contention.

The Australian Jewish Association's criticism of Penny Wong, accusing her of 'heading in a worrying direction' after she offered a small slither of support for Palestine, shows how difficult any meaningful discussion on a resolution in this crisis is, whether it's in an international forum, or for a domestic audience.

Dutton's approach has lacked subtlety and nuance, reflecting a concerning lack of depth in addressing the complex issues of the conflict. But this is Dutton at his worst: failing to avoid division, fear and loathing, because he knows no other way.

DUTTON'S DIVISIVENESS ON ISRAEL–PALESTINE

The domestic situation is becoming increasingly precarious, as tensions spill over into acts of violence and clashes between supporters of Israel and those standing in solidarity with Palestine. The recent firebombing of Burgertory, a burger shop owned by a pro-Palestinian advocate in the Melbourne suburb of Caulfield by purported supporters of Israel adds a dangerous dimension to the conflict. Although authorities denied political motivations—possibly to alleviate an already tense situation—there is a palpable risk of further escalation within the community.

In response to the attack, supporters of the Palestinian business organised a rally in Caulfield, unknowingly near a synagogue. Accusations of attempting to cause trouble arose, reflecting the heightened sensitivity surrounding the issue. Meanwhile, there have been calls from conservative members of the Jewish community to "prevent" Palestinians from entering Caulfield—as if to import the Israel brand of apartheid into Australia against people they do not like—indicating a disturbing level of polarisation within the community.

The incidents in Caulfield underscore the importance of political leaders treading carefully on international issues to prevent the exacerbation of tensions at a local level. Dutton's approach, geared towards inflaming divisions, aligns with his track record of utilising populist rhetoric on a wide range of issues: walking out during the Apology to the Stolen Generations in 2008; the "African gangs" rhetoric during 2018 and claiming the community was too scared to go out to restaurant in Melbourne; his concerns about non-white immigration and exploitation of terrorism issues.

This tendency to exploit divisive topics contrasts sharply with the need for subtlety and nuanced thought and, as the French politician Georges Clemenceau suggested, it's far easier to make war than peace, and the responsibility of a wise politician lies in fostering peace rather than perpetuating discord. Dutton's inclination towards trouble and division in domestic matters is evident across various contexts, and it raises questions about his suitability to navigate complex issues diplomatically.

The ongoing protests further highlight the stark contrast between the peaceful expressions of both pro-Israeli and pro-Palestinian sentiments. Demonstrations in Hyde Park, with thousands in attendance, demonstrated passionate but non-violent protests. While there have been instances of arrests, they have been minimal and related to minor infractions rather than serious offenses.

The importance of allowing peaceful protests, even on highly contentious issues, cannot be overstated. However, it necessitates responsibility from both organisers and participants to avoid exacerbating tensions. Dutton's failure to comprehend the distinction between disruptive yet peaceful protests and violent demonstrations further underscores the challenges in his approach.

In the midst of heightened emotions and deep-seated divisions, the call for political leaders to act responsibly and promote unity becomes more urgent than ever. The potential consequences of mishandling domestic tensions are immense, and the role of leaders in diffusing rather than escalating conflicts cannot be overstated.

DR. FRANCESCA ALBANESE'S BOLD WARNING ON ISRAEL–GAZA

During the week, Dr. Francesca Albanese, the United Nations Special Rapporteur on the occupied territories of Gaza and West Bank, visited Australia and addressed the National Press Club in Canberra.

In a series of exchanges with journalists from the mainstream media, Dr. Albanese unflinchingly addressed the severity of the crisis, going so far as to warn of the risk of genocide by Israel. Her responses challenged attempts to downplay the impact on civilians, emphasising the need for a nuanced understanding of the conflict. The exchanges also revealed the challenges faced by experts attempting to communicate the gravity of the situation amid differing interpretations.

The questions posed by journalists were poor and uninformed, chose the side of the Israel government, and deliberately misrepresented what she had actually said. The following exchanges are a sample, but a clear representation of the paucity of intellect that inflicts many journalists within the mainstream media, who mislead, misinform and search for the prize of "clickbait journalism", rather than informing the public:

> **Dr. Francesca Albanese:** "There is a risk of genocide being committed by Israel, and also the capacity to do that..."
> **Tom Connell (Sky News):** "if it wanted to, probably would have done, to be blunt about it—yes, it's a dire situation with civilians, but Israel did say civilians, 'please leave, this is where we're targeting'. So that wasn't them actually targeting civilians at that point."
> **Dr. Albanese:** "...I don't mean to be rude. But can you really keep a straight face as you asked me this question?"
> **Matthew Knott (Nine Media):** "You've said previously, that it should ultimately be up to Palestinians to decide who governs in Gaza, and that Israel should be open to making a peace deal with Hamas. Given that Hamas leaders since October 7, have said repeatedly that they would like to repeat these attacks, is that really possible? Is Hamas really a potential partner for peace? Or would the defeat or surrender of Hamas be part of any realistic peace agreement in Gaza?"
> **Dr. Albanese:** "Sorry, I cannot answer the question, because you are basically basing yourself on something that has been reported, that it has been completely distorted... you have some media who's really as manipulative as those in Italy! I said something else, that the military response cannot be war—must be peace, and the peace must be done with the Palestinians. I'm also speaking of a non-legal peace, at peace, reconciliation with the idea that Palestinians have same humanity and same entitlement to rights, freedom and dignity as the Israelis. I'm sorry, but this [what you've suggested] is not what I said—that has been completely distorted."

And the procession of gormless and uninformed journalists continued, only too happy to show their disregard for facts and information and, seemingly, to display their ignorance to a national audience. Dr. Albanese staunchly defended her choice of language, framing it within the context of international law and the existence of an apartheid regime, challenging journalists to refer to the apartheid convention for clarity.

Notably, Dr. Albanese's expertise and assertiveness provided a powerful counterpoint to the political dynamics at play. Her statements, delivered with conviction, resonated beyond the National Press Club, prompting reflection on the international stage.

However, as the discourse shifts from international perspectives to domestic considerations, the connection between Australia and Israel's military industries also needs to be considered. The potential use of Australian-made military hardware in the conflict raises ethical questions about Australia's role in supplying weaponry to a conflict zone. Have any Palestinian civilians been killed with Australian-supplied military hardware? It's likely. The lack of transparency around military exports to Israel, coupled with the substantial value of such exports, adds a layer of complexity to Australia's stance on the conflict.

The financial interests at play, evident in the significant military export licenses granted to Israel—52 so far during 2023, and over 350 since 2017—offer a potential explanation for the Australian government's unwavering support for Israel's "right to defend itself". The connection between political decisions and economic interests underscores the need for transparency in international relations, particularly when it comes to matters of conflict and human rights.

As the Israel–Gaza conflict continues to unfold, the dichotomy between international perspectives represented by figures like Dr. Francesca Albanese and domestic political considerations, influenced by economic interests, raises critical questions about Australia's role in the broader geopolitical landscape. The call for transparency in military exports and a reassessment of political stances in light of evolving circumstances becomes imperative in navigating the delicate balance between global ethics and national interests.

A DIPLOMATIC PARADIGM SHIFT AND MORE INTERNATIONAL ACCOUNTABILITY

In the context of the Israel–Gaza conflict, there is a critical need for a shift in approach in the management of international affairs. The reflexive use of claims of "anti-Semitism" to deflect criticism of the Israeli government, Benjamin Netanyahu, or the Israel military is not only counterproductive but may be working against the long-term interests of Israel itself. The international community must move beyond merely urging restraint and exert more substantial pressure on the state of Israel to bring about a resolution in Gaza: simply reiterating that Israel has a right to defend itself is simply avoiding the issue and won't result in any meaningful resolution.

Repeated calls for a resolution in the past month underscore the urgency of the situation. The international community's inability to resolve the Israel–Palestine conflict was compared with US President Jimmy Carter's tenure in the late 1970s, standing out as a rare instance of significant progress. Carter's tough approach, contrary to his public persona, demonstrated that Israeli leaders respond to firmness. The subsequent decades, marked by a lack of assertive international intervention, have contributed to the current impasse.

It is a sobering reminder that when political leaders are allowed unchecked power, they will act in their self-interest: history has confirm this basic fact. For Israel, this underscores the need for a change in approach within its political leadership. The international community must not shy away from demanding accountability and promoting a resolution that respects the rights and dignity of all involved.

President Carter's success in negotiating peace in the Middle East, resulting in the Camp David Accords, stands as a testament to the potential impact of resolute leadership. In a complex geopolitical landscape, it is essential to recognise that firmness, not complacency, is required to address deeply entrenched conflicts.

Noam Chomsky's characterisation of Israeli governments as "spoiled children" demanding their own way—a comment repeated by the President of Turkiye, Recep Tayyip Erdogan in 2011—aligns with the need for a recalibration of diplomatic strategies. The current desperation and internal challenges faced by Netanyahu further complicate the situation. As he confronts serious corruption charges and waning public support, his actions in the international arena become increasingly unpredictable and it's always best to treat a desperate political leader firmly.

In essence, the Israel–Gaza conflict reflects broader geopolitical challenges that demand thoughtful, assertive diplomacy. It requires a departure from conventional approaches and a commitment to addressing the root causes of the conflict. International pressure must be wielded judiciously, focusing on fostering a just resolution that considers the rights, security, and dignity of all parties involved.

As the situation continues to evolve, the world watches with a high level of concern, acknowledging the delicate balance required to navigate the complexities of the Israel–Gaza conflict. The need for international leaders to learn from history, leverage diplomatic tools effectively, and prioritise a just and lasting resolution remains paramount.

***

HMAS TOOWOOMBA INCIDENT REIGNITES TENSIONS IN AUSTRALIA–CHINA RELATIONS

25 November 2023

Last week, an incident involving the *HMAS Toowoomba* in the East China Sea has once again pushed Australia's relationship with China into the spotlight. While the exact details of the incident remain unclear, enough information has surfaced to fuel anti-China sentiments and provide the Liberal Party with an opportunity to ramp up national security concerns and play the race card, yet again. This episode has become another chapter in the ongoing saga of Australia–China relations, playing out against the backdrop of the diplomatic repair work led by Prime Minister Anthony Albanese and Foreign Minister Senator Penny Wong.

Over the past 18 months, Senator Wong has been worked to mend ties with China, aimed at reversing the fallout from accusations made by former Prime Minister Scott Morrison and former Home Affairs Minister, Peter Dutton, where they accused China of causing the COVID virus which, in turn, prompted hefty trade sanctions imposed against Australian exporters. Senator Wong's efforts have been primarily focused on repairing this rift, striving to restore normalcy to economic relations between the two nations.

However, the familiar divide along party lines persists—the Labor Party historically has fostered a co-operative relationship with China, while the Liberal Party remains suspicious, engages in xenophobia and seizes every opportunity to challenge the Labor government on matters of national security. It's a predictable and hostile pattern that suggests that the political tactics employed by the Liberal Party is unlikely to change in the foreseeable future.

The rhetoric from leader of the opposition, Peter Dutton, is aimed at taking Australia back to a bygone era of the 1950s, when language used to discuss China at the time was based on racist tropes and contained an endless threat of communism during the Cold War era, and Dutton seems to have a desire to return to an era when ideological lines were more clearly drawn.

This regressive stance becomes even more perplexing against the backdrop of recent diplomatic achievements: there have been great efforts to normalise relations with China, after the many issues caused by the Coalition during their latter time in office between the years of 2017–22, but it's evident that Dutton wants to portray himself as the "can-do guy", who can stand up to a superpower, irrespective of the domestic problems it may cause.

There is a disconnect in how the Liberal Party approaches its international relationships—seemingly overlooking the diplomatic issues Australia has with the United States and promoting a sycophantic stance, while adopting a confrontational stance toward China, despite the significant economic consequences and disruption to trade relationships.

There are still many questions about the *HMAS Toowoomba*'s presence do close to the China border and while it is presumed to have been there legally and validly under UN authority, doubts linger, underscoring the delicate nature of Australia's military posture in the region. The careful navigation of these geopolitical waters is crucial, with implications not only for Australia's standing but for global perceptions of its alliances and intentions.

SELECTIVE REPORTING AND MEDIA SENSATIONALISM

When incidents involving Australian vessels and the Chinese navy usually occur, the narrative often becomes muddled in the fog of limited information and the details are intentionally vague, leaving the public to infer the severity of the situation solely based on the involvement of China. It's a recurring theme that perpetuates the notion of China as a looming threat, a narrative that conveniently serves the political interests of conservative forces in Australia.

In the case of the recent *HMAS Toowoomba* incident, the initial reports portrayed the Australian warship as innocently cruising off the coast of Japan. However, the reality was more complex—the vessel was actually right on the edge of Chinese territory in the East China Sea, participating in a UN mission to monitor the trade embargo against North Korea. However, the proximity to Chinese territory raises questions about the intent behind the ship's presence, prompting speculation and demands for clarification.

And of course, the Chinese ship was described in the media as a "warship", while the *HMAS Toowoomba* was reported more innocuously as an Anzac-class frigate, whereas, in reality, both are classified as warships and are remarkably similar in design. This discrepancy in reporting illustrates the power of framing in shaping public perceptions, creating a narrative that doesn't align with the facts.

This selective reporting is not unique to the *HMAS Toowoomba* incident. In early 2022, when a Chinese vessel allegedly shone a military laser at an Australian vessel in the Arafura Sea, once again, details were sketchy and vague, yet the incident was ramped up with deliberate ambiguity, and heightened in national security concerns for the public in Australia. The media narrative tends to paint China as the aggressive antagonist, bullying Australia, the supposed naïve and innocent party, always "doing the right thing".

However, beneath the sensationalism lies a more nuanced reality. Naval interactions, like the shining of a military laser, can be interpreted as strategic messaging rather than outright aggression. These actions serve as a form of communication, signaling awareness and a readiness to respond if situations were to escalate. Quite often, it's a diplomatic game conducted at sea, a game of geopolitical posturing that extends beyond the headlines.

The challenge lies in deciphering these actions within a broader context, acknowledging the complexities of international relations. Both China and Australia have diplomatic channels to navigate such complexities, but the media and the Liberal Party often prefer a narrative of a hostile China rather than a nuanced relationship with occasional disagreements. The result is an inflated perception of events, distorting their actual importance and contributing to an oversimplified and sensationalised understanding of Australia's international relations.

LIBERAL PARTY'S OPPORTUNISM AND EXPLOITATION OF THE ISSUE OF CHINA

The political debate surrounding this East China Sea incident has become increasingly convoluted, with Dutton seizing the narrative, with the mainstream media framing events through the lens of the Liberal Party, positioning the party as a "government in exile", where every political event is interpreted from a Coalition perspective.

Deputy Liberal Party leader Sussan Ley's criticism of the Prime Minister's recent trip to China, accusing him of prioritising photo opportunities over discussing the naval incident with President Xi Jinping, stirred the political pot and, somehow because the lead narrative of the media, when in fact, the truth was otherwise.

"This certainly is an event that does do damage", said Albanese, "and we've made that very clear: this was dangerous, it was unsafe and unprofessional from the Chinese forces. We have put our very strong objections to China very clearly, very directly to all of the appropriate channels in all of the forums that are available to us."

Albanese also emphasised the importance of adhering to standard diplomatic practices rather than resorting to public megaphone diplomacy, a subtle jab at the previous approach taken by former Prime Minister Scott Morrison, whose actions exacerbated tensions with China, rather than relieve them.

However, the media headlines painted a different picture, emphasising a perceived lack of initiative on Albanese's part to address the issue with Xi Jinping, narratives that were primarily driven by political point-scoring comments from the Coalition, and somehow ending up in many media outlets, including *The Guardian*, the ABC, and particularly the *Daily Telegraph*, contributing to the sensationalisation of the incident.

Home Affairs Minister Clare O'Neil also underscored the seriousness of the matter, but went on to say: "we won't play politics; we won't say things about China to get a headline in Australian newspapers—this is a serious national security issue."

Yet, the statements from Dutton and Shadow Minister for Defence, Andrew Hastie, revealed a contrasting perspective. Dutton labeled the incident as "propaganda", emphasising the need to call out aggressive behaviour while balancing the importance of the relationship with China, while Hastie accused the Prime Minister of a "remarkable oversight" for not raising the issue directly with President Xi Jinping during the APEC summit.

This rhetoric aligns with a historical pattern for the Liberal Party, known for its strained relationship with China, manifested in what are, essentially, racist attacks. The belligerent tone, while resonating with the party's base and far right politics, raises concerns about its impact on Australia's broader interests. The perpetual narrative of fear and tension surrounding China serves the electoral interests of the Liberal Party but risks undermining the trade and more nuanced diplomatic relationships that have been carefully cultivated over the years, especially since 1972.

The AUKUS pact, which seems to be a resurgence of alliances which could be construed as the "white man's club" of Australia, United States and Britain, further complicates the diplomatic landscape. While the world has evolved since the days of Federation, the current trajectory appears to lean toward clinging to outdated political constructs, hindering Australia from forging new, bold partnerships in a changing global landscape.

In the midst of these political dramas, the role of Dutton stands out. His staunch approach, characterised by a willingness to confront China at the expense of diplomacy, raises questions about the long-term consequences for Australia's international relations if he were ever to become Prime Minister. As the nation navigates these complex waters, it remains to be seen whether the political rhetoric aligns with the country's broader interests or results in a diplomatic quagmire with far-reaching repercussions for both countries.

THE AUKUS PACT AND CREATING A MATURE RELATIONSHIP WITH CHINA

The context surrounding the recent naval incident in the East China Sea takes on added complexity when viewed through the lens of the AUKUS pact. While China acknowledges Australia as a valuable trading partner, the geopolitical landscape is marked by competition between China and the United States: that's where the main game is for China, and Australia is just a bit-player in this field. The AUKUS alliance introduces a new dynamic that raises suspicions in China, particularly when Australian warships venture close to areas of interest on the edge of the Chinese border.

Of course, this doesn't excuse the actions taken by the Chinese forces, especially the potentially harmful sonar signals that were directed at Australian divers who were, ostensibly, untangling fishing nets that become entangled in the underside of the *HMAS Toowoomba*. However, understanding the broader geopolitical context is crucial in evaluating such incidents. Unfortunately, this context has been notably absent in the reporting surrounding the naval encounter.

One aspect largely overlooked in Western media is a speech delivered by Xi Jinping at the recent APEC Summit. In his address, the Chinese president emphasised the importance of China and the United States getting along, advocating for mutual respect, coexistence, and co-operation.

> **President Xi Jinping:** "We, the largest developing country, and the largest developed country, the United States, we must get along with each other. China is ready to be a partner and friend of the United States. The two main fundamental principles that we follow in handling China–US relations are mutual respect, peaceful coexistence, and win–win cooperation. China never bets against the United States, and never interferes in its internal affairs. China has no intention to challenge the United States or to unseat it. Instead, we will be glad to see a confident, open, ever growing and prosperous United States.
> Likewise, United States should not bet against China, or interfere in China's internal affairs—whatever stage of development it may reach, China will never pursue hegemony or expansion and will never impose its will on others. China does not seek spheres of influence, and will not fight a Cold War or a hot war with anyone."

While skepticism about such statements is understandable—especially in the context of the Belt and Road Initiative and construction of military bases in the Spratly Islands, it marks a departure from the adversarial rhetoric of the Cold War. The words by Xi Jinping do not echo the confrontational stance exhibited by Soviet leaders such as Presidents Khrushchev and Brezhnev during that era, especially during the Cuban Missile Crisis in

1962. It is crucial to approach China with a care, but also with a recognition that the global political landscape has changed dramatically.

There needs to be a more mature and "grown-up" relationship with China and a shift away from a narrative of perpetual fear and suspicion. The desire to maintain a posture of being the "scared little child of Asia" is outdated and detrimental to Australia's interests in the long run. Dutton and his fellow conservative interests, however, appear reluctant to embrace this shift. Their preference for maintaining a certain narrative aligns with a perspective rooted in the past, fostering an environment where Australia is perpetually on edge. This approach is not in the best interests of a nation seeking to navigate the complexities of an ever-changing global landscape.

As Australia deals with the legacy of the past nine years of Coalition government, there is a call for a more forward-thinking and mature approach to international relations. Ignoring the need for a shift in perspective risks leaving the Liberal Party stranded in a time loop, disconnected from the evolving reality of the world. It remains to be seen whether conservative political leaders can adapt to the changing dynamics of global diplomacy or if they will continue to cling to narratives that no longer serve the nation's best interests.

***

DECEMBER

WILL COURAGE, CAUTION OR BRUTAL POPULIST POLITICS WIN THE NEXT ELECTION?

2 December 2023

The latest round of opinion polls indicates stronger support for the Liberal–National Coalition, with a recent Morgan poll revealing a 50.5 per cent two-party preferred voting support for the L–NP, leaving the Labor Party trailing at 49.5 per cent. And of course, there are the usual caveats of the inherent unpredictability of polls this far from an election—18 months away—and *the only poll that matters is the one on election day*. This has now developed into a trend, as all polls have shown a drop in the commanding levels Labor had recently held—between 53 and 61 per cent support up until September, now hovering around the 50 per cent mark.

While governments would prefer to be ahead in opinion polls, reflecting on the period between 2013 and 2022, during the Coalition's period in government, the polls often painted a different picture. Despite trailing in the polls for a substantial part of their tenure, the Coalition clinched victory in the closely contested elections of 2016 and 2019, underscoring the volatility and potential for last-minute shifts in political landscapes, despite what the opinions polls might be saying.

Notably, these recent polls suggest a rise in populist sentiment, fueled in part by the provocative rhetoric of the leader of the opposition, Peter Dutton, who had railed against issues ranging from parliamentary representation to national security, the Voice to Parliament, complaints about "wokeness", terrorism, and ramping up fear on China, appears to be garnering favourable results for the Coalition. The pervasive nature of this populist outrage is anticipated to persist in the political discourse for the foreseeable future, as it's clear Dutton has not much else to offer, certainly not much on the policy front, and with the backing of the mainstream media, it's clear that Dutton feels that this is the right political formula for success.

But is this a cause for panic in the Labor government? Even in light of opinion polls which have been more reliable since the debacle of inaccurate and misleading polls during the 2019 federal election, the question of their reliability remains, as well as acknowledgement that polling data alone does not guarantee an accurate prediction of an election outcome. Despite this current lead for the L–NP, projections—if they held until the next election—still indicate a more likely scenario of the Labor Party forming a minority government, rather than the Liberal–National Coalition being able to do this, adding an extra layer of uncertainty to the political landscape.

The other factor is that opinion polls tend to fluctuate, although that hasn't stop the mainstream media claiming these polls spell massive troubles for the Labor government, the *Sydney Morning Herald* publishing a headline: "Three signs of decay in the Albanese government", an unusual headline for a government that is only 18 months into its term, with the article suggesting that it's a government in terminal decline. In any case, the Morgan poll published today showed a bounce back for the Labor government, back up to 52.5 per cent in two-party preferred support, to 47.5 per cent for the L–NP, so it's obvious that many in the conservative media are jumping the gun.

While they are keen to amplify any negative issue for the Labor government—either real or imagined—if the media really wanted to ramp up controversy, they could look no further than the leadership of the Liberal Party.

It was only last week that there were rumours of a leadership spill within the Liberal Party, with speculations about potential successors such as Andrew Hastie, Paul Fletcher, Sussan Ley, Simon Birmingham and Jane Hume—even though the latter two reside in the Senate—but each of these candidates have their own set of challenges and considerations, competence and relevance being among those.

While there have been many predictions of Dutton's political demise—he's still there—the final two weeks of parliamentary sessions in November and December—this week and next—and known colloquially as the "killing season" in Canberra, might provide the stage for late year political dramas. If the opinion polls have been narrowing for Liberal–National Coalition, how might they fare with a leader who displays more gravitas, more depth and, at least, a more positive agenda? Could this issue be playing on the minds of Liberal Party members of parliament in the final parliamentary days of 2023?

LABOR'S MISSED OPPORTUNITIES AND THE CALL FOR A MORE AGGRESSIVE STANCE

Within the current Liberal Party leadership, there might be a dearth of quality leadership and lack of any policy substance and, in this situation, the Labor government should be in a commanding position, electorally. But it's not. While there have been criticisms that the Voice to Parliament referendum expended too much time and energy of government—and relinquishing political capital within gaining any political reward—there have been concerns that the Prime Minister has been focused on other political matters, rather than domestic issues, such as cost of living, housing, and inflation.

Certainly, these are causes for concern for the electorate, and these might be some of the reasons for a drop in Albanese's political support, but the main reasons relate to basic politics: the new Labor government failed to capitalise on its opponent's vulnerabilities, especially when they were in such a weakened state.

There's no doubt that the Liberal Party found itself in such a position after the 2022 federal election loss, and basic politics suggests that it's best to keep an opponent down, ensure an opposition's protracted struggle and make sure they cannot get up again.

However, the inherent challenges of being in government for the Labor Party have been compounded by the need to rectify the many issues that accumulated over the past nine years and were neglected by the Coalition. The business of government is difficult, but it's essential that a government monitors the actions of the opposition, and implements tactics to negate their role. While the Labor government may have proceeded with the task of government since May 2022, they may have inadvertently provided the tools and opportunities for the Coalition and Dutton, to regain political ground, and not capitalised on Dutton's political vulnerabilities. The Coalition government was laced with incompetence and corruption during most of its time in office between 2013–22. Why is the Labor government not trumpeting these failures on a daily basis? Where are the ringleaders who can promote this message to the electorate?

Albanese said that he wanted to model his leadership style on the Hawke government but while Bob Hawke governed effectively, he was also ruthless—as was Paul Keating—with his opponents during the 1980s, Andrew Peacock and John Howard. This suggests an imperative for the Labor government is for Albanese to adopt a more aggressive political stance, considering the historical tendency of the Liberal and National parties to play hardball politics.

The Coalition plays ruthless and brutal politics when they're in government—seemingly at the expense of good governing—and it partially explains their historical dominance in federal politics, where they have been in office for almost 70 per cent of the time since federation in 1901. Albanese needs to master this art of political warfare, otherwise, he'll be subsumed by Dutton's own brand of brutal politics, which is the art of obfuscation, misinformation and a base populist narrative. The narrative of the "cautious government" that Albanese espoused during the 2022 federal election campaign needs to be replaced with a bolder vision for where he and the Labor government wish to direct the country towards.

GLOBAL POPULISM AND THE CONTINUING DILEMMA OF THE "IDIOT KING" SYNDROME

In the global landscape of politics, outright populism and deception didn't go into retreat with the electoral losses of figures like Donald Trump in the U.S., Jair Bolsonaro in Brazil or closer to home, when Scott Morrison lost the election in 2022, or when Boris Johnson departed British politics earlier this year. The recent election in Argentina unveiled Javier Milei as the new President, also known as *el loco* (the "crazy man") into this line up—yet another leader with echoes of right-wing politics and associations with the far right, who seems to be a combination of all those predecessors who lost office, replete with wild "chainsaw" media stunts, a wild black hairstyle, and an outrageously eccentric personality.

Despite lacking the buffoonery of some these counterparts, Dutton shares an attachment to right-wing ideologies, raising questions about the global trend of electing leaders who lean towards ultra-conservatism, libertarianism, and rely on falsehoods, misinformation and disinformation, in collaboration with the conservative media.

Trump, Bolsonaro, Johnson, Morrison—and going back further to Tony Abbott—all lasted one term or less, arrived into power offering simple solutions to complex problems, and failed to solve any of them. And despite the consistent failures of these types of leaders to address and solve complex issues, they continue to be elected, posing a paradox that challenges the efficacy of established political systems.

Dutton, who perpetuates lies, fear, and division, all amplified by a media that hangs on his every word, continues this trend. In the current climate of Western democracies, where bombast often triumphs over substance, there are concerns about the effectiveness of traditional political approaches, and the Labor government, despite applying complex solutions to intricate problems, is failing to deal with the challenges of navigating the contemporary media landscape dominated by sensationalism and quick fixes.

The Labor government—and Albanese—needs to find a solution swiftly, and while a failure to do so might not result in them becoming the first one-term government in almost a century—a minority government is more likely in this scenario—it's best to adopt a different approach sooner, rather than later. The underlying message is that the electorate is after hope and certainty, but simplistic blame-shifting approaches that offer quick fixes seem to resonate—as can be seen with the rhetoric from Dutton—even if they ultimately exacerbate problems. If government is so easy, why didn't the government that Dutton was a part of for nine years, solve any of the problems they left behind?

Government is complex, but so is the challenge of countering the allure of populist leaders, and a multi-pronged approach involving a different type of political strategy might be needed to address the roots of these issues and appeal to a more politically savvy and discerning electorate.

***

THE DUPLICITOUS REPORTING OF GAZA AND SHIFTING PERSPECTIVES ON ISRAEL

2 December 2023

A concerning revelation has come to light in the war reporting in Gaza, raising questions about the objectivity of the mainstream media coverage on the conflict. Over 70 journalists and editors from mainstream media outlets have had "re-education" trips and junkets to Israel over the past decade funded by the Israeli government, with a significant majority of these individuals are affiliated with News Corporation, Nine Media, with some from the ABC and *The Guardian* as well.

Unsurprisingly, these effects and influence of these trips and junkets has resulted in media outlets taking actions against journalists who have expressed support for the Palestinian cause. Nine Media, in response to an open letter demonstrating solidarity with journalists covering the Gaza conflict, has banned journalists who endorsed the letter. While the ABC didn't ban journalists, it did issue a warning to its staff regarding the open letter, adding to the growing concerns about media impartiality. These developments follow a prior directive from the ABC, which explicitly banned the use of terms such as "genocide" and "apartheid" to describe the actions by Israel in Gaza and West Bank.

These directives were in response to the open letter initiated by the Media, Entertainment and Arts Alliance, which aimed to offer support and camaraderie for journalists covering the war in Gaza and also emphasised the importance of adhering to journalistic principles, including holding power accountable and accurate reporting on war crimes, genocide, ethnic cleansing, and apartheid, and suggesting that there was a risk of losing "the trust of our audiences if we fail to apply the most stringent journalistic principles and cover this conflict in full". It's hard to disagree with the contents of the open letter.

The backdrop to this media controversy is the ongoing conflict in Gaza, which has resulted in the deaths of over 55 journalists, with a notable number allegedly targeted by the Israeli Defense Forces. In the open letter, journalists were also expressing outrage over the loss of over 15,000 Palestinian lives, demanding that mainstream media uphold the fundamental tenets of journalism, such as reporting truthfully and freely on the realities of war.

News reporting in Australia has a discernible pro-Israel stance, which compromises the principles of an open and fair media. The conflict in Gaza, essentially ongoing since 1946 but reignited on 7 October when Hamas led an assault which killed 1,200 Israelis, has highlighted the need for objective journalism, particularly in democracies reliant on a free and open media environment.

Amidst these challenges, it is crucial to emphasise—yet again—that criticising a government, in this case, the Israeli government, should not be equated with hostility towards any particular religious or ethnic group. The complexity of the Israeli–Palestinian conflict extends beyond religious or ethnic lines, and journalists play a vital role in navigating these nuances while adhering to the principles of responsible reporting.

The issue has been further compromised to attempts by the Israeli government to use accusations of anti-Semitism as a means of stifling criticism and debate. The condemnation of anti-Semitism, anti-Arab sentiment, anti-Muslim attitudes and Islamophobia should be a given, and there needs to be a diversity of opinions within both the Palestinian and Israeli communities. However, concerns persist about the influence of the vocal Zionist lobby in Australia—small but loud—raising questions about the authenticity of accusations and the potential impact on unbiased reporting.

A FURTHER EROSION OF TRUST IN THE MAINSTREAM MEDIA: WHO DO WE TRUST?

The recent revelations about these close ties between the Israeli government and Australian journalists and media outlets continues a pattern of influence over media reporting, not only in Australia, but also in the United States and Britain. The Israeli lobby's substantial sway over the Australian media has become a focal point of scrutiny, with echoes of previous incidents highlighting these biases.

In 2014, when the Israel government instigated yet another conflict in Gaza, journalist Mike Carlton was pressured to resign from the *Sydney Morning Herald* for using offensive language in responses to Jewish readers—private correspondences—who criticised one of his articles on the conflict, and a cartoon by Glenn Le Lievre was removed due to claims of offensiveness by the Australian Jewish Association. These incidents underscored the existence of double standards in reporting on Israel and Palestine, where similarly offensive anti-Palestinian content, such as cartoons produced by News Corporations' Bill Leak, received little scrutiny. The perception that journalists may be compromised by their acceptance of sponsored trips from the Israeli government adds fuel to concerns about the integrity of media reporting on the conflict.

Figures such as Bevan Shields, editor at the *Sydney Morning Herald*, and Lenore Taylor, editor at *The Guardian*, have also received sponsored trips to Israel in the past. While the journalistic community defends their right to engage in such visits, the lack of disclosure raises questions about potential conflicts of interest.

Last week, at least two of the four panelists on the ABC's *Insiders* program were revealed to have traveled to Israel on sponsored trips: should the audience have been informed of this information? The editor of the *Herald Sun*, James Campbell, pushed his own one-sided views and racist attitudes when he commented: "Does you really think that refugees from the Ukraine would potentially [pose] security risks the way people from Gaza are? There's also an unfortunate truth that they are unlikely to hold sanguine views about Jews… people don't leave those sorts of attitudes when they hit the check-in".

Why should a journalist be allowed to push forward these divisive attitudes to a national audience? How much of Campbell's commentary is taken from the talking points provided to him by the Israel lobby in Australia? The broader concern is that journalists on sponsored trips or pressure from specific interest groups are likely to be swayed in their reporting due to their experiences, creating a distorted narrative that compromises journalistic integrity. There are comparisons to the "cash for comment" scandals in 1999, where the radio broadcasters Alan Jones and John Laws were paid—$18 million in total—to make favourable comments about corporations without disclosure, which ultimately forced changes to the *Broadcasting Services Act* to ensure tighter disclosure regulations. Should tighter rules be instigated for political reporting?

In 2019, the media industry launched a "Right to Know" campaign, claiming that governments has been "passing laws that make it harder and harder for people to tell the truth about what the government is doing in your name". Where is the public's right to know about where information that's being provided to the media is coming from? Shouldn't the public be aware of the distortions of this information and be informed about when the news is real or based on propaganda provided by the Israel government? The need for transparency in this area is essential: how would Australians react if other governments, such as Russia, were funding journalists and providing "re-education" tours to the Kremlin, to reshape perspectives on conflicts in countries such as Ukraine?

While there are instances where governments may sponsor journalists for positive reporting—trade shows or tourism purposes—the call for transparency is paramount and even in these instances, disclosure is usually provided. Journalists, when sponsored by governments, should disclose such ties to maintain trust in their reporting: even better; refuse the junkets in the first instance. This would allow audiences to better assess the potential influences on a journalist's perspective and encourage critical examination of the narratives presented. Ultimately, the hope is that a more transparent approach will lead to a media landscape that is less susceptible to external influences and better serves the public's right to unbiased information.

CONTROVERSIAL EDITORIAL CHOICES MAR THE ISRAELI–PALESTINIAN COVERAGE

Australian journalists have previously expressed support for colleagues in war zones, particularly in Ukraine, condemning Russian actions and President Vladimir Putin for instigating the invasion almost two years ago. However, there are no half-measures or equivocation about Ukraine: the ABC and Nine Media have published many articles accusing Russia of war crimes, genocide and ethnic cleansing—and rightly so—and there was no censorship imposed by news editors or management at the time. This perceived inconsistency in treatment has fueled the argument that similar scrutiny and denouncement should be applied to Israel for its actions in Gaza.

If Russia can be accused of war crimes and attempted genocide in Ukraine, the same standards should apply to Israel in the context of Gaza. The ABC's editorial decision to ban certain terms such as "genocide" and "war crimes" in reporting on Gaza and Israel was inappropriate, but if it's correct to accuse Russia of war crimes, then it must be correct to accuse Israel, because the actions committed by both the Russian and Israeli military forces appear to be identical, if not far more severe in Gaza.

The decisions of Nine Media and the ABC to interfere with the reporting of war on such a level is a failure of journalism, although it's evident that the public is becoming increasingly aware of such editorial decisions and seeking news and information from other more reliable avenues.

Social media is providing many platforms for a wider range of unfiltered opinions, allowing for more diverse perspectives on the Israeli–Palestinian conflict. Despite the challenges of navigating misinformation and confirmation bias, this is encouraging critical thinking and evaluation on the Middle East politics and shifting public opinions, however slightly, particularly among younger generations, and providing an opportunity re-evaluate essentially what has been a barrage of Israel government propaganda appearing in much of the mainstream media in Australia.

The geopolitical implications of the Israeli government's actions today are quite different to events from the past, which have usually been tacitly condoned by Western governments and after initial concerns, a level of indifference from the public: a faraway and confusing conflict can hold the attention span of the public for only so long.

However, there is a different global response in 2023. The Israeli government, under Benjamin Netanyahu, has overplayed its hand, losing its precarious and perfunctory political support in the Middle East region but potentially losing the substantial support it holds in Europe, the U.S. and within Australia, whose populations are becoming more outraged with the continuing tragic loss of innocent lives, and the continued domination of Israel in Gaza and the West Bank.

CEASEFIRE'S GLIMMER OF HOPE WIPED OUT

The recent ceasefire in Gaza, which Australia abstained from voting on just a few weeks ago, brought a glimmer of some hope amid the darkness of war. Initially planned for four days, the ceasefire was extended by an additional two days, and there were hopes that it could become a permanent agreement. United Nations Secretary–General António Guterres expressed optimism about the ceasefire, seeing it as an opportunity to increase humanitarian aid to the suffering population in Gaza.

However, this current ceasefire has since been broken by Israel and it's a reminder that there's still a long road ahead in this conflict, which has been substantially one-sided. The civilian casualties have been disproportionately high, with over 15,000 Palestinians killed since October, compared to 1,200 Israelis and, beyond the grim statistics, there's a pressing humanitarian crisis in Gaza that requires urgent attention.

The outcry against this conflict on the international stage has been larger than in previous Israeli conflicts, raising awareness and prompting outrage globally and the narrative surrounding the conflict, often controlled by mainstream media filters, is undergoing a transformation. The traditional controls on how stories are disseminated and framed are dissipating, indicative of the broader changes in media reportage and communication through social media and access of material, in general, through the internet.

While geopolitical changes move at a glacial pace, mainstream political parties in the Western world are facing challenges, both electorally and philosophically, and the disillusionment with established parties and their dwindling memberships becoming contributing factors. The changing narrative around the Palestinian people—once only portrayed in a negative light—is breaking down. Even among those who may not entirely support the notion of Palestine, there is a growing recognition that the situation is more complex than previously thought, that the situation cannot continue for ever and needs a long-lasting and peaceful resolution.

THE GEN Z AND MILLENNIAL IMPACT

The evolving landscape of public opinion on the Israeli–Palestinian conflict is significantly being influenced by social media, particularly among younger demographics. Platforms such TikTok and emerging independent media outlets in 2023 provide alternative perspectives beyond mainstream narratives. Younger audiences are less receptive to historical propaganda, and are increasingly critical of Israel's actions, perceiving them as practicing apartheid, attempting genocide, and likely committing war crimes.

This shift in perception is not confined to Australia but extends globally, prompting a re-evaluation of Israel and Palestine's dynamics. The Gen Z and Millennial demographic, in particular, are more likely to be advocating for international action against injustices, and this demographic's influence is spreading to other age groups, creating a sizable shift in popular opinion that may impact Middle East politics in the future. Beyond changing public sentiment, geopolitical factors are also at play. The slowly diminishing reliance on oil will reduce the strategic importance of Israel for Europe and the United States.

Recent developments at the United Nations, including Australia's vote against a resolution for Israel to withdraw from the occupied territories in the Golan Heights—as well as abstaining from a vote for a ceasefire—reveal a disparity between Australia's stated positions and its actions. While Australia supports the idea of a two-state solution, its voting record suggests a gap between rhetoric and practical steps.

Despite the international lobbying efforts of the Israel government and Zionist support groups in many countries, public support for the actions Israel is waning, and the consequences of overplaying their hand may be irreversible. The Israeli government's challenge now is to navigate this changing landscape, where reshuffling the deck may not guarantee a favourable outcome, leaving them with limited options to regain public favour. Obvious acts of war crimes, attempts at genocide, ethnic cleansing and apartheid will always outrage the international community, even if it has taken over 75 years to get to this stage.

***

THE ONGOING DECAY AND IDEOLOGICAL DECADENCE OF THE MEDIA

2 December 2023

In the ever-shifting landscape of Australian federal politics, the latest opinion polls have become a topic of intense media scrutiny, revealing a change in the public sentiment towards both the Prime Minister, Anthony Albanese and the leader of the opposition, Peter Dutton. While the polls suggest that Albanese and Dutton are as unpopular as each other—both showing a rating of minus 13 in the latest Newspoll figures—a significant gap persists when it comes to the preference for the Prime Minister.

There always has to be a caution against reading too much into polls this far ahead of an election, and the mainstream media, true to its nature, remains actively engaged in dissecting and interpreting the numbers and looking for any signs of turmoil within the Labor government, a pastime that always seems to be absent whenever the Coalition is in office.

The *Sydney Morning Herald*, recently took a bold stance with a headline article spotlighting what they perceive as "three signs of decay" within the Albanese government. However, the timing of such a critique raises questions about the validity of these assertions, especially considering that the current Labor government has only been in power for a relatively brief 18 months. How can a government be showing signs of decay after 18 months? What next, *rigor mortis* after two years?

These are ridiculous suggestions. Traditionally, governments are not deemed to be in a "state of decay" within such a short timeframe, and it's a political evaluation that lacks the necessary context. Problems and difficulties? Yes, most definitely, there are issues which have beset the Albanese government in a relatively short period of time. But none of these issues are irreversible and mid-term polls are usually not positive for first-term governments: what is the more surprising is that Albanese's polling numbers have stayed so high for so long.

The three purported signs of decay, as outlined by the *Sydney Morning Herald*, allude to critical aspects of governance. Firstly, the accusation of "policy inertia" suggests that the Labor government is struggling to articulate a forward-looking vision, but how can any government of any persuasion at the halfway point of their first term, still busy delivering on the agenda it promised at the *previous* election, be concerned about what it hopes to deliver in 2025 and beyond? Certainly, governments need to be aware of development of policy that attracts the electorate at subsequent elections—concurrent with the process of bedding down existing plans and agendas, as well as ongoing process of governing—but that stage hasn't been reached yet.

Secondly, the *Herald* points to a perceived lack of preparation and a poor response to events, citing a recent High Court ruling on unlawful immigration detention as a case in point, a decision which overturned another ruling from twenty years ago. It could be argued that the government should have had contingency legislative plans in place to deal with this decision—High Court rulings in the past have been notoriously unpredictable and despite there being a belief that there was a slim chance of the 2004 ruling being overturned—the government should have been prepared, both in terms of possible legislation and dealing with the politics of any potential fallout. But to claim a "lack of preparation and a poor response to events" based on one case—*one case!*—and on an issue that has negligible effect on the electorate—which conveniently feeds into Coalition talking points on national security—is a narrow and shallow political analysis.

The third sign of decay, revolves around the concept of "isolated leadership". Apparently, there are rumours of discontent within the Labor backbench and alleged tensions within the party are raising questions about the "cohesiveness of the government". And, as usual, these claims are based on anonymous sources and lack concrete evidence, a common criticism when evaluating the credibility of such reports.

This analysis has to be placed in the context that the *Sydney Morning Herald*, owned by Nine Media and chaired by former Liberal government treasurer Peter Costello, is displaying the anti-Labor bias that it usually offers in its analysis, and the political opinions expressed in most of the mainstream media often reflects the perspectives of their owners, a factor that requires careful consideration when interpreting the alleged "signs of decay" within the Albanese government.

As the debate over the government's performance intensifies within the mainstream media, it remains to be seen whether these early indicators of discontent will translate into a broader narrative of decay or whether the Labor government will navigate the challenges and emerge with an adequate political response. The pressures on the government are undeniable, yet the question of whether it can be labeled a "government in decay" is a lazy one, drawing varied opinions from political analysts and the electorate alike.

WHAT POLITICAL DECAY REALLY LOOKS LIKE

Within Australian federal politics, the interpretation of opinion polls and the subsequent media narrative often overshadows the substantive work conducted within parliamentary offices and electorates. Unquestionably, governments would prefer to have positive opinion polls all the time, but the better governments are not driven by polls: parliamentary business and managing public programs are a substantial part of the role of the Prime Minister, ministers and the government of the day. Certainly, despite what they all say publicly, politicians do inspect the polls, analyse them and interpret what they mean. But then they go off and do their work in their parliamentary offices, or out in the field in the electorate. While they take a *serious interest* in the polls, they are not *consumed* by the polls: there is a marked difference.

The media, on the other hand, has been relentless in amplifying the notion that the Albanese government is teetering on the brink of turmoil. Allegations of discontent within the backbench have been fervently disseminated, with the ABC and Nine Media leading the charge, suggesting that the government is in a "world of pain". However, seasoned political observers argue that such discontent is an anomaly for a new government, especially within the initial 18 months of its term.

Turmoil and decay is rarely a feature of first-term governments—that's not to say that they are without problems, especially if they have been out of office for close to a decade—but it is rare. Cabinet positions are rarely available to first-term MPs, where most are learning the art of being a politician and working out the practical nature and intricacies of politics and managing a political office, and they're not even in a position to be disgruntled and unhappy with the role they have as a backbencher: politics is based on rules of longevity and pecking orders, and a fresh-faced and new politician simply has to wait their turn. Certainly, if there were reports of dissent or disillusionment with the leadership in the second or third term of a government, that would be believable, because that's generally when it happens.

In addition, claims by Andrew Bolt from Sky News suggesting Albanese should "step down", is "not up to the job" and will face an imminent leadership change in the Labor government, ignores the mechanics of a leadership spill within the Labor government, which requires 75 per cent support from the Caucus, a threshold which is close to impossible. Critics argue that these reports are driven more by sensationalism than by a genuine assessment of the government's stability and performances.

As a comparison, what does a "decaying government" look like? The final years of the NSW Labor government between 2008–11, a level of decadence reached after 13 years in office; the NSW Coalition government between 2021–23, a level of incompetence reached after 10 years in office; the second term of federal Labor between 2011–13; the final years of mayhem in the federal Coalition between 2016–22, or the Howard government after they won their fourth consecutive election in 2004. All of these governments were long-term and had simply run out energy, become complacent or riven by internal divisions. *This is what decay looks like.* This point has not arrived for the Albanese—and that's not to say that it won't arrive at some point in the future, but it's very unlikely in this first term and certainly not the case at this point of time.

Prime Minister Albanese also doesn't have the same ideological, personal and political instabilities that many of his predecessors had: Rudd couldn't hold his party together with his esoteric personality and leadership style; Tony Abbott was consumed with ideological culture wars; Malcolm Turnbull and Scott Morrison led a divisive and divided Liberal Party; Julia Gillard had to contend with an even further divided Labor Party that was also dealing with the fallout from deposing Rudd and his continuing destructive presence in Parliament.

Albanese doesn't have any of these issues to contend with and appears to be more amenable to collaboration and operates within a more cohesive party structure. Albanese may yet need to deal with these issues: political parties, no matter how successful they might be or how well their government is travelling in opinion polls, will always have dissenting membership who are unhappy with the performances of their leader.

Certainly, there are issues that rank-and-file membership have been clearly unhappy with: the Labor government's responses to raising the Jobseeker rate in 2022; slow progress on social housing construction; the lack of debate over the AUKUS deal; Stage 3 tax cuts; the unchallenged support for the government of Israel when it's obvious to everyone that the Israel Defense Forces have committed war crimes against Palestinian people in Gaza—there is much for Labor members to be unhappy about, but this is not a government in decay—yet—despite what many in the mainstream media are suggesting, or indeed, hoping for.

Essentially, this is the narrative of discontent from a pro-conservative mainstream media doing their best to destabilise a government that has upset their ideological base and drawn the ire of the media editors and proprietors at News Corporation, Seven West Media and Nine Media, and increasingly, the ABC.

In the complex world of Australian politics, where optics and narratives vie for attention, the true and accurate measure of the Albanese government's trajectory will unfold over time, shaped by both its policy actions and the perception war waged in the media. Ultimately, it's the people in the electorate who decide, not the journalists and reporters compromised by their narrow commercial and ideological interests.

***

LABOR STRUGGLES WITH END OF YEAR IMMIGRATION CHALLENGES

9 December 2023

While the end of the year in Australian politics is coming to an end, the dramas for the federal government continue to unfold, casting a shadow over what they were hoping would be a quiet end to 2023. However, in the ever-turning world of politics, there is never a quiet moment, regardless of the which part of the year we are witnessing.

At the forefront was the contentious response to a High Court decision in early November, which decided that the indefinite detention of asylum seekers and stateless individuals is unlawful. The repercussions of this decision have sent shockwaves through the political community, prompting a frenzied race to enact legislation before the parliamentary curtains fall on the year. Yet, it is in the field of immigration and asylum policies that Australia often witnesses the creation on even more contentious—dangerous—and ill-conceived laws.

The Coalition, which has a penchant to politicise immigration at every opportunity, has been a driving force behind the formulation of draconian and, in some instances, unlawful legislation. However, the pendulum of blame swings both ways, as when the Labor Party is in government, they too engage in the same draconian practices to quieten the weighty debates surrounding immigration. This cyclical—and cynical—approach to policymaking has left many questioning the efficacy and morality of the legislative process, arguing that such a crucial matter should not be subjected to the whims of partisan politics.

What sets Australian immigration law apart is its distinctive nature; unlike most nations, Australia boasts comprehensive and complex legislation governing immigration rather than relying on policy frameworks. However, this complexity comes at a cost, as evidenced by the intricate web of immigration laws that empower the minister with the authority to overturn any decision. While there might be an argument that such a provision is necessary to address exceptional cases, there is the potential for abuse inherent in such unchecked power.

The intricate interplay of immigration legislation reveals the broader complexities of Australian politics—multiculturalism, once hailed as a triumph and one of Labor's significant policies—which had faced general bipartisan political support in the post-war era—has faced its share of challenges since 1996, when the Howard government was elected to office, which "always had trouble" with the concept of multiculturalism, deemed it to be a failure, and believed that migrants should "absorb the mainstream culture". Despite its undeniable success in fostering harmonious co-existence among diverse communities, the undercurrent of discontent has been fanned by conservative political leaders, and it's a dynamic that is ever present in contemporary Australian politics.

Australia, a nation built on the premise of a "fair go", seems to be struggling with the intricacies of immigration and multiculturalism as the year draws to a close, and the recent announcement by the Prime Minister, Anthony Albanese, to reduced immigration to "a sustainable level" is the epitome of this struggle, even though Labor is generally the political party that supports higher levels of immigration.

THE PERENNIAL ISSUE: EXPLOITING FEAR ON NATIONAL SECURITY, ASYLUM SEEKERS AND IMMIGRATION

Historically within Australian politics, the trifecta of national security, asylum seekers, and immigration has emerged as the Liberal and National parties' political stronghold. Like a well-worn script, they seize every opportunity to stoke fear and sow discord on these issues, transforming them into political weapons that consistently create political difficulties for Labor, whether they are in government or opposition. The strategy is clear: create an atmosphere of "fear and loathing" and paint asylum seekers as a "threat" that must be repelled at all costs, a narrative that plays into the Coalition's hands.

For the Labor government, navigating this terrain has become a political tightrope walk. Desperate to distance themselves from the spotlight of immigration and asylum policy, they engage in a delicate process of downplaying the issue, hoping it will simply fade into the background or the electorate will forget about the issues. Yet, no matter how tough or draconian the laws they propose might be, it's usually a futile effort. The Coalition, in conjunction with the media who are ever eager to sensationalise and support this conservative agenda, consistently conspire to portray Labor as weak and incompetent on matters of national security.

This isn't a novel predicament; the roots of this political strategy stretch back at least to 1998 and, in a broader historical context, to the 1950s during the Cold War, reaching a peak with the Petrov Affair, which was ruthlessly exploited by Prime Minister Robert Menzies just before the 1954 federal election. The Coalition, with a seemingly innate ability to exploit fears of outsiders, perpetuates a narrative that has been a fixture since the 1800s: the perpetual fear of invasion. The Chinese, in particular, have been a recurring bogeyman, a trope that has persisted for almost two centuries despite a lack of substantiated threats.

However, the historical pattern extends beyond the manufactured threat of a Chinese invasion. Even recent episodes, such as the 'African gang' narrative pushed by Peter Dutton in 2018, have proven to be largely baseless when challenged and scrutinised. Time and time again, the data reveals that immigrants contribute positively to the Australian landscape—economically, socially, and culturally. They become integral threads in the fabric of the community, fostering economic growth, creating jobs, and enriching the tapestry of multiculturalism. Despite these demonstrable benefits, the narrow-minded, racist voices continue to hijack the narrative, drowning out the nuanced truth with their divisive rhetoric.

As the politics struggles with these perennial issues, the challenge remains: can Australia move beyond the historical fear-mongering, and embrace a more inclusive and evidence-based approach to immigration and asylum policy? A nation such as Australia can rise above the shadows of its own history, dispelling the persistent myths that threaten to overshadow the reality of a diverse and dynamic society. But, it takes both sides of politics to be committed to this, and the tragedy is that if one side can see that there are significant political opportunities to be gained by this mayhem, the other side—Labor—will always be languishing in the catch-up lane.

A LACK OF PREPAREDNESS, REACTIVE POLICYMAKING AND SHAPING PERCEPTION

As the political fallout from the High Court decision continues to reverberate, an alternate narrative has emerged: that the government was caught off guard, unprepared for the shift in asylum seeker policy. The principle of political readiness—to always be prepared for the unexpected, a fundamental tenet of effective governance—seems to have eluded the government in this instance. Given the historical behaviour of the Coalition on such issues, there should have been a meticulous readiness for any judicial outcome, no matter how unlikely. While it could be argued that the government could hardly be blamed for not be prepared when the High Court didn't immediately release their reasons for overturning a previous ruling from 2004, the problem lay in their political responses.

The absence of such preparedness has given rise to a chaotic aftermath, where the government appeared to flounder in crafting an appropriate response. The consequence of this lack of foresight then manifested in the form of hastily created legislation, provided even more draconian measures for asylum seekers, which underscored the perils of reactive policymaking.

The government's failure to anticipate and prepare for this legal outcome has exposed a critical flaw, as the essence of politics lies not only in governance but also in deftly managing public perception. The Liberal Party, historically adept at diversionary tactics, typically resorts to discussing polarising issues such as the fruitless pursuit of nuclear energy, social division of transgender rights, or border security to divert attention when facing political challenges.

In contrast, Labor, often more competent in governance than political strategy and base politics, finds itself at a disadvantage in this arena. Effective governance necessitates not only sound policy decisions but also astute political management, political bastardry and manipulation—a balance that the Liberal–National Coalition, in certain aspects, seems to have mastered more proficiently, at the expense of good governance.

While allowances must be made for a new government finding its footing—in office for 18 months after being out of office for nine years—it is imperative to hold a government accountable for their actions. The public is less forgiving: they care less about who created the problems or what the problems are, they mainly want the problems resolved and will punish governments who either fail to resolve these problems or avoid their responsibilities altogether. Ministers, even those with previous experience in government, often struggle with shifting circumstances. However, this does not absolve them of responsibility, and vigilance from the public is paramount.

Amidst the turmoil, a misleading conservative narrative has surfaced, insinuating that the High Court decision has unleashed a wave of criminals into society and, by extension, is the fault of the Labor government. This perspective conveniently sidesteps the fact that majority of High Court justices were appointed by Coalition governments, and hold "black letter" legal opinions that align with a traditionalist interpretation of the law. The High Court applies the law according to the Constitution: it pays no interest to the politics of the days—nor should it—and assesses the case that it sees in front of it, based on its legal merits. In this recent High Court ruling, it was a unanimous 7–0 decision, including the four justices who were appointed by the Coalition.

The recent escape and subsequent capture of five asylum seekers who were recently released from indefinite immigration detention has also been subject to sensationalised media coverage. It is crucial to recognise that very few refugees are "criminals", and an objective analysis reveals that only a small minority of refugees run afoul of the law, in many cases, at a lower rate of recidivism than the general community. Contextual factors, exacerbated by prolonged detention and mistreatment, often contribute to such transgressions.

As the nation deals with the aftermath of the High Court decision, a nuanced and comprehensive approach is required—one that balances accountability, adherence to the Constitution, and an understanding of the complex factors influencing the behaviour of those seeking asylum. In scrutinising the government's response, citizens must remain vigilant in holding power to account, ensuring that justice is served without compromising the principles that define Australia's democratic fabric. In the current political environment—as it has been for much of Australia's history, which always defaults to a fear of outsiders and disdain for *the other*, this is a difficult task.

***

THE FRAGILE STATE OF CEASEFIRE IN GAZA AMIDST A HUMANITARIAN CRISIS

9 December 2023

In the wake of a shattered ceasefire in Gaza, tensions continue to escalate, drawing international attention and concern. Initially, there was a glimmer of hope for a lasting peace, but this optimism has been dashed by recent developments, when the Israeli Defense Forces broke the ceasefire—blaming this on Hamas, without providing proof—and resumed their operations, leading to an increased number of Palestinian casualties, including women and children, and a situation that is rapidly evolving into a humanitarian crisis.

James Elder, a spokesperson from UNICEF, provided a grim outlook on the conditions in Gaza, specifically the so-called "safe zones", which, in reality, are anything but safe. These areas lack basic necessities such as water, sanitation, and shelter, turning them into potential hotbeds for disease and suffering. Elder highlighted the dire situation in these zones, where basic facilities are woefully inadequate or entirely absent, exacerbating the plight of the displaced population.

The international community's response to this crisis has been a focal point of debate and the calls for more decisive action against Israel's actions in Gaza and the West Bank are growing louder. While they don't have great influence in current politics, Young Labor in Australia has passed a resolution urging the federal government to support an immediate ceasefire and to hold Israel accountable for its adherence to international law, as have 40 other Labor Party branches across Australia.

In the Australian Parliament last week, Labor MP Stephen Jones echoed these concerns, advocating for a peaceful resolution through a two-state solution, emphasising the importance of secure and internationally recognised borders for both Israelis and Palestinians and, importantly, stressed that peace is the only viable long-term solution to the ongoing hostility in the Middle East.

While these are fine sentiments—who doesn't want a ceasefire, except for the Israel government, their assorted lobbyists and the Liberal Party here in Australia—the ground realities paint a different picture. Despite the international outcry and political rhetoric, the situation in Gaza remains dire and this disconnect between political discourse and on-the-ground actions highlights the complexity and difficulty of resolving this long-standing conflict. Adding to the complexity is the intertwining of political ideologies and ethnic identities. The U.S. Congress's recent legislation equating anti-Zionism with anti-Semitism has sparked controversy, with a conflation of the two issues of political criticism of Israel and ethnic prejudice—even though the two are mutually exclusive issues—an oversimplification of a multifaceted issue, and a sign of further evidence of the influence the Israel lobby has within U.S. politics.

Both Israeli and Palestinian leadership face accusations of corruption and self-preservation at the expense of their people. The conflict, which disproportionately affects the innocent, is increasingly seen as a struggle between corrupt political factions rather than a representation of the will of the people. The pro-Netanyahu faction in Israel, in particular, faces diminishing moral and intellectual defences as the conflict continues and support within the international community is waning, and is testing the patience of the U.S., which seems to support any actions performed by the Israel government against Palestine, irrespective of how violent and destructive this action might be.

As the situation remains volatile, the hope for a return to ceasefire is more urgent than ever. The consequences of prolonged conflict are unpredictable, and the need for a peaceful resolution is paramount to prevent further loss and suffering.

AN INTERNATIONAL CONFLICT WITH LOCAL RAMIFICATIONS

In Australia, the conflict in Gaza is resonating deeply, particularly among the Jewish community, where these is a significant segment standing in opposition to Israel's actions. This divergence of opinion, often overshadowed by Australian media, is gradually gaining recognition. Louise Adler, the noted publisher and cultural figure, offered her perspective on her encounters with the Zionist lobby in Australia, which always seeks to suppress criticism of Israel and counters any negative perceptions.

Adler's experiences date back to the 2000s, beginning with a confrontation with the Israeli ambassador over a book she published as the CEO of Melbourne University Press—My Israel Question by Antony Lowenstein—the release of the book marked the start of her ongoing interactions with these lobby groups, and in this case, resulting in conversative politicians demanding her dismissal from the University of Melbourne.

Adler also highlighted the controversy surrounding the Adelaide Writer's Week, where the inclusion of Palestinian literary culture was also met with vehement opposition from the Israel lobby. Despite pressures, including calls for withdrawal of sponsorship and political interventions, the festival stood firm in its decision, underscoring the importance of representing diverse narratives, including those of Palestinians.

This situation is not a monolithic representation of Jewish opinion. Many Jewish individuals, both in Australia and globally, do not align with the Israeli government or its policies under Benjamin Netanyahu and Adler's willingness to expose the behaviour of the Zionist lobby underscores the diversity of thought within the Jewish community, as there would be in any other community.

While there should be an acceptance of a diversity of views and opinions, tolerance seems to be selective and based on the message that is being promoted. A poignant example of this selective acceptance was seen in the inner west of Sydney, where a woman, during the inauguration of the Lewis Herman Reserve by Prime Minister Albanese, held a sign featuring a hand-drawn watermelon—symbolising Palestinian resistance and identity—with the words "Shame Albo", was swiftly removed by police, while she was holding the sign, along with her one-year old-toddler. Forty years ago, Albanese would have been the one holding up the sign, agitating for the rights of Palestinian people and forcing a change in the politics of the Middle East.

While there have been criticisms of Albanese since this conflict erupted in early October, over a stance where Australia initially abstained from a U.N. resolution for a ceasefire in Gaza, as well as voting against another resolution calling for Israel to withdraw from its occupation of the Golan Heights—seen as a requisite and precursor to the two-state solution that has been envisioned for Israel and Palestine—Australia has now engaged in a *volte-face*, and has now supported a ceasefire, along with 152 other countries. It's unfortunate that it's taken the deaths of at least 18,000 civilians in Gaza for Australia to reach this step, an action that seemed so obvious to so many other people around the world.

Of course, this recent decision to support a ceasefire in Gaza will see different responses in different communities within Australia, but the domination that the Israel lobby has previous held over politics—when it comes to issues relating to Israel and Palestine—has seen a shift in recent months, as more people from within the Jewish community speak out in support of Palestine. These reflections and responses to the Gaza conflict illustrate the complexity and multiplicity of perspectives within both the

Jewish community and broader Australian society. They also highlight the ongoing struggle to balance political affiliations, personal convictions, and the demands of leadership in the face of global crises.

As the conflict in Gaza continues to unfold, the need for a comprehensive and humane approach to resolving it becomes ever more pressing. The voices of dissent and protest, both within and outside the affected regions, are crucial in shaping a future where peace and justice can prevail. This complex range of opinions and actions underscores the ongoing struggle to balance political power, personal convictions, and the urgent need for humanitarian intervention in a world increasingly fraught with conflict and division.

***

INDEX OF PEOPLE

A
Tony Abbott 16, 22, 24, 64, 75, 115, 155, 276, 306, 327, 383, 398, 421, 432
Louise Adler 440
Anthony Albanese 9, 11, 12, 13, 15, 17, 21, 30, 61, 71, 72, 77, 103, 122, 126, 128, 138, 139, 141, 149, 150, 166, 167, 170, 172, 174, 192, 196, 204, 205, 214, 215, 220, 228, 229, 241, 242, 243, 247, 257, 258, 262, 264, 265, 281, 282, 283, 285, 286, 289, 300, 303, 310, 311, 312, 337, 345, 351, 353, 358, 361, 371, 377, 382, 394, 397, 398, 399, 400, 401, 404, 406, 408, 409, 410, 412, 414, 415, 419, 420, 421, 429, 430, 431, 432, 433, 435, 441
Francesca Albanese 408, 409, 410
Janet Albrechtsen 268
Jacinta Allan 333
David Anderson 162
John Anderson 276
Daniel Andrews 24, 114, 130, 141, 233, 307, 329, 333
Bridget Archer 29, 75, 131
Jacinda Ardern 28, 29, 30
Julian Assange 11, 61, 62, 165, 166, 167, 168, 382
Stella Assange 165, 166, 167, 168
Steve Austin 135

B
Mike Baird 200
Steve Bannon 225
Mustafa Barghouti 350
Tony Barry 131
Peter Beattie 175
Kim Beazley 207
Gladys Berejiklian 199, 200, 201, 212, 222
Silvio Berlusconi 324
Mozammill Bhojani 245
Joe Biden 169, 376, 382
Simon Birmingham 204, 419
Bronwyn Bishop 276
Joh Bjelke-Petersen 102

Anna Bligh 177
Jair Bolsonaro 421
Andrew Bolt 30, 143, 242, 431
Dietrich Bonhoeffer 46
Behrouz Boochani 51
Richard Boyle 12, 61, 118, 120, 167
Stephen Bracks 175
Andrew Bragg 49, 277
Paul Brereton 210
Leonid Brezhnev 416
Russell Broadbent 75
John Brumby 177
Tony Burke 296, 384
Linda Burney 15, 353
Ita Buttrose 14, 227, 385

C
Cathy Callaghan 193
James Campbell 425
Kathryn Campbell 221, 223, 232, 247
Matt Canavan 60
Tucker Carlson 143
Mike Carlton 424
Bob Carr 115, 175
Jimmy Carter 86, 411
Michaelia Cash 209, 278, 311
Nicolae Ceaușescu 331
Jim Chalmers 11, 43, 44, 45, 46, 47, 72, 141, 151, 207, 220, 232, 249, 281
Ben Chifley 115
Noam Chomsky 411
Jesus Christ 27
Helen Clark 29
Nathan Cleary 335
Louise Clegg 156
Hillary Clinton 165
Bernard Collaery 61, 119
Peter Collins 173
Tom Connell 409
Roger Cook 177
Robert Corowa 55
Peter Costello 90, 430
Charles Court 102
Peta Credlin 143
John Curtin 115, 342, 381, 393

D
Zoe Daniel 258
Sam Dastyari 65

John Dawkins 190
Peter de Cure 173
Moira Deeming 109
Sandro Demaio 251
Katherine Deves 110, 155
Patrick Dodson 17
Stephen Donaghue 304
Mary Doyle 124
Mark Dreyfus 12, 21, 61, 78, 119
Shane Drumgold 267
Kirilly Dutton 196
Peter Dutton 10, 11, 16, 24, 33, 48, 51, 58, 71, 88, 104, 111, 115, 125, 129, 131, 146, 154, 155, 196, 205, 212, 216, 218, 224, 228, 232, 241, 245, 256, 258, 262, 272, 288, 291, 292, 294, 303, 306, 307, 309, 310, 311, 322, 336, 338, 343, 351, 356, 363, 366, 373, 377, 397, 400, 402, 406, 412, 418, 429, 436

E
James Elder 439
Recep Tayyip Erdogan 411
Herb Evatt 381

F
John Faulkner 230
Sarah Ferguson 350
Alan Finkel 88
Paul Fletcher 419
Israel Folau 226
Gary Foley 55
Francis Forde 381
Andrew Forrest 65, 280
Craig Foster 163
Bernie Fraser 139
Malcolm Fraser 88, 113, 231
Josh Frydenberg 220, 250

G
Katy Gallagher 21
Geoff Gallop 175
Andrew Gee 16
Julia Gillard 29, 383, 395, 432
Newt Gingrich 306
Adam Goodes 161
Mikhail Gorbachev 31
Stan Grant 161, 163, 164
Justin Greggery 40
Nick Greiner 200

Scott Grimley 230
António Guterres 376, 427

H
Mamdouh Habib 167
Ray Hadley 262
Pauline Hanson 276, 369, 403
Sarah Hanson-Young 162, 185
Brian Harradine 56
Peter Hartcher 88
Andrew Hastie 415, 419
Bob Hawke 243, 344, 395, 398, 420
Friedrich Hayek 298
Brad Hazzard 330
Ken Henry 139
John Hewson 113
David Hicks 167
Brittany Higgins 30, 67, 69, 211, 267, 268, 269
Chris Hipkins 31
Joe Hockey 24, 250
Christine Holgate 29
Catherine Holmes 98, 215
Katie Hopkins 110
John Howard 16, 19, 22, 24, 44, 58, 88, 113, 155, 176, 196, 238, 242, 257, 263, 337, 351, 382, 383, 394, 420
Jane Hume 146, 419
Ed Husic 377

J
Jandamarra 301
Peter Jennings 88
Boris Johnson 324, 389, 421
Alan Jones 276, 425
Stephen Jones 439
Alan Joyce 336
Barnaby Joyce 134, 135, 209, 276, 311

K
Matt Kean 277
Paul Keating 44, 60, 90, 94, 383, 394, 420
Kellie Jay Keen-Minshull 109
John Maynard Keynes 281
Nikita Khrushchev 416
King Charles 149, 163
King George 243
Matthew Knott 409
Tegan Kynaston 12

L

Jacqui Lambie 56
Marcia Langton 127, 128, 358
Mark Latham 19
John Laws 425
Bill Leak 424
Lavina Lee 88
Julian Leeser 17, 128, 163
Bruce Lehrmann 30, 67, 267
Glenn Le Lievre 424
Reneé Leon 81
Sussan Ley 47, 156, 197, 228, 265, 311, 351, 378, 414, 419
David Littleproud 271, 345
Philip Lowe 10, 50, 218, 219
Antony Lowenstein 440
Alexander Lukashenko 202
Melissa Lukashenko 356

M

Daryl Maguire 199, 200, 216
Chelsea Manning 165
Rodney Marks 277
Karl Marx 297
Chris Masters 180
Mariana Mazzucato 43, 251
David McBride 12, 61, 167
Mitch McConnell 306
Mark McGowan 141, 175
Bridget McKenzie 60, 209, 216
Nick McKenzie 180
Warwick McKibben 321
Nick McKim 110, 258
Robert Menzies 21, 115, 175, 436
Javier Milei 421
John Stuart Mill 82
Rachelle Miller 40
Chris Minns 114, 285, 315, 360
Neil Mitchell 234
Narendra Modi 169
Daniel Mookhey 114
Piers Morgan 149
Scott Morrison 9, 11, 22, 39, 81, 115, 132, 154, 155, 183, 200, 209, 216, 217, 221, 229, 247, 250, 253, 256, 264, 268, 282, 306, 311, 312, 336, 372, 373, 383, 389, 397, 398, 412, 415, 421, 432
Robert Mugabe 331
Warren Mundine 19, 34, 49, 55, 243, 276, 337, 344, 356, 363, 366
James Murdoch 325, 327
Lachlan Murdoch 142, 143, 186, 323, 324, 326, 327, 328
Rupert Murdoch 24, 30, 69, 79, 125, 161, 164, 204, 285, 316, 323, 324, 325, 326, 327
Paul Murray 30, 143
Murugappan family 35

N

Benjamin Netanyahu 13, 347, 407, 410, 427, 441

O

Barack Obama 86, 166
Kerry O'Brien 243
Barry O'Farrell 200
Andrew Olle 385, 386
Ehud Olmert 347
Clare O'Neil 50, 404, 415
Deborah O'Neill 230

P

Kerry Packer 144, 327
Annastacia Palaszczuk 141
Clive Palmer 176
James Paterson 311, 312
Fatima Payman 377
Andrew Peacock 113, 420
Noel Pearson 128, 335
George Pell 24
Pemulwuy 301
Dominic Perrottet 113
John Pesutto 111, 197
Michael Pezzullo 57
Arthur Phillip 243
Tanya Plibersek 73, 259
Barbara Pocock 173, 230
David Pocock 56, 123, 185
Christian Porter 217, 221, 247, 255
Enoch Powell 175
Bess Price 356
Jacinta Price 19, 34, 49, 55, 276, 337, 344, 356, 363, 366
Yevgeny Prigozhin 13, 202
Vladimir Putin 13, 85, 86, 204, 323, 376, 426
Christopher Pyne 90

R
Robert Ray 230
Ronald Reagan 275, 305
Teela Reed 163
Peter Reith 19, 344
Linda Reynolds 67, 209, 211
Mark Riley 399
Gina Rinehart 65, 297
Stuart Robert 81, 154, 183, 209, 216, 217, 221, 246, 247
Malcolm Roberts 388
Ben Roberts-Smith 179, 187
Bridget Rollason 333
Jay Rosen 115
Michelle Rowland 63, 227, 367
Kevin Rudd 46, 50, 58, 71, 186, 242, 300, 323, 383, 395
Philip Ruddock 403
Mick Ryan 88

S
Leigh Sales 385
Kos Samaras 355
Kyle Sandilands 12
Dr Kerry Schott 135
Leslie Seebeck 88
William Shackel 320
Dennis Shanahan 30
Greg Sheridan 30
Bevan Shields 425
Bill Shorten 215, 253, 288, 339, 340
Adam Smith 44, 297
Stephen Smith 166
Walter Sofronoff 267
David Speers 399
Bruce Springsteen 170
Jordan Steele-John 339
Justin Stevens 162
Amanda Stoker 276
Kerry Stokes 176, 179, 285, 316
Michael Sukkar 24, 341

T
Angus Taylor 75, 146, 156, 209, 228, 319
Lenore Taylor 425
Dan Tehan 335
Margaret Thatcher 275
Lidia Thorpe 34, 53, 56
Marg Thorpe 55

Robbie Thorpe 55
Greta Thunberg 320
Michael Towke 372
Donald Trump 142, 186, 203, 253, 290, 306, 323, 324, 389, 421
Alan Tudge 39, 209, 217, 221, 247, 255
Malcolm Turnbull 104, 115, 186, 272, 288, 323, 383, 432
Anne Twomey 18, 103

V
Aaron Violi 291
Carl von Clausewitz 85

W
Lloyd Walker 358, 359
Nicole Werner 197
Gough Whitlam 88, 95, 146, 189, 190, 391, 395, 398
Andrew Wilkie 132, 166
Richard Willingham 333
Witness K 61, 119
Penny Wong 13, 21, 204, 264, 348, 383, 398, 407, 412
Neville Wran 115, 175
Ken Wyatt 17

X
Xi Jinping 311, 399, 414, 415, 416

Y
Yagan 289, 301
Yunupingu 127, 128, 129

Z
Volodymyr Zelenskyy 86

www.ingramcontent.com/pod-product-compliance
Lightning Source LLC
Chambersburg PA
CBHW051416290426
44109CB00016B/1315